SOCIAL MEDIA MARKETING

Sara Miller McCune founded SAGE Publishing in 1965 to support the dissemination of usable knowledge and educate a global community. SAGE publishes more than 1000 journals and over 800 new books each year, spanning a wide range of subject areas. Our growing selection of library products includes archives, data, case studies and video. SAGE remains majority owned by our founder and after her lifetime will become owned by a charitable trust that secures the company's continued independence.

Los Angeles | London | New Delhi | Singapore | Washington DC | Melbourne

SOCIAL MEDIA MARKETING

Tracy L. Tuten & Michael R. Solomon

3RD EDITION

Los Angeles | London | New Delhi
Singapore | Washington DC | Melbourne

Los Angeles | London | New Delhi
Singapore | Washington DC | Melbourne

SAGE Publications Ltd
1 Oliver's Yard
55 City Road
London EC1Y 1SP

SAGE Publications Inc.
2455 Teller Road
Thousand Oaks, California 91320

SAGE Publications India Pvt Ltd
B 1/I 1 Mohan Cooperative Industrial Area
Mathura Road
New Delhi 110 044

SAGE Publications Asia-Pacific Pte Ltd
3 Church Street
#10-04 Samsung Hub
Singapore 049483

Editor: Matthew Waters
Associate editor: Lyndsay Aitken
Assistant editor, digital: Chloe Statham
Production editor: Nicola Carrier
Copyeditor: Gemma Marren
Proofreader: Sharon Cawood
Indexer: Silvia Benvenuto
Marketing manager: Alison Borg
Cover design: Sheila Tong
Typeset by: C&M Digitals (P) Ltd, Chennai, India
Printed in the UK by Bell and Bain Ltd, Glasgow

Library of Congress Control Number: 2017941079

British Library Cataloguing in Publication data

A catalogue record for this book is available from
the British Library

ISBN 978-1-5264-2386-3
ISBN 978-1-5264-2387-0 (pbk)

At SAGE we take sustainability seriously. Most of our products are printed in the UK using FSC papers and boards.
When we print overseas we ensure sustainable papers are used as measured by the PREPS grading system.
We undertake an annual audit to monitor our sustainability.

CONTENTS

LIST OF FIGURES AND TABLES

Figures

Tables

TABLE OF CASE STUDIES

(Continued)

(Continued)

Travel and Social Media: The Grand Ole Opry	Tourism, user-generated content, cross-platform campaign, social content	Case Zone, Part V—page 386–7
Native Advertising: Novel or Deceptive?	Sponsored content, in-feed advertising	Case Zone, Part V—page 388–9
Social Media Marketing in the Wedding Planning Industry	Word of mouth, customer reviews, social community, social media strategy	Companion website: https://study.sagepub.com/smm3e
Tito's Vodka Mini Case	Storytelling, brand community, Sprout Social, social listening, Tito's Vodka, engagement metrics	Chapter 6—page 204–5
A Social Media Conference Community	Sports, marketing, conferences, social, media, students, academia, PR	Case Zone, Part V—page 390
Authentic & Fake Consumers? Accepting the use of Native Advertisements in Social Media	Catphishing, influence, social media posts, fake product reviews, regulation.	Companion website: https://study.sagepub.com/smm3e
GoPro Mini Case	GoPro, personal heroism, social publishing, visual content, authenticity, community	Chapter 7—page 243
Nebraska State Historical Society Foundation: The Nebraska Marker Project Launch	social media campaign, social media zones, types of media outreach	Companion website: https://study.sagepub.com/smm3e
Burger King Complements MARCOM with #AngriestWhopper Social Game Mini Case	Burger King, Gamewheel, social gaming, app, advertising	Chapter 8—page 260–1
#NikeAirMaxDay: The Creation of a Social Brand Event	Community, content creation, social media sharing, gamification, social influencers, word of mouth, visual storytelling	Case Zone, Part V—page 391–3
Pokémon GO: A Revolution in Social Gaming	Social gaming, AR, in-app purchases, microtransactions, advergame	Case Zone, Part V—page 394–5
MantraBand Leverages User-Generated Reviews to Drive Sales Mini Case	MantraBand, Shopify, social commerce, Yotpo, UGC, app, customer reviews	Chapter 9—page 304–5
Social Media Is Gateway to eBook Sales Success: Amazon Kindle eBooks	Social community, self-publishing, social publishing, social commerce, content creation, social media presence	Case Zone, Part V—page 396–8

ABOUT THE AUTHORS

Tracy L. Tuten PhD, is Professor of Marketing at East Carolina University and also holds a Visiting Professor appointment with ICHEC Brussels Management School. Her first book, *Advertising 2.0: Social Media Marketing in a Web 2.0 World*, was followed by others on using social media and digital marketing for the enterprise, and the book, *Advertisers at Work*, which features interviews with luminaries in the field. Dr Tuten's publications have appeared in such journals as *Journal of Marketing Communications*, *Psychology & Marketing*, and *Journal of Business Research*. Prior to her appointment at ECU, she taught at Longwood University and at Virginia Commonwealth University, where her research efforts were recognized with VCU's Excellence in Scholarship award. A two-time Fulbright Scholar, she speaks all over the world on marketing topics. She's been recognized with teaching awards at her respective institutions and with national awards, such as the O'Hara Leadership Award in Direct & Interactive Marketing Education. In 2013, she was inducted into the Incredible Women of ECU series, which highlights female graduates of East Carolina University who have reached exceptional levels of achievement in their respective careers. She is one of only 110 women to achieve this distinction. Her influence in social media marketing is recognized with a consistent ranking in the top 20 listing of marketing professors and top 50 listing of authors of marketing books on Twitter (respectively) by *Social Media Marketing* magazine. Follow her at @brandacity on Twitter or follow her blog at www.tracytuten.com.

Michael R. Solomon PhD, is Professor of Marketing at Saint Joseph's University in Philadelphia, USA. Professor Solomon's primary research interests include consumer behavior and lifestyle issues, branding strategy, the psychology of fashion, and marketing applications of virtual worlds and other new media. His textbooks include *Consumer Behavior: Buying, Having, and Being*, *Marketing: Real People, Real Choices*, and *Better Business*. His most recent trade book, *The Truth about What Customers Want*, was published by FT (*Financial Times*) Press. Professor Solomon is frequently quoted in magazines and newspapers, including *Newsweek*, the *New York Times*, and the *Wall Street Journal*. He has served as a consultant to numerous corporations including Calvin Klein, Intel, Procter & Gamble, Microsoft, State Farm Insurance, and United Airlines on issues relating to consumer behavior, marketing strategy, advertising, and retailing.

PREFACE

As you sit in class, you're probably thinking about a lot of things. After all, you are a Master Multi-tasker. You've spent many of your waking hours (and maybe even some sleeping hours) tuning in to multiple media platforms at the same time. You're probably very comfortable surfing the Web, texting your friends, and perhaps talking on the phone while you sip a latte at the local coffee shop. We suspect you may even check Facebook Messenger during a lecture from time to time!

We have a name for people like you: Digital Natives. That's why this course on social media marketing is so important—it deals with the stuff you do all day long and shows you how to apply it to professional as well as personal activities. Unless you've been living in a cave, you know that platforms like Facebook are about more than just swapping stories with your buds. Marketers use them to talk to you as well—whether you want them to or not. Today marketers have a huge set of new tools to reach digital natives like you. In fact, for most companies now the question is not *whether* to include social media as part of the communications mix, but *how much* to use. Some organizations even question whether they need the "old school" platforms at all when they can easily reach millions of consumers around the world with the click of a mouse.

We don't go quite that far—social media complement other techniques but don't necessarily replace them. Still, there's a lot to learn about what's out there and the best way to integrate these new tools with the tried-and-true.

We hope this book will help you to figure all that out. We were proud (and a little scared) to publish the first textbook on social media marketing—and here we are with the third edition! With the first edition, our goal was to demonstrate how social media could and should take their place in the twenty-first-century marketer's toolbox. Now, a few years later, that has indeed happened! And what we know about social media marketing, both from an industry perspective and the academic's perspective, has developed. When social media marketing first entered the marketer's toolbox, the focus was on organic participation and relationship development. The media space itself was free, though, of course, there were labor costs involved. Now, social network sites have developed complex algorithms to customize each person's experience. For marketers, this means that while the organic participation is still preferred by consumers, advertising (paid media) must be part of the social media marketing mix. That's not the only development either. Technological capabilities have evolved in ways that influence how we access the social Web, the content we can create, and the experiences we can participate in and share. The penetration of smartphones and other connected devices is a major aspect of these developments.

When we first developed this book, most universities did not have a course on social media marketing. Today, many do and a select few have recognized that social media warrants its own concentration! This text will enable you to provide the content you—and your future employers—crave. Very simply, you need to know even more about social media than you do already. You need to know how to harness the power of these tools to succeed in business, nonprofit organizations, and pretty much any kind of situation that involves buyers and sellers, makers and users.

There are so many applications out there—where to start? We've organized the book around four zones of social media —communities, publishing, entertainment, and commerce. There are social media channels that serve multiple zones (Facebook is a prime example), but the zones capture the primary intent for participants in each zone. Social communities are about relationships. Social publishing is about sharing knowledge (even for everyday people). Social entertainment is about entertainment opportunities hosted in social media channels and with social media tools. Social commerce is about selling and buying and how social media plays a role in the purchase process. This framework will help you to make sense of the complex world of social media.

Our approach is simple: we start in Part I with a discussion of just what social media means, and how it's changing our lives. We explain the environment of social media that encompasses the Internet and Web, the social network sites that serve as channels of participation, the social software that facilitates our activities (including software that runs behind the scenes), and the devices through which we experience social media. We consider implications not only for consumers, but also for organizations that need to include social media as part of their strategic planning process. You'll learn about segmentation and targeting as it relates to consumers and prospective buyers in social media, in particular considering how audience engagement with social media may influence marketing strategies. We also review the characteristics of networks and online communities as these relate to every zone of social media by explaining how information spreads in a community, why influencers are valuable for seeding information, and the role of word-of-mouth communication in all of this.

In Part II, you'll learn the process for social media marketing strategic planning as well as the key organizational issues that must be considered when pursuing social media marketing strategies. You'll also learn the activities involved in planning specific tactics and executing on those tactics. This is one of the most exciting components of the third edition. The material models the very activities social media marketing managers perform on a daily basis. You'll be able to experience these activities and leave the course with hands-on knowledge you can take into your first job in social media marketing.

The text then dives into the four zones of social media. We start with community (e.g., Facebook, Instagram), then move on to publishing (e.g., user-generated content and branded content marketing shared via blogs, vlogs, Tumblr, etc.), entertainment (e.g., Candy Crush Saga, Spotify, YouTube), and finally commerce (e.g., ratings/reviews, Groupon, chatbots). Part IV explains how social media can serve as a source of marketing research and the key analytical approaches to harnessing information from social media. You'll also learn how to assess social media marketing outcomes in the final chapter on social media metrics. In fact, metrics is such a hot button for marketers, we've included a feature story in every chapter that includes the metrics used to assess the effectiveness of the strategy or tactic used. Every chapter also highlights an ethical issue or concern we face as marketers and consumers.

We've worked hard to bring a lot of current examples and "real-world" applications to the mix. That's a tough job when the landscape changes even as you write the book. The book includes the latest popular social communities, new examples, and the most relevant research that helps us to understand how to market using social media. Like social media, this text is very much a work in progress. We love hearing from readers in social channels! Enjoy the ride!

ACKNOWLEDGMENTS

James Allen said, "No duty is more urgent than that of returning thanks." This edition was made possible through the efforts of several people. We take this opportunity to express our sincere gratitude.

We thank Matthew Waters, our commissioning editor at SAGE. He recognized the value of this book in educating marketing students around the world about how to use social media marketing in a strategic way. We are very grateful for his vision and commitment. His staff, in particular Lyndsay Aitken, have been phenomenal in their availability, responsiveness, and attention. It's been a joy to work with this team.

No book comes to life without help from others and we would like to acknowledge the following individuals for their support, contributions, and assistance:

Paula Fisher worked tirelessly to aid in collecting relevant examples, updating vocabulary, and a host of other activities throughout the development process.

Mike Doherty helped design graphical representations of many of the concepts and models throughout the book. His understanding of the content and ability to relay concepts visually were critical to expressing complex and detailed information in an effective way.

Ashby Brame, a social media marketing manager herself, provided a sounding board, feedback, and more throughout the process.

Several professors also contributed by responding to survey questions about the past edition and sharing topics that were most important to them. We are grateful for their feedback, which served as a guiding force in this latest edition. We also thank Rob Kozinets for his review and kind words of affirmation. Gary Vaynerchuk of VaynerMedia has been a champion for social media marketing and we can think of no greater honor than to have his endorsement.

Many companies graciously provided content or other support for the text. We thank Social Media Examiner, Social Studio/Salesforce, Forrester Research, Altimeter, Sprout Social, Content Marketing Institute, HubSpot, Ignite Social Media, Hootsuite, AdEspresso, BrightSpark, eMarketer, Marketo, Buffer, CoSchedule, Nielsen, SocialBakers, Infegy, TeraData, Brandwatch, Curata, SimplyMeasured, Edelman Digital, Think with Google, Interactive Advertising Bureau (IAB), SmartInsights, Regalix, Ditch The Label, Vivaldi Group, Pew Research, NatCen Social Research, The Chartered Institute of Marketing, Content Strategy Alliance, Meltwater, SocialFish, SmartSheet, Accenture, and RadiumOne.

The book and companion website now feature several cases contributed by social media marketing professors from around the world. Their contributions elevate the book by providing additional learning activities for students, based on real company experiences. The following professors contributed case studies. We are delighted to share their work with you, and feel certain the case studies will be useful as you learn throughout this textbook.

- Donna C. Wertalik, Virginia Tech University: "Strategic Social Media Plan: First & Main, an Outdoor Shopping Mall" and "Strategic Social Media Plan for a University Business School"
- Karen Mishra, East Carolina University: "Social Advocacy Around the World"
- Ricardo Limongi França Coelho and Marcos Inácio Severo de Almeida, Federal University of Goiás – UFG, Brazil: "The Role of Digital Influencers in Social Media"
- Selcen Ozturkcan, Bahcesehir University: "The Rise and Fall of a Fake Psychologist as an Instagram Celebrity"
- Sarah Fischbach, California Lutheran University and Jennifer Zarzosa, Henderson State University: "Native Advertising: Novel or Deceptive?" and "Authentic & Fake Consumers? Accepting the Use of Native Advertisements in Social Media"
- Dr Julia Cronin-Gilmore and Randa Zalman, Bellevue University: "Nebraska State Historical Society Foundation: The Nebraska Marker Project Launch"
- Alan J. Seymour, University Lecturer Consultant: "A Social Media Conference Community"
- Kristen Smirnov, Whittier College: "Denny's Millennial Strategy"
- Sharon Justice, East Carolina University: "Social Media Marketing in the Wedding Planning Industry"
- Caley Cantrell, Virginia Commonwealth University Brandcenter and Brad Perry, Authentic: "Travel and Social Media: The Grand Ole Opry"
- Emma Reid, University of West of Scotland and Katherine Duffy, University of Glasgow: "#NikeAirMaxDay: The Creation of a Social Brand Event"
- Thomas Mueller, Appalachian State University: "Social Media is Gateway to eBook Sales Success: Amazon Kindle eBooks"
- Clay Gransden, Liverpool Hope University: "Pokémon GO: A Revolution in Social Gaming"
- Ilenia Confente and Paola Signori, University of Verona: "Mila: Leveraging Social Media for Market Research"
- Rania A. Pilidou, Consultant: "Combining Qualitative Marketing Research with Advanced Social Media Intelligence for Positioning"
- Jelena Filipović, University of Belgrade, "AcademLink—Information Before Socialization"

Last but not least, we thank our families who were patient, understanding, and kind, all the while managing a heavier load so that our focus could be on the writing.

ONLINE RESOURCES

 SAGE knowledge   Browse   Products   Search all SAGE Knowledge   🔍   LOGIN: Profile   **$SAGE** Publishing

Advanced

video

Electronic Word of Mouth
▶ Segment 1: Electronic Word of Mouth

$SAGE

🎬 Create Clip

TRANSCRIPT   SUMMARY

Auto-Scroll: ON   🔍   PDF

00:06   [Electronic Word of Mouth]

00:09   TRACY TUTEN: Electronic word of mouth, sometimes it's abbreviated EWOM. [Dr. Tracy Tuten, Professor of Marketing, East Carolina University] It literally means word of mouth communication that is communicated electronically, and it's quite broad when we think about it, because it could be word of mouth communication that is delivered through texting, through email, through comments on forums, any kind

00:33   TRACY TUTEN [continued]: of electronic communication, any of those channels. If it's word of mouth communication but person to person, peer to peer, Then it is EWOM, electronic word of mouth communication. And it could be something that's one to one, just the way you might, for instance, have a brand that you love, and you tell a friend about it as you're walking on the way to class.

Abstract

Professor Tracy Tuten discusses the principles how word-of-mouth communication in the digital world. Customer comments, reviews, and complaints are stored online in widely available, searchable formats.

$SAGE video shorts

VIDEO INFO   SEGMENT INFO   RELATED CONTENT

Video Info

Title: Electronic Word of Mouth

Subject(s): Marketing (general), Consumer Behavior, Social Media

Keywords: customers; email; informed decision making; internet; marketing concept; peer-to-peer; Search engines; text messaging

Duration: 00:02:04

Discipline: Business & Management

Content Type: Video Case

Publication Info

Publisher: SAGE Publications Ltd

Publication Year: 2016

Publication Place: London, United Kingdom

SAGE Original Production Type: SAGE Shorts

ISBN: 9781473988828

DOI: http://dx.doi.org/10.4135/9781473988828

Copyright Statement: (c) SAGE Publications Ltd., 2016

People

Academic: Tracy Tuten Ph.D.

Visit: https://study.sagepub.com/smm3e

$SAGE Course Cartridge makes it easy to import our quality instructor and student resources into your institution's virtual learning environment and to customize course content to meet your students' needs.

For instructors, for every chapter:

- PowerPoint slides
- Instructor manual
- Testbank of multiple choice questions
- SAGE premium videos on social media marketing
- Additional case studies

For students:

- Exclusive author video on social media marketing
- Author-selected YouTube video playlist
- Free SAGE journal articles and useful weblinks from the end-of-chapter notes in the book
- Additional case studies

PART 1

Foundations of
Social Media Marketing

The Social Media Environment

Learning Objectives

When you finish reading this chapter, you will be able to answer these questions:

1   What are social media? How are social media similar to, yet different from, traditional media?

2   How does the Social Media Value Chain explain the relationships among the Internet, social media channels, social software, and the Internet-enabled devices we use for access and participation?

3   What are the major zones of social media that make up the channels, modes, and vehicles for social media participation?

4   What is social media marketing? What marketing objectives can organizations meet when they incorporate social media in their marketing mix?

Greetings, Digital Native

When you woke up this morning, what was the first thing you did? Sure, you may have taken a moment to gulp down some juice or coffee, but odds are you also checked your mobile for texts that came in overnight. Maybe you set your Snapchat Story. Perhaps you scrolled through a few tweets or reviewed your Flipboard to see what's going on in the world. You certainly aren't alone: One recent survey of people from 31 countries reported 96% of them use their smartphone within an hour of waking up, often *before* they get out of bed.[1]

Face it—you're a **digital native**. If you're a typical student, you probably can't recall a time when the Internet was just a static, one-way platform that transmitted text and a few sketchy images. The term *digital native* originated in a 2001 article by Marc Prensky titled "Digital Natives, Digital Immigrants."[2] He tried to explain a new type of student who was starting to enter educational institutions. These students—students like you—were born in an era in which digital technology has always existed. You and your fellow digital natives grew up "wired" in a highly networked, always-on world. It's an exciting time—but it continues to change so constantly that we need to study it carefully.

Today the Internet is the backbone of our society. Widespread access to connected devices like personal computers, digital video and audio recorders, webcams, smartphones, and wearables like "smart watches" ensures that consumers who live in virtually any part of the world can create and share content. Worldwide, there are about 3.77 billion global Internet users today—that's roughly 50% of the world's population. Most Internet users, about 37% of the world's population, are active on at least one social network. That's nearly 2.8 billion people.[3] Of course, penetration does vary by global region, with the lowest penetration rates reported in Central Asia, Africa, and South Asia. Even these areas are expected to experience growth, at least in part due to Internet access via mobile phone. Mobile penetration is 108% worldwide and 34% of mobile users are active on social media via mobile applications. Curious about social media usage in a specific country? WeAreSocial, a global social media marketing agency, provides data on every country in the world in its Digital Yearbook.[4] Odds are you already participate in this wired world.

Information doesn't just flow from big companies or governments down to the rest of us; today each of us communicates with huge numbers of people by a click on a keypad, so information flows *across* people as well. This fundamental change in the way we live, work, and play is characterized in part by the prevalence of social media. **Social media** are the online means of communication, conveyance, collaboration, and cultivation among interconnected and interdependent networks of people, communities, and organizations enhanced by technological capabilities and mobility.[5] Does that sound like a complex definition? It is … because social media exist within a complex and rapidly advancing environment. We'll dive deep into the social media environment, but first let's explore the makings of a social media life—*your* life.

Living a Social (Media) Life

The Internet and its related technologies make what we know today as social media possible and prevalent. Every day the influence of social media expands as more people join online communities. Facebook, a **social utility** that offers synchronous interactions (which occur in real time, such as when you text back and forth with a friend) and asynchronous interactions (which don't require all participants to respond immediately, such as when you email a friend and get an answer the next day), content sharing of images, video, music, games, applications, groups, and more, has as of the time of this writing more than 2 billion active users worldwide.[6] What's more—more than 1 billion of those users are mobile users. If Facebook were a country, it would be the most populated in the world. Do you wonder why we called Facebook a social utility? A community that got its start as a social network, Facebook offers functionality far beyond basic relationship building. It not only competes with social channels ranging from video and photo sharing to blogs. Its Facebook Live, Marketplace, and Campaigns ensure it competes with e-commerce sites, news sources, and other advertising media channels. Facebook also owns the top two social messaging services, WhatsApp and Facebook Messenger, as well as the top photo and video-sharing network, Instagram.

People aren't just joining social communities. They are contributing, too! Let's take YouTube as an example. YouTube users (YouTube has over 1 billion users) upload more than 300 hours of video every single minute of every day.[7] That's roughly equivalent to 1,500,000 full-length movies uploaded weekly. YouTube hosts local versions in more than 88 countries and users can navigate YouTube in 76 different languages.[8] It's perhaps not surprising then to learn that YouTube users watch more than 3 billion hours of video each month (and more than half watch on mobile devices). Google the phrase "social media stats" and you'll see

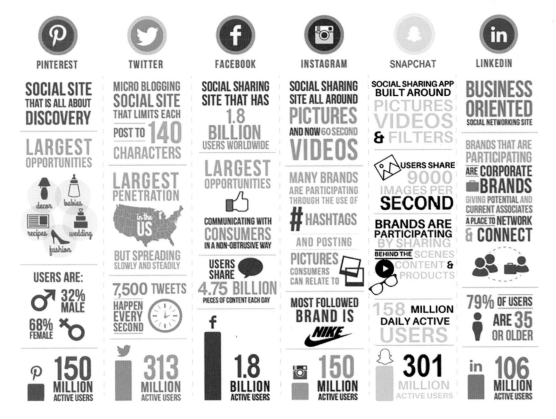

Figure 1.1   Fun Facts about Social Media's Most Popular Sites

Designed by: Mike Doherty

mind-boggling facts and figures about the number of people who use social media, what they're doing (and when) with social media, and their reach and influence. We've done that for you in Table 1.1. And take a look at Figure 1.1, an infographic that highlights fun facts about some of the most popular social sites.

Table 1.1   Mind-Boggling Social Media Stats

- It took radio 38 years to reach 50 million listeners. TV took 13 years to reach 50 million users. The Internet took 4 years to reach 50 million people. In less than 9 months, Facebook added 100 million users.[a]

- Just over 13% of Facebook users are in North America; more than a third of users are in the Asia-Pacific region.[b]

- 94% of companies use LinkedIn as their primary recruiting tool.[c]

- The top YouTubers, like PewDiePie and Lily Singh, earn millions of dollars each year.[d]

- Gen X (ages 35–49) spend the most time on social media – 6 hours and 58 minutes per week. Millennials (ages 18–34) come in second, spending 6 hours and 19 minutes of their time per week on social networks.[b]

- Only about $\frac{1}{5}$ of internet users worldwide use social media.[e]

- While Facebook dominates in size and penetration worldwide, Instagram dominates in user engagement. It averages 70 interactions per post per 1,000 users, while the other major social networks average under 10.[b]

- QQ, WeChat, and QZone, social networks with heavy user bases in Asia, are more popular than Tumblr, Instagram, Twitter, and Pinterest.[b]

Sources:
[a]Jake Hird, "20+ More Mind-blowing Social Media Statistics," eConsultancy Blog, August 17, 2009, https://econsultancy.com/blog/4402-20+-more-mind-blowing-social-media-statistics (accessed July 20, 2017)
[b]Dave Chaffey, "Global Social Media Research Summary," Smart Insights (2016), www.smartinsights.com/social-media-marketing/social-media-strategy/new-global-social-media-research (accessed February 2, 2017)
[c]Top 15 Recruiting Statistics 2014, Capterra Talent Management, http://blog.capterra.com/top-15-recruiting-statistics-2014 (accessed February 2, 2017)
[d]YouTube Statistics, YouTube, www.youtube.com/yt/press/statistics.html (accessed February 11, 2017)
[e]Mobile Messaging and Social Media 2015 Survey. Pew Research Center. www.pewinternet.org/2015/08/19/mobile-messaging-and-social-media-2015 (accessed February 11, 2017)

Social Behavior and the Philosophy of Participation

When we introduced the definition of social media earlier, we admitted it's a complicated idea. It's difficult to fully capture the realm of social media because of the expansive nature of sites, services, and behaviors that are a part of this rapidly expanding digital universe. There are simply too many social websites, too many things we can do online, and increasing access using a variety of devices to grasp it all at once.

More generally, however, we can think of social media as the way digital natives live a social life. To sum things up, it's all about a culture of participation; a belief in democracy: the ability to freely interact with other people, companies, and organizations; open access to venues that allow users to share content from simple comments to reviews, ratings, photos, stories, and more; and the power to build on the content of others from your own unique point of view. Here's just a brief look at some of the things you might do with social media:

- Share and document an event using live video.
- Watch television while discussing the program on social media.
- Create a blog to share your favorite recipes.
- Coordinate a book club meeting and negotiate a group discount on the book's purchase price.
- Mobilize a group of people to protest against an unpopular policy on your campus.
- Instant message or voice chat with friends to carry on a synchronous conversation online.
- Share an infographic with your friends.
- Locate the best vegan restaurant in a city you're visiting for the first time based upon reviews by other vegans.
- Make your own animated video and share it.
- Keep a travel diary of a trip abroad complete with photos, videos, journal entries, and destination ratings.
- Raise money for a charity or even find backers for a startup company who are willing to fund part of your costs.
- Find people you used to know and reconnect with them.
- Entertain yourself and your friends with short social games.

This list could go on and on. Our point? Social media enable active participation in the form of communicating, creating, joining, collaborating, working, sharing, socializing, playing, buying and selling, and learning within interactive and interdependent networks. It's an exciting time to be around!

The Infrastructure of Social Media

The environment of social media is like a volcano that suddenly erupts without warning. Within a few short years we've seen an ever-expanding domain of activities, channels, technologies, and devices that are changing how we think about our lives (e.g., in the old days a "friend" was someone you actually knew in person!). As a student of social media marketing, recognizing the parameters of the field and how the pieces of the puzzle fit together will benefit you as you develop skill at devising social media strategies and tactics. The **Social Media Value Chain**, shown in Figure 1.2, organizes this complex environment into its core components.

The value chain illustrates the core activities of social media participants and the components that make those activities possible. As a social media user, you are empowered to participate in any way you'd like, from just "lurking" on a site to scripting, filming, and uploading your own video stories. Those activities are made possible by the underlying *infrastructure* of social media's techno-social system.[9] Just as in the physical world where we need infrastructure in the form of roads, railroads, TV transmitters, and trained people to operate and maintain these structures, in digital environments the pieces that make up the social Web are crucial. These include the Web, the social channels and vehicles, the software that provides the programming we need to carry out these activities, the **devices** (iPads, smartphones, computers) we use, and of course the participants—the people and organizations whose contributions provide the content we all access. Let's take a closer look at each of these elements.

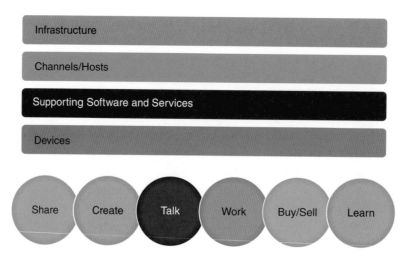

Figure 1.2   The Social Media Value Chain

The Web as Platform

Just as the Internet is a foundation for the Web, the Web is the foundation for social media. Because social media are not possible without this infrastructure, it is the first supporting component we identify in the Social Media Value Chain. To put it simply, the Internet is a network of connected data servers. Initially, the Web (what we now call Web 1.0) was a network of connected information. People browsing the Internet were merely consumers of the Internet's mostly static contents. Web 1.0 was the era of cognition, in which a network of data producers served information to primarily passive consumers. Web 2.0 marked a major shift by connecting *networks of people* in addition to networks of information.[10] Tim O'Reilly, founder of O-Reilly Media and the first to define Web 2.0, explained Web 2.0 as "developments in online technology that enable interactive capabilities in an environment characterized by user control, freedom, and dialogue."[11] Web 2.0 offered a cost-effective solution that provides access to rich data; the collective wisdom of its users; access to micro-markets; software that operates on multiple platforms (mobile phone, PDA, computer) and beyond (cloud computing); and user interfaces that are easy, accessible, and interactive.

From these advances blossomed the "social Web" and an era of communication, in which networks of networked communities have members who participate as consumers, creators, and co-creators. Each additional user adds value for all users. Economists refer to this as a **network effect**. Amazon's ability to recommend books to you based upon what other people with similar interests bought in the past gets better as it tracks more and more people who enter search queries and make purchases. When you're visiting a new city and want to find a great restaurant on Yelp, you feel more comfortable with a place that 1,000 diners recommend than one that only ten users rate. You get more value from Facebook as more of your friends also use the network. Network effects enable organizations to leverage the value of **crowdsourcing**, a process that harnesses the collective knowledge of a large group of people to solve problems and complete tasks. Organizations use crowdsourcing to benefit from the collective wisdom of crowds, but the network effect ensures that there is sufficient participation for the crowdsourced solution to be a good one.

Web 3.0, the **Semantic Web**, is the expected next stage. First envisioned by Tim Berners-Lee, this iteration of the Web makes it possible for people and machines to collaborate.[12] The Web will be a universal medium for data, information, and knowledge exchange. It will mark an era of collaboration—not only of people, but also of people and machines.[13] In other words, devices (yes, machines!) will be contextually, socially, and network aware and be able to dynamically create social connections between each other and connected people in order to offer services to each other and to jointly solve problems. In other words, social media will eventually serve to support **collective intelligence**.[14] While some elements of Web 3.0 exist—especially the presence of services made possible by social software, the capture of user-generated data, and the mining and processing of big data—it is not yet fully realized. We remain in a stage known as Web 2.x.

Social Software

So far we've learned that the social media environment supports many activities. But much of our experiences and what we are able to create or do online is due to a host of **social software** applications. These are computer programs that enable users to interact, create, and share data online. For virtually everything you'd like to do online, there is a social software program (or several) that can help you. Interested in planning an event? Use an event planner and invitation service like eVite.com. Want to keep a notebook of wedding ideas that you can share with your bridesmaids? Use Evernote.com, or create a board of hot new wedding gown styles on Pinterest (watch out for those hideous bridesmaids' dresses). Need to keep a news feed of all the latest happenings at your school? Use Paper.li or Google Alerts. Social software can facilitate interaction, content creation, sharing, syndicating, saving, analyzing, filtering, sorting, and searching data online. Such tools are certainly useful to individuals, communities, entrepreneurs, and businesses. Examples include Mixlr (for producing live radio shows and podcasts), Xtranormal (for video production), and Prezi (for presentations).

You've heard the phrase, "There's an app for that!" It's no wonder given that there are currently more than 1.2 billion apps available through digital stores like Google Play. Those **apps**, also known as **widgets** (usually downloadable or embeddable), are types of social software. In addition to apps, social software also encompasses application service sites that we call **social services**. Importantly, social software exists to facilitate *all* social media channels. There are applications for social community activities, publishing, entertainment, and commerce. Importantly, these apps largely enable mobile connectivity to our social spaces and activities. Blurring things further, open application programming interfaces (APIs) and other platform technologies have enabled countless third-party websites to integrate with social network sites. A more recent development is the **chatbot**, an artificial intelligence computer software program that simulates intelligent conversation via written or spoken text using a chat interface, such as Facebook Messenger or WeChat. Chatbots can provide a number of conversational services ranging from functional to fun.

EXHIBIT 1.1

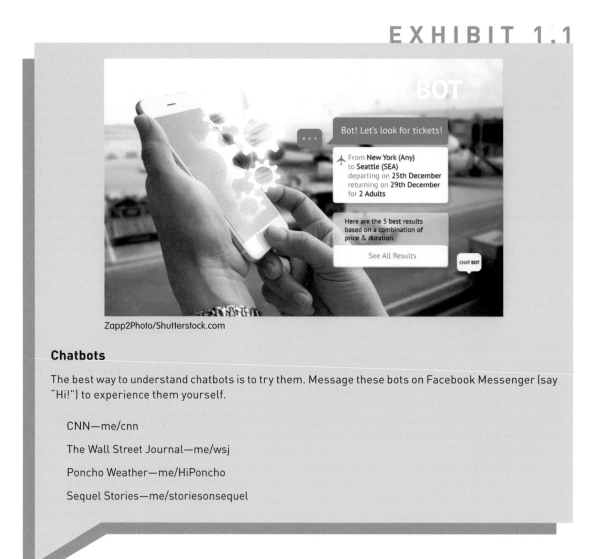

Zapp2Photo/Shutterstock.com

Chatbots

The best way to understand chatbots is to try them. Message these bots on Facebook Messenger (say "Hi!") to experience them yourself.

CNN—me/cnn

The Wall Street Journal—me/wsj

Poncho Weather—me/HiPoncho

Sequel Stories—me/storiesonsequel

Social software also operates behind the scenes in ways that affect your social media experience. Social sites use complex mathematical formulas called **algorithms** to personalize the content you see in your news feed, recommend friend connections, and more. Dominique Cardon, author of *What Are Algorithms Dreaming Of?*, likens algorithms to a recipe in that they are a series of instructions that produce a desired result.[15] When you browse nearby restaurants on your phone, view movie recommendations on Netflix, or check YouTube for how-to videos, algorithms likely played a role in the outcome.

Devices

Devices are pieces of equipment we use to access the Internet and the range of activities in which we participate online. We utilize hardware devices like tablet PCs, smartphones, smartwatches, Internet-connected game consoles, traditional laptops and desktops, and even televisions for social media access. As a consumer, we may focus primarily on connected devices like smartphones and other smart devices, especially those that provide mobile access to social media. Globally, 85.5% of social media users participate using a mobile device.[16] Today's smart devices also include refrigerators, thermostats, and even cars. **Wearables** are smart devices that can be carried or worn on one's body. They measure and capture data which can then be stored, shared, and further processed. Fitness wearables like Fitbit, which measure activity levels and share the information with online communities, have experienced the most adoption thus far, but they represent a small portion of wearable devices. For instance, Snapchat Spectators, camera-equipped sunglasses, enable users to take video and upload it to Snapchat with the touch of a button.

Even devices that aren't "smart" on their own can become so by using an **Internet of Things gateway**. The Internet of Things (IoT) refers to a paradigm in which all the objects around us could be connected anytime and anywhere.[17] Gateways are devices that can facilitate connection for objects without network capabilities. So far most applications are industrial, but expect to see consumer applications in surprising areas. Absolut, the vodka company, is experimenting with manufacturing its bottles as IoT-enabled objects! Smart devices are a first step in the evolution toward connecting machines as users, alongside people in social media.[18] Ultimately, social connection among machines will transform them from passive data-collecting devices into active members of a thriving digital ecosystem, capable of creating social connections, solving problems, and offering services.

People

Social media work only when people participate, create, and share content. Journalists, editors, and publishers still matter in social media, but so do everyday individuals. You see this visualized in Figure 1.2 as a series of activities typical in social media participation. This is why we hear so much about citizen journalists (amateurs who post about newsworthy events) and citizen advertisers (people who share their views about a product or service even though they're not affiliated with the company). Bloggers represent a unique hybrid form of "netizens" in that they may create and share content professionally or personally. Publishing a blog is surely a bigger commitment to sharing content than is posting a status update to your Facebook wall, but both actions generate content and add value to the social media environment. Still, people aren't the only actors in social media. As a techno-social system, other participants include businesses and brands, government organizations, community groups, media companies, content producers, and so on.[19]

Our coverage of the Social Media Value Chain isn't complete without a review of the social channels and related vehicles in and through which social media participation takes place. We address these channels, known as the **zones of social media**, next.

The Zones of Social Media

The word **media** has multiple meanings, but for our purposes we'll simply use it to refer to means of communication.[20] The media we use range from **mass media** (means of communication that can reach a large number of individuals) such as broadcast, print, and digital channels, to **personal media** (channels capable of two-way communication on a small scale) such as email, surface mail, telephone, and face-to-face conversations. Social media cross the boundaries of mass and personal media, so they enable individuals to communicate with one or a few people as well as to thousands or even millions of others.

Communication travels using a **medium** (or channel) such as word-of-mouth, television, radio, newspaper, magazine, signage, Internet, direct mail, or telephone. Within each medium, marketers can choose specific **vehicles** to place a message. For instance, within the medium of television, marketers may choose *The Walking Dead* as one vehicle to broadcast their message. *Cosmopolitan* and *Fast Company* are vehicles for the magazine medium. Social media are socially enabled online channels, and like other media, there are numerous vehicles within each channel.

Part of the complexity of social media is due to the sheer quantity of channels and vehicles, with new ones coming online all the time. These options are easier to compare and contrast if we group similar channels together. In so doing we can conveniently organize the social media space into a compact space that consists of what we call the four *zones of social media*. Figure 1.3 illustrates the four zones of social media channels, and we've organized the book around these groupings:

- Zone 1 is Social Community.
- Zone 2 is Social Publishing.
- Zone 3 is Social Entertainment.
- Zone 4 is Social Commerce.

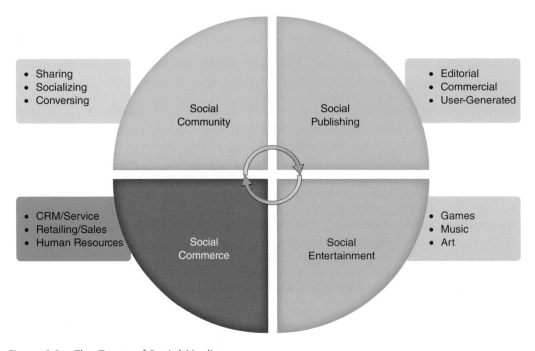

Figure 1.3   The Zones of Social Media

You'll note, as we discuss various uses of social media for personal and commercial purposes, that some areas overlap two or even more zones. That's the squishy nature of social media. All social media are networked around relationships, technologically enabled, and based on the principles of *shared participation*. The four zones framework isn't set in stone for this reason—but it is a very useful way to cut through the clutter and focus upon the most important functions of each social media platform—including those that haven't been invented yet.

Zone 1: Social Community

Social communities describe channels of social media that focus upon *relationships* and the common activities people participate in with others who share the same interest or identification. Thus, social communities feature two-way and multi-way communication, conversation, collaboration, and the sharing of experiences and resources. All social media channels are built around networked relationships, but for social communities the interaction and collaboration for relationship building and maintenance are the *primary* reason people engage in these activities. Many of the channels in which you already participate likely reside in this first zone. The channels in the social community zone include **social network sites**, **message boards** and **forums**, and **wikis**. All emphasize individual contributions in the context of a community, communication and conversation, and collaboration.

Social network sites (SNS) are online hosts that enable site members to construct and maintain profiles, identify other members with whom they are connected, and participate by consuming, producing, and/or interacting with content provided by their connections.[21] Profiles enhance the ability of members to develop a **social identity** when they add a profile picture or avatar, basic information about themselves, and other customizable options. Members maintain a **social presence** in the community that may indicate their availability, mood, friend list, and status. **Connections**, whom we might call *friends*, *followers*, or *fans*, communicate and share content in a variety of ways including *direct messages* (akin to email within the social network site), *wall posts* (posts to a profile, visible to others), and *chat* or *instant messaging (IM)* options. Thus, SNS offer both synchronous and asynchronous forms of communication, and the resulting content may be either permanent or temporary. Snapchat's surge in popularity is largely attributed to its disappearing messages. SNS add value to users by offering and/or enabling applications. Facebook offers thousands of apps, ranging from games to dating to weather forecasts to safety check-ins. Though the services provided by app functionalities heighten user engagement, the focus of SNS is on the individual communication and collaboration within the context of connections in the community. We'll delve deeper into these characteristics and uses of SNS and social communities in Chapter 6.

Given the dominance of Facebook and the other major players, it's easy to assume that there are only a small number of social networks. In fact, there are hundreds of SNS vehicles operating at present. You've surely heard of Instagram, Snapchat, LinkedIn, and Pinterest. But are you familiar with Steemit, DriveTribe, Whisper, Houzz, or Thumb? SNS exist to meet the needs of their users and many provide niche communities.

Forums are perhaps the oldest venue of social media. Essentially they are interactive, online versions of community bulletin boards. They focus entirely on discussions among members. Members establish profiles as they do in SNS and participate by posing content including questions, opinions, news, and photos. Others then respond and extend the conversation as they post responses; this results in a threaded discussion. There are thousands upon thousands of forums active online, most oriented around a common interest. For example, RC Universe (www.rcuniverse.com) is a vibrant community of remote-control hobbyists.

Wikis are collaborative online workspaces that enable community members to contribute to the creation of a useful and shared resource. Wikis can be about anything and everything. A wiki could be created by a family community to share and update family history, or by an appliance manufacturer that is trying to develop the perfect user manual. The software that supports the wiki enables multiple members to collaborate, edit, make comments, and share a variety of content.

Zone 2: Social Publishing

Social publishing is the production and issuance of content for distribution via social publishing sites. Social publishing sites aid in the dissemination of content to an audience by hosting content while also enabling audience participation and sharing. While social networks met the need for online communities, social publishing made it possible for people to share their content, user-generated content (UGC), without the barriers and gatekeeping of traditional publishing and broadcast models. It is a key reason we associate social media with democracy in that social publishing democratized content production and dissemination. That said, today, individual users are not the only social publishers. Professional content creators like journalists, traditional media organizations like newspapers, and brands develop content for and publish on social publishing sites. We categorize social publishers into four use groups: 1) individual users, 2) independent professionals, 3) professional contributors associated with organizations such as news media, and 4) brands. Brands use social publishing as a distribution and/or promotion mode in **content marketing** campaigns.[22]

The channels of social publishing that we will feature in Chapter 7 include blogs, microsharing sites, media sharing sites, and social bookmarking and news sites. Social publishing channels enable participation and sharing, just as social communities do. The distinction between these two zones is in the primary orientation. The orientation of social communities is networking while that of social publishing is knowledge-sharing.[23]

Blogs are websites that host regularly updated online content; they may include text, graphics, audio, and video. Blogs may be maintained by individuals, journalists, traditional media providers, or organizations, so they feature a wide range of topics. Thus, there are blogs that operate much like an online news source or magazine, a tabloid, or simply as an online personal diary. Blogs are social because they offer social share tools, and they are participatory because they include the option for readers to leave comments that can result in threaded discussions related to specific posts. Several services are available for formatting and hosting, including Blogger, WordPress, Squarespace, and Weebly.

Microsharing sites, also called **microblogging sites**, work much like blogs except that there is a limit to the length of the content you can post. A **microshare** could include a sentence, sentence fragment, embedded video, or link to content residing on another site. Twitter, the most well-known microsharing vehicle, limits posts to 140 characters. Others include Plurk and identi.ca.

Media sharing sites, like blogs, host content but also typically feature video, audio (music and podcasts), photos, and presentations and documents rather than text or a mix of media. Media sharing sites host content searchable by the masses, but within each vehicle are options for following content posted by specific people. Thus, media sharing sites are also networked. Here are some prominent vehicles within different types of media:

- Blogging: Tumblr, Blogger, Wordpress.
- Video sharing: YouTube, Vimeo, and Vsnap.
- Photo sharing: Flickr, Snapfish, and Instagram.
- Music and audio sharing: Audiofarm and Soundcloud.
- Presentations and documents: Scribd, SlideShare, SplashCast, BrightTalk, and SlideBoom.
- Social bookmarking services (i.e., sharing links to other sites): Diigo and Digg.

Zone 3: Social Entertainment

The zone of **social entertainment** encompasses events, performances, and activities designed to provide the audience with pleasure and enjoyment, experienced and shared using social media. The distinction between the zones of social publishing and social entertainment is the orientation: Knowledge-sharing versus entertainment-sharing. The topic of Chapter 8, these include social games, social music, video and social television. The social media channels supporting this zone include communities dedicated to entertainment like Spotify, as well as multi-zone social networks like YouTube and Twitter. At this stage in the development of social media, **social games** are by a substantial margin the most advanced channel in the social entertainment zone. These are hosted online and include opportunities for interaction with members of a player's network as well as the ability to **statuscast** (post updates to one's status) activities and gaming accomplishments to online profiles. Examples of social game vehicles include Candy Crush and Mafia Wars.

Zone 4: Social Commerce

Our fourth zone is **social commerce**. The topic of Chapter 9, social commerce refers to the use of social media in the online shopping, buying, and selling of products and services. Social commerce encompasses social shopping, social marketplaces, and hybrid channels and tools that enable shared participation in a buying decision. Thus, social commerce enables people, both networks of buyers and sellers, to participate actively in the marketing and selling of products and services in online marketplaces and communities.[24] **Social shopping** is the active participation and influence of others on a consumer's decision-making process, typically in the form of opinions, recommendations, and experiences shared via social media.[25] Channels include reviews and ratings (on review sites like Yelp or branded e-commerce sites), **deal sites** (like Groupon), **deal aggregators** (aggregate deals into personalized deal feeds), **social shopping markets** (online malls featuring user-recommended products, reviews, and the ability to communicate with friends while shopping like Wanelo), **social storefronts** (online retail stores that sometimes operate within a social site like Facebook with social capabilities), community marketplaces (peer-to-peer sites like Etsy), and social networks with sales conversion functionality. In addition, organizations can socially enable aspects of their traditional e-commerce websites by using tools such as **Facebook Connect** (a Facebook tool that allows users to log in to other partnering sites using their Facebook identities) and **share applications** (tools that let users share what they are buying). Figure 1.4 illustrates the four zones of social media along with several vehicles prevalent in each zone at this time.

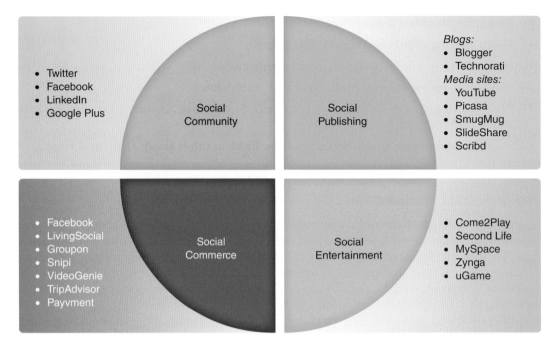

Social Community
- Twitter
- Facebook
- LinkedIn
- Google Plus

Social Publishing
Blogs:
- Blogger
- Technorati

Media sites:
- YouTube
- Picasa
- SmugMug
- SlideShare
- Scribd

Social Commerce
- Facebook
- LivingSocial
- Groupon
- Snipi
- VideoGenie
- TripAdvisor
- Payvment

Social Entertainment
- Come2Play
- Second Life
- MySpace
- Zynga
- uGame

Figure 1.4   Social Media Zones and Exemplar Vehicles

Monetization and Social Media

As wired individuals, we've come to rely on many of the social sites and services available online. And for marketers, social media have created one of the most exciting and efficient opportunities to reach target audiences. But have you ever thought about how those social sites earn revenues? Most sites still feature free access and a buffet of valuable tools and services. Yet those organizations have invested in potentially extensive development costs and time, hosting costs, and ongoing maintenance. Though it's standard business practice to invest capital to pave the way for future profitability, how do these organizations earn revenue if many of the platforms are free to use?

Business Models and Monetization

Just like other businesses, social media providers (whether they are social communities, utilities, software providers, or game and app developers) need a **monetization strategy**. **Monetization** refers to how a business earns revenue. It must make money if it is to survive. If a system requires substantial new investment as users adopt it, the break-even point for return on investment (ROI) is delayed even as it appears to be a success. This plan is part of a company's overall **business model**—the strategy and format it follows to earn money and provide value to its stakeholders. For example, Google derives most of the revenue from its widely used search engine (where you "google" a term to locate relevant online links) from the fees it charges advertisers to put their messages on the results pages. In contrast, eBay makes most of its money by taking a cut of the proceeds each time a seller fills an order from a buyer on its merchandise pages. Two different business models; both ways to return value to the sponsoring organization.

For decades now, media providers (e.g., the big networks, ABC, NBC, CBS, and Fox) and media conglomerates (e.g., Disney, Viacom, and Time Warner) relied heavily on a business model we call the **interruption-disruption model**. The goal is to create programming that is interesting enough to attract people to watch it or listen to it. Then, when they have your attention, they interrupt the programming to bring you a commercial message. They sell ad space to marketers who want to gain the attention of a targeted audience, and the audience allows this to happen in return for access to programming they want. The monetization strategy relies upon attracting as many people as possible to the content; the more who pay attention (or who at least tune in even though they may not be paying attention), the more the programmer can charge for the right to insert messages in that vehicle.

Many social media sites still use this same strategy of earning revenues from selling ad space (did you notice the text ads delivered alongside your Facebook news feed today?). Though some companies have other **revenue streams** (or source of income), typically through subscriptions to premium versions or fees for data, these are unlikely to replace the model of "ad space as revenue." Despite the value of services and content found online, the culture of the Web is one of open and free access.

Psychic Income

Should you have to pay for online content? Believe it or not, way back in the old days (i.e., before 1999) it never occurred to consumers that they should *not* pay for content. That's when a college student named Shawn Fanning introduced the Napster site that enabled music lovers to share tracks for free. That party lasted only two years before legalities caught up with the service, but by then the cat was out of the bag. Now, many people (not to point fingers, but especially college students) believe that "information wants to be free," and they gravitate toward technology that enables them to download songs, newspapers, and, yes, even textbooks without cost.

As attractive as that sounds, in the long run an entirely free world probably isn't feasible. Remember the old expression, "there's no such thing as a free lunch"? At the end of the day, *someone* has to pay for content and services. Music artists and novelists (and, yes, even textbook authors) can't create and receive nothing in return (for long, anyway). However, the currency that we exchange doesn't necessarily have to be money. For example, if you post a restaurant review on Yelp you won't get a check in the mail for your comments. But you may get "paid" by the satisfaction of sharing your foodie opinions with the uneducated masses. You may even receive a rating on some sites that designates you as a star reviewer. These are forms of **psychic income** (perceived value that is not expressed in monetary form) that help to grease the wheels of social media. Also referred to as **social currency**, people and brands need to earn a reputation for providing high value—whether that value comes from information, relevance, and/or entertainment.[26]

Social Media Marketing

Let's take a step back: **marketing** is the activity, set of institutions, and processes for creating, communicating, delivering, and exchanging offerings that have value for customers, clients, partners, and society at large.[27] The classic view is that organizations accomplish these goals through a **marketing mix** that includes the so-called Four Ps: Product, Price, Promotion, and Place (or distribution).

As social media marketing techniques continue to sprout around us, today we need to add a fifth P: Participation. It's fair to say that just as social media are changing the way consumers live on a daily basis, so too these new platforms transform how marketers go about their business. Whether our focus is to improve customer service, maintain customer relationships, inform consumers of our benefits, promote a brand or related special offer, develop a new product, or influence brand attitudes, new social media options play a role. **Social media marketing** is the utilization of social media technologies, channels, and software to create, communicate, deliver, and exchange offerings that have value for an organization's stakeholders. We can see this definition play out in emerging trends in social media. While social media marketing initially influenced brands' promotional plans, more recent business applications include social funding (e.g., Kickstarter for funding new business ventures) and social indexing (e.g., preference data from social users from sources like Google+).[28]

Marketing Communication: From Top-Down to Bottom-Up

Just as the horizontal revolution changed the way society communicates, the advent and adoption of social media change the way brands and consumers interact. Traditional marketing focuses on **push messaging** (one-way communication delivered to the target audience) using a large dose of broadcast and print media to reach a mass audience. There are minimal opportunities for interaction and feedback between customers and the organization, and **boundary spanners** (employees who interact directly with customers) mediate these dialogues. The brand message is controlled in a top-down manner by brand leadership within the organization.

Even as digital technology developed in the 1990s and beyond, marketers still essentially applied the traditional Four Ps model to reach customers. Over time they embraced the Internet as an environment for promotion and distribution. **E-commerce** began to blossom as an alternative to other forms of promotion such as television or radio. Consumers increasingly began to learn about products online—and to purchase them online as well. E-commerce sites are websites that allow customers to examine (onscreen) different brands and to conduct transactions via credit card.

This explosion in e-commerce activity was a boon to manufacturers, retailers, and non-profit organizations because it offered greater speed, cost efficiencies, and access to **micromarkets**. A micromarket is a group of consumers once considered too small and inaccessible for marketers to pursue. Suddenly it became feasible for even a small company that offered a limited inventory to reach potential customers around the globe. The Internet enables efficient access to these markets, and in turn allows customers to search for very specialized products (e.g., music tracks by bands that recorded bass line music in Sheffield, England, between 2002 and 2005, or steampunk science fiction novels written by K.W. Jeter). This allows marketers to offer **niche products** that appeal to small, specialized groups of people.

As it became clear that the Internet was not going to go away, marketers flocked to cyberspace. However, most of them still applied the familiar model of the Four Ps to the digital domain. This form of marketing, **tradigital marketing**, is characterized by improvements in interactivity and measurement, but it retains the primarily vertical flow of power in the channels of communication and distribution. Digital online messages made it possible for consumers to respond directly to an online **display ad** by clicking through to the e-commerce website. **Search advertising** grew during this time too, making it possible for online advertising to target both mass and niche audiences. Direct marketers widely adopted email marketing as a complement to direct mail and telemarketing.

Despite these developments, modes of communication were still primarily vertical, one-way "mass communication," largely impersonal, and delivered from one to many. Whether you read the front page of the *New York Times* online at www.nytimes.com, on the New York Times app on your phone, or peruse the physical newspaper at your kitchen table, the content from the publisher is delivered vertically through the channel of communication.

Both traditional and tradigital marketing work on the basis of the interruption-disruption model we discussed earlier. This means that the source of a communication delivers messages to audiences whether they want to receive them or not, and regardless of whether these messages are directly relevant to their unique needs. By design, an advertising message interrupts some prior activity: a commercial for L'Oréal mascara suddenly appears during the latest episode of *Real Housewives*, or perhaps a pop-up bubble asks you to click on a link to learn more about low rates on car insurance while you browse a website.

Why would Internet users tolerate these disruptions as they surf the Web? For the same reason television viewers and radio listeners have for decades. The ad as interruption that provides a stream of revenue for the media provider, also enables this sponsor to provide the content of interest at little or no cost to the audience. Television programming exists to draw audiences, which enables the network to sell space to advertisers who wish to reach that audience. The audience in turn accepts the presence of the advertising in order to consume the desired programming. This "you scratch my back and I'll scratch yours" relationship also describes traditional Internet advertising: before you can watch a full episode of *The Walking Dead* on your laptop, you might sit through a 15-second ad for Verizon Wireless.

In contrast, social media empower consumers. It isn't enough to interrupt the consumer experience and steal a few moments of attention. With social media marketing, the ability for consumers to interact and engage with brands is greatly enhanced. Social media channels give consumers unparalleled access. Consumers discuss, contribute, collaborate, and share—with brands and with each other. The culture of marketing has shifted to an informal one focused on the belief that customers are in control.[29] Marketing guru Peter Drucker once famously said, "The purpose of a business is to create a customer." With the reach and community influence of social media, we can expand this definition: the purpose of a business is to create customers who create other customers. *That participation in the process is the new fifth P of marketing.*

In the few years of social media's existence, social media marketing has expanded rapidly as much for its efficiency given its low absolute costs as for its potential business applications as a tool for garnering customer attention, managing customer relationships, developing new product ideas, promoting brands, driving store (online and offline) traffic, and converting consumers to customers. Social media are not a substitute for traditional marketing communications, but they are also more than a complement to traditional methods, as you'll see throughout this book. This shift from traditional to tradigital to social media is illustrated in Figure 1.5.

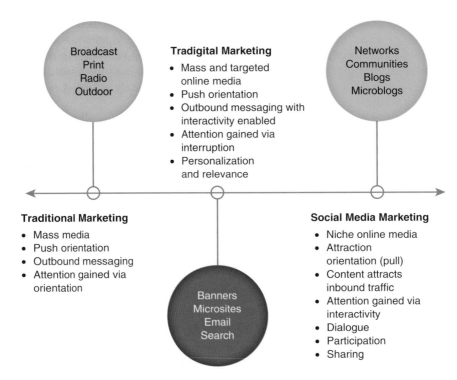

Figure 1.5   The Evolution of Marketing Communications

Social Media Achieves Marketing Objectives

As social media marketing has accelerated over the last few years, the objectives organizations can accomplish have also expanded. Figure 1.6 shows the percentage of marketers using social media marketing to accomplish objectives across a range of marketing activities that include promotion and branding, customer service, relationship management, retailing and commerce, and marketing research. Just as the digital lives of consumers intersect across the four zones of social media, brands reach consumers in those same spaces to build awareness, promote themselves, and encourage users to try them. Let's take a closer look at some of the ways they do this.

Promotion and Branding

Marketers have many possible techniques to promote goods, services, ideas, places, or people. Though there are potentially dozens of specific promotion objectives marketers may seek to accomplish, there are two overarching objectives relevant to the use of social media marketing as part of a brand's promotional mix:

1   Extend and leverage the brand's media coverage.
2   Influence the consumer throughout the decision-making process.

When it comes to acquiring space in media to distribute brand messages, marketers have access to three core types of media: (1) paid, (2) owned, and (3) earned. Marketers

	% Using	B2B Product	B2B Services	B2C Product	B2C Services
Brand awareness and brand building	46.1%	45.3%	48.9%	45.6%	43.9%
Acquiring new customers	31.4%	27.0%	30.4%	36.8%	40.4%
Introducing new products and services	28.9%	29.9%	27.4%	35.1%	24.6%
Retaining current customer	28.4%	26.3%	24.4%	33.3%	38.6%
Brand promotions (e.g., contests, coupons)	28.4%	27.7%	27.4%	38.6%	22.8%
Improving employee engagement	20.1%	17.5%	23.0%	15.8%	24.6%
Marketing research	14.7%	12.4%	14.8%	17.5%	17.5%
Identifying new customer groups you currently don't target	13.7%	14.6%	14.1%	15.8%	8.8%
Identifying new products and service opportunities	11.1%	8.8%	14.8%	7.0%	12.3%
Improving current products or services	7.2%	6.5%	8.9%	5.3%	7.0%

Figure 1.6   Top Priorities for Businesses Using Social Media Marketing

are assessed monetary fees for **paid media**, including purchasing space to deliver brand messages and securing endorsements. Paid media are traditionally the purview of **advertising**, defined as the paid placement of promotional messages in channels capable of reaching a mass audience. **Public relations**, the promotional mix component tasked with generating positive publicity and goodwill, may also utilize paid media in the form of sponsorships. Television commercials, radio ads, magazine print ads, newspaper ads, billboards, Internet display ads, and **search engine marketing (SEM)** all represent examples of paid media that may be incorporated in a brand's promotional plan. As we'll see in later chapters, other emerging formats include paying for messages in online games like Happy Pets or offering branded virtual goods to inhabitants of virtual worlds. And traditional sales promotions such as coupons and contests get a new life on social media platforms.

Owned media are channels the brand controls. Corporate websites and e-commerce sites, corporate blogs, advergames, and alternate reality games (ARGs) all represent forms of owned media. Just as Zara's brick-and-mortar retail stores are owned and controlled by the organization, so is its website.

Earned media are those messages that are distributed at no direct cost to the company and by methods beyond the control of the company. **Word-of-mouth (WOM) communication** (called **influence impressions** in social media) and publicity are important forms of earned media. Companies release content through press releases and paid channels, participate in community events and causes, create stunts designed to generate media attention and buzz, and offer exceptional service quality, all with the hope that a brand message will spread. Table 1.2 explains the forms of paid, earned, and owned media possible in each of the zones of social media marketing.

Table 1.2   Types of Media

Zone	Paid Media	Earned Media	Owned Media
1: Social Communities	• Ads • Native ads • Paid influencers	• Conversations in communities • Shared content • Influence impressions • Likes, followers, fans	• Brand-owned social networks
2: Social Publishing	• Endorsements • Sponsored content • Branded channels in media sharing sites	• Embeds • Comments • Shares • Links • Search rankings	• Corporate blogs • Branded content • Brand-controlled media sharing sites
3: Social Entertainment	• Ads in games or on social entertainment sites • Sponsored social entertainment experiences	• In-game interactions • Engagement in social TV	• Advergames • Branded ARGs • Branded entertainment
4: Social Commerce	• Sales promotions • Retargeted ads on social sites	• Reviews and ratings • Recommendations and referrals • Group buys • Social shopping interactions	• Social storefronts

Do you notice a category missing? That's right. There are forms of marketing that are truly controlled by a social vehicle but that are not paid, earned, or owned. David Armano of Edelman PR calls this media location, "social embassies."[30] For instance, a brand's Facebook profile content is controlled by the brand. Does that sound like owned media? Think again. Facebook dictates the type of content that can be posted. This distinction when the media source is "free" has become more relevant of late as Facebook and other social network sites have favored paid advertisers in news feed announcements over organic posts. We'll talk

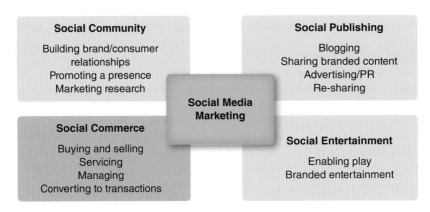

Figure 1.7   Marketing Applications Across the Social Media Zones

more about this in Chapter 6. But for now, this lack of control is why social media experts advise against building your brands on rented land. It's also why it's important to recognize forms of media that do not fall neatly in our buckets of paid, earned, and owned media.

A major objective related to using social media marketing for promotional purposes is to assist in moving the consumer through the purchase process. Marketers target various stages of this cycle to increase brand awareness, enhance brand liking and image, build brand equity, incite desire, and move consumers to action. They can influence consumer attitudes and movement through the process with promotional messages targeted throughout the social media channels.[31] Figure 1.7 illustrates how marketers can use each zone of social media.

Let's take a brief look at how social media marketing works at each stage of the purchase process:

1   *Increase awareness*: brands can increase awareness with social media marketing by maintaining an active presence in the social spaces where target consumers "live" and by integrating social media into the marketing mix. Unilever brand Knorr's #LoveAtFirstTaste campaign matched singles with similar food preferences, then set them up on dates, where they had to feed each other (and agree to be recorded). The campaign included an interactive flavor-profile quiz, a campaign landing page and a series of social videos, including a popular YouTube video.

2   *Influence desire*: social media promotions can be used much like advertising, catalog marketing, and feature events to persuade consumers to recognize a sense of desire. The fashion brand Lilly Pulitzer posts each new collection on Facebook, Flickr, and YouTube. Visitors can tour pictures of its designs, fresh from each photo shoot. It's like being in the pages of *Vogue*.

3   *Encourage trial*: social media can even be used to support sampling and loyalty programs. **Sampling** means to offer a free trial of a product; these are usually mailed to consumers' homes or distributed in stores or on the street. Social media can be used to recruit interested prospects to qualify for samples. Celestial Seasonings used this approach to distribute 25,000 samples of its new tea flavors. Called Share The Magic, Facebook followers were asked to share how tea adds magic to their day and, in return, Celestial Seasonings sent a free sample and a coupon.

4   *Facilitate purchase*: social media serve as a distribution channel and venue for many sales promotion incentives, including deals and group offers. Many customers "like" or follow brands in social networks in order to qualify for special deals. Here's a recent tweet from Taco Bell: "We're on @Snapchat. Username: tacobell. Add us. We're sending all our friends a secret announcement tomorrow! #Shhh." Friends were rewarded with coupons.

5   *Cement brand loyalty*: social media venues offer engaging activities for consumers that can ensure they spend more time with the brand, hopefully resulting in higher levels of brand loyalty. Look no farther than social games that offer rewards for the most loyal visitors. That's just what grocery chain Lidl accomplished in the UK with its ingenious Social Price Drop campaign on Twitter. The campaign was designed to let its social media followers control pricing for select products during the holiday season. The more followers talked about an item on Twitter, such as the "Christmas lobster," the more that item's price dropped.

Customer Relationship Management and Service Recovery

Despite all the hype we hear constantly about social media being the "new advertising," there are in fact other applications where these techniques will play an increasingly important role. For one, customer relationship management, or CRM, also finds a home here. CRM practices focus on what we do with a customer after the first sale; it's far more difficult (and expensive) to attract new customers than to keep old ones. That's why many organizations work hard to maintain contact with their customers and to provide additional products and services to them over time. Often they rely on sophisticated databases that keep an ongoing record of what a person buys and other pertinent information so that he or she will receive customized follow-up messages and offers that are likely to meet unique needs. Salesforce. com is among the leading business solutions for social CRM.

MINI CASE STUDY

American Express Innovates with Social Media Marketing

American Express (AMEX) is a leader when it comes to social media marketing. Despite targeting consumers, businesses, and merchants, AMEX is social media savvy. It leverages three zones of social media marketing—social community, social publishing, and social commerce. The brand has too many social media marketing campaigns to review them all, but let's take a look at some of its campaigns in each zone.

Among its most successful social media marketing initiatives is its efforts for small businesses including the development of Small Business Saturday and its Open Forum community. Small Business Saturday developed as a campaign to drive traffic for merchants to help them compete against large retailers during Black Friday, which is the busiest shopping day of the year. Not only did AMEX successfully create and brand the Saturday following Black Friday as a day to shop in local small businesses, it also lobbied for the day to become an official day. Part of the strategy included providing resources like marketing toolkits to help small businesses succeed so AMEX created Open Forum. Open Forum is a collaborative social community American Express created for small business owners. Members can access how-to guides, articles, and research provided for community members, contribute content, and engage in discussions with other members. While American Express is also active on Facebook, Twitter, YouTube, and other social networks, Open Forum is its own social community. Branded communities are one of the strategies discussed for companies using the zone of social community. The content published in the Open Forum belongs to the zone of social publishing and it includes UGC (user-generated content) and branded content from contributors and American Express.

AMEX develops engaging content for its brand fans and shares that content across its social network profiles. For instance, the #AmexArchive initiative told visually exciting stories of the brand's heritage and values, leveraging an extensive bank of digitized archive content. An #AmexArchive image of the first purple paper American Express Card from 1958 got the most likes the brand ever received on Instagram. For its 163rd birthday, American Express celebrated with a virtual Twitter party, using the hashtag #163Candles. American Express created and shared images of birthday cake personalized with fans' and followers' names to those who wished the brand a "Happy Birthday" or tweeted with the #163Candles hashtag.[32]

The brand also encourages people to use its campaign hashtags, some of which are tied to specific American Express products. For example, the hashtag #everydaymoments is tied to promotional efforts for the American Express Everyday credit card.

AMEX has been especially innovative in the zone of social commerce. One of its most successful social commerce efforts is its @AskAmex Twitter profile for customer service requests. It also developed a social app and program called Link, Like, Love. Once card members registered for the app on Facebook, they would receive special offers like discounts. When they accepted an offer, American Express asked if they wanted to share it with their Facebook friends or Twitter followers.[33] The app facilitated brand awareness as people saw Facebook and Twitter postings about their friends' use of American Express and Link, Like, Love. It facilitated purchase through the sales promotions offered via the Facebook app. It also achieved advocacy from users in that the posts were akin to a testimonial.

iStock.com/adamdodd

Encouraged by the powerful business results generated by the Link, Like, Love program, American Express released GoSocial, which allowed merchants to draw up their own offers and distribute them through American Express' social channels. Then, American Express provided participating merchants with data on the number of redeemed offers, the average purchase value, and the total amount of sales.[34]

The latest social commerce initiative by AMEX is its own Facebook Messenger bot!

AMEX Bot provides real-time notifications on balances and benefits and services, all delivered via Facebook Messenger.[35] The messages will also seek to help customers streamline purchases like restaurant recommendations paired with hotel reservations.

Results and Outcomes

How effective is American Express when it comes to social media marketing? The metrics suggest these campaigns have been powerful for the brand. For instance, the Twitter birthday party resulted in nearly 6 million impressions on Twitter and more than 500 mentions of @AmericanExpress in just the first six

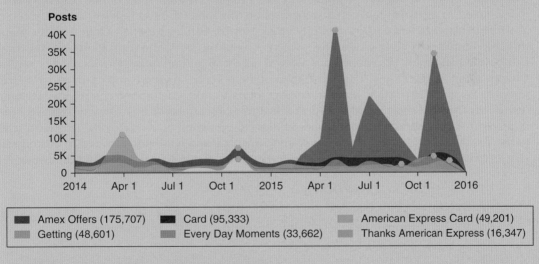

Figure 1.8   Tweet Volume by AMEX Campaign

Source: Morgan Johnstonbough, Positive Responses Follow American Express's Entrance into Customers' Everyday Lives Online and Offline, Crimson Hexagon, www.crimsonhexagon.com/blog/how-credit-card-companies-can-drive-consumer-interest-using-social-insights

Reproduced with kind permission of Morgan Johnstonbaugh, Crimson Hexagon, an enterprise social media analytics company (www.crimsonhexagon.com)

(Continued)

(Continued)

hours of the "party."[36] A study of more than 600,000 tweets that mentioned American Express by Crimson Hexagon, a social media analytics provider, found that total post volume increased by 272% over a two-year period.[37] Sentiment in the posts were mostly positive (41%) and neutral (53%) and minimally negative (6%). Conversations were driven primarily by AMEX offers, more so than the #everydaymoments hashtag and campaign, as shown in Figure 1.8.

Beyond the Arc, an agency that specializes in social media research, studied more than 20,000 Facebook comments about the Link, Like, Love app. Most of the offers promoted specific merchants. Engagement was highest when offers were substantial (e.g., 50% off). Free shipping offers weren't successful at generating likes and posts.[38]

Because of this digital focus, it's not surprising that CRM lends itself to social media applications. **Social CRM** embraces software and processes that include the collective intelligence of a firm's customers to more finely tune the offer and build intimacy between an organization and its customers.[39] When brands embrace social CRM, they use social media as they were meant to be used. Why do we make this claim? Just as we learned that earned media can result from creative and interactive social messages, companies that do a good job of maintaining strong brand-to-customer relationships will benefit from earned media, as those customers in turn share information and recommendations with their networks.

But this is a sword that cuts both ways. It's ideal when all of our interactions with customers are positive. Unfortunately, things sometimes go wrong. When they do, today's social consumers won't hesitate to share their nasty experiences with others on social platforms. They'll vent their frustrations in the most public of ways. A great example is the sad story of one man's plane trip that resulted in a busted guitar that went viral on YouTube ("United Breaks Guitars" video on YouTube).[40] After he tried unsuccessfully to get United Airlines to repair or replace his guitar, this disgruntled passenger created his own version of the story and set it to music—the video he uploaded about his experience was viewed nearly 10 million times. Obviously this was not a happy event for the airline. This illustration of the potential negative impact on a firm's image underscores how important it is for organizations to take customers' complaints seriously (especially those who are inclined to post about their experiences). It is also vital to have a plan in place to initiate **service recovery** when things do go wrong (and they will). This term refers to the actions an organization takes to correct mishaps and win back dissatisfied customers.[41] One helpful set of guidelines that some companies use is known as the **LARA framework**:[42]

- **Listen** to customer conversations.
- **Analyze** those conversations.
- **Relate** this information to existing information within your enterprise.
- **Act** on those customer conversations.

Service recovery typically has to happen quickly if it's going to have any impact. A firm that can identify a problem in the system (e.g., a product recall, a snowstorm that will ground flights) can nip it in the bud by letting customers know that it's aware of the issue and is taking steps to address it. That's a big reason why social media can play such a big role in CRM: the platforms they can use allow them to communicate quickly and efficiently to large groups of customers or to customize messages to individuals who require follow-up. For example, companies such as Carphone Warehouse, Zappos, Best Buy, and Comcast have turned to Twitter to conduct their social CRM: they can monitor trending topics and pre-empt problems if they find that a lot of people are tweeting about them (in a bad way). If necessary, they can send their own tweets to explain what happened and provide solutions.

Marketing Research

Social media open exciting new windows for marketing research. Whether to collect insights for the discovery stage of the creative process or to gather ideas for new product development, social media provide new tools to listen to customers as they discuss their lives, interests, needs, and wants. In fact, this social media marketing activity is called **social listening**.[43] Social listening may be used for social CRM, service recovery, competitive analysis, or even ideas for new product development. We'll learn more about conducting research with social media in Chapter 10. Which channels of social media are relevant for social media market research? Potentially all of them, but profile data, activities, and content shared in social communities and content shared via social publishing vehicles are especially valuable for researchers.

Retailing and E-Commerce

The last major application for social media marketing is that of retailing and e-commerce. We've already shared ways that brands can incent trial and purchase using social media promotions. If you are like most consumers, you've used your share of online ratings and reviews before you made a purchase decision. But did you know that you can go shopping in social storefronts or browse on e-commerce sites that enable real-time chat with your friends? That's right. Groups of friends can shop together even when everyone is online— and not necessarily in the same physical location. When brands use social media marketing as a retailing space, create a venue for and/or encourage consumer reviews and ratings of products, and enable applications that help friends shop together online, we're solidly in the social commerce zone. This will be our focus for Chapter 9.

CRITICAL REFLECTION

How Algorithms Influence Reality

Algorithms are instructions for solving a problem or completing a task. Recipes are algorithms, as are math equations. Computer code is algorithmic. The Internet runs on algorithms and all online searching is accomplished through them. The apps on your smartphone are algorithms. Computer and video games are algorithmic storytelling. Anytime you are offered automated suggestions—whether people you may wish to friend on Facebook, programs to watch on Netflix, products to consider on Amazon, possible romantic matches on Tinder, restaurant recommendations on Yelp (we could go on)—algorithms are responsible.

Algorithms help gadgets respond to voice commands, recognize faces, sort photos, and build and drive cars. Algorithms are mostly invisible aids, augmenting human lives with convenient knowledge delivered on demand. However, sometimes the application of algorithms created with good intentions leads to unintended consequences. As you might have guessed, criminals exploit algorithms for hacking and cyberattacks. Algorithms are also blamed for unfortunate issues in the currency and stock markets.

(Continued)

(Continued)

Vintage Tone/Shutterstock.com

But algorithms are the subject of this critical reflection feature because of the effect they may have on your experience using social media—and ultimately on your life. In fact, some are calling this the Age of Algorithms.[44] Algorithms are primarily written (by coders) to optimize efficiency and profitability without much thought about the possible societal impacts of the data modeling and analysis. A study of experts by Pew Research explained that in algorithmic design, humans are viewed simply as an "input" to the process, rather than as real, thinking, feeling, changing beings. This is already problematic, but is likely to become more so as algorithms begin to write the algorithms. At that point, the robots will decide the rules by which the algorithms produce solutions.

Bart Knijnenburg, a professor at Clemson University, explained: "Algorithms will capitalize on convenience and profit, thereby discriminating [against] certain populations, but also eroding the experience of everyone else. The goal of algorithms is to fit some of our preferences, but not necessarily all of them: They essentially present a caricature of our tastes and preferences." He went on to say, "My biggest fear is that ... it will be simply too convenient for people to follow the advice of an algorithm (or, too difficult to go beyond such advice), turning these algorithms into self-fulfilling prophecies, and users into zombies who exclusively consume easy-to-consume items."[45]

Perhaps zombie is an exaggeration but the risk of living in a filter bubble is real. What is a filter bubble? Akin to living in a bubble, unable to experience the world, algorithms can limit our exposure to new information and different experiences, while influencing our beliefs and emotions with the content that is served to us.[46] Is this risk real? In fact, it's already happening. Your news feed in Facebook is controlled by an algorithm designed to personalize the content you see based on your preferences and past behavior. There are benefits—it means you see more of the stories you have liked in the past, from people and brands you've interacted with most, with the goal of enhancing your experience. It is this filtered access to our social network that inspired the question, "Is social media even social anymore?"

Do you see the flaw? The flow of content you see isn't random or even in real time. It is filtered such that you are increasingly less likely to see stories from people with whom you haven't engaged for a while. You will see more stories from people you agree with and less from people who might have a different opinion. Over time, you could adopt a very distorted view of the world. You also will be limited in new experiences. The information presented by algorithms will never surprise you with something you never thought you'd do, watch, or see because the solutions are based on your past behavior.

That is, unless the solutions are manipulated. What's that? You trust the information you get online? Not so fast. Facebook scientists collaborated on an experiment called the Contagion Experiment. One sample of Facebook users were served consistently negative stories and another sample saw positive content. Did the content influence the recipients? You bet it did. Those in the negative group began posting content that suggested they were in a bad mood and those who saw positive content posted happier messages. In other words, not only may our experiences be influenced by algorithms, our perception of our experiences may as well.

Careers in Social Media

Now you've seen how individuals and organizations including businesses, non-profits, and governments use social channels. As organizations learn the value of social media for marketing, new jobs come online every day to accommodate the need for skilled social media marketers. Interested? Consider the list of social media jobs in Table 1.3.

Table 1.3   Jobs in Social Media

Job Title	Job Duties
Social Media Marketing Manager	Develop and execute plans to engage and acquire superior recommendations/content for services via grass roots recruiting of influencer and social engagement strategies.
	Ensure timely delivery of superior answers/recommedations to users by working closely with influencers and local experts.
	Execute the viral marketing plan, engage bloggers and neighborhood leaders, as well as drive word-of-mouth programs.
	Support the active outreach program to recruit local influencers, local experts, bloggers and brands to add their recommendations and invite their customers to endorse them on Romio.
	The ability to select the very best sources of superior best of the best service recommendations.
Social Media Insights Analyst	Listen, monitor and analyze social media content to create reports which include metrics and insights which help the client to make business decisions and drive strategies.
	Present reports and measurement frameworks to clients.
	Create reporting templates based on client requirements. Get sign off from clients on the templates.
	Support development and deployment of new social media measurement frameworks and KPIs.
	Assist in training and mentoring new team members and client service teams in their understanding of social media measurement/insights.
	Maintain familiarity with social media tools.
	Create advanced queries to glean insights for research reports.
	Add value to the existing deliverables by bringing in new methodologies and processes.

(Continued)

Table 1.3 (Continued)

Job Title	Job Duties
Social Media Assistant	Write awesome social media posts.
	Work closely with and report directly to the Social Media Marketing Manager.
	Stay current with emerging digital marketing and social media trends and best practices.
	Report on the team's awesome work with Google Analytics and other tracking tools.
	Create beautiful Instagram imagery.
	Brainstorm – contribute thoughtful ideas during team meetings.
	Assist with other agency projects.
	Assist with managing vendor relationships.
	Leverage social media tools to streamline your day.
	Create and upload content into Wordpress websites.
	Basic skills needed:
	You have a mega ton of intellectual curiosity
	Digital marketing is your dream job
	You are passionate about social media
	You don't see obstacles, you see opportunities
	Organized
	Great writing skills
	Knowledge of Photoshop, WordPress website structure, technology platforms
	Interested in analytics, metrics and KPIs
	Deadline-driven
	Strategic, creative and proactive
	Skilled at Excel, Powerpoint and/or Keynote, Numbers, Pages
	Happy, sense of fun
Social Media Marketing Specialist	Develop social media content for a variety of clients in a wide array of fields.
	Work with our design and web team to conceptualize and bring to life amazing social media creative campaigns.
	Work with the web development team to create content for pages.
	Offer strategic input for campaign execution.
	Create Facebook & Instagram ad campaigns.

CHAPTER SUMMARY

What are social media? How are social media similar to, yet different from, traditional media?

Social media are the online means of communication, conveyance, collaboration, and cultivation among interconnected and interdependent networks of people, communities, and organizations enhanced by technological capabilities and mobility. Like traditional media, social media include several channels, and within each channel there are specific vehicles. For example, television is a broadcast media and is a vehicle within the medium of television. Social communities are a channel of social media and LinkedIn is a vehicle.

How does the Social Media Value Chain explain the relationships among the Internet, social media channels, social software, and the Internet-enabled devices we use for access and participation?

The Social Media Value Chain explains that social media are made up of core activities and supporting components. The core activities include the things people do with social media such as converse, share, post, tag, upload content, comment, and so on. The support components include the Web 2.0 infrastructure, social media channels, social software, and the devices we use to interact with social media.

What are the major zones associated with social media that make up the channels, modes, and vehicles for social media participation?

The major channels of social media include social communities, social publishing, social entertainment, and social commerce. Each channel incorporates networking, communication functionality, and sharing among connected people, but they each have a different focus. Communities are focused on relationships. Publishing features the sharing and promotion of content. Entertainment channels are geared to fun and shared uses of social media. Commerce addresses the shopping functionality of social media applications.

What is social media marketing?

Social media marketing is the use of social media to facilitate exchanges between consumers and organizations. It is valuable to marketers because it provides inexpensive access to consumers and a variety of ways to interact with and engage consumers at different points in the purchase cycle.

What marketing objectives can organizations meet when they incorporate social media in their marketing mix?

There are several marketing objectives achievable utilizing social media marketing techniques. Branding and promotion, research, and customer service and relationship management objectives are all viable using social media.

REVIEW QUESTIONS

1   How do you define social media? Social media marketing?

2   What are the supporting components of the Social Media Value Chain?

3   What role did Web 2.0 play in the development of social media?

4   What is crowdsourcing?

5   What is social software? Give two examples.

6   How are devices and the Internet of Things (IoT) related?

7   What are the four zones of social media? How do social media compare to traditional media?

8   Explain the concept of psychic income, also known as social currency.

9   How can brands use social media to develop earned media value?

10   What is social CRM? How is it different from traditional CRM?

EXERCISES

1   What is a monetization strategy? Visit Twitter.com and explain how Twitter monetizes its business. Do the same for Snapchat.

2   Should online services like Facebook and Google Docs be free? Poll your classmates and friends (including your social network) to find out what they think should be free. Use the polling features available on Facebook to conduct your poll. What do the results say about the possible monetization strategies available to social media providers?

3   Watch the Ted Talk in which Eli Pariser explains the risk of a world lived in a filter bubble. Do you think the convenience of algorithmic solutions warrant the risks to human experience? Is social networking even social anymore? You can find the video on the Ted Talks site at www.ted.com/talks/eli_pariser_beware_online_filter_bubbles?language=en

4   Create an account at About.Me. Your account will serve as the basis for your social footprint. Begin to link your existing social media accounts to your footprint page. Identify other social communities in which you should develop profiles. Even for channels you choose not to use, you may wish to reserve your profile name.

5   Brands include social media lingo in ads designed for traditional media. The practice is known as *borrowed interest*. For example, an ad using this tactic might leverage the word "like" and a thumbs-up symbol or include the word "hashtag" in conversation. Are these "ripoffs" of social media culture effective? Explain.

6   Social funding sites like Kickstarter promise to use crowdsourcing to fund worthy projects. Visit Kickstarter and assess the participation in a project. What do you think spurs participation in the funding process?

CHAPTER NOTES (access all weblinks listed here at: https://study.sagepub.com/smm3e)

1 Paul Lee and Cornelia Calugar-Pop, "Global Mobile Consumer Survey 2016," Deloitte, www2. deloitte.com/global/en/pages/technology-media-and-telecommunications/articles/global-mobile-consumer-survey.html# (accessed February 11, 2017).

2 Marc Prensky, "Digital Natives, Digital Immigrants," *On the Horizon*, 9:5 (October 2001), 1–6.

3 WeAreSocial, 2017 Digital Yearbook, http://wearesocial.com/uk/blog/2017/02/2017-digital-year book (accessed February 11, 2017).

4 Ibid.

5 There are several definitions of social media proposed by experts in the field. In preparing this definition, we've aggregated the most commonly referenced characteristics of social media and also sought to align the definition with those of traditional media.

6 Facebook Statistics, http://newsroom.fb.com/company-info (accessed July 20, 2017).

7 YouTube Statistics, www.youtube.com/yt/press/statistics.html (accessed February 11, 2017).

8 Kit Smith, "36 Fascinating YouTube Statistics," Brandwatch, June 8, 2016, www.brandwatch.com/ blog/36-youtube-stats-2016 (accessed February 2, 2017).

9 P.G. Shotsberger, "The Human Touch: Synchronous Communication in Web-Based Learning," *Educational Technology*, 40:1 (2000), 53–6.

10 Fuchs, Christian, Wolfgang Hofkirchner, Matthias Schafranek, Celina Raffl, Marisol Sandoval and Robert Bichler, "Theoretical Foundations of the Web: Cognition, Communication, and Co-operation. Towards an Understanding of Web 1.0, 2.0, 3.0," *Future Internet*, 2:1 (2010), 41–59; Celina Raffl, Wolfgang Hofkirchner, Christian Fuchs, and Matthias Schafranek, "The Web as Techno-Social System: The Emergence of Web 3.0," http://fuchs.uti.at/wp-content/uploads/web3.pdf (accessed June 2, 2017).

11 Tim O'Reilly, "What Is Web 2.0?" O'Reilly Media, September 30, 2005, http://oreilly.com/web2/ archive/what-is-web-20.html (accessed December 31, 2010).

12 Nigel Shadbolt, Wendy Hall, and Tim Berners-Lee, "The Semantic Web Revisited," IEEE Intelligent Systems, 21:3 (2006), 96–101.

13 Marina Pticek, Vedran Podobnik, and Gordan Jezic, "Beyond the Internet of Things: The Social Networking of Machines," *International Journal of Distributed Sensor Networks*, 12:6 (2016), http://journals.sagepub.com/doi/full/10.1155/2016/8178417 (accessed June 2, 2017).

14 Tim O'Reilly and John Battelle, "Web Squared: Web 2.0 Five Years On," Web 2.0 Summit (2009), https://conferences.oreilly.com/web2summit/web2009/public/schedule/detail/10194 (accessed February 2, 2017).

15 Cardon, Dominique, *What Are Algorithms Dreaming Of?* (Paris: Seuil, 2015).

16 Dave Chaffey, "Global Social Media Research Summary," Smart Insights (2016), www.smart insights.com/social-media-marketing/social-media-strategy/new-global-social-media-research (accessed February 2, 2017).

17 Pticek, Podobnik, and Jezic, "Beyond the Internet of Things: The Social Networking of Machines."

18 Blake Morgan, "Absolut Enters the Internet of Things," *Forbes*, February 16, 2016, www.forbes.com/sites/blakemorgan/2016/02/16/absolut-enters-the-internet-of-things/#6f2695a21652 (accessed June 2, 2017).

19 Fuchs et al., "Theoretical Foundations of the Web."

20 The Free Dictionary, www.thefreedictionary.com/medium (accessed June 8, 2014).

21 D.M. Boyd and N.B. Ellison, "Social Network Sites: Definition, History, and Scholarship," *Journal of Computer-Mediated Communication*, 13:1 (2007), http://jcmc.indiana.edu/vol13/issue1/boyd.ellison.html (accessed June 2, 2017).

22 "What Is Content Marketing?" Content Marketing Institute, http://contentmarketinginstitute.com/ (accessed June 2, 2017).

23 Nick Couldry and Jose van Dijck, "Researching Social Media as if the Social Mattered," *Social Media and Society*, 2:1 (2015), http://journals.sagepub.com/doi/full/10.1177/2056305115604174 (accessed June 2, 2017).

24 Mark Ralphs, "Built In or Bolt On: Why Social Currency Is Essential to Social Media Marketing," *Journal of Direct, Data, and Digital Marketing Practice*, 12:3 (2011), 211–15.

25 Tracy Tuten, "Social Media Marketing Glossary," http://tracytuten.com/social-media-marketing-glossary (accessed March 2, 2017).

26 Ralphs, "Built In or Bolt On: Why Social Currency Is Essential to Social Media Marketing."

27 American Marketing Association, "Definition of Marketing," www.marketingpower.com/aboutama/pages/definitionofmarketing.aspx (accessed December 31, 2010).

28 Park Sung-Min, "New Business Applications for Social Networking," *SERI Quarterly*, January 2012, 121–6.

29 David Armano, "How Social Digital Is Your Company?", *Harvard Business Review* October 19, 2011, https://hbr.org/2011/10/how-social-digital-is-your-com (accessed March 3, 2017).

30 Ibid.

31 Yogesh Joshi, Liye Ma, William Rand, and Louiqa Rashid, "How Social Media Drives Brand Engagement and Sales," MSI Insights, Marketing Science Institute, December 20, 2013, www.msi.org/articles/how-social-media-drives-brand-engagement-and-sales/?utm_source=20141&utm_medium=Email&utm_campaign= Insights (accessed February 2, 2014).

32 Christopher Heine, "AmEx's Social Data Shows That Nostalgia Is Just Swell," AdWeek October 11, 2013, www.adweek.com/digital/amexs-social-data-shows-nostalgia-just-swell-153053 (accessed June 3, 2017).

33 Beyond The Arc, "Can Social Media Become a Platform for Social Commerce? American Express Case Study: Applying Social Media Analytics to Evaluate *Link, Like, Love*," Case Study, http://beyondthearc.com/wp-content/media/cases/BTA-CaseStudy-Amex-Jan2012.pdf (accessed June 3, 2017).

34 Mikolaj Jan Piskorski, *A Social Strategy: How We Profit from Social Media* (Princeton, NJ: Princeton University Press, 2014).

35 Khari Johnson, "American Express Has Launched its Facebook Messenger Bot," Venture Beat, September 9, 2016, https://venturebeat.com/2016/09/09/american-express-has-launched-its-facebook-messenger-bot (accessed June 3, 2017).

36 Heine, "AmEx's Social Data Shows That Nostalgia Is Just Swell."

37 Morgan Johnstonbough, "Positive Responses Follow American Express's Entrance into Customers' Everyday Lives Online and Offline," Crimson Hexagon, www.crimsonhexagon.com/blog/how-credit-card-companies-can-drive-consumer-interest-using-social-insights (accessed June 3, 2017).

38 Beyond The Arc, "Can Social Media Become a Platform for Social Commerce?"

39 Michael Fauscette, "What Is 'Social' CRM Anyway?" January 26, 2009, www.mfauscette.com/software_technology_partn/2009/01/what-is-social-crm-anyway.html (accessed September 8, 2010).

40 Josh Bernoff, *Empowered* (Cambridge, MA: Harvard Business Press, 2010).

41 Maria Ogneva, "Why Your Company Needs to Embrace Social CRM," *Mashable*, May 21, 2010, http://mashable.com/2010/05/21/social-crm (accessed September 7, 2010).

42 Ibid.

43 Eric Melin, "Arby's Biggest Social Win Ever Comes From Listening," *Social Media Today*, January 31, 2014, www.socialmediatoday.com/eric-melin/2130416/arby-s-biggest-social-win-ever-comes-listening (accessed February 3, 2014).

44 Lee Raine and Janna Anderson, "Code-Dependent: Pros and Cons of the Algorithm Age," Pew Research Center, February 8, 2017, www.pewinternet.org/2017/02/08/code-dependent-pros-and-cons-of-the-algorithm-age (accessed June 2, 2017).

45 Cited in ibid.

46 Eli Pariser, "Beware Online 'Filter Bubbles,'" Ted, March 2011, www.ted.com/talks/eli_pariser_beware_online_filter_bubbles?language=en (accessed June 2, 2017).

Visit **https://study.sagepub.com/smm3e** for free additional online resources related to this chapter.

2

Social Consumers

Learning Objectives

When you finish reading this chapter, you will be able to answer these questions:

1 Why do social media marketers need to understand the behavior of consumer segments? What are the bases of segmentation used to group consumers?

2 What are the elements of social identity? How do individuals build their social identities? How are these identities relevant to marketers?

3 What behaviors are exhibited by people using social media? To what extent are people participating in the four zones of social media?

4 How can we explain the motives for participation in social media activities? What attitudes are most relevant for our understanding of social consumer behavior?

5 What are the most important segments of social media consumers? What do they tell us about targeting users of the social web?

Segmentation and Targeting for Social Media Marketing

Marketers rely upon consumer insights to plan effective social media marketing strategies. Whether planning a campaign that will be executed entirely in social media or one for which social media is one component of an integrated marketing communications (IMC) campaign, understanding the needs, beliefs, and behaviors of the target market is key. Marketers use these insights to develop buyer personas that facilitate the strategic planning process. This is the focus of Chapter 2. We'll review the basics of segmentation, discuss individual and group behaviors in social media and why those behaviors occur, and detail segments found in social media communities.

Profiling the Targeted Segments

Marketers value social media marketing strategies and techniques, but social media marketing will work only to the extent that these new media platforms can reach the customers organizations want to talk to in the digital space. Marketers target specific segments whose needs they believe the brand is capable of satisfying in exchange for meeting organizational objectives. **Market segmentation** is the process of dividing a market into distinct groups that have common needs and characteristics. Segmentation enables marketers to achieve a trade-off between the efficiency of treating all customers the same and the effectiveness of addressing all customers' unique characteristics. Marketers use several variables as the basis to segment markets, including geographic, demographic, psychographic, benefits sought, and behavior. These characteristics represent the **bases of segmentation** marketers use when they divide a population into manageable groups.

Marketers utilize these variables to segment and to identify target audiences regardless of what kind of strategy will be used. But when it comes to social media marketing, we need to also take into account how prospective customers can be segmented according to their digital lives. Although it may seem like everyone is online, and most everyone is on Facebook, the extent to which a person's life is digital varies based on his or her lifestyle, personality, demographics, and even his or her geographic and economic conditions. For B2C (business-to-consumer) marketers, understanding these segments and how their attitudes and behaviors differ is a critical component in devising an effective social media marketing strategy. Marketers use this information and insight to develop profiles that help marketers make better campaign choices. Likewise, B2B (business-to-business) marketers also benefit from segmentation-driven targeting. Let's briefly review the bases of segmentation and try to understand how these variables translate into the online world.

Geographic Segmentation

Geographic segmentation refers to segmenting markets by region, country, market size, market density, or climate. For example, North Face can expect to sell more parkas to people who live in winter climates, whereas Roxy will move more bikinis in sunny vacation spots. Geographic segmentation is increasingly relevant to social media marketers, not only due to location-based targeting based on a business's distribution channel, but also because social media increasingly incorporate **GPS technology**, a satellite system that provides real-time location and time information.

This innovation aids local businesses that can use the technology to target specific people based on physical presence. Services such as Yelp position themselves as geotargeted social media. Yelp became popular for its user-generated reviews of local businesses. In fact, Yelp users have contributed more than 120 million reviews of local businesses.[1] Its mobile app helps users search for nearby businesses with the added value of reviews, ratings, and photos. Businesses can partner with Yelp to target Yelp users with advertising and in-app coupons. This is where segmentation strategy comes into play.

For social media marketers, there are three geolocation techniques: geofencing, geotargeting, and beaconing.[2] **Geofencing** is like a virtual line around a defined geographic space. As people with a geolocation mobile app enter the defined area, they can be targeted with ads or offers. For example, if you have a smoothie shop at the mall, you could set up a geofence around the mall and parking lot. As soon as people (with their devices enabled) come into that geofenced area, you can show them an ad with a deal. It's this same kind of functionality Snapchat uses to offer Snapchat geofilters—visual overlays that relay the "where" and "when" a Snap was taken. **Geotargeting** is similar to geofencing but the geographic parameters are more general, such as 50 miles from a zip code. The third type is **beaconing**, which has a very small range and is best for targeting locations within a store.

EXHIBIT 2.1

Yelp's Geotargeting Adds Value

Source: Tom Humbarger, "Why Is Yelp Important to Your Business?" Tom Humbarger's Social Media Musings (April 22, 2010), https://tomhumbarger.wordpress.com/2010/04/22/why-is-yelp-important-to-your-business

Reproduced by kind permission of Tom Humbarger

(Continued)

(Continued)

Yelp's mobile app averages more than 20 million unique users per month. As Yelp mobile app users enter targeted geographic areas, local businesses in that area can reach out to them with special offers and interactive promotions such as free drinks or discounts. In fact, this is perhaps the most relevant aspect of geographic segmentation for social media marketers—it provides actionable strategies that engage on the social, mobile level. Importantly for the local merchants who use the service, Yelp offers a business "dashboard" that includes customization options for the business's page information and promotional offers, metrics on the number of Yelp views, notifications of new reviews, and message functionality for communicating with reviewers and heavy users.[3] Though Yelp began primarily as a review site to help people find local businesses, it now incorporates transactional services as well. These include Eat24, YelpNow, SeatMe, and Request-A-Quote. Such services enable Yelp to close the gap in the consumer decision-making process between information search and evaluation of alternatives and purchase. The services also provide another stream of revenue, in addition to advertising, for Yelp. Worried about privacy? We address privacy later in this chapter.

Demographic Segmentation

When marketers employ **demographic segmentation** they utilize common characteristics such as age, gender, income, ethnic background, educational attainment, family life cycle, and occupation to understand how to group similar consumers together. For example, General Mills creates specialized campaigns for different demographic segments, such as when it launched QueRicaVida.com as an online platform for Latina moms. B2B marketers also use demographic variables for segmentation but the variables of interest will relate to company size, industry vertical, buyer type, and other characteristics useful for describing businesses. Facebook, Twitter, and LinkedIn have made it easy for businesses to target prospects by offering targeting specifications based on information like interests, job title, company size, revenue, and more.

How can demographic segmentation benefit social media marketers? Let's take a look at a campaign from Secret deodorant.

EXHIBIT 2.2

Secret's Mean Stinks Campaign

How would you describe Secret's target market demographically? That's easy—females, aged 12 and up, in North America. Traditionally, a brand such as Secret would target women with print ads in magazines appropriate by age group. In this case, though, Secret has taken a very different route; its strategy highlights the importance of considering demographic characteristics. Here's an overview of the campaign. Mean Stinks is an anti-bullying campaign sponsored by Secret deodorant. The campaign provides support literature to inform girls and their parents about the dangers of bullying and how to combat those dangers. But more, the campaign has become a community, a channel for creative expression, and a rallying cry of importance to teen girls and their moms. It started simply with a Facebook page and a call to action—girls who believed that "mean stinks" would pinky swear against bullying. How? By painting their pinkies blue! The Facebook page acquired hundreds of thousands of likes in short order. Since then, the campaign has evolved. Using the theme #gangupforgood, Secret empowered girls to use their blue pinkies to let others know they would not bully. Secret then leveraged this content, and its own, in the social community zone (zone 1) and the social publishing zone (zone 2). Profiles are active in Twitter, Facebook, Instagram, and Pinterest. A microsite publishes user-generated content from the social communities, and a YouTube channel and Vimeo (zone 2) channel provide both Secret-produced videos to help parents and teachers combat bullying and user-generated videos.

Is this campaign an effective way to reach the target market? The approach suggests the Secret brand really understands the challenges of being female. This is a key component of demographic targeting. It's about more than the basic facts. The marketer takes the demographic knowledge and uses it to understand the needs of the market.

Keith Homan/Shutterstock.com

Psychographic Segmentation

Psychographic segmentation approaches slice up the market based on personality, motives, lifestyles, and attitudes and opinions. These variables may be used alone or combined with other segmentation bases such as demographics. Psychographics tend to provide the richest picture of a consumer segment in that the descriptions of psychographic segments help marketers to know the real person making the consumption decisions.

Let's consider a practical application of psychographics in the social media space. The greeting card industry has experienced declining sales for some time now. Instead of cards, people may send emails, e-cards, or even just a Facebook post! A large-scale study by Unity Marketing identified four psychographic segments among greeting card buyers.[4] Unfortunately for the greeting card industry, a segment called "Alternative Seeker," the largest group the study identified, is also the most eager to use an alternative to the traditional card. Alternative Seekers view social media as an answer to staying in touch with friends and family on both a daily basis and on special occasions such as birthdays and holidays.

Unity's report warns that greeting card companies are at risk as people use social media as a replacement to traditional cards. But this change presents an opportunity for others. Apps like Cool Greeting Cards and justWink create a variety of virtual greeting cards that can be delivered on Facebook and other social networks. Even Starbucks enabled a Twitter app that lets you give a cup of coffee to someone with a simple tweet!

Benefit Segmentation

Benefit segmentation groups individuals in the marketing universe according to the benefits they seek from the products available in the market. For example, in the auto industry people who buy hybrids and electric cars look for different benefits from a car than those who buy muscle cars or SUVs. For business prospects, benefits sought might be about "how soon can it be delivered?" or "can the purchase be invoiced?". Brands may use social media to identify benefits customers want. That's how McDonald's identified the demand for its new "All Day Breakfast" menu—more than 80,000 tweets specifically mentioned the need for breakfast options all day.[5] What benefits do consumers want from their interactions with brands in social media environments? There are competing schools of thought on this issue. Some industry experts argue that consumers want to have meaningful relationships with the brands they use frequently, and particularly with those brands they consider lovemarks. This term, developed at Saatchi & Saatchi, refers to brands that inspire passionate loyalty in their customers. Saatchi & Saatchi even maintains a website that encourages people to nominate the brands that inspire them in different categories. For example, brands in the beverage category include Guinness, Inca Kola, and Boost Juice.[6] You can nominate your own favorites at www.lovemarks.com.

Others believe consumers seek a more functional relationship with brands, but will offer loyalty for those that meet their needs. This is the view taken in research on the social currency of brands.[7] **Social currency** measures the ability of brands to fit into how consumers manage their social media-centric lives. Based on the premise that social consumers are defined by the extensive use of technology and social media, limited time and attention for decision-making, and a desire for value and utility, the social currency construct assesses brand contribution to several desirable benefits. How do consumers respond to brands with high social currency? The study, which assessed 90 brands over five industries, found that people were more likely to choose these brands and more willing to pay a price premium.

MINI CASE STUDY

The Power of Social Currency

The *Power of Social Currency* study was designed to measure the ability of brands within retail, fashion, automotive, food and beer to adapt to the ways consumers manage their social lives.[8] The report asserted that brands often struggle to keep up with changing consumer preferences. To succeed in social currency, brands should focus on initiatives across seven dimensions that help consumers manage their lives more effectively and efficiently. The modern social consumer is defined by a number of different characteristics that contribute to a desire for social currency benefits:

- manage their lives and achieve their goals using technology across context and culture
- make decisions with limited attention, time and effort
- use social media for information and entertainment, and
- comparison shop for cheaper and/or more convenient alternatives.

The dimensions of social currency are explained in Figure 2.1. The study evaluated brands across the dimensions, assigning an index score for each.

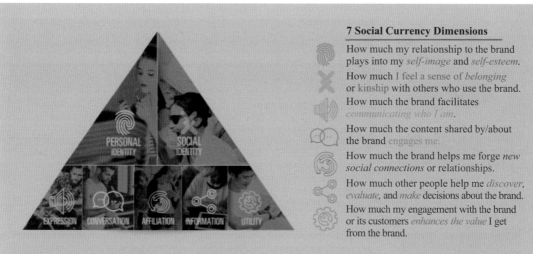

7 Social Currency Dimensions

How much my relationship to the brand plays into my *self-image* and *self-esteem*.

How much I feel a sense of *belonging* or kinship with others who use the brand.

How much the brand facilitates *communicating who I am*.

How much the content shared by/about the brand *engages me*.

How much the brand helps me forge *new social connections* or relationships.

How much other people help me *discover, evaluate,* and *make* decisions about the brand.

How much my engagement with the brand or its customers *enhances the value* I get from the brand.

Figure 2.1   Dimensions of Social Currency

Reproduced with kind permission of the Vivaldi Group (http://vivaldigroup.com)

Results and Outcomes

The top ten brands in social currency were Nike, Subway, Olive Garden, Southwest Airlines, Honda, Levi's, Wendy's, Under Armour, Chili's, and Toyota. Nike scored an indexed social currency composite score of 119—a weighted composite of the brand's results on the seven dimensions. The scores are interpreted to mean that Nike provides social currency benefits at a 19% higher rate than the average of the other 90 brands included in the study.

The results suggest brands can use social media engagement with customers to build the relationship—conversing, sharing, caring, and interacting in each other's lives over time (just like people do). We'll take a deep look at how brands can engage consumers using social communities (zone 1) in Chapter 6.

Behavioral Segmentation

Behavioral segmentation divides consumers into groups based on their actions. Exemplary variables include product research sources, the nature of the purchase, brand loyalty, usage level, frequency of purchase, and distribution channels used. Notice that these very same variables are valuable for B2B segmentation. When it comes to social media, marketers may use behavioral information such as how much time prospective customers spend online and on social media, what activities they participate in on social media, which social networks they use, and the devices they use to access social media as segmentation variables.

Marketers use these bases of segmentation to construct **buyer personas**. A persona is a snapshot of your ideal customer that tells a story using the information you used for segmentation (i.e., demographic, geographic, psychographic, benefits sought, and behavior). This 'bio' provides a composite sketch of the desired target marketing. With personas, marketers are better able to identify, understand, acquire, engage, and retain the target audience. For example, Geckoboard, a company offering data visualization software for

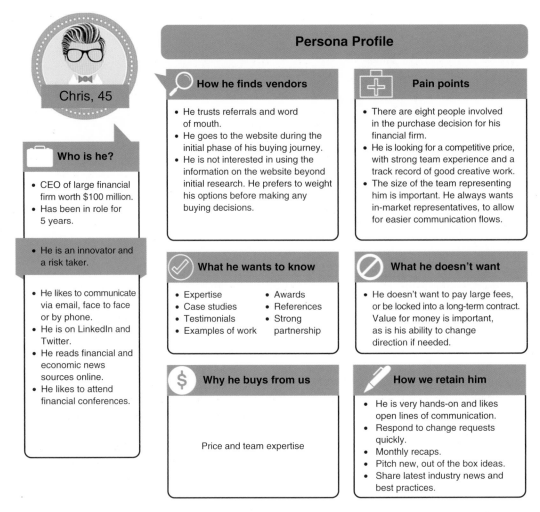

Figure 2.2   Buyer Persona

social media analytics, describes its buyer persona as a young to middle-age founder or chief executive level decision-maker, at an organization in a high-growth, digital business with 11–200 employees, located in the United States, Western Europe, Australia, or Canada.[9]

Social Identity

Facebook? YouTube? Flickr? Twitter? Which of these sites do you make a part of your digital life? What are you sharing? Thoughts, opinions, activities, photos, videos? When and from where? On the go with a mobile device? From a fixed location using a stationary computer? These days, the answer is most or all of the above. We all have an image of ourselves, or a sense of who we are; this is called our **self-concept**. From a psychological perspective, **social identity** is the part of our self-concept that results from our perceived membership in a group.[10] We can break this rather abstract-sounding notion into two components. First, we think of ourselves as members of some groups but not others. At any point in time, what we're doing and where we are brings one of our groups front of mind. When playing a video game, for instance, we might see ourselves as a member of an affinity group of gamers. We probably won't be identifying with people who like baking. Second, we belong to many, many groups—some formal, some informal; some aspirational, some actual. If we are aware of our membership and the group is important to us, it can affect our social identity. What does this have to do with social media? When we participate in social media, we are engaging with one or more groups. From the broadest view, posting on Instagram is an interaction with the group of Instagram users.

Our online activities and the information we post document and express our social identity—the way we represent ourselves via our social connections, community membership, participation, and shared text, images, sounds, and video—to others who access the Web. Consequently, social identity can influence where, when, how, and what you contribute as a social media participant.

Marketers are interested in your social identity—along with other information useful for segmenting and targeting you, like your demographic characteristics, your interests and lifestyle, your personality traits, where you live and work, your shopping behaviors offline and online, and so on. Where do they get this data? From a host of sources—smart marketers will license data from multiple sources to build a dataset useful for marketing analytics. One of the sources is social data. As you participate online, you leave behind residue, sometimes called social exhaust. The residue becomes a source of **big social data (BSD)**, data generated from technology-mediated social interactions and actions online, which can be collected and analyzed.[11] When marketers assess this information, the portrait they paint of you is *their view* of your social identity. Altimeter defines the marketer's view of social identity as "the information about an individual available in social media, including profile data and ongoing activity."[12] In other words, social identity is the way marketers view you given your social media activities.

Just as direct marketers have long known that a more complete customer profile can lead to better targeting of offers, marketers now recognize that utilizing social data can further enrich these profiles. Marketers can use this information to identify new leads, convert prospects to customers, resolve service issues, and more. For example, if a brand can associate an Instagram user who posts a picture with a complaint caption with a customer who has purchased often in the past, it can resolve the complaint, retain the customer, and build higher customer lifetime value. Altimeter believes using social identity data helps brands to build richer customer profiles, efficiently use marketing budgets, and engage across channels. Brands can use social identity data at all points in the purchase funnel, whether they seek to identify prospects, nurture leads, tailor recommendations, follow up with customers to enhance retention, or reward loyalty.

Social Touchpoints: The DNA of Social Identity

Let's take a closer look. Perhaps in a typical day you wake up using an alarm clock app on your smartphone. After you snooze the alarm, you might check your news feed on Facebook Mobile. You leave home and head for school. In transit, you stay connected with your smartphone or even an Internet-enabled car if you drive a new Ford. You might search for reviews on the best place for coffee along your route, or the cheapest source of gas. When you get to class, your professor might ask you to work collaboratively in a wiki on a class assignment or bookmark research for a group project using an app like Evernote. Later that night, you might watch *The Tonight Show* with Jimmy Fallon. You get ready for your evening shift at work. When Jimmy tweets out the hashtag for tonight's Hashtag Game,

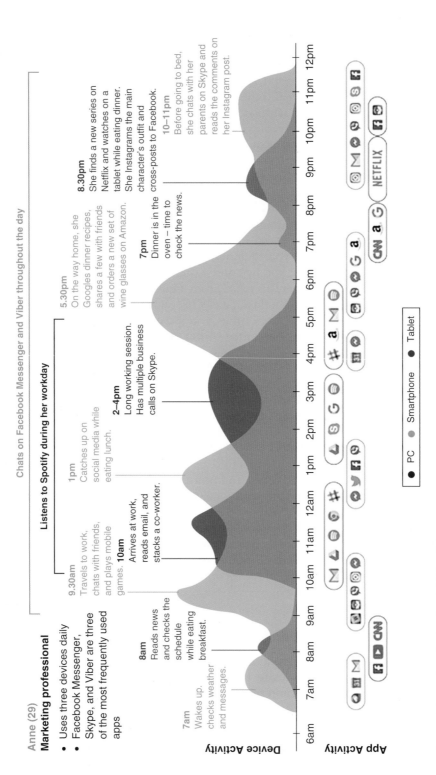

Figure 2.3   A Day in the Social Life of Anne

Source: Mike Read, A Day in the Life of a Consumer, Verto Analytics, 2017. Used with permission.

you turn to Twitter to play along, hoping to be among those chosen to be on the show. See what we mean? Everywhere you go, as long as you have an Internet-enabled device, social media can be a part of your daily life. The opportunities exist as **social media touchpoints**. You can see the possibilities for these touchpoints in Figure 2.3. These touchpoints leave impressions, and they make up the data that marketers use to paint your social identity.

Social Footprints

A footprint is the impression or mark an object makes when it occupies a physical space. Depending upon the surface material, the impression may remain sometime after the indentation was created—when a budding graffiti artist happens upon a patch of drying cement, the rest is history! Similarly, a **social footprint** is the mark a person makes when he or she is present in a social media space. As we visit websites and web communities, we leave a digital trail behind. This social footprint may be subtle or obvious depending upon the quantity and frequency of visits and the activities in which we participate. For example, when you visit your friend's Facebook profile and learn that she's a fan of Juicy Couture, you learn something about what matters to her. This information is one aspect of her social footprint.

Figure 2.4 illustrates a social footprint for one person, Jennifer Jacques. Professionally, Jenn is an editor (the first female editor in the entire industry!) for Bearing Arms, a Second Amendment news site. She's a well-known gun rights advocate, and often interviewed by the media. Personally, she's a wife and mother. Her favorite hobby is hunting. How is Jenn's identity reflected in her social footprints? In zone 1, Jenn has a sizeable presence including a personal Facebook page, a Facebook page dedicated to hunting (www.facebook.com/jenn.d.jacques), and a Facebook fan page (www.facebook.com/2AJennJacques). She connects to her professional community using LinkedIn (www.linkedin.com/in/jennjacques). With personal friends, she also uses SnapChat (jennjacques). In zone 2, Jenn maintains her own website (https://jennjacques.com) and tweets links to her content as well as other information she wants to share with her followers (https://twitter.com/JennJacques). She also posts photos on Instagram (www.instagram.com/jennjacques75). In zone 3, Jenn enjoys using Pinterest (www.pinterest.com/JennJacques75) and when she has a few moments of downtime she plays the social game, Trivia Crack. In zone 4, Jenn is primarily a consumer of social content. She relies on reviews and ratings shared online for many of her purchases, but she hasn't utilized group deals like Groupon, or other social shopping elements. Across all four zones, Jenn leads a very social life. As a full-time writer and a mother, Jennifer doesn't have much time for social entertainment, but she occasionally participates in a game of Words with Friends.

You may or may not leave as many footprints as Jennifer, but you certainly leave your share. Like Hansel and Gretel who dropped breadcrumbs to mark their way in the forest, you leave traces as you interact online and especially as you share social content. Have you ever "liked" a site, an article, or a product? Footprints. Did you ever shop online? More footprints. Comment on YouTube videos? Download podcasts from iTunes or upload pictures on Instagram? That's right ... more footprints. Records of your activities may make up a lifestream (assuming you share enough detail with regularity), which is essentially a diary you keep through your social media activities.

Your footprints become a source of the big social data (we'll cover how marketers use the data in Chapter 10). The footprints are useful for making predictions about people—even broad, seemingly innocuous measures, such as the number of times you've logged into Facebook, and number of likes, comments, and shares. According to Michal Kosinski, a Stanford-based researcher who coordinates a collaborative research study of the Facebook

Figure 2.4   Jenn's Social Footprints

footprints of 8 million volunteers, social footprints can effectively predict surprisingly personal traits—including whether your parents are divorced![13] Sceptical? You can see for yourself—The Psychometrics Centre at the University of Cambridge hosts an online demo at https://applymagicsauce.com/demo_likes.html. Simply log in with your Facebook profile and the API will use your profile data to make a series of predictions about your personality traits, leadership potential, intelligence, life happiness, political, religious, and sexual orientations, and more.

Your Social Brand

You deposit social footprints throughout the social communities you visit. Many social communities require registration as a member of the community in order to access services and join in community activities. Lacking visible bodies, people actively construct profiles that reflect how they want to be identified in social media spaces. Your username in social communities is a **handle** or nickname, just like those truck drivers used on their old-fashioned CB radios. It may be a pseudonym or your real name. Although many digital natives use pseudonyms that can hide real identities and maintain some privacy, others choose handles that describe something about them in shorthand as they try to build a following. We can think of these IDs as our **digital brand name**. Rather than hide one's identity, they heighten the meaning associated with one's name. For example, digital media guru Jennifer Leggio, a prominent blogger for ZDNet, uses the handle "mediaphyter" to represent her social digital footprint.

Before settling on a handle, be sure that you aren't **handle-squatting**. This term refers to the use of a digital brand name by someone who really doesn't have a claim to the brand name. Sometimes another person may have a legitimate claim to the name—many of us have names that are not unique. For instance, there are hundreds of men named David Jones in the world. In that case, use of the handle doesn't constitute squatting. On the other hand, a quick search of Twitter for actor Hugh Jackman turns up several people listings, including @RealHughJackman, @JackmanHugh, @HughJackman, and @H_Jackman, among others. Only one is the "real" Hugh Jackman—the others are probably handle-squatters.

Next, you should find out whether your desired username is available in the many social communities. Services like Namechk.com make this easy. A sign of the times—parents are using services like this to choose baby names (to find a unique name) and then registering their newborns in social networks to reserve the handle!

Your Social Brand in the Age of Selfies

The first selfie was shared in early 2011, and in just a few years, the hashtag #selfie has been used on Instagram more than 185 million times![14] A **hashtag** is a word or phrase comprised of letters, numbers, and/or emoji preceded by what was once referred to as the pound symbol (#). That's just one social vehicle and one hashtag. People use the hashtag #me just as much! Your selfies are indicators of your social brand and, like your handle, they differ from many other sources of information that make up your social identity. Aspects of your identity over which you have a great deal of control are thought to be active, while activities associated with typical participation in social channels are thought to be more passive.[15] The less control you have over the information, the more passive it is in terms of influencing your identity. A selfie is one of the most active aspects because you are in control. You may take several shots, but you publish only the ones you like—if you publish at all.

We'll explain later in this chapter how marketers can use the information that makes up your social identity to target you more effectively, but what does your social identity say to others? To your friends, family, employers, teachers? That's the question Andy Beal addresses in *Repped*, a book designed to show people how to protect their own reputations in a social economy.[16] Why is it important? Because, as we discussed in Chapter 1, social media is a reputation economy. Brian Solis perhaps said it best: "Think about it this way. When you look in the mirror, you see a reflection of who you are right now. What if you could transform that reflection each day into someone you hoped to see staring back at you?"[17] You can with the choices you make. Solis suggests that people conduct their own social activity audit. Sound like a useful activity? It should. It's a personal version of a **social media audit**, the exercise marketers use to assess the situation and their competitors' social presence! A personal audit should categorize social media activity according to the values expressed in the social engagement:[18]

- *Vision*: a vision post answers the questions, "Did I learn something? Was I inspired?"
- *Validation*: a validation activity answers the question, "Am I accepted by a group?"

- *Vindication*: a vindication post informs others, "I am right."
- *Vulnerability*: a vulnerability post opens one's self to others, "I am approachable."
- *Vanity*: a vanity post reveals a tendency to narcissism, "Look at me. I am all that."

Footprints should reveal a social identity that is balanced. We all have aspects of these values inside. But when our footprints are focused more in certain areas, we may inadvertently paint a distorted picture of ourselves.

Once you've completed the audit, you will be ready to cultivate a personal brand identity using social media. Daniel Tolliday of the Social Media Examiner poses five questions—the answers will guide your choices as you build your social brand:[19]

- What goal are you seeking to accomplish?
- What do you want to be known for?
- What groups and people are active in your desired field and which social media channels do they use?
- What can you do to communicate your desired social brand identity while also differentiating yourself from others?
- What visual elements will support the image you want to establish?

Who knows! You could become the next "it" social media influencer. That's one of the exciting benefits of social media. Anyone with a unique point of view can gain a following. To summarize, your *social footprint* leaves evidence of where you are and where you've been. Your *lifestream* is the journal of your digital life. Taken together, they make up your social brand, what marketers call your social identity. When you look at this evidence, we think you'll agree: *You are what you share!*

CRITICAL REFLECTION

Which Right Matters Most? The Right to Know or the Right to Privacy?

We've warned that reputation is everlasting in the realm of social media. But is that really so? The Court of Justice of the European Union thinks differently. Under the Data Protection Directive, its so-called Right to be Forgotten ruling, the Court declared that people have a right to control, at least to some extent, the access others have to digital information about them.[20] In other words, if you don't like some of the information that makes up your social identity, just ask Google that it not be found! And, yes, your public activities in social communities are indexed! Try Googling yourself to see what others could see. While you may appreciate this "do-over" approach to burying past mistakes, it creates tension between the right to privacy and that of free speech. Japan's top court recently ruled on a right to be forgotten case and determined that the country's legal system prioritizes the public's right to know over privacy.[21] Denying a plaintiff's bid to remove search results on Google about his child pornography-related criminal record, the high court said that search engines assist users in obtaining necessary information from massive volumes of data and, therefore, play pivotal roles in modern society's internet-based information distribution. The court listed six factors to guide future cases in determining which should be superseded—freedom of speech or privacy:

1   nature and content of information resulting from search engine search

2   plaintiff's damages

3   plaintiff's social status and power

4   searched articles' objective and meaning

5   societal conditions

6   necessity of posting searched information.

Rawpixel.com/Shutterstock.com

EXHIBIT 2.3

Annette Shaff/Shutterstock.com

Companies Use Selfies Too!

Dallas Pets Alive is just one of several brands, like Toyota, Mastercard, Disney, and Tarte Cosmetics, leveraging the popularity of selfies in marketing campaigns. Dallas Pets Alive decided to use the #selfie trend to find homes for homeless mutts. How? With its #Muttbombing campaign! The campaign features real dogs available for adoption. The dogs are featured in "photobombs" using selfies of area celebrities and local people grabbed from Instagram. See the campaign at www.muttbombing.com.

Motives and Attitudes Influencing Social Media Activities

Web users increasingly participate in social networks such as Facebook, play online social games (turn-based, multi-player games designed to be played within social networks) such as Candy Crush within the network community, watch videos, listen to music, comment on the posts of friends, update status messages, and share content. Likewise, brands are active on these sites as they add content and try to converse with consumers. Research from GfK identified the top social activities:[22]

- visiting a friend's profile page
- commenting on a friend's post
- sending a private message
- watching a video
- posting pictures
- liking a post
- updating status
- following, liking, or becoming a fan of something or someone
- playing a social game.

What motives are behind participation in social media? Chances are there are many reasons that drive your activity in social communities. Some of these motives probably seem like no-brainers, but others may surprise you. These are the most common impulses researchers have identified:

- **Affinity impulse**: social networks enable participants to express an affinity, to acknowledge a liking and/or relationship with individuals and reference groups. Affinity relates to the affective dimension of social identity.[23] When you use Facebook to stay in touch with high school friends and to make new friends, you are responding to the affinity impulse.[24] This is also referred to as a social function. When people contribute to social communities for this reason, they do so to form friendships and feel a sense of belonging.[25] The affinity impulse is related to a person's desire for **social capital**. Social capital refers to the resources created by the building and maintaining of relationships in social networks.[26]

- **Personal utility impulse**: while we tend to think of social media participation truly as community participation, some do consider, "What's in it for me?" This is the personal utility impulse and it may be one of the most important motives for brands to acknowledge. Studies of participation in social communities report that utility, whether in the form of information seeking, incentive seeking, entertainment seeking, or convenience seeking, is a major motive for social media activity.[27] The findings are congruent with others utilizing a uses and gratification approach to understanding social media behavior.[28] For instance, one study found that 60% of Internet users used social media as a source of health-related information. Participants consulted online reviews of doctors, hospitals, and medical treatments; posted reviews of their own experiences; and posted questions in social networks.[29]

- **Contact comfort** and **immediacy impulse**: people have a natural drive to feel a sense of psychological closeness to others. Contact comfort is the sense of relief we feel from knowing others in our network are accessible. Immediacy also lends a sense of relief in that the contact is without delay. Do you feel lost without your mobile phone? Do you feel anxious if you haven't checked Facebook recently? When you reply to a message, do you keep checking for a response? These are indicators of your need for contact comfort and **contact immediacy**. Social media users even seek contact comfort and immediacy from brands. One study found that nearly 40% of respondents believed brands were very likely to engage with them on social networks and 25% expected a response within an hour of leaving a comment on a brand's Facebook or Twitter page.[30] In another study, participants named timeliness and speed of response and sense of connection among the attributes they associate with the most successful brands using social media.[31]

- **Altruistic impulse**: some participate in social media as a way to do something good. They use social media to "make the world a better place," and "pay it forward." The altruistic impulse is also aided by the immediacy of social media, and this value has been played out in the **immediate altruistic responses (IAR)** of social media users to aid calls during crises such as the earthquake relief for Haiti or Japan.[32] Individuals want to do good and do it quickly—social media make it easier to contribute in the form of a cash donation or a service to the community. The altruistic impulse serves a value-expressive function in that it enables individuals to express their own moral beliefs through their social media behavior.[33] Altruism can also explain negatively valenced social media activities including **altruistic punishment**, in which social media users seek to draw attention to a company or person whose behavior is unacceptable to the social community.[34] Beware of the difference between the altruistic impulse and affinity and validation impulses. Known as **virtue signaling** (and sometimes "hashtag activism" or "slacktivism"), people may give token support for a cause with a simple post-share or like.[35] The altruistic impulse is intrinsically motivated. If the underlying motive is to affirm a relationship, publicly build one's image, or shame others, altruism is not the social media motive at play.

- **Curiosity impulse**: when people use social media to gain new knowledge and stimulate intellectual interests, **epistemic curiosity** is the driver.[36] Another form of curiosity is the **prurient impulse**. Online, we can satisfy our curiosity by "following" people on Twitter and visiting their profiles. Surely it is the prurient impulse that led millions of Twitter users to follow Kim Kardashian's daily tweets while millions of others relentlessly track the ups-and-downs of Justin Bieber—will he prevail, or crash and burn?

- **Validation impulse**: social media focus intently on the individual. You can share as much or as little of your opinions and activities as you like, and comment on those of others. This focus on the self highlights the validation impulse, in other words, feeding one's own ego. That's why the validation impulse is sometimes referred to as the ego-defensive function. This function is thought to be particularly relevant as people seek to eliminate perceived external threats and eliminate self-doubts.[37] Certain behaviors are affiliated with people driven by the validation impulse. These include the prevalence of selfies among the mix of posts, a tendency to check to see if posts received likes, a tendency to overshare, and a tendency to impression manage (e.g., promoting the perfect life).[38] These were among the behaviors noted by researchers in a study that investigated types of narcissism in social media. Particularly on Facebook and Twitter, people may use posts to show superiority (particularly by expressing opinions) or to participate in exhibitionism. That's why Brian Solis, a thought leader in the realm of social media, advises to guard against the dreaded disease, "accidental narcissism." Perhaps it's no wonder then that an analysis of Twitter posts found that 80% were posted by "meformers" and just 20% by informers.[39] Meformers post updates primarily related to themselves such as commentary on their daily mood and activities, while informers post updates that share and/or link to information. Though informers were less prevalent, the study revealed that they have twice the number of followers as meformers.

Though all of these motives have been linked to social media participation, one study suggested that the validation motive, and especially the aspect related to developing a desirable image, is the dominant driver of social media activities.[40] Whether a conscious decision or not, image management is a major factor in social media participation. Particularly when one is narrowcasting (i.e., communicating with just one person) rather than broadcasting (i.e., communicating with multiple people), people will avoid sharing content that makes them look bad.[41] How can we know if our friends are revealing their "true selves" to us online? The answer may be in the content—a study of true self-expression on Facebook found that people who felt comfortable sharing their "true self" tended to post personally revealing and emotional content.[42] Earlier we encouraged you to audit your social media activities and to consider using social media to brand yourself. As part of the exercise, you may want to consider how much separation between personal friends and professional colleagues you prefer and whether you will use social media as a tool for enhancing your professional reputation. The choices you make will result in one of four strategies to guide the boundaries you set between personal and professional contacts while accomplishing your goal.[43] Figure 2.5 illustrates the four strategies and includes recommendations to guide your social media activity.

	Integration	**Separation**
Self-verification	**Open boundary management behaviors** Open your profiles to personal and professional contacts	**Audience boundary management behaviors** Exclude professional contacts from your social media profiles
Self-enhancement	**Content boundary management behaviors** Open your profile to friends and colleagues, but manage the content that you post	**Hybrid boundary management behaviors** Keep personas separate by managing both audience and content

(Vertical axis label: **Self-evaluation Motives**)

Figure 2.5   A Framework for Understanding Social Sharing Boundaries

Reproduced with kind permission of the Academy of Management

Despite these motives for participation, there are also motives for not participating! This is reflected in the rise of **social identity suicide**. Why do people delete their social identities? Research suggests that people who commit social identity suicide are concerned about privacy.[44]

Privacy Salience: How Much Do They Know and How Much Do You Care?

It's helpful for marketers to understand motives for social media participation and sharing as we make strategic marketing decisions, but the residue left behind from your social footprints is also of value. That residue big social data makes up the social identity information that marketers can use to augment other customer information, conduct research, target advertising and other promotions, and more.

Are you concerned about privacy as it relates to your social media activities? The extent to which one worries about privacy and the risks related to the collection, unauthorized secondary use, errors in, and improper access of personal data is known as privacy salience. Interestingly, privacy salience doesn't necessarily explain whether social media users take steps to protect their privacy. Because of the disparate relationship, researchers call the phenomenon the **privacy paradox**.[45] The privacy paradox describes people's willingness to disclose personal information in social media channels despite expressing high levels of concern for privacy protection. How can we understand this contradiction? One explanation views privacy concerns as a two-part system: System 1 is **intuitive concern** and System 2 is **considered concern**.[46] Intuitive concern is an emotional gut reaction to a possible privacy invasion, while considered concern involves identifying possible privacy risks, estimating the potential costs of privacy invasions, and deciding if any benefits offset those costs. Thus, it is possible for social media users to have high intuitive concern and yet determine that the risk doesn't warrant action.

Privacy concerns also take on multiple forms including social privacy and institutional privacy. **Social privacy** refers to concerns about disclosing personal information to others. Institutional privacy is privacy from the use of data by the institution providing the service and third parties. Research suggests that people are taking steps to protect their social privacy. Common strategies include using privacy settings to restrict access, excluding personal contact information, untagging and removing photographs, and limiting contacts to known others. While it's still common to disclose (and perhaps overshare) intimate information, people may feel comfortable sharing because they've taken steps to protect social privacy.

Some suggest that privacy is viewed differently by different generations. In particular, today's teens exhibit lower levels of privacy salience. According to Pew, teens share a lot of information in social channels:[47]

- 92% have posted their real name to the profiles they use.
- 91% have posted a selfie.
- 82% have posted their birth date.
- 71% have posted the name of the school they currently attend.
- 71% have posted the name of the town in which they live.
- 64% who use Twitter have a public profile.
- 53% have posted their email address.
- 20% have posted their mobile phone number.
- 16% have allowed sites to auto-post their location.

Why so much sharing? It may be the view of the social context. If social media communities are viewed as private, the expectation is that social norms will prevent inappropriate use of the content and people should feel comfortable disclosing sensitive information. If these spaces are viewed as public rather than private communities, users may disclose more carefully, recognizing that the content may have a broad reach beyond the intended audience. People, particularly young people, may view social media profiles as forms of "produced self" and tend to see social communities as public venues.[48] In other words, people may view privacy in social media settings as networked privacy. With **networked privacy**, people understand that their personal information is likely to be compromised by technological and social violations and that any protective behaviors they may invoke are likely to be insufficient. People may develop an attitude of "privacy cynicism" as a coping mechanism, leading to a resigned neglect of behaviors that would protect privacy.[49] Another explanation is that social media users use a mental cost-benefit approach to justify negating their privacy concerns when trust is high, marginal risk is low, and the entities collecting the data aren't overtly present.[50]

Privacy salience may also vary by cultural region. A study by marketing research firm Ipsos found just that! You might be surprised by the outcome, though. When asked for a descriptor of how much they share online, nearly one in four people around the world said they share everything.[51] The United States, Canada, the United Kingdom, France, and Germany all under indexed while countries such as Saudi Arabia over indexed. There may be a relationship between Internet penetration and oversharing. Nearly all of the countries reporting oversharing are in areas with lower Internet penetration, while the countries that undershare are primarily European, where Internet penetration is high.[52]

Social Media Segments

Because social media are such new areas, marketers are still figuring out just how to use them, and to what extent they should rely on these platforms when they identify their target markets and try to communicate with them. One brand may add a social media piece to a broader strategy when it creates a Facebook page, whereas another may replace virtually all of its traditional advertising with "new media" messages. Decisions regarding just how much to rely on social media and how to design programs that will be effective require us to understand as much as we can about just who participates in social media and how they may differ from one another.

Understanding these nuances will help you to ensure that the social media marketing strategies and tactics you plan have a shot to resonate with the target market. There are countless examples of social media marketing campaigns that have failed. In fact, Gartner, a research firm specializing in technology, claims that half—that's right, 50%—of social media campaigns fail.[53] Why the huge number of bombs? Probably a major reason is simply that the social strategy is not matched to the target audience. A contest that requires players to upload original video content will not succeed with a target market that primarily consumes content but does not create its own. A promotion for a free song download offered on Twitter will not work if the band's fans tend to hang out on SoundCloud instead. A stunt from Skittles to feed live streams from social media communities to its website will not appeal to parents if the live feed includes profanity inappropriate for their children. Let's take a look at several social segmentation models, each of which offers insights about social media users.

Social Technographics

Forrester Research introduced the concept of **Social Technographics** based on research it conducted on the social and digital lives of consumers. This work became the foundation for a book, *Groundswell*, by Charlene Li and Josh Bernoff.[54] From that first study, Forrester identified six types of people (of those online) based on how those people use and interact with social media. Categories included joiners, spectators, creators, critics, collectors, and conversationalists. The types were not exclusive—some people fit into more than one category based on their activities. The behaviors are still useful but as the population of social media users became increasingly savvy and engaged, Forrester revised the model to incorporate an overall score of social media usage. The new framework emphasizes that people rely on social media at varying degrees throughout the stages of purchase decisions.[55]

The Social Technographics score reflects how actively a segment uses social tools, how important those tools are within the stages of the customer life cycle, and how willingly they engage with brands in social media. The score ranges from 0 to 100 and includes four types of social media users: 1) social skippers, 2) social snackers, 3) social savvies, and 4) social stars.

- **Social stars** (scores of 60+) demand social interactions with your company. These consumers constantly use social media to connect with companies, brands, and products. For stars, social media is the preferred choice for interaction with and about brands and products. What's more, with their high discretionary spending via multiple channels including mobile, social stars are valuable customers to acquire.

- **Social savvies** (scores of 30 to 59) expect social interactions with your company. Social media is still a part of their everyday lives and they frequently use social media to connect with companies, brands, and products.

- **Social snackers** (scores of 10 to 29) appreciate social interactions with your company. They don't shy away from branded social interactions, but neither do they seek them out — meaning that marketers targeting this audience should treat social tools as a secondary part of their marketing plans.

- **Social skippers** (scores of 0 to 9) spurn social interactions with your company. They rarely use social media to connect with companies, brands, and products. Skippers prefer to interact with companies through established channels such as email, catalogs, and brick-and-mortar stores — so marketers targeting this audience should put as few resources as possible into their social efforts. You may be surprised to learn that skippers are more than 20% of the general population, but don't worry. Skippers tend to be older, brand-switchers who spend the least on discretionary products, and resistant to marketing.

As you might expect given variations in social media usage globally, Social Technographics scores also vary. For instance, in Asia, Indian and Chinese consumers living in metropolitan areas have the highest scores. Though South Korea is typically described as a country with heavy social media penetration and usage, Koreans had a lower average Social Technographics score. This is attributed to the popularity of the mobile messaging app KakaoTalk.[56]

Social Technographics also provides scores by customer life cycle stage, to enable brands to better choose objectives for social media marketing. Figure 2.6 illustrates a sample report based on the average scores for online adults in the US.

The Social Technographics Score

This score gauges how important social tools are to an audience's customer life cycle and where in the life cycle social tools have the greatest impact.

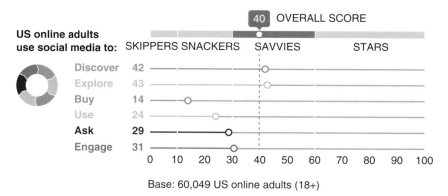

Base: 60,049 US online adults (18+)

Figure 2.6   Forrester's Social Technographics Model

Source: The Data Digest: Forrester's Social Technographics 2016, August, blog by Gina Fleming (http://blogs.forrester.com/gina_fleming/16-08-03-the_data_digest_forresters_social_technographics_2016)

- The **discover** score measures the extent to which the target audience uses social media to learn about new brands as well as how likely they are to spread the word about their favorite products and services. High discover scores also reflect an openness to the experiences afforded via social media. When marketing to a segment with high discover scores, the zones of social community, social publishing, and social entertainment are all viable.

- The **explore** score gauges whether social media can be used to create purchase intent. This number measures how actively your audience consumes social content when they're considering products and making purchase decisions. High explore scores suggest social media marketing tactics focused in Zones 2 and 4—the zones of social publishing and social commerce.

- The **buy** score tracks whether social media is likely to be used to make purchases. It measures how often your audience clicks a "buy" button on social sites. In other words, it measures the likelihood of conversion using social media, the ultimate goal of the zone of social commerce. Forrester's research suggests that even people who are social stars are still resistant to completing transactions in social media.

- The **use** score measures whether social media can stimulate increased product usage. It measures how common it is for a target segment to share product and service experiences, such as sharing what songs they're listening to on Spotify or comparing their workouts to that of other Fitbit users. When use scores are high, brands can benefit from organic word-of-mouth communication and encourage the audience to contribute brand-related UGC and reviews and ratings—leveraging the zones of social community, social publishing, and social commerce.

- The **ask** score reflects whether social media is a valued channel for customer support. It measures how commonly the segment turns to social media for help using the products and services they buy, such as asking for help on Twitter or looking up how-to videos on YouTube. When ask scores are high, the zones of social community, social publishing, and social commerce are useful.

- The **engage** score gauges whether social media will be useful to build customer relationships. It measures the target segment's use of social media to connect with their favorite brands (i.e., their lovemarks). High engage scores suggest social media marketing strategies that include the zone of social community.

The Social Consumption/Creation Matrix

Another segmentation framework, the Social Consumption/Creation Matrix, categorizes social media user types according to their degree of social media consumption and creation.[57] While a more simplistic representation of social media users, the framework effectively captures the dual roles of creation and consumption. Consumption of social media content is the most prevalent activity but must be served by the more taxing creation of content. While brands and media publish social media content, research suggests that social media users have a proclivity for content created by other users. Considering user propensity, from low to high, for content creation and consumption results in a four-segment matrix, depicted in Figure 2.7: 1) attention seekers, 2) devotees, 3) entertainment chasers, and 4) connection seekers.

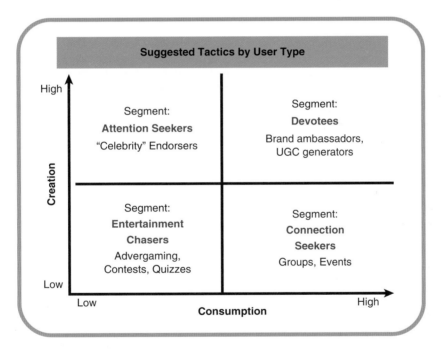

Figure 2.7   The Social Consumption/Creation Matrix

Reproduced with kind permission of the *Journal of Marketing Management*—Taylor and Francis

- **Attention seekers** have large networks, high social capital, and the ability to create and promote social content. These are the social media influencers we discussed earlier in the chapter—regular people whose social media activities have created a celebrity-like following for them. They are motivated by the validation impulse and are ready to participate in conspicuous, brand-initiated interaction.
- **Devotees** are ideal brand ambassadors, because they want to interact with brands and are eager to share their opinions. Like attention seekers, they are talented content

creators, but because devotees are also active content consumers, other social media users may perceive them as more authentic and genuine.

- **Entertainment chasers** are characterized by a low level of both creation and consumption. These are passive users with short attention spans who restrict their investments of time and effort unless there is a reward offered as an incentive. They respond best to social media marketing efforts in the zone of social entertainment including videos, quizzes, polls, and games.

- **Connection seekers** are the largest segment of social media participants. They make up the foundation of any social community. Though they are low content creators, their ongoing engagement is critical to the health of social communities. Motivated by the affinity impulse, connection seekers want to socialize and build relationships. For brands, the social media marketing activities associated with the zone of social community will be most effective for nurturing connection seekers.

The Social Consumption/Creation Matrix provides clear guidance to marketers given the characteristics of each segment. The framework is based on research conducted among Facebook users, but clearly the implications are valuable across social channels.

A Typology of Social Utility

Researchers from Ryerson University in Toronto took a different approach to categorizing social media segments using user propensity to socialize and seek information in social media communities. By categorizing social media users into passive or active information

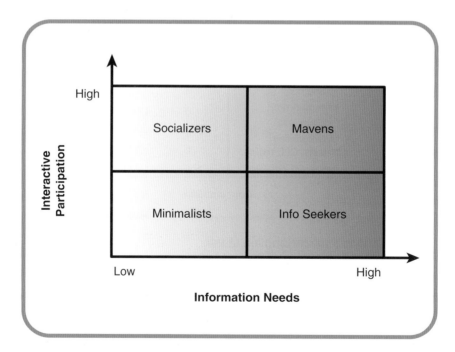

Figure 2.8   A Typology of Social Utility

Reproduced with kind permission of the *International Journal of Internet Marketing and Advertising*—Inderscience Publishers

seekers and passive or active participants, four segments were identified, as shown in Figure 2.8: 1) Minimalists, 2) Info seekers, 3) Socializers, and 4) Mavens.[58] Brands must interact socially in the zone of social community to target Socializers and Mavens, and actively provide content (content marketing in the zone of social publishing) for Info Seekers and Mavens. Minimalists are the least engaged, presumably because their needs for affiliation and information are lower than those of the other segments.

Pew Internet Technology Types

The Pew Internet & American Life Project published a paper called "The Mobile Difference."[59] As increasing numbers go online and participate in social communities from mobile devices, this Pew report sought to better understand consumer views of mobile Internet access. In the study, participants were asked about their attitudes toward a variety of online activities as well as their motives. What resulted was a typology of ten digital lifestyles for the American consumer. In this scheme, digital lifestyle groups are based on two characteristics: (1) whether they hold a positive or negative view of **digital mobility** and (2) their relationships with assets (gadgets and services), actions (activities), and attitudes (how technology fits in their lives).

Pew defines digital mobility in terms of whether the individual welcomes mobility as a way to delve further into digital communications or keeps Internet communication technologies at a distance. Five groups have an increasing reliance on mobile technologies as a way to connect with others online; the other five groups are "stationary" in their use of Internet communications. The research suggests that when it comes to social media strategies, marketers should target those with positive views of mobility. The use of social media is associated with their use of the Internet and mobile devices, whereas the stationary groups are less likely to be heavily engaged in social media. Table 2.1 summarizes the ten groups Pew identified.

Table 2.1   Pew Internet Technology Types

Motivated by Mobility

- **Digital collaborators**: Digital collaborators have the most gadgets of any group and use them to work, play, create, and share by visiting social networks with their mobile devices. Key demographics: mostly male, late 30s, well educated, relatively high incomes.

- **Ambivalent networkers**: Ambivalent networkers use mobile devices to visit social networks and for texting, but they also feel like people need breaks from so much connectivity. Key demographics: male (60%), young (late 20s), ethnically diverse.

- **Media movers**: Media movers create content such as photos and share them on social networks using their mobile devices. For them, digital is all about being social and connecting with others. 46% have a social network profile. They are managers of content and have a high attachment to the Internet. Key demographics: male (56%), mid-30s, family oriented, middle income.

- **Roving nodes**: This group wants to be connected but primarily for work. They use texting and email and rely upon their mobile devices for productivity. Social networking is not a key concern. This group relies on voice communication, texting, and email for communication. Key demographics: female (56%), late 30s, well educated, high incomes.

- **Mobile newbies**: This group is relatively new to mobile connectivity to the Internet. Overall, they are more focused on old media than new. Key demographics: female, 50s, lower educational and income levels.

(Continued)

Table 2.1   (Continued)

Stationary Media Preferred

- **Desktop veterans**: Content to use desktop computers with high-speed Internet access. Key demographics: male, mid-40s, well educated, relatively high incomes.

- **Drifting surfers**: Infrequent online users who wouldn't mind giving up the Internet and their mobile phone. Key demographics: female, early 40s, middle income.

- **Information encumbered**: This group suffers from information overload. They prefer old media such as television to the Internet. Key demographics: men (66%), early 50s, average education, lower-middle income.

- **Tech indifferent**: This group is made up of light users of the Internet who would be willing to give up their digital connectivity. Key demographics: female, late 50s, lower income.

- **Off the network**: This group is made up of people who do not use the Internet and do not have mobile phones. They may have had some experience in the past, but did not choose to continue participation. Key demographics: low-income seniors.

Source: adapted from John Horrigan, "The Mobile Difference," Pew Internet & American Life Project, March 2009, http://pewinternet.org/Reports/2009/5-The-Mobile-Difference-Typology.aspx (accessed March 27, 2010)

Microblog User Types

Microblogs like Twitter are thought to differ from other social networks. Members may seek to align by interests rather than relationships. The patterns go even deeper though, as Pew Research Center found in its study of Twitter topic networks.[60] It discovered six specific archetypes of social media participation in its analysis of Twitter conversations:

1. Polarized crowds
2. Tight crowds
3. Brand clusters
4. Community clusters
5. Broadcast networks
6. Support networks.

The two most critical for marketers are brand clusters and support networks, but before we get into that, let's take a look at the meaning of each archetype. Polarized crowds are people who are passionately discussing an issue. There are two sides and people do not cross the party lines! Tight crowds are characterized by highly interconnected people such as hobbyists, fans, or professional groups. Brand clusters are talking about brands but the people talking are not talking with each other. Community clusters typically feature news relevant to specific groups. Broadcast networks exist when many people repeat prominent news. The news sources are the hub, but the news is spread through retweets. The support network is one in which customer complaints are handled by one or more members. It produces a hub-and-spoke structure but the members are largely disconnected. Brand clusters are relevant for social media marketers because these conversations are occurring around brand topics. There is an opportunity to engage. The support network archetype is relevant to brands seeking to use social media as a customer service channel.

CHAPTER SUMMARY

Why do social media marketers need to understand the behavior of consumer segments? What are the bases of segmentation used to group consumers?

Segmentation is the process by which the total available market is clustered into groups, based on similarities. Once a target segment is selected, the segmentation characteristics of the group provide insights marketers use to design effective marketing offers. The traditional bases of segmentation marketers rely upon are still useful in social media applications. Geographic segmentation is segmenting by market location or location characteristics. In particular, social media tools with geotargeting such as Foursquare are useful to businesses that employ geographic segmentation. Demographic segmentation includes common personal characteristics such as age, gender, income, and educational attainment. Benefit segmentation is based on the benefits consumers seek from products. Some brands are developing mobile apps to provide added value to consumers; we call these branded applications brand butlers. Behavioral segmentation uses consumer behavior as the basis for segmentation. Psychographic segmentation utilizes personality, activities, interests, and opinions to categorize individuals. Many of the existing social media segmentation schemes available to date are psychographic in nature.

What are the aspects of social identity? How do individuals build their social identities? How are these identities relevant to marketers?

Social identity is the information marketers collect using our social footprints (the residue from our social media activities). We build our social identities anytime we share online. Marketers can use this information to augment other consumer data.

What behaviors are exhibited by people using social media? To what extent are people participating in the four zones of social media?

Increasingly our lives are spent online checking email, shopping, banking, watching videos, playing games, and socializing in social networks. In zone 1, consumers interact and communicate with others in their networks. In zone 2, we publish our own content as well as consume the content produced by others (both commercial and user-generated). If you've watched videos on YouTube, you've spent part of your online activity in zone 3. Playing games online is a major activity of zone 3 and shopping online is a prelude to zone 4.

How can we explain the motives for participation in social media activities? What attitudes are most relevant for our understanding of social consumer behavior?

There are several motivations for consumer participation in social media activities. The affinity impulse is our need to acknowledge a liking or relationship with individuals or reference groups. The prurient impulse is the curiosity we feel—curiosity that can be fed by observing social media activity. Contact comfort is our need to feel close to others. The immediacy impulse is our need to have contact without delay. The altruistic impulse is the need to do something good for others. The validation impulse is the need to feed our own egos.

What are the most important segments of social media consumers? What do they tell us about targeting users of the social Web?

Several typologies of digital consumers exist, including the Social Technographics profiles from Forrester Research, the Social Consumption/Creation Matrix, The Typology of Social Utility, Pew Internet Technology Types, and the archetypes of Twitter participation. Each provides insight into online social behavior. In particular, each model explains some aspect of social media usage and the needs that drive behavior.

REVIEW QUESTIONS

1   Define social currency. What is the significance of a brand with high social currency?

2   What behaviors help us to segment social media participants and how can we describe those segments?

3   What is a social identity?

4   Define the major variables marketers use to segment consumers, and provide an example of how each variable can be applied in a social media application.

5   What are the primary motives that drive social media participation?

6   Explain the Social Technographics Score and the resultant four types of social media users.

7   Why is the concept of mobility relevant to social media marketers?

8   What differences exist between the Pew Internet Technology Types who are motivated by mobility and those who prefer stationary media?

9   What is privacy salience? Why is it of concern to social media marketers? What is the difference between social privacy and institutional privacy?

EXERCISES

1   Begin to create your social brand. Make a list of your social network profiles. Note the type of content you've shared recently and how others may perceive you if their impression of you was based solely on the information you shared in social media. Then evaluate your presence using the personal audit suggested by Brian Solis. Are you painting the social identity you wish to portray?

2   Which of the four social media user types identified by the Social Technographics Score would you classify yourself as? What would this mean for marketers targeting you?

3   Find an ongoing social media marketing campaign. Assess the components of the campaign in terms of whether and to what extent it offers a participation route for the Social Technographics segments. How could the campaign be improved to better engage people of varying levels of social media involvement?

4   Visit Twitter and read the stream of user posts (this is known as the tweet stream) for a few minutes. Can you see activities related to the archetypes in the chapter? How are you able to identify them?

5   Visit https://applymagicsauce.com/demo and use your Facebook profile to analyse your social identity.

6   How do you feel about privacy? Do you take steps to protect your social privacy? What about your institutional privacy? Ask a few friends and establish a plan to protect your privacy that fits with your own view.

CHAPTER NOTES (access all weblinks listed here at: https://study.sagepub.com/smm3e)

1   D. Kaplan, "Yelp Revenue Jumps on National Performance Ads, Transactions," GeoMarketing from Yext, February 10, 2017, www.geomarketing.com/yelp-revenue-jumps-on-national-performance-ads-transactions (accessed March 2, 2017).

2   M. Stelzer, "Mobile Local Marketing: Reaching the Mobile Customer," Social Media Examiner. February 3, 2017, www.socialmediaexaminer.com/mobile-local-marketing-reaching-the-mobile-customer-rich-brooks (accessed March 2, 2017).

3   Ibid.

4   "Changing Demographics and Psychographics of the Greeting Card Market Reveal New Opportunities—and Challenges—for Card Marketers and Retailers," *Market Wire*, February 4, 2010, www.marketwired.com/press-release/changing-demographics-psychographics-greeting-card-market-reveal-new-opportunities-challenges-1189051.htm (accessed July 3, 2017).

5   Ethan Wolff-Mann, "Why McDonald's Is Tweeting at Everyone Who Asked for All-Day Breakfast," *Time*, September 4, 2015, http://time.com/money/4022979/mcdonalds-twitter-all-day-breakfast (accessed June 6, 2017).

6   Lovemarks, www.lovemarks.com/index.php?pageID=20015&lmcategoryid=17&additions=2&require=100 (accessed May 21, 2010).

7   Vivaldi Group, *The Power of Social Currency*, August 2016, http://vivaldigroup.com/en/wp-content/uploads/sites/2/2016/09/Social-Currency-2016_Main-Report.c.pdf (accessed March 2, 2017).

8   Ibid.

9   Laura Tyson, "Buyer Personas: Why and How We Use Them for Focus," July 14, 2016, www.geckoboard.com/blog/buyer-personas/#.WLIpLPnyuUl (accessed June 7, 2017).

10 D. Khajeheian, "Intercultural Peers' Effect on Social Identity of Social Media Users: A Critical Study of Consumer Socialization Theory," *Journal of Business and Economics*, 7:3 (2016), 467–73.

11 E. Olshannikova, T. Olsson, J. Huhtamäki, and H. Kärkkäinen, "Conceptualizing Big Social Data," *Journal of Big Data*, 4:3 (2017).

12 Andrew Jones, "Leveraging Social Identity," A Market Overview Report, Altimeter, June 12, 2014, http://getcommandpost.com/assets/2014/07/Leveraging-Social-Identity-Altimeter-Group.pdf (accessed June 7, 2017).

13 Cited in Christina Dong, "What Our Digital Footprint Says About Us," August 27, 2015, http://news.stanford.edu/2015/08/26/social-media-kosinski-082515 (accessed June 7, 2017).

14 Ambuj Gupta, "I. Me. My Selfie," Simplify360, http://simplify360.com/i-me-myselfie-ebook (accessed July 30, 2014).

15 "A History of the Selfie," *BBC News Magazine*, June 6, 2013, www.bbc.com/news/magazine-22511650 (accessed July 30, 2014).

16 Andy Beal, Repped: 30 Days to a Better Online Reputation (CreateSpace, 2014).

17 Brian Solis, "Hello, It's Nice to Meet You Again: Your Digital Reputation Precedes You," February 18, 2014, www.briansolis.com/2014/02/digital-reputation-precedes (accessed March 5, 2014).

18   Brian Solis, "This So-Called Digital Life: Re-Evaluating the Value of Social Media," October 27, 2013, www.briansolis.com/2013/10/re-evaluating-the-value-of-social-media (accessed July 30, 2014).

19   Daniel Tolliday, "How to Use Social Media to Build Your Personal Brand," July 21, 2015, www.social mediaexaminer.com/use-social-media-to-build-your-personal-brand (accessed February 8, 2017).

20   Rory Cellon-Jones, "EU Court Backs 'Right to Be Forgotten' in Google Case," May 13, 2014, www.bbc.com/news/world-europe-27388289 (accessed July 30, 2014).

21   Toshio Aritake, "Japan Supreme Court Denies Right to Be Forgotten Bid," Bloomberg BNA, February 8, 2017, www.bna.com/japan-supreme-court-n57982083500 (accessed June 7, 2017).

22   *The GfK MRI Psychographic Sourcebook*, GfK MRI, December 2015, www.mri.gfk.com/file admin/user_upload/microsites/MRI/GfK_MRI_Psychographic_Sourcebook_Dec_2015.pdf (accessed June 7, 2017).

23   Tien Wang, "Social Identity Dimensions and Consumer Behavior in Social Media," *Asia Pacific Management Review*, 22:1 (2017), 45–51.

24   A. Quan-Haase and A.L. Young, "Uses and Gratifications of Social Media: A Comparison of Facebook and Instant Messaging," *Bulletin of Science, Technology and Society*, 30:5 (2010), 350–61.

25   T. Daugherty, M. Eastin, and L. Bright, "Exploring Consumer Motivations for Creating User-Generated Content," *Journal of Interactive Advertising*, 8:2 (2008), 1–24.

26   M.A. Hodis, R. Sriramachandramurthy, and H.C. Sashittal, "Interact With Me on My Terms: A Four Segment Facebook Engagement Framework for Marketers," *Journal of Marketing Management*, 31:11–12 (2015), 1255–84.

27   Yongjun Sung, Yoojung Kim, Ohyoon Kwon, and Jangho Moon, "An Explorative Study of Korean Consumer Participation in Virtual Brand Communities in Social Network Sites," *Journal of Global Marketing*, 23 (2010), 430–45.

28   Quan-Haase and Young, "Uses and Gratifications of Social Media."

29   R. Thackeray, B.T. Crookston, and J.H. West, "Correlates of Health-Related Social Media Use Among Adults," *Journal of Medical Internet Research*, 15: 1 (2013).

30   Andrea Lehr, "Why People Unfollow Your Brand on Social Media-New Data," HubSpot, March 6, 2015, https://blog.hubspot.com/marketing/unfollow-social-media-stats#sm.0004b7ol91cduds6tl j2qb4zw13aj (accessed June 7, 2017).

31   "Shunning Your Customers on Social Media?" The Q2 2016 Sprout Social Index, http://sprout social.com/insights/data/q2-2016 (accessed June 7, 2017).

32   Scott Brown, "Scott Brown on How Twitter + Dopamine = Better Humans," *Wired*, April 19, 2010, www.wired.com/magazine/2010/04/pl_brown_karma (accessed August 7, 2011).

33   Daugherty, Eastin, and Bright, "Exploring Consumer Motivations for Creating User-Generated Content."

34   Katja Rost, Lea Stahel, and Bruno S. Frey, "Digital Social Norm Enforcement: Online Firestorms in Social Media," PLOS One, 11:6 (2016).

35   Hall, Mitch, "Stop Virtue Signaling and Help Someone," The Federalist, June 23, 2016, http://thefederalist.com/2016/06/23/stop-virtue-signaling-on-social-media (accessed March 2, 2017).

36   A. Strobel, "Epistemic Curiosity and Need for Cognition: Assessment and Correlates," *Personality and Individual Differences*, 60, Supplement (April 2014).

37   Daugherty, Eastin, and Bright, "Exploring Consumer Motivations for Creating User-Generated Content."

38 Elliot Panek, Yioryos Nardis, and Sara Konrath, "Mirror or Megaphone? How Relationships Between Narcissism and Social Networking Site Use Differ on Facebook and Twitter," *Computers in Human Behavior*, 29 (September 2013), 2004–12.

39 Mor Naaman, Jeffrey Boase, and Chih-Hui Lai, "Is It Really About Me? Message Content in Social Awareness Streams," Proceedings of the 2010 ACM Conference on Computer Supported Cooperative Work, CSCW 2010, Savannah, Georgia, USA, February 6–10.

40 Sylwia Z. Cisek, Constantine Sedikides, Claire M. Hart, Hayward J. Godwin, Valerie Benson, and Simon P. Liversedge, "Narcissism and Consumer Behaviour: A Review and Preliminary Findings, *Frontiers in Psychology*, 5:232 (2014), www.ncbi.nlm.nih.gov/pmc/articles/PMC3968766 (accessed June 7, 2017).

41 Alixandra Barasch and Jonah Berger, "Broadcasting and Narrowcasting: How Audience Size Affects What People Share," *Journal of Marketing Research*, 51:3 (2014), 286–99.

42 Gwendolyn Seidman, "Expressing the 'True Self' on Facebook," *Computers in Human Behavior*, 31 (February 2014), 367–72, www.sciencedirect.com/science/article/pii/S0747563213004020 (accessed June 7, 2017).

43 Ariane Ollier-Malaterre, Nancy P. Rothbard, and Justin M. Berg, "When Worlds Collide in Cyberspace: How Boundary Work in Online Social Networks Impacts Professional Relationships," *Academy of Management Review*, 38:4 (2013), 645–69.

44 S. Stieger, C. Burger, M. Bohn, and M. Voracek, "Who Commits Virtual Identity Suicide? Differences in Privacy Concerns, Internet Addiction, and Personality Between Facebook Users and Quitters," *Cyberpsychology, Behavior, and Social Networking*, 16:9 (2013), 629–34.

45 Alyson Leigh Young and Anabel Quan-Haase, "Privacy Protection Strategies on Facebook," *Information, Communication, and Society*, 16:4 (2013), 479–500.

46 Chanda Phelan, Cliff Lampe, and Paul Resnick, "It's Creepy, But It Doesn't Bother Me," *Proceedings of the 2016 CHI Conference on Human Factors in Computing Systems* (CHI '16), ACM 2016, New York, USA, pp. 5240–51.

47 Mary Madden, Amanda Lenhart, Sandra Cortesi, Urs Gasser, Maeve Duggan, Aaron Smith, and Meredith Beaton, "Teens, Social Media, and Privacy," May 21, 2013, *Pew Research Center*, www.pewinternet.org/2013/05/21/teens-social-media-and-privacy (accessed June 7, 2017).

48 Sonia Livingstone, "Taking Risky Opportunities in Youthful Content Creation: Teenagers' Use of Social Networking Sites for Intimacy, Privacy and Self-Expression," *New Media Society*, 10:3 (2008), 393–411.

49 C.P. Hoffmann, C. Lutz, and G. Ranzini, "Privacy Cynicism: A New Approach to the Privacy Paradox," *Cyberpsychology: Journal of Psychosocial Research on Cyberspace*, 10:4 (2016).

50 Sonja Grabner-Kräuter and Sofie Bitter, "Trust in Online Social Networks: A Multifaceted Perspective," *Forum for Social Economics*, 44:1 (2015), 48–68; E. Hargittai and A. Marwick, "'What Can I Really Do?' Explaining the Privacy Paradox with Online Apathy," *International Journal of Communication*, 10 (2016), 3737–57; A.E. Marwick and D. Boyd (2014) "Networked Privacy: How Teenagers Negotiate Context in Social Media," *New Media & Society*, 16:7 (2014), 1051–67.

51 Caitlin Dewey, "Where Do People Overshare Most Online? Hint: It's Not the U.S.," *The Washington Post*, May 30, 2013, www.washingtonpost.com/news/worldviews/wp/2013/05/30/where-do-people-overshare-most-online-hint-its-not-the-u-s/?utm_term=.14fc2529fc54 (accessed June 7, 2017).

52 Ibid.

53   Caroline McCarthy, "Analyst: Half of 'Social Media Campaigns' Will Flop," CNET News, October 6, 2008, http://news.cnet.com/8301-13577_3-10058509-36.html (accessed December 20, 2010).

54   Charlene Li and Josh Bernoff, *Groundswell: Winning in a World Transformed by Social Technologies* (Cambridge, MA: Harvard Business Press, 2008).

55   J. Liu and G. Fleming, "Social Technographics® Defines Your Social Approach and Tactics," *The Social Marketing Playbook for 2017*, Forrester Landscape Report, July 29, 2016, www.forrester.com/report/Social+Technographics+Defines+Your+Social+Approach+And+Tactics/-/E-RES128037 (accessed June 7, 2017).

56   "Asian Social Media Behaviors Diverge Significantly," CMO Innovation, December 5, 2016, www.enterpriseinnovation.net/article/asian-social-media-behaviors-diverge-significantly-1366708412 (accessed June 7, 2017).

57   Hodis, Sriramachandramurthy, and Sashittal, "Interact With Me on My Terms."

58   M.K. Foster, A. Francescucci, and B.C. West, "Different Strokes for Different Folks: Why Different User Groups Participate in Online Social Media," *International Journal of Internet Marketing and Advertising*, 7:2 (2012), 103.

59   John Horrigan, "The Mobile Difference," *Pew Internet & American Life Project*, March 2009, http://pewinternet.org/Reports/2009/5-The-Mobile-Difference-Typology.aspx (accessed March 27, 2010).

60   Marc Smith, Lee Rainie, Itai Himelboim, and Ben Shneiderman, "Mapping Twitter Topic Networks: From Polarized Crowds to Community Clusters," *Pew Research Center*, February 20, 2014, www.pewinternet.org/2014/02/20/mapping-twitter-topic-networks-from-polarized-crowds-to-community-clusters (accessed May 2, 2014).

Visit **https://study.sagepub.com/smm3e** for free additional online resources related to this chapter.

Network Structure and Group Influences in Social Media

Learning Objectives

When you finish reading this chapter, you will be able to answer these questions:

1 How are social networks structured?

2 What are the characteristics of online communities?

3 What role do influencers play and what are their sources of power and social capital?

4 How do ideas travel in a community?

Community Structure

Though infrastructure, channels, devices, and social software make social media possible, it's people like you that make it a living, breathing part of everyday life. Social media are first and foremost about *community*: the collective participation of members who together create value. Defining exactly what an online community is and what it isn't has been a difficult task for researchers. Though different approaches exist, we'll refer to online communities as a group of people who come together for a specific purpose, who are guided by community policies, and who are supported by an online vehicle or host that enables virtual communication among members.

In some ways, online communities are not much different from those we find in our physical environment. The Merriam-Webster Dictionary (online version, of course) defines community as "a unified body of individuals, unified by interests, location, occupation, common history, or political and economic concerns." In fact, one social scientist refers to an online community as a cyberplace where "people connect online with kindred spirits, engage in supportive and sociable relationships with them, and imbue their activity online with meaning, belonging, and identity."[1]

Community participation is facilitated online by sites that serve as hosts or vehicles (the second layer of infrastructure in the Social Media Value Chain we covered in Chapter 1) for communication and collaboration between members. These hosts, whether social network sites, forums, or message boards, provide a virtual space—a cyberplace—and functionality to support member connectivity and participation in one or more of the zones of social media. Chances are you are already using Facebook and other host sites like these!

- Qzone
- Taringa
- Sina Weibo
- VK
- YouKu

Across all four zones, the value of social media is tied to network effects and group influence. For this reason, we cover the structural elements of networks, the creation and flow of content, and the sources of influence in social communities as a foundation.

Networks: The Underlying Structure of Communities

When we first presented the Social Media Value Chain to you, we emphasized that all of social media is networked. Though we'll talk more in the next chapter (and throughout the text) about social network sites, in fact *all social communities are networks of social networks*. Social network sites, defined as "networked communication platforms in which participants 1) have uniquely identifiable profiles that consist of user-supplied content, content provided by other users, and/or system-provided data; 2) can publicly articulate connections that can be viewed and traversed by others; and 3) can consume, produce, and/or interact with streams of user-generated content provided by their connections on the site," serve as the most prevalent form of host in social media.[2] Networks underlie the premise of social media and the network effect is key to understanding the value of social communities for social media marketing. The **network effect** explains that the relative value a community offers its members is tied to its membership. Before we move on, let's cover the basics of **social network theory**, the theory that explains how networks (whether online or off) work.

Social Networks

A **social network** is a set of socially relevant nodes connected by one or more relations.[3] **Nodes** are members of the network (whom we also refer to as **network units**). When we think of community, we tend to think of people, but members of a network can be organizations, articles, countries, departments, or any other definable unit. A good example is your university alumni association. The association is a community of networked individuals and organizations. Members are connected by their relationships (or **ties**) with each other. Relationships are based on various affiliations such as kinship, friendship and affective ties, shared experiences, professional relationships, and shared hobbies and interests. They may be reciprocal or unidirectional. Friend, follower, fan, link, and contact are all terms used to denote relationship connections in social communities.

Connected nodes in a network experience **interactions**; these are behavior-based ties such as talking with each other, attending an event together, or working together. If you have a conversation on Twitter, you are a node engaging in an interaction with another node. These interactions create **flows** among connected nodes. Flows are exchanges of resources, information, or influence among members of the network. For example, on Facebook you share news, updates about your life, opinions on favorite books and movies, photos, videos, and notes. As you share content, you create flows among those in your network. In social media these flows of communication go in many directions at any point in time and often on multiple platforms—a condition called **media multiplexity**.[4] Flows are not simply two way or three way, they may involve an entire community, a list or group within a network, or several individuals independently.

Flows of communication also occur outside the community platform. While the online community exists within a web space, the flows of communication may extend to other domains such as emails, text messages, virtual worlds, and even face-to-face **meetups** where members of an online network arrange to meet in a physical location. Increasingly we find that social connections online result in face-to-face connections offline. For marketers, flows are especially important because they are the actionable components of any social network system in terms of the sharing of information, delivery of promotional materials, and sources of social influence. **Word-of-mouth communication** flows from node to node. Whether the flow changes behavior or attitudes depends on the social influence of the initiating node. The extent of social influence (where one person's attitudes or behavior change as a result of others' attempts) varies depending upon the power or attractiveness of other nodes. We'll take a deep look at influence and how someone develops it later in the chapter.

Social networks can be diagrammed to illustrate the interconnections of network units. Socilab offers LinkedIn members a mapping tool that creates a visual representation of

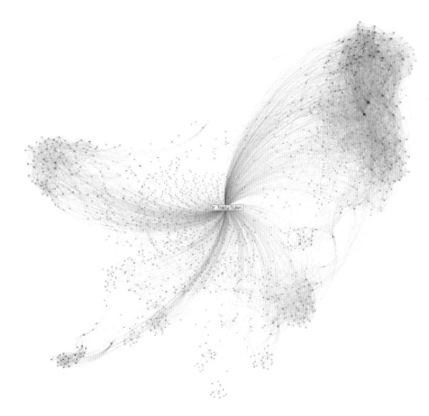

Figure 3.1   A LinkedIn Network Map Visualization

members' social graphs at www.socilab.com. Figure 3.1 illustrates a LinkedIn member network. Circles in the image represent nodes (members of LinkedIn) who are connected via ties. LinkedIn also supplies information on degrees of separation between members. People with direct connections are separated by one degree. A friend of a friend has a two degree separation, and so on.

How many degrees of separation are you from your favorite movie star or most admired business leader? Six degrees or less. That's the concept known as the six degrees of separation—the idea that anyone on Earth is connected to anyone else in just six steps or less.[5] So through just five other people or less, you're effectively connected to anyone and everyone—whether those people are the Queen of England, Mark Zuckerberg, and Cristiano Ronaldo. The theory originated from a 1929 short story called Chains, in which one of the characters challenges the others to find another person on Earth that he cannot connect himself to through fewer than five intermediaries, but wasn't tested scientifically until decades later. Based on the math, the concept is plausible. Assuming everyone knows at least 44 people, and that each of those people knows an entirely new 44 people, and so on, the math shows that in just six steps everyone could be connected to 44^6, or 7.26 billion people—more than are alive on Earth today. But we owe the real breakthrough in scientific support for the theory to a college game called "Six Degrees of Kevin Bacon."

EXHIBIT 3.1

The Six Degrees of Kevin Baron

Inspired when binge-watching *Footloose* and other movies starring Kevin Bacon, a group of college friends created the game Six Degrees of Kevin Bacon to illustrate the six degrees of separation.[6] The game requires players to link celebrities to Bacon, in as few steps as possible, via the movies they have in common. The game took off, spreading much like the memes of today. Bacon leveraged the ubiquity of the game to launch SixDegrees.org, a charitable organization that connects celebrities with good causes for fundraising purposes. The Six Degrees game has also inspired a website, The Oracle of Bacon, where you can play yourself! The site assigns each celeb a "Bacon number" to show the number of degrees of separation between the two. Google is even in on the game—users can simply type "Bacon number" in the search field, followed by an actor's name, to produce the same result.

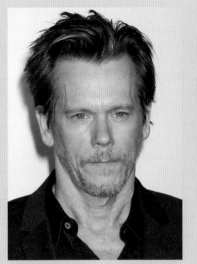

Ga Fullner/Shutterstock.com

The Characteristics of Online Communities

All communities, whether they exist online or in the physical world, share important characteristics: participants experience a feeling of membership, a sense of proximity to one another (even though in online groups other members' physical selves may be thousands of miles away), and in most cases some interest in the community's activities. Social network sites, and other social vehicles, provide value for community members by establishing a virtual location and the functionality needed for members to connect, communicate, and collaborate.

Presence

Though online communities exist virtually rather than at a physical location, the better ones supply tangible characteristics that create the sensation of actually being in a place. This is particularly true for virtual world communities that include three-dimensional depictions of physical spaces, but it also applies to visually simplistic online communities such as message board groups. **Presence** refers to the effect that people experience when they interact with a computer-mediated or computer-generated environment.[7] Social media sites enhance a sense of presence when they make the environment look and feel real.[8]

Purposive Value and Social Objects

Virtual communities do not develop and thrive without a foundation of commonality among the members. Just as your offline communities revolve around family, religious beliefs, social activities, hobbies, goals, place of residence, and so on, your online communities also need commonalities to create bonds among the members. These groups come together to allow people to share their passions, whether for indie bands, white wines, or open-source apps. Community content (whether simple dialogue, shared recipes, event photos, or something else entirely) is generated, shared, consumed, fortified, and promoted by community members. The contributions of members add value for the general membership group.

Social object theory suggests that social networks will be more effective if there is a way to activate relationships among people and objects.[9] In this perspective an object is something of common interest and its primary function is to mediate the interactions between people. All relationships have social objects embedded in the relationship. In the online world, a site such as Facebook provides venues for several object formats to ensure that relationships can thrive within the site's framework. One factor that drives Facebook's stunning success is that it offers so many objects for users to share; these include photos, live video, events, quizzes, and so on.

Other social network sites provide a more specialized or focused set of objects. For example, consider how each of the following SNS incorporates objects as part of its mission. On Instagram users participate because they want to share photos. These images are the objects that give meaning to the platform and motivate people to visit. Video is burgeoning. It's no wonder that social media vehicles that previously focused on photos have expanded to include video. Instagram and Snapchat are two examples.

EXHIBIT 3.2

Dogster and Social Object Theory

Source: www.dogster.com

Social object theory explains that shared objects give meaning to a social vehicle and motivate member engagement. On Diigo, the objects are URLs (Uniform Resource Locators). On Yelp, the objects are businesses. On Dogster, the objects are our canine companions. On Whisper, secrets are the object.

Object sociality, the extent to which users can share an object in social media, clearly relates to an audience's unique interests.[10] It ties the site relationships to a specific object such as photos of people's dogs or bookmarked websites that provide details about the history of alternative music. The audience becomes specialized, at least to a degree. Importantly, though, SNS oriented around object sociality are likely to be passion-centric. That is, the people who join those communities probably not only share an interest in the object in question; chances are they are passionate about the object. We all know people who devote countless hours to a hobby or who (to an outsider) seem insanely obsessed about the fine details of *Star Wars* characters, vintage wines, or warring guilds in *World of Warcraft*.

In industry terms, vertical networks are sites designed around object sociality. The term refers to the narrow, deep focus of SNS that differentiate themselves because they center on some common hobby, interest, or characteristic that draws members to the site. These vertical networks do not attract the same traffic typical of general sites, but one might argue that the members are more involved because of the common interest that initially brought them to the site. They function much like so-called niche markets in the physical world. The term niche refers to marketplaces that offer a relatively small number of items to buyers who tend to be loyal to these outlets (e.g., big-and-tall men's stores or tandem bicycles built for two).

Standards of Behavior

Communities help members meet their needs for affiliation, resource acquisition, entertainment, and information. Above all else, communities are active! Whether online or offline, they thrive when the members participate, discuss, share, and interact with others as well as recruit new members to the community. Virtual communities need norms, or rules that govern behavior, in order to operate effectively. Some of these rules are spelled out explicitly (as when you agree to the terms of use when joining various SNS) but many of them are unspoken. In general, **norms** are mental representations of appropriate behavior in a community. Social norms are created, shared, and sustained by community members because they promote behavior that benefits the collective.[11] Without these rules, we would have chaos. Imagine the confusion if a simple norm in the offline world such as stopping for a red traffic light did not exist!

In social communities, members learn norms through socialization. For instance, researchers attempting to explain the prevalence of aggression expressed online, including vulgarity, insults, bullying, slander, and trolling found that expressed aggression was more common in social communities in which peer comments were also aggressive.[12] Some of the more prevalent forms of aggression are flaming, doxing, and trolling. **Flaming** refers to posts written with ALL CAPITAL LETTERS TO EXPRESS ANGER. **Doxing**, a cyber offence that is illegal in the UK, refers to identifying and publishing private information about someone as a form of punishment or revenge.

Trolling refers to the deliberate provocation of conflict by posting messages that are inflammatory, controversial, insulting, and/or provocative.[13] Trolls are not your average social media user taking advantage of an opportunity to vent or complain. They are online bullies; trolling is a hobby to them. Michael Brutsch, a Reddit troll, is an example.[14] Using the handle Violentacrez, Brutsch created offensive subreddits (topic groups on Reddit) with the goal of enraging other Reddit users. Some of the sections Violentacrez created were Chokeabitch, Rapebait, Misogyny, and Jailbait. Unfortunately for marketers, it's become a popular game among trolls to bait brands. If they succeed in eliciting an emotional response, they screenshot it and post it. Whether a marketer or an individual unlucky enough to be the target of a troll, experts recommend ignoring the troll unless the attacks become sufficiently severe to warrant reporting the troll to the social community and blocking the troll.[15]

As you can see, some norms prevent negative behaviors that are pretty minor; others relate to more serious matters. And while norm enforcement is typically thought of as sanctions against community members, social media make it possible for communities to attempt sanctions against people and businesses beyond the community, as in the case of shaming and online firestorms.[16] David Brooks, a writer for the *New York Times*, explains that shaming, attempting to make people feel bad by posting many negative comments, marks a shift in the culture of social communities. In the past, people would recognize their bad behavior by the guilt felt by their conscience. Now, Brooks claims, people are expected to respond to the voice of the community.[17]

In addition to social norms, standards of behavior may also be influenced by anonymity and by explicit agreements between the community and individual members. Open access sites enable anyone to participate without registration or identification. This can be valuable for participation on sensitive topics as well as for ease of use. However, open access also lowers the barriers for misbehavior because it ensures anonymity to users. Just as people tend to "act out" at a costume party when no one knows who they really are, visitors to these sites may post things they might avoid if others knew their real identity.[18] The social contract is the agreement that exists between the host or governing body and the members. You engage in a social contract when you indicate agreement to a "terms of use" clause for a site. Social contracts set forth expectations for user behavior as well as for the host or governing body. Some sites such as Facebook, however, come under fire when they make changes to the social contract without user input. The specific concern is typically for the protection of membership privacy.

Groups and Subcultures

Within a social community, groups and subcultures can thrive. We've seen this since the early days of research on virtual communities and into the present with the many netnographic studies of niche groups. These communities and subcultures have always existed but often remained on the fringe, unable to reach a critical mass due to logistical inaccessibility to like-minded others. Social media enable these once remote subcultures to network and collaborate.[19] The result is flourishing **crowdcultures** around almost any topic: anime, minimalism, Paleo diets, marathon runners, libertarianism, and more. The potential influence of these communities is illustrated by the phenomenon of crowdsourcing, when tasks are completed collaboratively by a large group of people such that the resulting value far exceeds that which could have been contributed by any single participant.

Members affiliate with communities with which they identify but the source of commonality could be anything—a mission, location, interest, characteristic, and so on. The choice to affiliate is tied to one's social identity, which we introduced in Chapter 2. Social identity is that part of an individual's self-concept that is related to group membership and it helps us to understand participation in social communities. Participation can be thought of as **intentional social action** in the context of a group.[20] Described as "we-intentions", participation is influenced both by individual attitudes and characteristics and the context and norms of the group.

Participation

Community members seek out ways to be connected. The site encourages new members to connect. It's critical to encourage participation among new members; these contributions continue to build the value of the platform for all members. If a social media site starts to lose visitors, it resembles a deserted mining town in the Old West—empty saloons, banks, and stores with (digital) tumbleweed blowing across the streets. Your level of activity is based on a mix of four elements of the people with whom you are connected, the content (called artifacts) you produce on the site, the feedback you receive from others, and the distribution of the artifacts and feedback throughout the network.[21] Of these, the biggest predictor of whether someone will become active in a social network space, regardless of the site's primary function, is the presence of a critical mass of friends. If your friends are present and active in the space, you probably will be too because you will have someone with whom to interact and to reward you for your participation.

Of these four elements of social network site participation, three are dependent upon the nodes in your network. If your contacts are not active in your experience, your own activity in the network will be stunted because you won't have people with whom to interact, you won't receive sufficient feedback, and your content will not be redistributed. Some nodes will have more connections than others and some will take part in more interactions. These nodes will tend to have greater influence in the network. We'll talk more about influence and the types of nodes later in this chapter. Interactions are participative in nature—they are shared activities among members in the network.

For an online community to thrive, a significant proportion of its members must participate. Otherwise the site will fail to offer fresh material and ultimately traffic will slow. In addition to its importance in community health, participation fuels engagement—the ultimate desired state of being in social media (and a topic we cover more in Chapter 4). The meaning of engagement has been the focus of great scrutiny among marketing scholars. Engagement as "a psychological state that occurs through interactive, co-creative consumer experiences with a focal agent/object" highlights the role of participation (in interactive, co-creative experiences) and the context (in this case, the social community).[22] Participation can be a challenge, though, because most users are lurkers, people who review site content but don't actually contribute. Researchers estimate that only 1% of a typical community's users regularly participate and another 9% do so only intermittently. The remaining 90% just observe what's on the site, so they don't add a lot of value—other than adding to the number of "eyeballs" the site can claim when it tries to convince advertisers to buy space.

Sound familiar? This disparity roughly parallels the larger pattern we often observe in marketing contexts called the 80/20 rule—that roughly 20% of a brand's users buy 80% of the product.

Marketers label these faithful "heavy users." In many groups or consumer segments, a relative handful of people account for most of the activity; this hard-core group is often the most valuable for organizations to touch because they are the real movers and shakers. Thus a person's participation is influenced by 20% or less of their network. What do the most effective communities do to promote participation? According to *The Platform Revolution*, three factors are responsible: 1) magnetism (i.e., members are attracted to the community and vice versa), 2) user-generated content (members are proactive in contributing content), and 3) value creation (by participating, members co-create value, thus improving the experience).[23]

Social Capital

When people form community relationships, these affiliations allow them to accumulate resources that they can "trade" for other things. In the offline business world, we clearly see how this process works in the golf subculture. Although many people do love to hit that ball around, the reality is that a lot of business is transacted on the course and executives profit from their membership in this community (some business schools even offer academic courses on "golf etiquette"!).

We call these resources **social capital** because their value lies in providing access to others.[24] The resources may be actual or virtual, and they may be held by a group or an individual. For instance, they might include useful information, relationships, the ability to organize groups, employment connections, and more.[25] Do you know anyone who landed a job interview due to the intervention of a friend of a friend? This is an example of social capital at work—especially since jobseekers who know larger numbers of people who already work at high-level jobs are more likely to be able to trade on these connections. Social capital tends to be a limited and protected resource. To return to the golf example, at many country clubs it's not enough just to be rolling in money: you also need to be recommended by current members so that the organization controls (fairly or not) just who gets to hobnob on the links and in the locker room.

Typically, a community is healthier and more desirable when it is able to offer a lot of social capital as an inducement for people to join. Communities build capital through reputation and structure. **Reputational capital** is based on the shared beliefs, relationships, and actions of those in the community such that norms, behaviors, and values held and shared by individuals ultimately support a community reputation. You can think of this like a big, beefy nightclub bouncer who decides whom he will admit past the velvet rope. In fact, like exclusive country clubs, online gated communities that selectively allow access to only some people may offer a high degree of social capital to the lucky few who pass the test.

EXHIBIT 3.3

Raya Members Have Social Capital

RAYA, an exclusive dating network, is an example of an online gated community that carefully curates members to weed out the unattractive. Described as "Tinder for famous people," applicants are screened using selection criteria including Instagram followers, personal recommendations, and individual characteristics (think looks, creativity, and income).

Let's use Klout as an example to understand how online social capital works. Klout is a social reputation indicator that measures relative influence across several social communities including Twitter, Facebook, LinkedIn, and Foursquare. Klout assigns a Klout Score between 0 and 100 to each user, with higher scores denoting greater levels of influence in social media.

Network size, member activity, activity quality indicators such as network feedback like number of "favorites," and information flows from a member through his or her network all serve as variables to calculate a Klout score (https://klout.com/brandacity). Network size is a variable because it promotes the viability of the *network effect* we discussed in Chapter 1 and the chance that content will cascade through the community. Member activity reveals the importance of participation. Quality indicators and information flow serve as evidence of value and relevance. All of this is based on community participation. If and when people participate less in a given social community, the social capital of influencers in that community will diminish as well. As social capital declines, the community experiences decline in its own strength as measured by participation, adherence to norms, perceived reputation, and trust among members.[26] Hopefully you can see that influencers in a community have a lot at stake in keeping the community active and even growing it.

Interestingly, this is the very phenomenon researchers at Princeton University used to predict the ultimate demise of Facebook.[27] Just as we discussed the way viral content spreads like a disease, we can also view community participation and membership much like the spread of infection. Using data on the adoption and abandonment of memberships and activity in MySpace, the study built a model using Google Trend data on social network search queries. The model suggested that social networks follow a life cycle (much like a product life cycle) through which social communities will grow, mature, and ultimately decline. The prediction that Facebook would lose 80% of its active members went viral, and Facebook researchers responded with their own study of Princeton enrollment. Using data from Google Scholar and a similar approach to modeling, Facebook's team built a model illustrating that Princeton would lose all student enrollments by 2021.[28] Given the low probability of the latter prediction, Facebook was able to humorously debunk the Princeton study. Nonetheless, it is true that Facebook's meteoric growth is stabilizing, especially as many younger people abandon it in favor of more private networks like Snapchat and for "dark social" options like texting.

EXHIBIT 3.4

Is Facebook's Future Uncertain?

Although billions of people worldwide love to share on Facebook, not everyone wants details about their private lives to be available to lurkers (especially to curious parents). In recent years sites like

(Continued)

(Continued)

SnapChat that delete posts after a certain amount of time have gained in popularity. What do you predict to be the future of Facebook?

franviser/Shutterstock.com

Strong and Weak Ties

Emotional support is one form of social capital. For example, people who struggle to lose weight or fight addictions often prevail because they are part of a group that helps them with these battles, such as Weight Watchers or Alcoholics Anonymous. We call this kind of emotional support **bonding social capital**.

This resource easily accrues online because of our accessibility to people who can help us with a variety of issues even though we may not know them personally. In contrast, our **core ties**, those people with whom we have very close relationships, may or may not be in a position to provide solutions to some problems we face (or we may not want them to know about these in some cases).[29] Interestingly, through the course of giving and receiving bonding social capital, we may come to develop core ties, or at least **significant ties** (somewhat close connections, but less so than core ties), with others in the community.

Online communities can also provide other kinds of support. This is particularly true of those that increase the accessibility of so-called **weak ties**. This term refers to contacts with people where your relationship is based on superficial experiences or very few connections. For instance, you have a **strong tie** with your best friend. Perhaps you and she went to high school together and so you have a history of shared experiences and friendships from your past. You then attended college classes together and again you were able to share experiences. You also joined the same sorority so you are bound by your relationship in the context of the organization. In this relationship, there are at least three connection streams between you and your friend that extend over several years and multiple shared experiences—we'd say this is a fairly strong tie.

In contrast, you likely have *weak ties* among your Facebook friends, many of whom are just casual acquaintances or even friends of a friend whom you've never met. Weak ties may also be more prevalent when someone is connected to several otherwise dispersed networks of people. In other words, rather than being central in a few tightly connected networks, the person serves as a node in several relatively unconnected networks.[30]

However, we can assure you that weak ties also have value. They may provide **bridging social capital**, the value we get from others who provide access to places, people, or ideas we might not be able to get to on our own.

In fact, many of the connections we make on SNS are not active ties at all. Rather, they are **latent ties**: pre-existing connections that we've discarded.[31] **Maintained social capital** refers to the value we get from maintaining relationships with latent ties. You've probably heard your parents say they've reconnected with old high school friends on Facebook ("I can't believe how bald he is now!"). This is a perfect example of latent ties—as we move through life, some people stay in our lives, but others lose relevance as we develop and change. SNS are valuable connectors for latent ties because they represent a low-involvement, low-effort channel to maintain these bonds. In fact, researchers discovered that college students use Facebook as a way to preserve their network of latent ties.[32] Some of your high school friends may have chosen the same university you did. Others went elsewhere. With sites such as Facebook, you are easily able to stay in touch with these friends, despite the shift in lifestyle and geographic location. Those connections may come in handy if you visit an unfamiliar place or need to find a job.

Note: earlier we talked about weak and strong ties in communities. Latent ties are not necessarily weak ties. Your BFF in the sixth grade was once a strong tie, but she might now be a latent one. Before the social media era, it's likely you would have just lost track of her unless you both happened to hobble into your 25th class reunion. Now, you can keep your old connections on the radar screen, even if you don't necessarily talk or write to them on a regular basis. SNS enable members to maintain relationships across tie types.

EXHIBIT 3.5

Influencer, Casey Neistat, Used Social Capital for Good

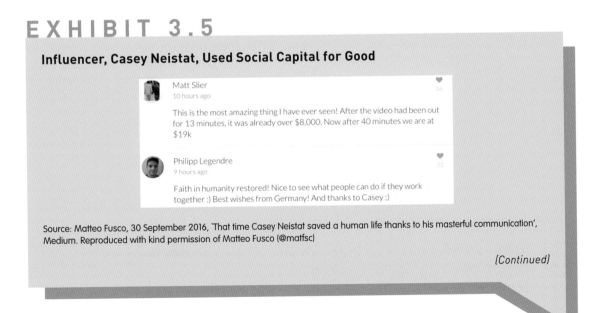

Matt Slier
10 hours ago

This is the most amazing thing I have ever seen! After the video had been out for 13 minutes, it was already over $8,000. Now after 40 minutes we are at $19k

Philipp Legendre
9 hours ago

Faith in humanity restored! Nice to see what people can do if they work together :) Best wishes from Germany! And thanks to Casey :)

Source: Matteo Fusco, 30 September 2016, 'That time Casey Neistat saved a human life thanks to his masterful communication', Medium. Reproduced with kind permission of Matteo Fusco (@matfsc)

(Continued)

(Continued)

Influencers can use their social capital for good. That's what happened when Casey Neistat, a YouTuber with more than 5 million subscribers, used his daily vlog to ask for help on behalf of his friend, UPS driver, and frequent guest Marlan Franklyn.[33] Marlan had been paying his sister's medical expenses to treat her severe kidney disease personally but could no longer shoulder the burden alone. Casey suggested a GoFundMe campaign to crowdsource the needed money—$125,000.

Watch Casey's plea here: https://youtu.be/nELmgVd0dWw

Within a few hours, Marlan's GoFundMe campaign was trending. Within four days, nearly 10,000 people from around the world had donated, exceeding the goal by several thousand dollars.

The Rise of Influencers

Although consumers get information from personal sources, they do not usually ask just *anyone* for advice about purchases. If you decide to buy a new sound system, you will most likely seek advice from a friend who knows a lot about this topic. This friend may own a sophisticated system, or may subscribe to specialized magazines such as *Stereo Review* and spend her free time browsing through electronics stores. However, you may have another friend who has a reputation for being stylish and who spends his free time reading *Gentleman's Quarterly* and shopping at trendy boutiques. You might not bring up your sound system problem with him, but you may take him with you to shop for a new fall wardrobe.

Opinion leaders (also known as **influencers** or **power users** in some communities) are people that others view as knowledgeable sources of information.[34] They have a strong communication network that gives them the ability to affect purchase decisions for a number of other consumers, directly and indirectly. Five characteristics help to describe them: (1) activists, (2) connected, (3) impact, (4) active minds, and (5) trendsetters.[35] In other words, opinion leaders develop a network of people through their involvement in activities. They are active participants at work and in their communities. Their social networks are large and well developed. Others trust them and find them to be credible sources of information about one or more specific topics. They tend to have a natural sense of intellectual curiosity that may lead them to new sources of information.

Opinion leaders exist in all social communities. It is a natural pattern for some members to be more active and to acquire positions of authority within a group, whether offline or online. The source of the influence itself, however, originates from the power bases an influencer may possess.

How can someone acquire power? French and Raven identified in their classic article, "The Bases of Social Power", several sources of power individuals can accrue in organizations.[36] These sources of power include:

- **Reward power**: one's ability to provide others with what they desire.
- **Coercive power**: the ability to punish others.
- **Legitimate power**: organizational authority based on rights associated with a person's appointed position.

- **Referent power**: authority through the motivation to identify with or please a person.
- **Expert power**: recognition of one's knowledge, skills, and ability.
- **Information power**: one's control over the flow of and access to information.

Of course, marketers always want to identify opinion leaders and get them on their team. These people often are the linchpin in a communications strategy; once an opinion leader decides he or she loves your product, it's just a matter of time before others in that person's networks hear about it as well. Thus for purchase decisions, opinion leaders are extremely valuable information sources due to their social power:[37]

- They are technically competent so they possess expert power.
- They prescreen, evaluate, and synthesize product information in an unbiased way, so they possess knowledge power.
- They are socially active and highly interconnected in their communities.
- They are likely to hold positions of leadership. As a result, opinion leaders often have legitimate power by virtue of their social standing.
- They tend to be similar to the consumer in terms of their values and beliefs, so they possess referent power. Note that although opinion leaders are set apart by their interest or expertise in a product category, they are more convincing to the extent that they are *homophilous* rather than *heterophilous*. **Homophily** refers to the degree to which a pair of individuals is similar in terms of education, social status, and beliefs. Homophily can predict collaborative online relationships and connectivity, whether in professional collaborations like a new product development project or in reciprocal kindnesses among friends in an online network of musicians.
- Effective opinion leaders tend to be slightly higher in terms of status and educational attainment than those they influence but not so high as to be in a different social class.
- Opinion leaders are often among the first to buy new products, so they absorb much of the risk. This experience reduces uncertainty for the rest of us who are not as courageous. Furthermore, whereas company-sponsored communications tend to focus exclusively on the positive aspects of a product, the hands-on experience of opinion leaders makes them more likely to impart *both* positive and negative information about product performance. Thus, they are more credible because they have no "axe to grind."

Though opinion leaders exist in social communities, these communities have also given rise to a different type of influencer—the microcelebrity (also called micro-influencers). Microcelebrities build influence using a self-presentation technique that involves establishing a sense of intimacy with their audiences by sharing content in one or more social communities.[38] Though these influencers are self-branding, the technique ensures they are perceived as authentic, transparent, and relevant.[39] Compared to traditional celebrities, microcelebrities have smaller audiences; they are classified as social personalities with 1,000 to 100,000 followers, but they often have higher engagement rates and more influence in their communities.[40] Unlike traditional celebrities, who may have large audiences across several social network sites, these influencers tend to specialize in one community. Over time, their audiences can grow. Kayla Itsines, a fitness trainer from Australia, is an example. She regularly shares before and after photos of women who follow her fitness protocol

8 Social Media Archetypes

The Balanced Life

Description: This type of influencer eats well, exercises and still makes time to live an all-round healthy lifestyle.
Brands that use this archetype: Bai, Under Armour, Beta Brand
Exemplar: Jessenia Vice turns negatives to positives and focuses her podcasts and Instagram posts on fitness, motivation, and overcoming adversity.

The Friend Zone

Description: Online friend squads that create comedic content focused on collaboration across channels.
Brands that use this archetype: Lego, Hotpockets
Exemplar: LankyBox is led by two comedic influencers – Adam & Justin. Their content is funny and family-friendly.

Fashionista Coach

Description: These influencers are fashion icons with their own personal identity.
Brands that use this archetype: Kate Spade, Adidas, Victoria Secret
Exemplar: Karlie Kloss, former Victoria's Secret Angel and fashion model, uses her unique insight into the world of fashion to inspire fashionistas around the world.

Gaming Hero

Description: Gaming heros amass followers seeking entertainment as well as tips and techniques to improve their own games.
Brands that use this archetype: Warner Brothers, Motorola, Red Bull
Exemplar: Mari Takahashi, who uses the handle AtomicMari, shows that Gaming Heros aren't always male.

The Charismatic Cook

Description: These influencers are relatable and fun, evolving from the Zen-like online chefs and food stylists of years past.
Brands that use this archetype: Blue Apron, Kraft Foods, Wolf
Exemplar: Mariam Ezzeddine (@CookinwithMima) shares inspirational and healthy recipes and photos on Instagram.

The Adventurer

Description: The adventurer creates a lifetime narrative of storylines that blend across journeys and borders.
Brands that use this archetype: GoPro, Northface, Patagonia, Travelocity
Exemplar: Megan Jerrard (@MappingMegan) has traveled the world sharing her adventures via her blog, Instagram, Twitter, and Facebook.

The Fitspiration

Description: The Fitspiration archetype makes you want to move, sharing workout and stretching tips.
Brands that use this archetype: Lululemon, GNC, SmartWater
Exemplar: Anllela Sagra, a Colombian fitness guru, shares workouts and fitness inspiration on Instagram and YouTube.

The Beauty Expert

Description: The beauty expert is a master of hair and/or makeup. This glamazon will show you how to get the look from beginning to end.
Brands that use this archetype: Maybelline, MAC, Suave, Nivea
Exemplar: Manny Gutierrez (@mannymua733) highlights beauty tips like how to line the perfect brow on YouTube and Instagram.

Figure 3.2 Archetypes of Social Media Influencers

Source: adapted from Marty Swant, "6 Social Media Archetypes for the Modern-Day Brand Influencer," Adweek, October 30, 2016, www.adweek.com/digital/6-social-media-archetypes-modern-day-brand-influencer-174335/ (accessed June 12, 2017)

(Bikini Body Guide), as well as training videos, and pictures of healthy food on Instagram. Her following is now in the several millions; even *Time* magazine heralded her positive influence motivating women to make better fitness choices as a "virtual movement."[41]

Figure 3.2 describes a few of the archetypes that characterize social media influencers and examples of the types of brands that work with each archetype. This won't be our only discussion of the role of influencers in social media marketing. Brands partner with influencers to seed campaigns, drive impressions, and increase the likelihood that campaign content will go viral.

MINI CASE STUDY

Influencer Marketing

Influencer marketing is one of the fastest growing strategies for marketers, and agencies like Linqia, Grapestory, and Everywhere have developed to match marketers and influencers and plan effective influencer campaigns. Influencers provide reach for marketers but there are other benefits as well. A study of marketers using influencers in campaigns revealed a plethora of reasons for the rising popularity of influencer marketing.[42] When asked why they chose to work with influencers, 73% of participants noted that the influencers were relevant to their target audience; 72% wanted to leverage the influencers' authenticity and trusted voice; and 60% sought to spark audience engagement.

Working with influencers is also an efficient way to create content for social media. Traditionally, brands pay professional content creators (e.g., photographers, videographers, writers) to produce content, whether it be a blog post, photo, video, how-to article, or recipe. This can be expensive and time consuming. When brands work with influencers, content is typically a part of the deal. According to the study, 50% of marketers pay influencers a flat rate to produce each piece of content, in the same way that they would engage a professional content producer. On average, this typically costs 2.6 times less than working with a professional for a similar output. It also allows the marketer to categorize the production as a "working spend" because the influencers are sharing the content with their audiences. **Working spend** is a term used to describe investments that reach the target audience such as advertising and event marketing. **Non-working spend** is any cost attributed to creating campaign assets, planning, or managing the campaign. Lacey Meece, strategist for Ragu, explained: "Something as simple as a recipe ends up being an excruciatingly long and expensive process when professionally produced. First, we have to pick a product to feature, then hire a food scientist that charges a per recipe fee. Next, we bring in photographers and videographers to shoot the visuals. Working with influencers is far more efficient—they each have their own style and voice and can quickly churn out authentic recipes, photos, and videos at scale."[43] Ragu partnered with lifestyle influencer, Dzung Duong of the popular YouTube channel Honeysuckle to develop recipes for its Homestyle line of sauces.

Creating enough good content is a major challenge for social media marketers. Influencers add value by not only reaching more consumers but also creating content that can be repurposed for use across a brand's social media channels. Most marketers are repurposing influencer-generated content: 84% post influencer content on the brand's organic social media accounts and 72% drive attention to the content using paid social media.

Are influencers effective? Nestlé's Gerber thinks so. When Gerber launched its Lil' Beanies™ product and wanted to drive awareness and trial in key markets through Publix, Target, Walmart, and Kroger, it chose influencers as a key part of the social media strategy. The navy-bean-based snack for toddlers

(Continued)

(Continued)

Monkey Business Images/Shutterstock.com

has two grams of protein per serving, is non-GMO and contains no artificial flavors or colors. The advertising budget for the product launch was small and the strategy needed to showcase the brand's value proposition.[44] Using mommy bloggers as influencers was the perfect solution.

The hook? Lil' Beanies is a great snack for toddlers. Who were the influencers? Several influencers participated including Kristy of Mommy Hates Cooking, Shannon of Mom Without Labels, and Susie of Not Quite Susie Homemaker. The bloggers clearly labeled the blog posts as sponsored but also shared their stories with the brand. As important as conveying the positive nutritional information was, the bloggers were able to illustrate that their kids liked the snack. Check out their posts to see how the influencers promoted the product while staying true to their followers.[45]

Results and Outcomes

Effective? We'd say so! The campaign resulted in a reach of more than 56 million impressions and 260,000 interactive engagements. It also produced more than 9,000 pieces of content that could be repurposed in Gerber's social media activities. The product achieved a 5% sales lift during the campaign, suggesting that the campaign drove sales as well as awareness.[46]

Flow: How Ideas Travel Online

Earlier we saw that social communities are built on networks, and these networks include nodes that are connected by ties through which content and experiences flow. We also learned that the nodes of influencers are valuable because of the large number of people they can reach with their social power.

Understanding what flows occurred and how extensively the flows were disseminated through influencers was first based on a framework called the **two-step flow model of influence**.[47]

More recent research has tweaked that basic idea; now it suggests that influence can be driven by both influencers and by interactions among those who are easily influenced. These people communicate the information vigorously to one another and also participate in a two-way dialogue with the opinion leader as part of an **influence network**. These conversations create **cascades** of information, which occur when a piece of information triggers a sequence of interactions (much like an avalanche), as Figure 3.3 shows.

A message originates at Level 1 and is sent by the influencer to his or her contacts (Level 2). The message may travel on from some Level 2 contacts to their contacts (Level 3), and so on. With the ease of sharing via social media, the power of the network effect, and the flow of influence, word-of-mouth communication can spread with or without influencers.

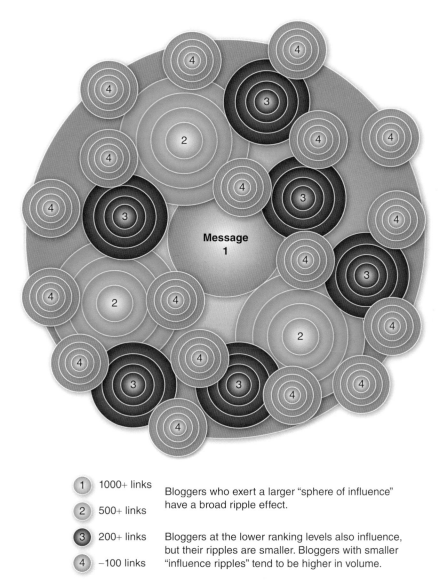

1. 1000+ links
2. 500+ links

Bloggers who exert a larger "sphere of influence" have a broad ripple effect.

3. 200+ links
4. −100 links

Bloggers at the lower ranking levels also influence, but their ripples are smaller. Bloggers with smaller "influence ripples" tend to be higher in volume.

Figure 3.3   An Influence Network

Word-of-Mouth (WOM)

When the information spread via flow is product information shared node-to-node, person-to-person, it is called **word-of-mouth (WOM) communication**. Despite all of the money marketers pump into lavish ads, WOM is far more powerful: it influences two thirds of all consumer goods sales. In one survey, 69% of interviewees said they relied on a personal referral at least once over the course of a year to help them choose a restaurant, 36% reported they used referrals to decide on computer hardware and software, and 22% got help from friends and associates to decide where to travel.[48]

If you think carefully about the content of your own conversations in the course of a normal day, you will probably agree that much of what you discuss with friends, family members, or coworkers is product related: when you compliment someone on her dress and ask her where she bought it, recommend a new restaurant to a friend, or complain to your neighbor about the shoddy treatment you got at the bank, you engage in WOM.

Marketers have been aware of the power of WOM for many years, but recently they've been more aggressive about trying to promote and control it, instead of sitting back and hoping people will like their products enough to talk them up. The ease of sharing WOM via social media and other digital channels is a key reason. Companies such as BzzAgent (www.bzzagent.com) have thousands of online "agents" who try new products and spread the word about those they like.[49] And many sophisticated marketers today also precisely track WOM.

EXHIBIT 3.6

Engagement Labs Measures WOM Online and Off

With word-of-mouth conversation driving $6 trillion in annual consumer spending, marketers need to know what people are saying. Online conversations are important, but offline conversations are too. Engagement Labs' TotalSolution combines in-depth social listening with comprehensive offline conversation measurement tools, delivering a TotalSocial scorecard in 17 major industry categories.[50]

According to the report "Hearing the Voice of the Consumer: UGC and the Commerce Experience," online word-of-mouth communication is the most preferred source for 90% of shoppers making a purchase. It even outranked search engines and promotional emails and was so valuable for some that they are willing to pay more and wait longer for shipping for products that are organically endorsed by others.[51] Online WOM consistently correlates with sales in empirical studies, but its influence varies.[52] When shared via social media, it tends to be more influential when those exposed to the message believe they are similar to the person sharing the information. In contrast, similarity doesn't seem to play a role in the relative influence of online WOM on e-commerce platforms (e.g., Amazon.com).[53] It is also more influential when products are novel, rather than well established in the market.

Keep in mind that word-of-mouth can be a double-edged sword for marketers. Just as positive WOM can enhance attitudes and sales, negative WOM can harm. Furthermore, consumers weigh **negative word-of-mouth** more heavily than they do positive comments. According to a study by the White House Office of Consumer Affairs, 90% of unhappy customers will not do business with a company again. Each of these customers is likely to share his or her grievance with at least nine other people, and 13% tell more than 30 people about their negative experience.[54]

Over time, negative WOM has increased relative to positive WOM such that there is a higher volume of negative messages online.[55] Reach is also potentially high because social media allows users access to many others, even beyond their own network, because of the cascading flow of information. Though, research suggests that the valence of WOM shared may depend upon the interpersonal relationship between sender and receiver.

When interpersonal closeness is high, negative WOM is more likely to be shared; when low, positive WOM is more likely. The research suggests that the effect is due to high interpersonal closeness activating the goal to protect others, and low interpersonal closeness activating the goal to enhance the self.[56]

These brand-specific conversations also have value in terms of their media equivalent, known as the **ad equivalency value**. In other words, when brands use paid media, they have an estimate of the value of the advertising in the form of the fees they paid to place the ads. But in social media, most of our promotional value comes from earned and owned media. Therefore, we may try to establish a value and relate that value to the cost of buying equivalent paid media. This is the meaning of ad equivalence value—what would the value of the mention be if it had come through a paid advertising placement rather than a volunteered comment?

Forrester Research labels these brand-specific mentions "influence impressions." We generate influence impressions whenever we discuss brands openly online. In advertising lingo, an **impression** refers to a view or an exposure to an advertising message. In social media, brands may benefit from influence impressions as well as ad impressions. An influence impression is an exposure to a brand via another person—in other words, it's the impressions that are generated through social sharing. Forrester estimates that each year, among US consumers, 256 billion influence impressions are generated as people talk about their lives with each other, telling stories and experiences that invariably include brands.[57] Further, the brand activity in the social media space, whether in the form of tweeting, blogging, social networking, or virtual commerce, encourages people to incorporate this information into their own communication exchanges.

Opinion leaders in social communities are most likely to deliver these influence impressions: only 6.2% of social media users are responsible for about 80% of them. Forrester calls these influencers **mass connectors**, paying homage to Malcolm Gladwell's popular book *The Tipping Point*. Gladwell posits that three factors work to "tip" a trend, in other words to ignite interest in an idea, behavior, or product: the law of the few, stickiness, and the power of context.[58]

1   The law of the few proposes that three types of people help to spread viral messages:

  • **Mavens** are people who are knowledgeable about many things.

  • **Connectors** are people who know many people and communicate with them.

  • **Salespeople** are people who influence others with their natural persuasive power.

2   If an idea is sticky, this means it has memorable impact and it stays with us for a long time. Indeed, web designers use the term "stickiness" to describe the extent to which a website captures people's interest so that they stay on the site for a long time.

3   Lastly, Gladwell acknowledges that ideas spread more easily when conditions are right—that's the power of context.[59]

The Viral Spread of Social Content

When content, whether a simple opinion, video, or trend, spreads through social networks rapidly, we say that it *went viral*. Viral content may or may not be branded, but it will be content that a large number of people in one or more social communities deemed relevant, valuable—or just plain too bizarre not to share with friends. Those community members then influenced the spread of the content by sharing it with their own social graphs and by participating in WOM about the content.

EXHIBIT 3.7

Viral Content Inspires Memes

Recent examples of viral content include the videos Chewbacca Mom, Damn Daniel, and LipSyncBattle.

www.youtube.com/watch?v=y3yRv5Jg5TI

www.youtube.com/watch?v=_LUX70mXcEE

When viral content evolves within a social community, it becomes a meme. A **meme** is a snippet of cultural information that spreads person to person until eventually it enters the general consciousness. These snippets may include songs, phrases, ideas, slang words, fashion trends, or shared behaviors. An example of a meme is the more than 4 million Mannequin Challenge videos available on YouTube. After the initial video spread, people around the world made their own versions (e.g. www.youtube.com/results?search_query=mannequin+challenge).

It's easy to understand how a meme spreads if you use the medical analogy of a virus: memes spread among consumers in a geometric progression, just as a virus starts off small and steadily infects increasing numbers of people until it becomes an epidemic. The leap from person to person occurs as people share and imitate the meme. The memes that survive over time tend to be distinctive and memorable. The most enduring ones evoke earlier memes that may relate to legends and well-known stories and tales. For example, the *Star Wars* movies evoke prior memes that relate to the legend of King Arthur, religion, heroic youth, and 1930s adventure serials.

Memes have even inspired their own community on Reddit called the Meme Economy, in which memes are discussed using stock market jargon. It inspired a website, https://memetrades.com, where memes are bought, sold, or held like stocks in a stock market. The buy/sell trades serve as an indicator of a meme's future spread.

EXHIBIT 3.8

Rickrolling: A Classic Meme

Have you ever clicked on an exciting link or potentially explosive news story, only to find yourself watching the 1987 Rick Astley hit "Never Gonna Give You Up"? Then you've been rickrolled, my friend. A classic bait-and-switch scenario, the meme is as popular now as it's ever been. The first rickroll happened in 2007 when visitors to the YouTube trailer for the video game *Grand Theft Auto IV* were instead served Astley's video. YouTube got in on the fun itself one April Fool's Day when the site rickrolled every user who viewed a clip on its homepage.[60] Since then millions of people have been rickrolled. See some of the best examples (including one by the White House Twitter account) at http://mentalfloss.com/article/55468/11-epic-rickrolls.

CRITICAL REFLECTION

Social Media as an Outlet for Cyberbullies

David Molak was a teenager who suffered months of anonymous, cyberbullying insults about his appearance. His parents transferred him to a new school in the hope of relief, but the bullying continued. Eventually, David took his own life. David's story spread after his brother, Cliff, posted news of David's suicide and a plea against cyberbullying on Facebook, writing, "In today's age, bullies don't push you into lockers, they don't tell their victims to meet them behind the school's dumpster after class, they cower behind user names and fake profiles from miles away constantly berating and abusing good, innocent people."[61] Unfortunately David's story is not that unusual.

According to anti-bullying charity Ditch The Label cyberbullying is generalized abuse delivered via digital means, which is typically targeted towards the appearance, interests, intelligence or previous posts of the recipient.[62] Ditch The Label explains that cyberbullying is not a separate issue from traditional bullying; but rather an expansion of the platforms on which it exists. Reported rates of cyberbullying vary, with as high as 87% of youth being exposed and 34% being direct recipients.[63] Victims of cyberbullying are more likely to abuse drugs and/or alcohol and smoke cigarettes as a form of self-medication.[64] Teen targets of cyberbullying are nearly twice as likely to have attempted suicide compared with teens who

(Continued)

(Continued)

have not experienced cyberbullying.[65] And the forms of cyberbullying that hurt adolescent victims most are social media posts and pictures. While cyberbullying seems to be most prevalent among teens, it also affects adults, even in the workplace.[66] Even Lady Gaga recently spoke out about her frustration with attacks she faces from trolls on Twitter.[67]

Ditch The Label partnered with Brandwatch to evaluate 19 million tweets from the US and the UK to better understand the phenomenon:[68]

- Politics is the topic most likely to receive bullying remarks, followed by topics relating to sport and food. However, innocuous posts about music, television, and travel also received bullying responses.

- Cyberbullying on Twitter is most prevalent on Sundays and between 6 pm and 8 pm.

- Sports fans and executives were over-represented in bullying tweets, while teachers and scientists were less likely to participate in cyberbullying tweets.

- The majority of insults on Twitter related to intelligence (33%) and appearance (20%).

- Female trolls tend to attack the victim's intelligence (dumb, stupid) or appearance (fat, ugly), while males were more likely to use homophobic insults.

Responding to people who troll escalates the conflict. Research found that responding to bullying tweets escalated the conflict in 44% of cases, compared with only 3% of positive outcomes.

Of course, Twitter is not the only social network site for cyberbullies. A study of cyberbullying on Facebook found that trolls targeted victims with public and private comments, photographs, and status updates using comments about romantic relationships, sexual activity, friendships, and appearance.[69]

Ditch the Label offers support for victims of cyberbullying via its website at www.DitchtheLabel.org.

So, what's the verdict? Are online communities as strong—or stronger—than the traditional kind? The jury is still out. One study of civic engagement and social networks found that online communities neither hindered nor encouraged the sharing of community resources.[70] The Pew Internet & American Life Project offered positive support for the role online networks can play; it noted that the Internet provides us with access to the right people with the right information. In fact, the Pew report even showed that the more we see members of our network in person and talk on the phone, the more likely it is that we will *also* communicate with those people online.[71] The more connected you are, the more connected you will become!

 CHAPTER SUMMARY

How are social networks structured?

Online communities are built on foundations of networks. These networks are made up of nodes connected by ties. The nodes experience interactions and flows of resources, information, and influence occur between nodes. Some nodes are more influential than others. Some ties are stronger than others. Some information flows more deeply and widely. The network effect explains that the relative value a community offers its members is tied to its membership.

What are the characteristics of online communities?

Communities are often built around social objects—objects of mutual interest among community members. Social communities thrive on conversations. They instill a sense of presence for those who participate. Community members share a collective interest, and governance is based on democracy. Community members follow standards of behavior that may be presented as rules and as norms accepted by the membership. Social norms are created, shared, and sustained by community members because they promote behavior that benefits the collective. Participation is necessary for the health of the community but most members are not active. Community participation is typically characteristic of the 80/20 rule whereby only a small percentage of members participate for the benefit of all.

How do ideas travel in a community?

Information travels in the community via flows between nodes in the network. Word-of-mouth communication about brands, known as influence impressions, travel this way. It is a natural pattern for some members to be more active and to acquire positions of authority within a group, whether offline or online. Opinion leaders have more influence in communities and consequently information shared by opinion leaders may be more influential and spread farther and deeper through the social network. The content may go viral. When a viral piece of information enters the general consciousness of the community and is adapted by the community members, it is called a meme.

What role do influencers play and what are their sources of power and social capital? What types of ties do we have to others in our communities?

Opinion leaders possess sources of social power such as expert power, reward power, and authority power. Social capital refers to the valuable resources people (individually or in groups) have within the context of a community. The capital may be actual or virtual and can include reputational capital, bonding social capital, bridging social capital, and maintained social capital. People's networks always include strong and weak ties. Both have value. Even weak ties can create social capital for network members. Maintained social capital refers to the value we get from maintaining relationships with latent ties.

REVIEW QUESTIONS

1   What is the underlying structure of a network?

2   How does information flow in a network?

3   What are the characteristics common to communities, whether offline or online?

4   Explain the meaning of social capital.

5   What is an opinion leader? What sources of power might accrue to opinion leaders?

6   Why are social communities relevant for word-of-mouth communication?

EXERCISES

1   Visit an online community like Playstation Community or Lego Ideas. What do you see in common among these communities? What's different? Does each so-called community really seem to be a unified group with a common culture? Explain.

2   Review the list of friends you have on Facebook. How many of your friends are "weak ties" and how many are "strong ties"? Identify the relationship bonds you share with those in your strong tie group. Does Facebook help you to strengthen both kinds of relationships? Why or why not?

3   Identify a current meme and track its origin, or create your own meme using a meme generator like www.memecreator.org.

4   Search Instagram for hashtags related to a brand (e.g., #dunkindonuts). What kinds of influence impressions appear for the hashtag you searched? Can you identify key influencers who are sharing tweets with this specific hashtag?

5   Discussion: How can we explain the Six Degrees of Kevin Bacon game as an example of social network theory?

CHAPTER NOTES (access all weblinks listed here at: https://study.sagepub.com/smm3e)

1   Barry Wellman, "Physical Place and Cyberplace: The Rise of Personalized Networking," *International Journal of Urban and Regional Research*, 24:2 (2001), 227–52.

2   Nicole Ellison and Danah Boyd, "Sociality through Social Network Sites," in William H. Dutton (ed.), *The Oxford Handbook of Internet Studies* (Oxford: Oxford University Press, 2013), pp. 151–72.

3   Alexandra Marin and Barry Wellman, "Social Network Analysis: An Introduction," in John Scott and Peter J. Carrington (eds), *The Sage Handbook of Social Network Analysis* (London: Sage, 2011), pp. 11–25.

4   C. Haythornthwaite, "Social Networks and Internet Connectivity Effects," *Information, Communication & Society*, 8 (2005), 125–47; Nathan Miczo, Theresa Mariani, and Crystal Donahue, "The Strength of Strong Ties: Media Multiplexity, Communication Motives, and the Maintenance of Geographically Close Friendships," *Communication Reports*, 24:1 (2011), 12–24.

5   Fiona MacDonald, "Are We Really All Connected by Just Six Degrees of Separation? Here's What Science Has to Say," 27 August 2015, www.sciencealert.com/are-we-all-really-connected-by-just-six-degrees-of-separation (accessed June 12, 2017).

6   Ibid.

7   T.B. Sheridan, "Further Musings on the Psychophysics of Presence," *Presence: Teleoperators and Virtual Environments*, 5 (1994), 241–6.

8   Matthew Lombard and Theresa Ditton, "At the Heart of It All: The Concept of Presence," *Journal of Computer Mediated Communication*, 3:2 (1997), http://jcmc.indiana.edu/vol3/issue2/lombard.html (accessed December 31, 2010).

9   K. Knorr-Cetina, "Sociality with Objects: Social Relations in Postsocial Knowledge Societies," *Theory, Culture & Society*, 14:4 (1997), 1–30.

10 Ibid.

11 Michael Morris, Ying-yi Hong, Chi-yue Chiu, and Zhi Liu, "Normology: Integrating Insights about Social Norms to Understand Cultural Dynamics," *Organizational Behavior and Human Decision Processes*, 129 (2015), 1–13.

12 Leonie Rösner and Nicole C. Krämer, "Verbal Venting in the Social Web: Effects of Anonymity and Group Norms on Aggressive Language Use in Online Comments," *Social Media and Society*, 2:3 (2016), http://journals.sagepub.com/doi/full/10.1177/2056305116664220 (accessed July 3, 2017).

13 Luis Gerardo Mojica, "Modeling Trolling in Social Media Conversations," (2016) arXiv:1612.05310 [cs.CL].

14 Adrian Chen, "Unmasking Reddit's Violentacrez, the Biggest Troll on the Web," The Daily Dot, December 11 2015, www.dailydot.com/news/unmasking-violentacrez-biggest-reddit-troll (accessed July 3, 2017).

15 "When to Ban Social Media Trolls and Prevent Harassment," Adweek, January 27, 2017, www.adweek.com/digital/peter-friedman-liveworld-guest-post-trolls (accessed July 3, 2017).

16 K. Rost, L. Stahel, and B.S. Frey, "Digital Social Norm Enforcement: Online Firestorms in Social Media," PLoS ONE, 11:6 (2016).

17 David Brooks, "The Shame Culture," *New York Times*, March 2, 2016, www.nytimes.com/2016/03/15/opinion/the-shame-culture.html?_r=0 (accessed July 3, 2017).

18 Rösner and Krämer, "Verbal Venting in the Social Web."

19 Douglas Holt, "Branding in the Age of Social Media," *Harvard Business Review*, March 2016, https://hbr.org/2016/03/branding-in-the-age-of-social-media (accessed July 3, 2017).

20 R.P. Bagozzi, and U.M. Dholakia, "Intentional Social Action in Virtual Communities," *Journal of Interactive Marketing*, 16:2 (2002), 2–21.

21 Sheridan, "Further Musings on the Psychophysics of Presence."

22 J.R. Brodie, L. Hollebeek, B. Juric, and A. Ilic, "Consumer Engagement: Conceptual Domain, Fundamental Propositions and Implications for Research", *Journal of Service Research*, 14:3 (2011), 252–71.

23 Geoffrey G. Parker, Marshall W. Van Alstyne, and Sangeet Paul Choudary, *Platform Revolution: How Networked Markets Are Transforming the Economy—and How to Make Them Work for You* (New York: W.W. Norton & Company, 2016).

24 James S. Coleman, "Social Capital in the Creation of Human Capital," *The American Journal of Sociology*, 94 (1988), 95–120.

25 Nicole Ellison, Charles Steinfield, and Cliff Lampe, "The Benefits of Facebook 'Friends:' Social Capital and College Students' Use of Online Social Network Sites," *Journal of Computer-Mediated Communication*, 12 (2007), 1143–68.

26 John Cannarella and Joshua Spechler, "Epidemiological Modeling of Online Social Network Dynamics," January 2014, working paper, Princeton University, http://arxiv.org/pdf/1401.4208.pdf (accessed January 27, 2014).

27 Ibid.

28 Josh Constine, "Facebook Hilariously Debunks Princeton Study Saying It Will Lose 80% Of Users," TechCrunch, January 23, 2014, https://techcrunch.com/2014/01/23/facebook-losing-users-princeton-losing-credibility (accessed July 3, 2017).

29 Lee Rainie, John Horrigan, Barry Wellman, and Jeffrey Boase, "The Strength of Internet Ties," Pew Internet & American Life Project, January 25, 2005, www.pewinternet.org/Reports/2006/The-Strength-of-Internet-Ties.aspx (accessed June 23, 2010).

30 McKinsey & Company, "The Strength of Weak Ties," Report, www.mckinsey.com/insights/high_tech_telecoms_internet/the_strength_of_weak_signals?cid=other-eml-nsl-mip-mck-oth-1403 (accessed February 12, 2014).

31 Fred Stutzman, "Activating Latent Ties," May 2007, http://chimprawk.blogspot.com/2007/05/activating-latent-ties.html (accessed December 31, 2010).

32 Ellison, Steinfield, and Lampe, "The Benefits of Facebook 'Friends.'"

33 Matteo Fusco, "That Time Casey Neistat Saved a Human Life Thanks to his Masterful Communication," Medium, September 30, 2016, https://medium.com/@matteofusco/that-time-casey-neistat-saved-a-human-life-thanks-to-his-masterful-communication-7767b5f44562#.mugvlup6h (accessed July 3, 2017); Marlan's GoFundMe campaign is closed but you can read more about his sister and see the final campaign results at www.gofundme.com/2rckwss (accessed July 3, 2017).

34 Ed Keller and Jon Berry, *The Influentials* (New York, Simon & Schuster, 2003).

35 Ibid.

36 J.R.P. French and B. Raven, "The Bases of Social Power," in D. Cartwright and A. Zander (eds), *Group Dynamics* (New York: Harper & Row, 1959).

37 Shahid Ali Chaudhry and Waseem Irshad, "Opinion Leadership and Its Role in Buyer Decision Making," *Academy of Contemporary Research Journal*, 2:1 (2013), 16–23; Raghuram Iyengar, Christophe Van den Bulte, John Eichert, Bruce West, and Thomas W. Valente, "How Social Networks and Opinion Leaders Affect the Adoption of New Products," *New Theories*, 3:1 (2011), 17–25.

38 A. Marwick, and D. Boyd, "To See and Be Seen: Celebrity Practice on Twitter," *Convergence*, 17:2 (2011), 139–58.

39 Susie Khamis, Lawrence Ang, and Raymond Welling, "Self-Branding, 'Micro-Celebrity' and the Rise of Social Media Influencers," *Celebrity Studies* (2016), 1–18.

40 Edelman Digital, *2017 Trends Report*, http://edelmandigital.com/wp-content/uploads/2016/12/2017-Edelman-Digital-Trends-Report.pdf (accessed June 12, 2017).

41 Heather Saul, "Instafamous: Meet the Social Media Influencers Redefining Celebrity," *The Independent*, 27 March 2016, www.independent.co.uk/news/people/instagram-model-natasha-oakley-iskra-lawrence-kayla-itsines-kendall-jenner-jordyn-woods-a6907551.html (accessed July 3, 2017).

42 Linqia, *The Value of Influencer Content 2017*, www.linqia.com/wp-content/uploads/2017/04/The-Value-of-Influencer-Content-2017_Final_Report.pdf (accessed June 12, 2017).

43 Ibid.

44 Ibid.

45 "Toddler Playdate with Gerber Lil' Beanies," Mommy Hates Cooking, www.mommyhatescooking.com/toddler-playdate-gerber-lil-beanies (accessed July 3, 2017); "Toddler Snacking with Gerber Lil' Beanies," Mom Without Labels, September 25, 2016, http://momwithoutlabels.com/ (accessed July 3, 2017); "Fuel Playtime All Summer with Gerber Lil' Beanies!" Not Quite Susie Homemaker, June 24, 2016, www.notquitesusie.com/2016/06/fuel-playtime-summer-gerber-lil-beanies.html (accessed July 3, 2017).

46 Linqia, *The Value of Influencer Content 2017*.

47   Elihu Katz and Paul F. Lazarsfeld, *Personal Influence: The Part Played by People in the Flow of Mass Communication* (New York: The Free Press, 1955).

48   Douglas R. Pruden and Terry G. Vavra, "Controlling the Grapevine," MM (July–August 2004): 23–30.

49   BzzAgent, http://about.bzzagent.com/word-of-mouth/index/about-bzzagent (accessed December 31, 2010).

50   Keller Fay, "Engagement Labs Launches New TotalSocial™ Measurement Solution," Engagementlabs, August 9, 2016, www.engagementlabs.com/press/engagement-labs-launches-new-totalsocial-measurement-solution (accessed July 3, 2017).

51   Deena Amato-McCoy, "Study: User-Generated Content Influences Most Purchase Decisions," Chain Store Age, June 19, 2017, www.chainstoreage.com/article/study-user-generated-content-influences-most-purchase-decisions (accessed July 3, 2017).

52   Ana Babić Rosario, Francesca Sotgiu, Kristine De Valck, and Tammo H.A. Bijmolt, "The Effect of Electronic Word of Mouth on Sales: A Meta-Analytic Review of Platform, Product, and Metric Factors," *Journal of Marketing Research*, 53:3 (2016), 297–318.

53   Ibid.

54   Chip Walker, "Word-of-Mouth," *American Demographics* (July 1995), 38–44; Albert M. Muñiz, Jr., Thomas O'Guinn, and Gary Alan Fine, "Rumor in Brand Community," in Donald A. Hantula (ed.), *Advances in Theory and Methodology in Social and Organizational Psychology: A Tribute to Ralph Rosnow* (Mahwah, NJ: Erlbaum, 2005).

55   Kelly Hewett, William Rand, Roland T. Rust, and Harald J. van Heerde, "Brand Buzz in the Echoverse," *Journal of Marketing*, 80:3 (2016), 1–24.

56   David Dubois, Andrea Bonezzi, and Matteo De Angelis, "Sharing with Friends Versus Strangers: How Interpersonal Closeness Influences Word-of-Mouth Valence," *Journal of Marketing Research*, 52:5 (2016), 712–27.

57   "Introducing Peer Influence Analysis: 500 Billion Peer Impressions Each Year," Empowered, April 20, 2010, http://forrester.typepad.com/groundswell/2010/04/introducing-peer-influence-analysis.html (accessed December 31, 2010).

58   Malcolm Gladwell, *The Tipping Point* (Boston, MA: Little, Brown, 2000).

59   Ibid.

60   "The History of RickRolling: Infographic," *Huffington Post*, June 1, 2010, www.huffingtonpost.com/2010/06/01/the-history-of-rickrollin_n_596064.html (accessed December 31, 2010).

61   Mark Patinkin, "Mass. Cyberbullying Verdict Sends Right Message," *Providence Journal*, June 17, 2017, www.providencejournal.com/news/20170617/mark-patinkin-mass-cyberbullying-verdict-sends-right-message (accessed July 3, 2017).

62   Ditch The Label, "Cyberbullying and Hate Speech," Brandwatch, 2016, www.brandwatch.com/dtl-cyberbullying-viz-2016 (accessed July 3, 2017).

63   K. Eichorn, "Cyberbullying Triples According to New McAfee '2014 Teens and the Screen Study,'" McAfee, June 3, 2014, www.mcafee.com/us/about/news/2014/q2/20140603-01.aspx (accessed July 3, 2017).

64   Valerie A. Earnshaw, Marc N. Elliott, Sari L. Reisner, Sylvie Mrug, Michael Windle, Susan Tortolero Emery, Melissa F. Peskin, and Mark A. Schuster, "Peer Victimization, Depressive Symptoms, and Substance Use: A Longitudinal Analysis," *Pediatrics*, May 2017, http://pediatrics.aappublications.org/content/early/2017/05/04/peds.2016-3426 (accessed July 3, 2017).

65   Ibid.

66   Gary Namie, *2017 WBI U.S. Workplace Bullying Survey*, Workplace Bullying Institute, www.work placebullying.org/wbiresearch/wbi-2017-survey (accessed July 3, 2017).

67   Kaitlin Reilly, "Lady Gaga Explains Why Cyberbullying Is Such a Problem," Refinery29, June 29, 2017, www.refinery29.com/2017/06/161518/lady-gaga-internet-trolls-advice-cyberbullying (accessed July 3, 2017).

68   Ditch The Label, "Cyberbullying and Hate Speech."

69   Nicholas Brody and Anita L. Vangelisti, "Cyberbullying: Topics, Strategies, and Sex Differences," *Computers in Human Behavior*, 75 (2017), 739–48.

70   Josh Pasek, Eian More, and Daniel Romer, "Realizing the Social Internet? Online Social Networking Meets Offline Civic Engagement," *Journal of Information Technology & Politics*, 6:3–4 (2009), 197–215.

71   Keith Hampton, Lauren Sessions, Lee Rainie, and Kristen Purcell, "Social Networking Sites and Our Lives," Pew Research Center, June 16, 2011, www.pewinternet.org/2011/06/16/social-net working-sites-and-our-lives (accessed July 3, 2017).

Visit **https://study.sagepub.com/smm3e** for free additional online resources related to this chapter.

PART 2

Social Media Marketing Strategy and Planning

Social Media Marketing Strategy

Learning Objectives

When you finish reading this chapter, you will be able to answer these questions:

1 Where does social media marketing planning fit into an organization's overall planning framework?

2 What are the phases of social media marketing maturity? How does social media marketing change for companies as they shift from the trial phase to the transition phase and eventually move into the strategic phase?

3 What are the steps in social media marketing strategic planning?

4 How can organizations structure themselves to support social media marketing?

5 What are the key components of an organizational social media policy, and why is it important to have such a policy in place?

Strategic Planning and Social Media Marketing

Honda is buying into social media, big time. The company has strategically utilized several different social media channels and vehicles in recent years and coordinated these with more traditional tactics like paid broadcast media to maximize impact. The company has an active presence in social communities including YouTube, Facebook, Instagram, and Twitter, but also runs targeted campaigns on niche community networks like Snapchat and Pinterest. Honda partnered with Salesforce to manage its social media activity and ensure it could be responsive with fans around the world who use social media to reach out to the brand. It also uses Adobe Marketing Cloud to facilitate local adaptations of its social media content for different world regions and ensures consistency by providing social media tools for dealers to use in local and regional communications. We'll hear more about Honda's approach to social media marketing in this chapter.

For marketers like those at Honda, **strategic planning** is the process of identifying objectives to accomplish, deciding how to accomplish those objectives with specific strategies and tactics, implementing the actions that make the plan come to life, and measuring how well the plan met the objectives. The process of strategic planning is three-tiered, beginning at the corporate level, then moving to the business level, and lastly moving to the functional areas of the organization, including marketing. Planners first identify their overall objectives (e.g., "raise consumer awareness of our brand by 10% in the next year") and then develop the specific tactics they will use to reach those goals (e.g., "increase our spending on print advertising in targeted publications by 15% this year"). A **marketing plan** is a written, formalized plan that details the product, pricing, distribution, and promotional strategies that will enable the brand in question to accomplish specific marketing objectives. Table 4.1 provides a sample of an overall marketing plan structure.

Table 4.1   The Structure of a Typical Marketing Plan

The Marketing Plan Outline	Questions the Plan Addresses
A PERFORM A SITUATION ANALYSIS **1 Internal Environment**	• How does marketing support my company's mission, objectives, and growth strategies? • What is the corporate culture and how does it influence marketing activities? • What has my company done in the past with its: Target markets? Products? Pricing? Promotion? Supply chain? • What resources including management expertise does my company have that make us unique? How has the company added value through its offerings in the past?
2 External Environment	• What is the nature of the overall domestic and global market for our product? How big is the market? Who buys our product? • Who are our competitors? What are their marketing strategies? • What are the key trends in the economic environment? The technological environment? The regulatory environment? The social and cultural environment?
3 SWOT Analysis	• Based on this analysis of the internal and external environments, what are the key Strengths, Weaknesses, Opportunities, and Threats (SWOT)?

The Marketing Plan Outline	Questions the Plan Addresses
B SET MARKETING OBJECTIVES	• What does marketing need to accomplish to support the objectives of my firm?
C DEVELOP MARKETING STRATEGIES **1 Select Target Markets and Positioning**	• How do consumers and organizations go about buying, using, and disposing of our products? • Which segments should we select to target? If a consumer market: what are the relevant demographic, psychographic, and behavioral segmentation approaches and the media habits of the targeted segments? If a business market: what are the relevant organizational demographics? • How will we position our product for our market(s)?
2 Product Strategies	• What is our core product? Actual product? Augmented product? • What product line/product mix strategies should we use? • How should we package, brand, and label our product? • How can attention to service quality enhance our success?
3 Pricing Strategies	• How will we price our product to the consumer and through the channel? • How much must we sell to break even at this price? • What pricing tactics should we use?
4 Promotional Strategies	• How do we develop a consistent message about our product? How do we best generate buzz? • What approaches to advertising, public relations, sales promotion, and newer forms of communication (such as social networking) should we use? • What role should a sales force play in the marketing communications plan? How should direct marketing be used?
5 Supply Chain Strategies	• How do we get our product to consumers in the best and most efficient manner? • What types of retailers, if any, should we work with to sell our product? • How do we integrate supply chain elements to maximize the value we offer to our customers and other stakeholders?
D IMPLEMENT AND CONTROL THE MARKETING PLAN **1 Action Plans (for all marketing mix elements)**	• How do we make our marketing plan happen?
2 Responsibility	• Who is responsible for accomplishing each aspect of implementing the marketing plan?
3 Time line	• What is the timing for the elements of our marketing plan?
4 Budget	• What budget do we need to accomplish our marketing objectives?
5 Measurement and Control	• How do we measure the actual performance of our marketing plan and compare it to our planned performance and progress toward reaching our marketing objectives?

On second thought, what's wrong with jumping right into the game? Why should we take the time to plan? Although it's tempting to just follow our instincts, it turns out there is tremendous value in planning. Dumb luck and sweat take you only so far. Planning ensures that an organization understands its markets and its competitors. It helps to ensure that organizations are aware of the changing marketplace environment. When organizational partners participate in the planning process, they are better able to communicate and coordinate activities. Planning requires that objectives are set and agreed upon, which improves the likelihood of those objectives being met. It enhances the ability of managers to allocate limited resources using established priorities. Perhaps most of all, planning enables success to be defined. Success or the lack thereof becomes a measurable outcome that can guide future planning efforts.

It's increasingly common for organizations to include a heavy dose of social media in their marketing plans. The annual *Social Media Marketing Industry Report* provides data on the use of social media marketing by B2B and B2C marketers around the world. The most recent report revealed that 90% of marketers feel social media is important to their marketing initiatives.[1] Whether large or small, B2B or B2C, most businesses recognize that social media should be integrated into their marketing plans. According to the *2016 Social Media Marketing Industry Report*, 81% of businesses have integrated their social media efforts in their marketing plans. Most are doing so for branding and demand-generation purposes, but social media marketing is also valuable for managing customer service interactions and conducting market research. This upward trend will continue in the coming years.

It makes sense to include social media marketing in a brand's marketing plan. Social media marketing has many applications for marketers. Social media can be a delivery tool to build buzz and word-of-mouth communication. It can efficiently deliver coupons and other special promotional offers. Social platforms can be the primary venue for the execution of contests and sweepstakes. They can collect data to build databases and to generate sales leads. Social media can also serve as efficient channels to manage customer service relationships and to conduct research for new product development. Not to mention, social media are relatively inexpensive ways to increase the reach and frequency of messages that are otherwise delivered via more traditional, big media methods.

Because the creative applications related to social media are somewhat unique, we will suggest an approach for developing an in-depth social media marketing strategy much as advertising plans (also known as integrated marketing communications (IMC) plans or marcom plans) provide in-depth detail on the execution of the (traditional) promotional portion of a brand's marketing plan. In the early days of social media marketing, many plans were developed for stand-alone campaigns that were not fully integrated into the brand's promotional mix. Today, social media marketing campaigns may serve as stand-alones and/or be a fully integrated media choice in the brand's marcom plan. For simplicity, we approach the sample plan from the perspective of planning a stand-alone campaign. Table 4.2 provides the structure of a social media marketing plan. We'll begin this process as we explore the strategic development of social media marketing plans. Then we'll cover the steps in strategic planning for social media marketing. Finally, we'll discuss structural approaches organizations can take to be prepared to execute their plans.

The Phases of Social Media Marketing Maturity

If you keep up with industry news, you might be tempted to think that *every* brand has a social media strategy. Each day seems to bring new stories about a marketing campaign

Table 4.2   A Social Media Marketing Plan Outline

I Conduct a situation analysis and identify key opportunities

- Internal Environment

  1. What activities exist in the overall marketing plan that can be leveraged for social media marketing?
  2. What is the corporate culture? Is it supportive of the transparent and decentralized norms of social media?
  3. What resources exist that can be directed to social media activities?
  4. Is the organization already prepared internally for social media activities (in terms of policies and procedures)?

- External Environment

  1. Who are our customers? Are they users of social media?
  2. Who are our competitors? What social media activities are they using and how are social media incorporated in their marketing and promotional plans?
  3. What are the key trends in the environment (social, cultural, legal and regulatory, political, economic, and technological) that may affect our decisions regarding social media marketing?

- SWOT Analysis

  1. Based on the analysis, what are the key strengths, weaknesses, opportunities, and threats (SWOT)?

II State objectives

  1. What does the organization expect to accomplish through social media marketing (promotional objectives, service objectives, retail objectives, research objectives)?

III Gather insight into target audience

  1. Which segments should we select to target with social media activities?
  2. What are the relevant demographic, psychographic, and behavioral characteristics of the segments useful in planning a social media marketing strategy?
  3. What are the media habits, and especially the social media habits of the segments?

IV Select social media zones and vehicles

  1. Which mix of the four zones of social media will be best to accomplish our objectives within the resources available?

- Social community zone strategies

  a. What approach to social networking and relationship building should we use? How will we represent the brand in social networks (as a corporate entity, as a collection of corporate leadership, as a brand character)? What content will we share in this space?

- Social publishing zone strategies

  a. What content do we have to share with audiences? Can we develop a sufficient amount of fresh, valuable content to attract audiences to consume content online?

(Continued)

(Continued)

b. What form should our blog take?

c. Which media sharing sites should we use to publish content? How should we build links between our social media sites, owned media sites, and affiliates to optimize our sites for search engines?

- Social entertainment zone strategies

a. What role should social entertainment play in our social media plan? Are there opportunities to develop a customized social game or to promote the brand as a product placement in other social games? Is there an opportunity to utilize social entertainment sites such as MySpace as an entertainment venue?

- Social commerce zone strategies

a. How can we develop opportunities for customer reviews and ratings that add value to our prospective customers?

b. Should we develop retail spaces within social media sites? If we socially enhance our own e-retailing spaces, what applications should be used?

c. How can we utilize social commerce applications like group deals to increase conversions?

V Create an experience strategy encompassing selected zones

1. How can we develop social media activities that support and/or extend our existing promotional strategies?

2. What message do we want to share using social media?

3. How can we encourage engagement with the brand in social spaces?

4. How can we encourage those who engage with the brand socially to act as opinion leaders and share the experience with others?

5. In what ways can we align the zones used as well as other promotional tools to support each other? Can we incorporate social reminders in advertising messages, in store displays, and other venues?

VI Establish an activation plan

1. How do we make the plan happen?

2. Who is responsible for each aspect of implementing the plan?

3. What is the timing of the elements in the plan?

4. What budget do we need to accomplish the objectives?

5. How do we ensure that the plan is consistent with the organization's overall marketing plan and promotional plan?

VII Manage and measure

1. How do we measure the actual performance of the plan?

with social media elements. On ads, storefronts, and business cards, we see "Follow me" calls to action as organizations large and small flock to Twitter and Facebook.

Although it seems everyone is talking about social media, it's one thing to claim you *use* social media and quite another to say you have a *strategy* that incorporates social media. In the former case, a group can turn to social media activities to stage **stunts** (one-off ploys designed to get attention and press coverage) or as **activation tools** to support other marketing efforts. For example, when Skittles let its social media presence take over its website, that was a stunt. But when Starbucks runs social media promotions, it integrates these promotions with the overall campaign in place. The most engaging brands using social media for marketing will ensure that all communications are consistent with the brand's image, while using social media as an element for experimentation and engagement with short-term campaigns as well as use in omni-channel marcom campaigns.

As organizations develop in their social media marketing maturity, they plan systematically to ensure social media marketing activities are consistent with their marketing and marketing communications plans and are capable of meeting specific marketing objectives. By this we mean that, as a result of time and experience, we tend to see that applications that start as one-time "experiments" often morph into more long-term and carefully thought-out elements that the organization integrates with all the other communication pieces it uses to reach customers.

Nevertheless, many marketers currently use social media marketing tactics without that level of maturity. A major study of marketers in both Europe and North America found huge differences in the level to which respondents use social media and integrate them with their other initiatives. Many still just experiment with baby steps (like creating a Facebook page) rather than include social media as a fundamental component of their marketing strategy.[2] Companies are eager to benefit from social media, but many are still in the process of figuring out just how these approaches can go beyond the novelty stage and actually help them to meet their objectives. Companies can be thought of in terms of their level of maturity in social media marketing, of which there are three phases: trial, transition, and strategic.[3] Let's take a closer look at each phase.

Trial Phase

The trial phase is the first phase of the adoption cycle. Organizations in the trial phase test out social media platforms, but they don't really consider how social media can play a role in the overall marketing plan. In these early days, most groups focus on learning to use a new form of communication and exploring the potential for social media as a venue.

It isn't necessarily a bad thing to test the waters of social media. Companies need, especially early on, to experiment—to play in the sandbox, so to speak. Doing so helps them to brainstorm ideas to use social media and understand what it takes to succeed in this brave new world. However, the problem with the trial phase is that many companies do not treat it as an exploratory stage of what is really a multi-stage process. Instead they just jump right in and focus only on cool new ways to communicate. Think this couldn't happen? According to the *2016 Social Media Marketing Industry Report*, 41% of marketers have been using social media less than two years.

EXHIBIT 4.1

The Transition Stage of Social Media Marketing

Chris Parypa Photography/Shutterstock.com

British Airways is an example of a brand in the transition stage of social media marketing. It uses Twitter as a brand presence and customer support channel but doesn't consistently manage complaints. How do we know? Consider this example. A customer of British Airways, frustrated about his lost luggage (using his Twitter handle @hvsvn), posted a "promoted tweet" (that's paid media in a social vehicle) advising people to avoid flying with British Airways due to its horrendous service. The company didn't respond for eight hours! When it did, it tweeted that customer service hours were standard business hours—9 to 5—and asked that the customer direct message (DM) his baggage claim information to them. What would you think? You got it. Twitter is 24/7. Brands don't have the option of being on only eight hours per day.[4] Issues like this can be amplified by influencers. We tend to think of brands partnering with influencers to increase the reach and spread of positive content. But if influencers have a negative experience, their complaints spread as well.

British Airways learned this the hard way when television star Phillip Schofield documented the delays and lack of support from BA employees during a computer system failure that left thousands stranded at Heathrow. Schofield posted a selfie to Instagram with the crowded chaos in the background and tweeted what some called an "epic rant" to @britishairways too.[5] Schofield wasn't the only BA customer using social media to complain to BA that day, but his activity is especially relevant because of his multi-million person fan base.

Transition Phase

As organizations mature in their use of social media marketing, they enter a **transition phase**. During this phase, social media activities still occur somewhat randomly or haphazardly but a more systematic way of thinking starts to develop within the organization.

In the transition stage, brands are on the right track but may not have fully formed a strategic approach. For instance, the brand may have established social media profiles and be using them regularly but still make mistakes. A common one is the use of automation to schedule social media posts and replies. This means that some of the responses to tweets or Facebook posts (or other social media comments) are programmed. In the industry, these automated responses are useful for workflow management but users view automation as fake, referring to the practice as **social media zombies**. In and of itself, that's not bad. Automation can help brands be responsive. But if overused or used ineffectively, people will know. And they will resent it.

Strategic Phase

When an organization enters the final strategic phase, it utilizes a formal process to plan social media marketing activities with clear objectives and metrics. Social media are now integrated as a key component of the organization's overall marketing plan. While making a strategic commitment to social media marketing takes time, it also comes with benefits. Marketers report increased brand exposure, brand attitudes, and even sales driven from social media marketing. Of course, this isn't necessarily easy, even for marketers with substantial experience using social media—40% say that social media marketing is more difficult now than it was in the past.[6] A need to show the ROI for marketing activities coupled with a fluid social media environment create challenges.

CRITICAL REFLECTION

Bots Among Us

Bots are algorithms acting in social media networks. Their capabilities offer potential value to marketers and consumers. For instance, bots can make recommendations, provide information, facilitate purchases, and interact in conversations with surprising authenticity. The automation provides efficiencies for marketers. Many of us have interacted with bots. There are already thousands of them on Facebook Messenger, WeChat, and other social channels. Some are clearly labeled, particularly when used as a branded app like the one TripAdvisor offers on Facebook Messenger. Research on consumer attitudes toward chatbots suggest that people are open to using chatbots but want their accuracy to improve and security measures to protect credit card data and other personal information bots may have access to.[7]

That's not the whole story though. Some bots are disguised and to the average social media user, the bots seem like a real person. In fact, 30% cannot identify bots from real users on social networks.[8] The risk? Bots can influence perceptions and sentiment, the spread of information, and cause all kinds of trouble.[9] A simple example? Barack Obama is frequently praised for his strong Twitter following. But, estimates suggest that more than 50% of Obama's followers are actually bots!

Bots can send spam, make bogus offers, deliver messages with malware, and more. Scammers are well aware of this phenomenon. Security research firm Cloudmark has documented the rise of a flirtatious bot called "TextGirlie." After obtaining a victim's name and telephone number from their social media profile, TextGirlie would send the victim a personalized message asking them to continue the conversation in an online chatroom. A few coquettish exchanges later and the victim would be asked to click on a link to an adult dating or web cam site. Bots can be programmed to post

(Continued)

(Continued)

kithanet/Shutterstock.com

fake messages to sway public opinion. It's a problem known as 'astroturfing', in which a seemingly authentic swell of grass-roots opinion is in fact manufactured by a battalion of opinionated bots.[10] The ramifications of astroturfing are in fact so serious that the US Department of Defense has developed an app, called BotOrNot, which can determine whether a Twitter account is run by a bot. The application provides a predictive analysis based on account activity and tweet semantics, which suggests whether the account operator is likely to be a human or a bot.

The threat is real—estimates suggest that 15% of Twitter accounts are actually bots. To put that in perspective, that's about 50 million Twitter "users." Bots stay busy too. One study found that more than 60% of all Internet traffic is actually generated by bots.

Richard Wallace, a creator of bots for customer service and other marketing uses, explains that the most realistic bots can convince people that they are human. Bot designers compete for the Loebner Prize, a contest in which chatbots try to convince judges that they are human. Twitter and other social networks have detection systems to identify bots, but the systems are no match for well-designed bots. A group of researchers showed just how easy it is to infiltrate Twitter as long as the bots looked and acted like real Twitter users. They created 120 bot accounts, making sure each one had a convincing profile complete with picture and attributes such as gender. After a month, they found that almost 70% of the bots were left untouched by Twitter's bot detection mechanisms. What's more, the bots were pre-programmed to interact with other users and quickly attracted thousands of followers.

Another problem with bots? As artificial intelligence (AI) programs, bots learn from their surroundings and interactions. This is meant to be an advantage, but there are risks too. Savvy trolls can manipulate what bots learn. That's what happened with Microsoft bot, Tay. Tay was a conversation bot created for Twitter. She was designed to learn from conversations and then use what she learned. Trolls began to converse with the program in ways to trick it into becoming racist, ignorant, and even cruel. Within a day, the program was tweeting out offensive posts and Microsoft shut the bot down.[11]

Social Media Campaigns: The Strategic Planning Process

Those organizations that have moved beyond the trial and transition phases of social media marketing maturity develop strategic plans for social media that incorporate components of the social media mix as channels to accomplish marketing objectives. As we saw in Table 4.2, the process consists of the following steps:

- Conduct a situation analysis and identify key opportunities.
- State objectives.
- Gather insight into and target one or more segments of social consumers.
- Select the social media channels and vehicles.

- Create an experience strategy.
- Establish an activation plan using other promotional tools (if needed).
- Execute and measure the campaign.

Situation Analysis

The first step in developing the plan is much the same as it is in the creation of traditional strategic plans—research and assess the environment. Good social media planning starts with research on the industry and competitors, the product category, and the consumer market. Once this research is compiled, strategists try to make sense of the findings as they analyze the data in a situation analysis.

The situation analysis details the current problem or opportunity the organization faces. It will typically include a social media audit. In addition to the standard things marketers need to know, the social media audit ensures the team understands the brand's experience in social media. The audit will assess the brand's past social media activity including whether profiles are consistent with the brand image, frequency of activity, types of activity, responsiveness, engagement, and other measures of effectiveness. Free tools that are useful for auditing social media activities are LikeAlyzer, Fan Page Karma, and AgoraPulse. Audit reports can also be created using paid vendor services like those from Sprout Social, Sysomos, and others. Figure 4.1 provides a template for beginning a social media audit.

In addition, a review of the brand's SWOT analysis will highlight relevant aspects of the firm's internal and external environment that could affect the organization's choices, capabilities, and resources. This acronym refers to *strengths, weaknesses, opportunities,* and *threats* that the firm should consider as it crafts a strategy. The internal environment refers to the strengths and weaknesses of the organization—the controllable elements inside a firm that influence how well the firm operates. The external environment consists of those elements outside the organization—the organization's opportunities and threats—that may affect its choices and capabilities. Unlike elements of the internal environment that management can control to a large degree, the firm can't directly control these external factors, so management must respond to them through its planning process.

A key aspect of the external environment is the brand's competition. Analyzing competitive social media efforts and how the target market perceives those efforts is a must-do in social media marketing planning. It can be done in much the same way as the social media audit—except the focus is on the competing firms. You can use an internal system or a **cloud service** such as RivalMap (www.rivalmap.com) to organize competitive information and to monitor news and social activity. When you use RivalMap, you can maintain a search of competitive activity and news mentions online for a small fee. Figure 4.2 illustrates a template for tracking a social media competitive analysis. For a very thorough example of a competitive analysis, see the Infegy report, "Brand Analysis: Coca-Cola versus Pepsi," which assesses effectiveness as well as brand activity in social media.[12] A competitive social media analysis should answer the following questions:

- In which social media channels and specific vehicles are competitors active?
- How do they present themselves in those channels and vehicles? Include an analysis of profiles, company information provided, tone, and activity.
- Who are their fans and followers? How do fans and followers respond to the brand's social activity?

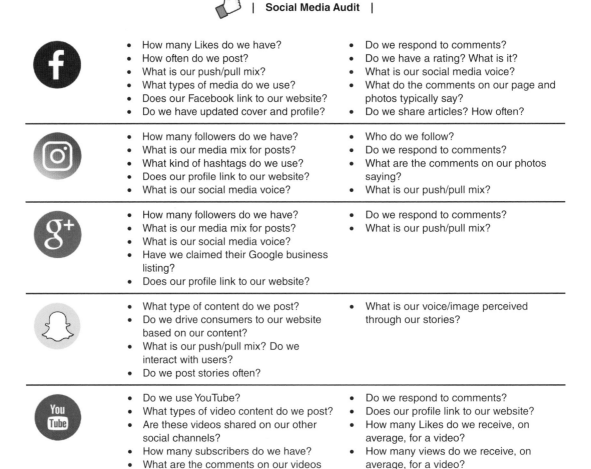

| Social Media Audit |

- How many Likes do we have?
- How often do we post?
- What is our push/pull mix?
- What types of media do we use?
- Does our Facebook link to our website?
- Do we have updated cover and profile?

- Do we respond to comments?
- Do we have a rating? What is it?
- What is our social media voice?
- What do the comments on our page and photos typically say?
- Do we share articles? How often?

- How many followers do we have?
- What is our media mix for posts?
- What kind of hashtags do we use?
- Does our profile link to our website?
- What is our social media voice?

- Who do we follow?
- Do we respond to comments?
- What are the comments on our photos saying?
- What is our push/pull mix?

- How many followers do we have?
- What is our media mix for posts?
- What is our social media voice?
- Have we claimed their Google business listing?
- Does our profile link to our website?

- Do we respond to comments?
- What is our push/pull mix?

- What type of content do we post?
- Do we drive consumers to our website based on our content?
- What is our push/pull mix? Do we interact with users?
- Do we post stories often?

- What is our voice/image perceived through our stories?

- Do we use YouTube?
- What types of video content do we post?
- Are these videos shared on our other social channels?
- How many subscribers do we have?
- What are the comments on our videos saying?

- Do we respond to comments?
- Does our profile link to our website?
- How many Likes do we receive, on average, for a video?
- How many views do we receive, on average, for a video?

Figure 4.1   Social Media Audit Template

Importantly, marketers have many approaches to solving problems and taking advantage of opportunities. Here we are concerned with the organization's use of social media, but still, the planner should ask the question, "Given the situation and the problem identified, is social media marketing the appropriate approach?" Especially for organizations that are still in the trial phase, it's tempting to focus on social media "gimmicks," even if other less trendy tactics might in fact be more effective. So, a word of caution: social media often provide effective solutions to marketing problems, but beware of blindly using these tools.

To see how the early stages of the strategic planning process work in the real world, let's return to our example, Honda. Honda uses social media as part of its integrated marcom campaigns for Honda and each sub-brand (e.g., CRV, Civic, Ridgeline) and also creates independent social media initiatives. It does so in a way that resonates with specific social media vehicles like Twitter, Instagram, YouTube, Pinterest, and Tumblr. Honda is one of the most well-known brands in the world, named 20th on the Forbes most valuable brands list. That's not all; the brand has won awards for most trusted car brand, best value brand, and best overall brand! But, Honda faces stiff competition online and offline.

Figure 4.2   Social Media Competitive Analysis Template

Table 4.3   Honda's Social Media SWOT Analysis

Strengths:	Weaknesses:
• Loyal customers • High brand equity • Affordability • Quality products • High levels of coverage across all forms of media • Financial resources for marketing communications	• Difficulty standing out in a highly competitive marketplace • Reputation issues due to recalls • Reputation issues related to being an old-school brand
Opportunities:	**Threats:**
• Social media as a cost-efficient channel • Affiliations with causes and lifestyle passions • Growth in social entertainment and social commerce options	• Strong brand competition from competitors like Toyota • Economic concerns may slow spending on high-price purchases • Environmental concerns over gas consumption and pollution

Identify Social Media Marketing Objectives and Set Budgets

In this stage of the process, the planner elaborates on what is expected of the social media campaign and what financial and human resources are available to meet those objectives. An **objective** is a specific statement about a planned social media activity in terms of what that activity intends to accomplish. The content of the objective will vary based on the situation and the problem at hand. For instance, the campaign may be designed to amplify other marketing communication efforts the organization uses. Let's say, for example, the brand co-sponsors a concert series. This series is an event marketing strategy built into the overall marketing communications plan. But the organization realizes that promoting the event using social media can build pre- and post-event buzz. In this case, the objective (to create heightened awareness of the event among target customers) relates to other activities in the organization.

The basic assumption is that the campaign can accomplish the desired marketing objectives. What are some examples of the basic marketing objectives social media marketers pursue? Here are some important ones:

- Increase brand awareness.
- Improve brand or product reputation.
- Increase website traffic.
- Amplify or augment public relations work.
- Improve search engine rankings.
- Improve perceived customer service quality.
- Generate sales leads.
- Reduce customer acquisition and support costs.
- Increase sales/sales revenue.

In this stage of planning, it's important to state the objectives in a way that will help the planner to make other decisions in the planning process and eventually to measure the extent to which the objective was accomplished at specific points into the campaign. A well-stated, actionable objective should include the following characteristics:

- Be specific (what, who, when, where).
- Be measurable.
- Specify the desired change (from a baseline).
- Include a time line.
- Be consistent and realistic (given other corporate activities and resources).

Here's an example of an actionable objective: To increase site stickiness in the retail areas of our site by 100% (from five minutes browsing to ten minutes per site visit) with the addition of social commerce sharing applications by the end of the third quarter. The statement of the objective should include specific elaboration on the individual goals the brand wishes to achieve over the course of the campaign, taking care to state these goals such that they are specific, measurable, realistic, and time-lined. We don't know Honda's precise objectives but we can gauge that Honda seeks to generate engaging

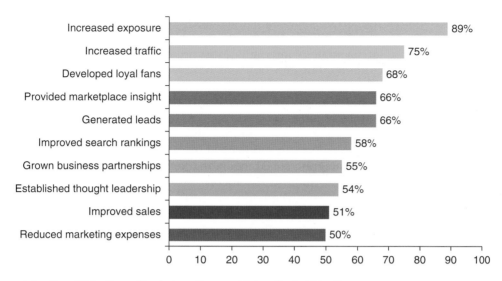

Figure 4.3   Top Objectives Marketers Pursue Using Social Media

Source: Stelzner, *2016 Social Media Marketing Industry Report*, p. 17

Reproduced with kind permission of the Social Media Examiner

content for popular social networks, build its fan base in social communities, build brand equity, and increase top-of-mind awareness.

There should be a focus on resources. You've probably heard people say that the main benefit of social media marketing is that it's free? When brand managers work with agencies to plan traditional advertising campaigns, the cost of media placement can seem overwhelming. With that as a point of comparison, one can see why many might think of social media marketing as the free alternative to advertising. Even for brand participation in social network sites, social media are not free. In planning a social media campaign, a budget must be allocated that ensures sufficient resources to accomplish the goals—just like in a traditional ad program. Granted, the media costs are often much lower compared to, say, a national television campaign. But there are other costs associated with social media. Charlene Li, a leading social media strategist, once said, "Social media trades media costs for labor costs."[13]

What does Li's comment mean? To a large extent, the social communities in which brands engage consumers are indeed free to play spaces in terms of *media costs*. But there are other costs we must take into account. Content must be generated, shared, and managed, and the time that that takes requires funding. Strategies in some social media channels of our social media framework require development costs (in-house or with a vendor or agency) such as customizing profiles and developing social games, branded applications and widgets, and microsites. Organic reach is increasingly difficult for brands to achieve as well. The result is an increase in the use of advertising (paid media) on SNS. At the end of the day, there's no such thing as a free lunch!

Most organizations to date allocate only a small portion of their marketing budgets to social media. Current estimates are under 10%! Though that budget is expected to nearly double in the next five years! Where will this money be spent? Primarily organizations are staffing for content management, ensuring that time is available for content development, blogging, and monitoring of social channels and paying for social advertising. As we described in Chapter 1, the job of social media manager, akin to that of a brand manager, is becoming more commonplace. This person has the role of overseeing, managing, and championing the social media strategy internally. Most organizations now have a dedicated team for social media marketing, but 80% of teams have fewer than four people.[14] Typical roles include that of social media strategist, community manager, social media analyst, and social media associate. In addition, organizations may budget for software and services to manage social media accounts, manage projects, analyze effectiveness, automate tasks for efficiency, host content, monitor social conversations and collect data, and facilitate content creation. Agencies and other providers can supplement the work of the social media manager (or team) with ideas, ways to integrate social media marketing with the rest of the brand's marcom plan, technical expertise, and measurement.

As with everything else in business, the budget is critical—without funding, the organization can't initiate or maintain the campaign. How much should it allocate? When it comes to social media campaigns, budgets run the gamut from a few hundred to hundreds of thousands of dollars. For instance, Honda reportedly shifted its budget for communications on cable television networks to fund its social entertainment initiative.

Many companies approach social media marketing budgets as a percentage of their ad spends, which in turn are assigned by planners within the organization according to one of several formulae. The percentage of ad spend method assigns a set portion of the overall advertising budget for the organization to social media activities. Some use a variation, where they allocate a percentage of online marketing funding to social media.

Two other methods are used by companies. The competitive parity method uses competitors' spending as a benchmark. Like advertiser share of voice, competitive parity is based on the belief that spending the same or more on social media marketing will result in a comparable change in share of attention for the brand. When it comes to social media, though, share of voice takes on a new dimension; social media include conversations about the brand from other sources. In contrast, with advertising, increasing share of voice is accomplished by simply purchasing more media time for advertisements.

With social media marketing, the costs of different approaches and platforms vary widely, and even a large spend may not result in widespread buzz or content sharing and viral spread. The resulting share of voice depends in part on the extent to which fans and friends share the message with their own networks. Lastly, the objective-and-task method considers the objectives set out for the campaign and determines the cost estimates for accomplishing each objective. This method builds the budget from a logical base with what is to be accomplished as the starting point.

Profile the Target Audience of Social Consumers

Social media marketing plans, like any marketing plan, must target the desired audience in a meaningful and relevant manner. To do this requires the development of a social media profile of the target audience. The target market for the brand will have been defined in the brand's marketing plan in terms of demographic, geodemographic, psychographic, and product-usage characteristics. The target audience's social profile will take this understanding of the market one step farther. It will include the market's social activities and styles, such as their level of social media participation, the channels they utilize and the communities in which they are active, and their behavior in social communities. You learned about the elements of segmentation and targeting and the use of personas in Chapter 2.

The strategic planner must assess what it means to speak to the audience in the social media space. Who is the core target? How can we describe the key segments of that core target? To whom will the conversations in social media be directed? Of which social communities are the consumers a member? How do they use social media? How do they interact with other brands? The insights from the consumer profile that was done for a brand's overall marketing and marcom plans will be useful to understand the overall profile of the target market.

However, the planner also must understand how and when his or her customers interact in online social communities, as well as which devices they use to do so. In developing a consumer profile, the planner may plot out a typical day for the social media user as well as gather information on the Internet activities of the audience.

Honda's profiles will align with its sub-brands. The target audience for the Honda Civic is different than that for the Honda CRV, and so on. Honda uses the insights about each persona to guide specific campaigns and interactions across its social media activities.

Select Social Media Channels and Vehicles

Once the organization understands who it wants to reach, it's time to select the best **social media mix** to accomplish this. The zones of social media make up the channel and vehicle choices available for a social media mix. Similar to a more traditional marketing mix, the social media mix describes the combination of vehicles the strategy will include to attain the organization's objectives.

The social media mix options lie among the four zones we've already discussed: relationship development in social communities, social publishing, social entertainment, and social commerce. Within each zone are many specific vehicles that may be best suited to reach a certain audience. For instance, to meet the desired objectives and the social media patterns of a target audience that includes college students, the planner may determine that the campaign should include social networking, social publishing, and social games. The media vehicles might include Facebook, YouTube, and Flickr. Social publishing may utilize a corporate blog and document sharing sites such as Scribd. Brands can leverage the popularity of games, music, and video using the zone of social entertainment. It's also a good idea at this stage of planning to map out how the campaign will build earned media and utilize paid and owned media synergistically.

EXHIBIT 4.2

Honda's Experience Strategy Invited Fans to Design Stunt Track

To promote the newest Civic Coupe, Honda created a UGC campaign for Instagram. Instagram's user profile matches the persona for Honda Civic's target audience and UGC campaigns inspire engagement. The experience? Fans helped design the world's first crowdsourced stunt track, the Dream Track.[15] Filled with obstacles like bowling pins, pinball bumpers, and—strangely—donut cannons, the track

(Continued)

(Continued)

was a culmination of suggestions from Honda fans all over the world. Fans could submit ideas using Facebook, Twitter, and Instagram. Fans whose ideas were picked for the stunt track got a shout out from Honda. Once the Dream Track was finalized, Honda created photos and videos featuring a professional stunt driver showing off the Civic's capabilities on the Dream Track. The content was shared on Instagram. The concept aligned with Honda's marcom campaign, The Power of Dreams, while effectively engaging the Civic target audience. Not only was the choice of experience and social vehicles appropriate given the target persona, the campaign was designed for propagation. Fans who contributed ideas were invested in the campaign and likely to share the campaign content with their friends.

Reproduced by permission of American Honda Motor Co., Inc.

Honda utilizes many of the zones of social media and multiple vehicles within each zone. The choice of zone and vehicle is based on the nature of the marketing objective and the persona characteristics, as well as how best to bring the experience strategy to life. See Figure 4.4 for a summary of Honda's zone activity.

Create an Experience Strategy

If we were planning an advertising campaign, the next step would be to identify a creative message strategy. Message strategy refers to the creative approach we will use throughout the campaign. This should flow from the brand's positioning statement—a single written statement that encapsulates the position the brand wishes to hold in the minds of its target audience. Positioning statements succinctly capture the heart of what the brand is and what the sponsor wants it to become. Reviewing the position is a necessary step in preparing a social media marketing strategy, because the social media activities the campaign plans and executes need to consistently support the desired message.

Can you identify the brands that go with these positioning statements?[16]

1   The computer for the rest of us
2   Networking networks
3   The world's information in one click
4   Personal video broadcasting network

Answers: (1) Apple, (2) Cisco, (3) Google, (4) YouTube

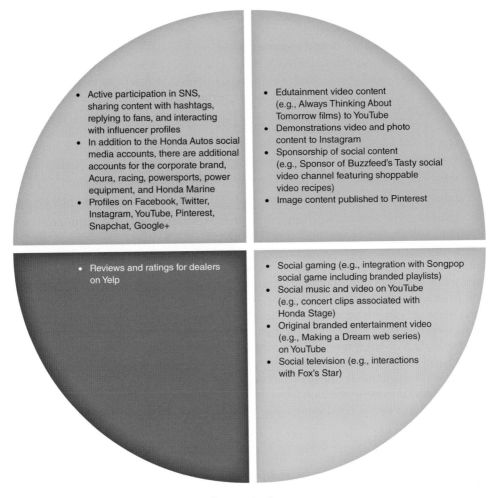

Figure 4.4 Honda's Zones of Social Media Marketing

The message strategy should also be appropriate to meet the campaign's objectives. It is developed from a creative brief—a document that helps creatives channel their energy toward a sound solution for the brand in question. In planning for social media marketing campaigns the design process works similarly; the planners create a brief to guide the development of the campaign. But—because unlike traditional media, social media focus on interactive experiences, social sharing, and engagement—the brief has a somewhat different structure and goes by a different name. Some planners call this document an experience brief.

The concept of an experience brief evolved from the work of website developers who consider the direct impact on users when they design site architecture, imagery, copy, and other site features. Griffin Farley, a strategy planner, uses a different term. He describes the planning document for social media as a propagation brief.[17] He explains that propagation planning means to plan not for the people you reach, but for the people that *they* will reach. In other words, the audience produces more audience. Traditional advertising promotes a message to a passive audience, and that audience is the target. Social media invite an interactive experience with an audience of influencers who will then share the brand's message and invite others to the experience.

Researchers conceptualize **brand experience** as the sensations, feelings, thoughts, and behaviors evoked by brand-related stimuli when consumers interact with brands, whether during exposure to brand messaging, shopping and service interactions, or product consumption.[18] The four dimensions of brand experience point to important elements in experience design:

- To trigger the sensory dimension, the experience should engage the senses, especially visual.

- To evoke the affective dimension, the experience should be emotional.

- To activate the behavioral dimension, the experience should enable physical action.

- To stimulate the cognitive dimension, the experience should stimulate curiosity, problem-solving, or other intellectual motive.

Based on the brand experience dimensions, social media marketing strategies should use visual elements like video, emotional creative appeals (like humor, love, guilt, nostalgia, and fear), and interactive features. Surprisingly, research suggests that brands have focused on functional messages in social media marketing, far more than emotional messages. In one study of top brands using social media, nearly 90% of the brands studied used functional messages but only 57% used interactivity and 43% used emotional appeals. The study found that engagement and influence were both positively influenced by emotional appeals and interactivity, while functional appeals had no effect at all.[19]

To develop a social experience worthy of participation and worthy of sharing, social media planners ask and answer several questions.[20] The answers become the basis for the brief:

- *What are the campaign goals and/or communication tasks?* Objectives have been set for the campaign and the use of social media identified as a possibility. Here the planner reviews these decisions and provides a succinct overview of the goals.

- *How is the brand positioned? What is unique and special about its position in the marketplace?* As in a traditional creative brief, any campaign work should leverage the brand's positioning strategy and build on the brand's strengths.

- *Who is the target audience?* You've profiled the target already. Now consider what you want the audience to do. Do you want them to talk to the brand? Create and share content? Spread the message to their network? On what devices (e.g., iPad, smartphone, desktop) will they interact with your brand? What could you offer of value in exchange for their cooperation?

- *Is there another group of people who can persuade the target audience to follow them?* This group is your influencers—the people who will propagate your message. Why would these people want to share your message with others? What's in it for them?

- *What are the existing creative assets? How can the brand's creative assets foster a social experience?* Most brands already have some **creative assets** that drive their paid and owned media. For example, a well-known and popular brand spokescharacter such as the GEICO gecko is a creative asset that the insurance company has developed in its traditional advertising, so he might be employed in a social media campaign to give the company a head start in terms of consumer recognition as it tries to break through the clutter of competing messages. The planner should list the creative assets that already exist and identify the assets he or she still needs to extend the brand's story. How can the creative assets already available be used and/or leveraged in a social media context?

- *How can we integrate with other branded media being used by the organization, and how long do we have to execute?* This is a question that references how the campaign can integrate best with the brand's paid and owned media.

- *What experiences are possible given target market needs and motives, the available channels, and the creative assets?* How can we design these experiences to maximize device portability and access? Creative assets used in social media campaigns should inspire activity and interactivity. These questions ask what types of activities could be engaging for the target audience using multiple devices and worth sharing with their network.

- *What content will be needed?* Social media are content-driven. What content will be relevant to the campaign and what will be the source? Comments? Questions and polls? Video? Images? Stories? Apps?

- *How will experience engagement be extended and shared throughout the social channels?* For instance, will engagement activity auto-post to status updates (e.g., "Tracy created a Honda playlist on Songpop")?

After the planner goes through the process of discovery and briefing to provide these "must-knows" to the creative team, the creative team will then enter the stage of ideation or concepting. *Discovery* is the term used to describe the research stage of the plan. Planners may rely on secondary and primary research as they seek to discover insights that will be useful to the creative team. These insights will be presented to the team during the briefing. The creative team will spend time brainstorming ideas and developing possible concepts for the campaign. Eventually the chosen ideas will be further refined and designed, and prototypes or mock-ups will be developed. These preliminary executions can then be used for internal review, usability testing, and other pre-testing.

When a brand begins to interact in social spaces, a key decision is how to represent the brand's social persona. This means planners need to define how the brand will behave in the social Web, what voice will be used, and even how deeply the brand will interact in the social space with customers. The decisions made should support the brand's position in the market. To introduce that persona, brands have several creative options. They may involve humanizing the brand (again, think of the GEICO gecko); showing a vulnerability to the customer and working as a steward to customer service (think Dell); or providing a value to the customer whether that value be function, information, or entertainment (think Nike). In Honda's case, the brand's position is brand as corporate entity.

Additionally, the makeup of the brand's social persona may vary. Other brands, such as Zappos, utilize different employee voices in social communities so the online retailer's persona is the sum of its employees. Still others have represented the brand with a person, but with a single individual charged with the brand's social reputation. The brand's mascot may take the social stage as Travelocity has done with its Roaming Gnome. Some brands present themselves as funny, comedic, thought leaders, and friends. There is no right or wrong social persona—it should ultimately be a social representation of the brand's position and of course be consistent with how the brand presents itself in other contexts.

EXHIBIT 4.3

Honda's Brand Personality Shines in Social Media

Honda's brand personality is reflected in its social media banter. In addition to brand fans, Honda's presence in zone 1—social community— also includes engaging in conversations with other popular brands on Twitter. Honda sent antagonistic remarks to 15 powerful brands in a humorous way designed to spark engagement and conversation. Take a look at a message Honda tweeted to Oreo. This was smart engagement! The tweet was clever, funny, and relevant! What car owner hasn't felt the frustration of crumbs left over from an in-transit snack? Plus, because the brands Honda teased all have large, active fan bases on Twitter, Honda was able to reach a large audience—but without the cost of paying influencers.

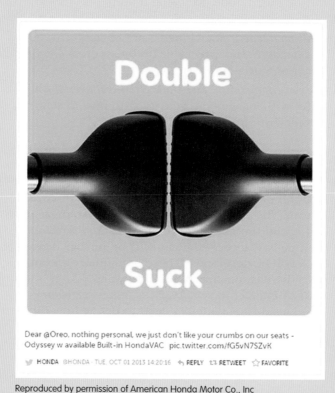

Dear @Oreo, nothing personal, we just don't like your crumbs on our seats - Odyssey w available Built-in HondaVAC pic.twitter.com/fG5vN7SZvK

🐦 HONDA @HONDA · TUE. OCT 01 2013 14:20:16   ↩ REPLY ⇄ RETWEET ☆ FAVORITE

Reproduced by permission of American Honda Motor Co., Inc

Integrate With Other Promotional Components and Establish Activation Plan

Traditional media campaigns typically live a designated lifespan with timing tied to the accomplishment of specific objectives. For social media, though, campaigns are not necessarily events with fixed start and stop dates. Conversations in communities continue over time, and a brand's social media marketing presence should do this as well. This is particularly true for brands that rely on social media for customer service and customer relationship management. Some of the most famous social brands, like Dell and Zappos, are "always on" with their social media campaigns. They aim to project a constant presence in the communities in which they participate. Honda uses a mix of short-term campaigns and ongoing presence. Other organizations have also done this.

EXHIBIT 4.4

Honda Makes Social Community Meaningful

Brand-created experiences are one of the most effective tactics for building consumer engagement. Honda connects with its loyal customers through its "Honda Loves You Back" social media strategy — by rewarding them with perks like sports tickets, massages, and food giveaways.[21] Once the Honda Facebook page reached 1 million followers, the company began searching the Facebook pages of brand fans, looking for unique stories. They soon discovered Joe, a Honda owner who was approaching 1 million

Reproduced by permission of American Honda Motor Co., Inc

miles on his 1990 Honda Accord. Working with RPA, its Los Angeles-based ad agency, Honda devised a native video campaign to introduce Joe to the Honda community — with a unique twist. RPA posted its first video, "Meet Million Mile Joe," on Honda's Facebook and YouTube pages, where fans could track Joe's mileage and encourage him along the way. The second video captured a great surprise for Joe: a hometown parade in his honor, culminating with a gift of a new Accord. News stations across the country began carrying the story that night, creating earned media impressions on- and offline. The campaign earned more than 44 million unique impressions in earned media, several hundred thousand views of the YouTube videos, and drove positive sentiment and social conversations about Honda.

Execute and Measure Outcomes

In the final stage of the strategic planning process, we implement the plan and measure the results. In Chapter 11, we'll go into detail about the *metrics* we can use to assess the effectiveness of social media campaigns. The data gathered on all aspects of the social media plan are used to provide insight for future campaigns.

MINI CASE STUDY

Honda's Social Media Strategy Features Storytelling

Honda's social media marketing strategy encompasses multiple campaigns told across zones and channels, supporting integrated marketing communications initiatives and executing unique social experiences. Best practices recommend brands develop content for social media that is authentic, engaging, valuable for the audience, creative, and experiential. Ultimately, brands must inspire the audience to participate and to share the experience with others. Honda's Serial One campaign accomplished all this and more.

Reproduced by permission of American Honda Motor Co., Inc

In 1969, Honda made its first entry into the American car market, with the compact N600 two-door sedan. The N600 remains a storied piece of Honda's history, a firm tie to Americana and the heyday of muscle cars. But those first vehicles were thought lost, until just a few years ago, when a mechanic named Tim Mings discovered the last N600. Dubbed "Serial One," for its unique model number N600—1000001, the car was a lime-green, undriveable wreck. Mings' restoration of Serial One became a rare opportunity for Honda to tell the story of its humble beginnings, protect a historical artifact, and connect with Honda fans, restoration enthusiasts, and classic car buffs.

Camera crews documented every step of Mings' work to restore Serial One, a year-long process that captured pivotal moments from Serial One's first engine start since being rebuilt to the revelation of Serial One fully restored at the Japanese Classic Car Show. The story of Serial One's restoration was shared in a 12-part video documentary series, published at a dedicated microsite, www.serialone.com, and on Honda's YouTube channel and Facebook page.[22] The hero content was promoted across Honda's other social channels using the hashtag, #HondaSerialOne, and augmented with GIFs, interview clips, and other shareable story elements.

In sharing the story of Serial One, Honda also told the story of Honda's renegade spirit. The N600 was Honda's very first automobile and the granddaddy of every Honda on the road today. The American market didn't believe Honda could make a car, but the N600 was, ultimately, the reason Honda became the household name that it is today. When all was said and done, Honda not only got to tell the story of the N600 over the course of a year, but also launched a brand movement that social fans everywhere fell in love with. Serial One's success was built on an authentic experience in zone 2—the zone of social publishing—that was activated with posts and conversations in zone 1—the zone of social community.

Results and Outcomes

Honda's Serial One initiative was truly one-of-a-kind. Sentiment was overwhelmingly positive. The launch video alone received 48.7 million impressions across Honda's social platforms with a total of 206 million PR impressions and features from online publications such as Motor Trend, Jalopnik and Yahoo! Autos. The videos held the attention of viewers, as evidenced by a completion rate of 81%. Week by week, people followed along to check in on Serial One's progress, as indicated by the project's average engagement rate of 4.8%. Over the yearlong restoration, the Serial One content kept fans interested and engaged all the way to the final video, which received more than 39 million PR impressions. Now that Serial One is complete—with a new ceramic white paint job—it has taken a place of honor at the Honda Museum, where admirers can check out Mings' handiwork in perpetuity. And hopefully, occasionally rev its engine.

As we've seen, many organizations are still "social media wannabes." They're at an early stage in the process and feeling their way in a new environment. So perhaps we can forgive them for the common mistakes they tend to make. Here are some of the biggest offenders:

- *Staffing*: the initial imperative when it comes to social media marketing is to simply get there—to have a presence in the community of interest. But focusing on presence can result in brand assets that are underutilized and underperforming in terms of the objectives set for the campaign. Organizations in the trial and transition phases tend to focus on establishing Facebook profiles and Twitter accounts, or perhaps on planning a UGC contest. These companies take an "if you build it, they will come" *Field of Dreams* approach, without addressing ways to build and maintain **traffic** and interest. Ultimately though, social media marketing is built on the community, content, and technology inherent to social media. To make it successful, the brand must be active in the space— and that means committing staff time to posting, responding, and developing content.

- *Content*: a related issue is the failure to introduce new, fresh, and relevant content. Developing interactivity, emphasizing relevance, monitoring the asset for needed maintenance, responding to visitor feedback, and providing new content will keep the asset fresh and inspire a curiosity to return among the core audience. Importantly, these components of successful social media marketing require an ongoing commitment of human resources.

- *Time horizon*: social media work differently than do traditional advertising, and may require patience before results are delivered. Although a television campaign can utilize a heavy buy early in its media plan to incite near immediate awareness and build momentum, social media are just the opposite. It can take months for a social media campaign to build awareness (and there are plenty of social media failures that never gained traction). Assuming the plan itself is sound, organizations must be patient while the community embraces the content and the relationship. Although the results may take longer to see, the overall effectiveness and efficiency of the social media model can be well worth the patience and resources required.

- *Focus of objectives*: it's not uncommon for organizations to focus on action steps rather than desired outcomes from social media. In other words, they take a short-term tactical approach rather than a long-term strategic approach. An inappropriate objective might read: "Increase engagement by responding to comments on Twitter and Facebook within 24 hours of posting, posting three status updates per business day, and adding links to social media accounts on the corporate blog." Do you see the error? The emphasis is on the action steps the social media manager will complete (tactical) but there's no focus on what the social media activities should *do* for the brand. There is no value in doing social media marketing for the sake of social media—the value lies in accomplishing marketing objectives. Social media are more than the "flavor of the month"—they have the potential to provide lasting and measurable benefits when campaigns are done right.

- *Benefits to users*: social media live or die on the quality of the content a platform offers to users. That content must add value to the social community. A social media marketing plan answers the question: How will we distribute our content using social media channels? But it also must answer other questions: How can we engage our target audiences in social media communities? What content is valued by our audiences? Do they want content that informs? Entertains? How can we develop an ongoing stream of relevant, fresh content?

- *Measurement*: organizations fail to properly measure results. Marketing consultant Tom Peters famously observed, "What gets measured gets done." As social media marketing has developed, some evangelists have encouraged new disciples to keep the faith, emphasizing the growth and popularity of the media as reason enough to develop a presence in the space. In the long term, that's just not good enough. For organizations to succeed in social media marketing, measurement is critical. Measuring outcomes ensures that the organization is learning from what worked and what didn't. Importantly, as organizations begin to shift more marketing dollars from traditional advertising to social media marketing, managers will seek out comparisons on metrics such as ROI between social media and other media options.

Managing Social Media Marketing in the Organization

So there we have it—a framework to plan a social media marketing campaign. In Chapter 5, we'll take a closer look at the tactics social media marketers use and how social media teams plan for the daily, weekly, monthly, and annual activities. But social media teams aren't the only employees who play a role in social media. Other divisions may interact with the social media team to share brand assets, meet information technology needs, address customer concerns, design creative materials, evaluate risk and potential legal liabilities, identify prospects, coordinate sales and special offers, develop human resource recruitment materials, and so on. In other words, social media teams will likely interact with marketing, sales, customer support, information systems, web design, legal, human resources, and finance. In addition, employees can be valuable brand advocates in social media channels. But they can also cause problems. Stories abound of employees who tweeted an insult on an impulse that reflected poorly on the employer brand and harmed customer relationships. To address the roles employees play across the organization, companies rely upon social media policies.

The Social Media Policy

Companies need to develop, adopt, and publicize a social media policy among employees. A social media policy is an organizational document that explains the rules and procedures for social media activity for the organization and its employees. Just like you, many employees are already engaged in social media. They may be active on social network sites and microsharing tools like Facebook and Twitter. While employees may use social media to communicate with friends and access entertainment opportunities (maybe even when they're supposed to be working!), there's a good chance they will mention their employers and maybe even vent about office politics or shoddy products. Managing that risk is a must for companies. And many companies will recognize that these employees can act as powerful brand ambassadors when they participate in social media. As we mentioned, Zappos takes advantage of the fact that many of its employees participate in social media vehicles—and these enthusiastic team members promote the company in the process.

Of course, there's no guarantee that an employee (at least on his or her own time) will necessarily say only glowing things about the company. Brands use formal documents to ensure that the company is protected in a legal sense and also to encourage employees to participate in ways that are consistent with the brand's overall strategy. Here are excerpts from three companies' policies:[23]

- *Microsoft*: if you plan to tweet about any professional matters (such as about the business of Microsoft or other companies, products, or services in the same business space as Microsoft), in addition to referencing your alias@microsoft.com email address, whenever possible use the service's profile or contact information to assert that you are a Microsoft employee and/or affiliated with a specific group/team at Microsoft.

- *Sun Microsystems*: whether in the actual or virtual world, your interactions and discourse should be respectful. For example, when you are in a virtual world as a Sun representative, your avatar should dress and speak professionally. We all appreciate actual respect.

- *Intel*: consider content that's open-ended and invites response. Encourage comments. You can broaden the conversation by citing others who are blogging about the same topic and allowing your content to be shared or syndicated … If you make a mistake, admit it. Be upfront, and be quick with your correction. If you're posting a blog, you may choose to modify an earlier post—just make it clear that you have done so.

EXHIBIT 4.5

Honda's Social Media Policy

Honda's basic guidelines are for Honda associates, suppliers, vendors, consultants and individuals employed by a third party and assigned at Honda, who are participating in social media activities related to Honda's brands and business activities. The full policy is available online.[24] Five key points are highlighted in the policy:[25]

Honda recognizes that our dedicated associates and business partners are often our best advocates and that your engagement in online conversations may help inform and positively influence the public's perception of the company. When engaging in social networks, industry blogs, forums, wikis and other similar sites, your actions, writing and content are not only a reflection of you,

(Continued)

(Continued)

iStock.com/Weekend Images Inc.

but also of Honda. Remember that you are an ambassador for Honda and all of its brands, so think before you post, and consider that online comments may exist forever.

- Be transparent—If you have something to say, use your real name. When commenting about something related to our industry, state who you are and your role in the company or on the project. Be clear that you are not an authorized representative speaking on behalf of the company. (See full disclosure/disclaimer obligations.)

- Be deferential—Do not post or engage with comments and/or "likes" on any official Honda public communication channels unless you are an authorized spokesperson for the company. Only authorized associates or teams communicate on behalf of Honda through the company's sites and properties.

- Be credible—When electing to share your personal opinions about Honda on "non-Honda" sites, be thoughtful about your comments, how they reflect on Honda's position and your role in the company. Keep your focus on the topic at hand and be credible in your area of expertise.

- Be vigilant—It is your obligation to protect Honda's confidential or proprietary information including policy, product details, financial records, trade secrets and business plans. Do not share anything publicly that might be considered sensitive in nature.

- Be considerate—Think before you publish a comment that could be perceived as disrespectful. Never disparage a competitor, customer, supplier, partner, our company or your colleagues. Do not engage in a battle of words or make it personal. If in doubt, do not do it.

The Word of Mouth Marketing Association (WOMMA) developed a quick guide to designing a digital social media policy, shown in Table 4.4. Its purpose is to guide how the organization, its employees, and agents should share opinions, beliefs, and information with social communities.[26] Not only is it good business, it can also help prevent legal problems. The WOMMA guide encourages organizations to make several decisions and include those in an organization-wide social media policy. Organizations must decide upon:

- *Standards of conduct*: standards of conduct in a social media policy refer to the basic expectations for employee behavior in social communities. At a minimum, WOMMA recommends that the standards require that all online statements about the business be honest and transparent. Deceptive, misleading, or unsubstantiated claims about the organization or its competitors must not be issued. Further, good manners must be used in social communities (no ethnic slurs, personal insults, rumors, lies, or other offensive statements).

- *Disclosure requirements*: transparency is key in online communities. Employees must disclose that they are affiliated with the organization. If they are receiving material compensation or gifts in exchange for posting, this must be disclosed. Disclosing affiliations ensures that readers can still find the posts credible and trustworthy. WOMMA recommends that bloggers include a simple statement: "I received [insert product name] from [insert company name] and here is my opinion …" In addition, when using posts on social networks, WOMMA recommends that the poster use hashtags to disclose the nature of relationships reflected in the posts: #emp (employee/employer), #samp (free sample received), #paid (paid endorsement).

- *Standards for posting intellectual property, financial information, and copyrighted information*: many of the potential legal problems within social media relate to the inappropriate sharing of information. WOMMA recommends that organizations keep all intellectual property and private financial information confidential. Prior to posting copyrighted information, appropriate permissions should be collected.

Table 4.4 WOMMA Guidelines

Key Aspects of the WOMMA Disclosure Form

Personal and Editorial Blogs

- I received _____ from _____ sent me _____
- Product Review Blogs
- I received _____ from _____ to review
- I was paid by _____ to review

Additionally for product review blogs, WOMMA strongly recommends creating and prominently posting a "Disclosure and Relationships Statement" section on the blog fully disclosing how a review blogger works with companies in accepting and reviewing products, and listing any conflicts of interest that may affect the credibility of his or her reviews.

Providing Comments in Online Discussions

- I received _____ from _____
- I was paid by_____
- I am an employee [or representative] of_____

Microblogs

Include a hash tag notation, either:

- #spon (sponsored)
- #paid (paid)
- #samp (sample)

Additionally, WOMMA strongly recommends posting a link on your profile page directing people to a full "Disclosure and Relationships Statement." This statement, much like the one WOMMA recommends for review blogs, should state how you work with companies in accepting and reviewing products, and list any conflicts of interest that may affect the credibility of your sponsored or paid reviews.

Status Updates on Social Networks

- I received_____ from_____
- I was paid by_____

(Continued)

Table 4.4   (Continued)

Key Aspects of the WOMMA Disclosure Form

If status updates are limited by character restrictions, the best practice disclosure requirement is to include a hash tag notation of either #spon, #paid or #samp. Additionally, WOMMA strongly recommends posting a full description or a link on your social network profile page directing people to a "Disclosure and Relationships Statement." Note that if an employee blogs about his or her company's products, citing the identity of the employer in the profile may not be a sufficient disclosure. Bloggers' disclosures should appear close to the endorsement or testimonial statement they are posting.

Video and Photo Sharing Websites

Include as part of the video/photo content and part of the written description:

- I received_____ from_____
- I was paid by_____

Additionally, WOMMA strongly recommends posting a full description or a link on your video and/or photo sharing profile page directing people to a "Disclosure and Relationships Statement."

Podcasts

Include, as part of the audio content and part of the written description:

- I received_____ from_____
- I was paid by_____

Additionally, WOMMA strongly recommends posting a full description or a link directing people to a "Disclosure and Relationships Statement."

Source: http://womma.org/main/Quick-Guide-to-Designing-a-Social-Media-Policy.pdf (accessed September 30, 2011)
Reproduced with kind permission of http://womma.org

An Organizational Structure to Support Social Media

Who "owns" social media within an organization? Some brands assign the responsibility to a discipline "silo" such as the marketing department, whereas others rely upon a **center of excellence model** that pulls people with different kinds of expertise from across the organization to participate. This eliminates the internal political issues relating to who in the company has primary responsibility for social media so it's easier to integrate social media applications with other marketing initiatives.

Aside from the organizational structure to support social media marketing efforts, businesses must make decisions on the level of resources to dedicate. Social media are ongoing conversations across potentially several communication vehicles. Some businesses dedicate multiple employees to manage the conversation calendar whereas others assign a single person. The organizational task is to assign the least number of resources needed internally and then supplement those resources with help from the organization's social media agency resources.

There are five basic models for social media structure:[27]

- Organic
- Centralized
- Hub and Spoke-Coordinated

- Multiple Hub and Spoke—Dandelion
- Holistic Honeycomb

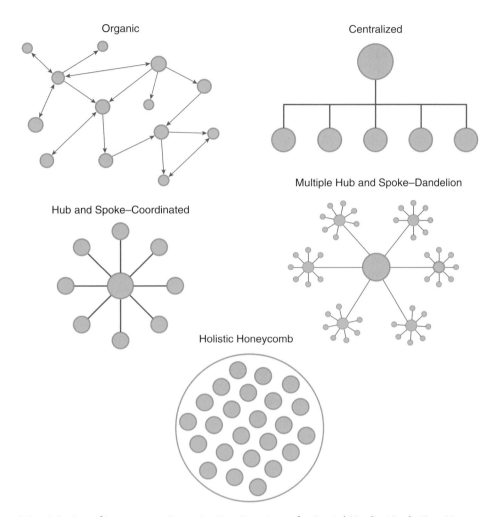

Figure 4.5   A Series of Images on Organization Structures for Social Media Marketing Management

Source: http://www.web-strategist.com/blog/2010/04/15/framework-and-matrix-the-five-ways-companies-organize-for-social-business
Images courtesy of Altimeter, a Prophet Company.

1   In the centralized structure the social media department functions at a senior level that reports to the CMO (Chief Marketing Officer) or CEO (Chief Executive Officer) and is responsible for all the social media activations. The potential problem here is that all social media activity may not be adequately represented. Is customer care going to be good if social media marketing is housed under marketing rather than customer service?

2   In the organic structure no one person owns social media. Instead, all employees represent the brand and work social media into their roles. This is implemented through training and used across the organization. The danger here is that the

content can end up off message. Any employee can sign up to respond to customer queries on Twitter. That means the company cannot control what employees say. Therefore, the company must have a well-developed social media policy in place to guide employee behavior in social communities.

3 In the hub and spoke (also called the coordinated) model, a team of people who are cross-functionally trained are ready to address various social media needs. This is currently the most popular structure for social media management.

4 The dandelion model is essentially a multi-layered hub and spoke model. It is appropriate for companies with strategic business units (SBUs) that still represent a core brand.

5 The holistic model is currently the least used. It truly refers to a structure within which all employees are empowered to use social media, use social media, and do so according to the company's strategy.

Social Media Management Systems

Regardless of the structure a company uses or the policy it develops, it must also devise a day-to-day system for managing social media activities, tracking content from development to distribution, managing social ad campaigns, analyzing effectiveness, monitoring and listening, and capturing and analyzing social data for market research. Companies may also use vendors to aid in social customer relationship management (social CRM), host owned social sites, generate reviews and ratings, facilitate influencer marketing tactics, and provide content. In particular, companies benefit from incorporating cloud services for social media management, social monitoring and listening, social ad management, and social media analytics and modeling. Whether on a small or large scale, one of the most used systems is Hootsuite. Notably, Hootsuite offers a special program for university users that includes an option to become Hootsuite Certified.

A Framework for Strategic Social Media Marketing

The framework for social media marketing depicted in Figure 4.6 describes an organization's use of social media marketing along four dimensions: 1) scope, 2) culture, 3) structure, and 4) governance[28].

- *Scope*: does the organization use social media marketing internally and externally to collaborate with stakeholders or is social media predominantly limited to use as an external communications channel? The answer categorizes organizations as defenders, who use social media marketing primarily as a one-way communication tool to entertain consumers or to inform stakeholders, or as explorers, who seek collaboration with many different stakeholders such as clients, employees, and suppliers.

- *Culture*: is the organization's culture conservative (traditional with a focus on mass communications) or modern (permeable, open, flexible)?

- *Structure*: are the organization and departmentalization of the social media marketing assignments hierarchical or networked?

- *Governance*: does the organization define social media regulations and employee practices (autocracy) or allow norms to develop organically (anarchy)?

Decisions on social media marketing should be guided by the firm's internal influencers (e.g., general vision, mission, corporate goals, corporate culture, available resources), which in turn should be in line with external influencers (e.g., communities, competition, government regulation). The framework doesn't suggest a right or wrong choice. Rather, depending upon the organization's overall strategic focus and stakeholders, social media marketing should be organized for fit and congruence with the organization's design.

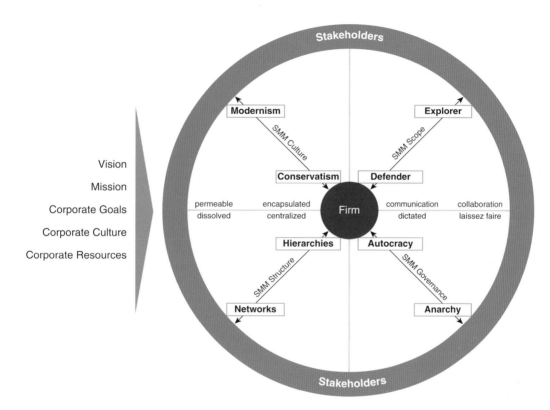

Figure 4.6   Strategic Social Media Marketing Framework

Source: Reto Felixa, Philipp Rauschnabelb, and Chris Hinsche, "Elements of Strategic Social Media Marketing: A Holistic Framework," *Journal of Business Research*, 70 (January 2017), 118–26. Reproduced with kind permission of the *Journal of Business Research*—Elsevier

 CHAPTER SUMMARY

Where does social media marketing planning fit into an organization's overall planning framework?

Social media marketing should be a part of an organization's marketing plan. Like integrated marketing communications plans, organizations may also develop stand-alone plans offering greater social media marketing.

What are the phases of social media marketing maturity? How does social media marketing change for companies as they shift from the trial phase to the transition phase and eventually move into the strategic phase?

The phases of social media marketing maturity are trial, transition, and strategic. In the trial phase, organizations are pursuing social media tactics in an ad hoc manner, with a focus on gaining experience in social media. The tactics are not well linked to the organization's overall marketing plan and may be haphazardly executed. Organizations in the transition phase think more systematically about how to plan social media activities that support marketing objectives. When an organization enters the final, strategic phase, it utilizes a formal process to plan social media marketing activities with clear objectives and metrics. Social media are now integrated as a key component of the organization's overall marketing plan.

What are the steps in social media marketing strategic planning?

The social media marketing strategic planning process consists of the following steps:

- Conduct a situation analysis and identify key opportunities.
- State objectives.
- Gather insight into and target one or more segments of social consumers.
- Select the social media channels and vehicles.
- Create an experience strategy.
- Establish an activation plan using other promotional tools (if needed).
- Manage and measure the campaign.

How can organizations structure themselves to support social media marketing?

Companies can structure themselves as centralized, decentralized, hub and spoke, dandelion, or holistic. Each option represents a trade-off of control and responsiveness. Organizations can also use social media management systems.

What are the key components of an organizational social media policy, and why is it important to have such a policy in place?

Policies may include several guidelines such as standards of conduct, disclosure requirements, and standards for posting intellectual property, financial information, and copyrighted information. Companies need policies to ensure that social media activity is consistent with the overall brand.

REVIEW QUESTIONS

1   Why do some organizations enter the trial phase without planning and research? Is there value in getting social media experience before social media marketing becomes part of the marcom plan?

2   Explain the phases in the social media marketing maturity life cycle.

3   What are the forms of organizational structure used by companies embracing social media marketing? What are the pros and cons of each?

4   Explain the steps in the social media marketing strategic planning process.

5   What approaches to budgeting can be used by organizations planning for social media marketing?

EXERCISES

1 Visit www.thecoca-colacompany.com/socialmedia where you'll find Coca-Cola's social media policy, or find the policy for another company. Identify the key components WOMMA recommends be included in a corporate social media policy. How could the policy be improved?

2 Identify a social media campaign for a favorite brand. In what experiences does the campaign invite you to take part? In what zones does the strategy lie? Does the campaign include share technologies to ensure your activities are shared with your network?

3 Explore Hootsuite Academy, a training service for Hootsuite, a social media management system.

CHAPTER NOTES (access all weblinks listed here at: https://study.sagepub.com/smm3e)

1 Michael Stelzner, *2016 Social Media Marketing Industry Report*, Social Media Examiner, www.socialmediaexaminer.com/wp-content/uploads/2016/05/SocialMediaMarketingIndustryReport2016.pdf (accessed June 16, 2017).

2 "The State of Marketing 2010," *Unica*, www.unica.com/survey2010 (accessed August 10, 2010).

3 Marketing Sherpa explained these three phases in its *Social Media Marketing Benchmark Report* (2010), http://content.marketingsherpa.com/heap/SocialMediaMarketing2010EXE.pdf (accessed June 12, 2017), which surveyed 2,300 marketers. This report has not been updated. Since that time, Altimeter has conducted a similar study and identified five phases of development; see Altimeter, *The Evolution of Social Business* (2013), http://altimetergroup.wpengine.netdna-cdn.com/wp-content/uploads/2013/03/Altimeter_Evolution_Social_Business_FINAL_030613.pdf (accessed June 12, 2017). However, we believe that the path to social media marketing maturity is best understood following Marketing Sherpa's model.

4 David Moth, "The Top 16 Social Media Fails of 2013," *Econsultancy*, https://econsultancy.com/blog/63901-the-top-16-social-media-fails-of-2013#i.13hfu23ibbfs9x (accessed July 20, 2014).

5 Martin Robinson, "We Told You This Would Happen!" *Mail Online*, July 18, 2016, www.dailymail.co.uk/news/article-3695151/Philip-Schofield-melts-Heathrow-check-computer-failure-hits-BA-passengers-starting-summer-holidays.html (accessed June 12, 2017).

6 Michael Stelzner, *2014 Social Media Marketing Industry Report*, Social Media Examiner, May 19, 2014, www.socialmediaexaminer.com/social-media-marketing-industry-report-2014 (accessed May 30, 2014).

7 Michelle Krasniak, "Chatbots and Social Media: New Research," Social Media Examiner, March 17, 2016, www.socialmediaexaminer.com/chatbots-and-social-media-new-research (accessed June 12, 2017).

8 Chris Baraniuk, "How Online Chat Bots Are Already Tricking You," BBC, June 9, 2014, www.bbc.com/future/story/20140609-how-online-bots-are-tricking-you (accessed June 12, 2017).

9 Finger, Lutz, "Do Evil—The Business of Social Media Bots," *Forbes*, February 17, 2015, www.forbes.com/sites/lutzfinger/2015/02/17/do-evil-the-business-of-social-media-bots/#6df7bc75fb58 (accessed June 12, 2017).

10 Jayson Veley, "Twitter and Other Social Media Networks Are Run by Millions of Robots That Attack Anyone Who Threatens the Status Quo," March 16, 2017, www.evil.news/2017-03-16-

twitter-and-other-social-media-networks-are-run-by-millions-of-robots-that-attack-anyone-who-threatens-the-status-quo.html (accessed June 12, 2017).

11 Jayson Demers, "The 7 Worst (and Most Amusing) Mistakes Brands Have Ever Made on Social Media," *Forbes*, May 2, 2016, www.forbes.com/sites/jaysondemers/2016/05/02/the-7-worst-and-most-amusing-mistakes-brands-have-ever-made-on-social-media/#73454ced6a5c (accessed June 12, 2017).

12 Infegy, *Brand Analysis: Coca-Cola Versus Pepsi*, Report, http://cdn2.hubspot.net/hubfs/1716 283/Reports/Brand-Analysis-Coca-Cola-vs-Pepsi_Report-by_Infegy.pdf?t=1490652833765 (accessed June 12, 2017).

13 Jay Baer, "The 6 Dangerous Fallacies of Social Media," Convince & Convert, www.convince andconvert.com/social-media-strategy/the-6-dangerous-fallacies-of-social-media (accessed July 3, 2017).

14 Kate Taylor Mighty, *How to Build a Social Media Strategy Dream Team*, ebook, Hubspot, December 13, 2016, https://blog.hubspot.com/marketing/build-social-media-strategy-team (accessed June 12, 2017).

15 Carlow Pacis, "The 13 Best Instagram Marketing Campaigns of 2016," Business 2 Community, December 22, 2016, www.business2community.com/214instagram/13-best-instagram-marketing-campaigns-2016-01742750#PjArZfPjZgk7C0IE.99 (accessed June 12, 2017).

16 Leslie Jump, "Marketing Artifacts: Brand Positioning Statements?" February 7, 2007, www.marketer blog.net/2007/02/marketing_artif.html (accessed August 11, 2010).

17 Griffin Farley, "Propagation Planning," May 3, 2010, http://griffinfarley.typepad.com/propagation (accessed December 1, 2010).

18 J. Brakus, Bernd Schmitt, and L. Zarantonello, "Brand Experience: What Is It? How Is It Measured? Does It Affect Loyalty?" *Journal of Marketing*, 73 (2009), 52–68.

19 Christy Ashley and Tracy Tuten, "Creative Strategies in Social Media Marketing: An Exploratory Study of Branded Social Content and Consumer Engagement," *Psychology & Marketing*, 31 (2), 15–27.

20 Adapted from Griffin Farley, "Revised Propagation Planning Brief," May 3, 2010, http://griff infarley.typepad.com/propagation/2010/05/revised-propagation-planning-brief.html (accessed December 1, 2010).

21 *The Future of Branded Entertainment*, Report, Canadian Media Production Association, April 2014, www.omdc.on.ca/Assets/Research/Research+Reports/The-future-of-branded-entertainment/The-future-of-branded-entertainment_en.pdf (accessed June 12, 2017).

22 I. Sherwood, "Honda's Historic Car Restoration Racks Up Half a Million Views," Campaign, October 19, 2016, www.campaignlive.com/article/hondas-historic-car-restoration-racks-half-million-views/1412646#c4Tvqq0mJhWpS2hJ.99 (accessed June 12, 2017).

23 Kimberly Smith, "A Step-by-Step Guide to a Successful Social Media Program," MarketingProfs, 2009, p. 9, www.d.umn.edu/~jvileta/MProfs_Social_Media_Program_Guide.pdf (accessed June 12, 2017).

24 "Corporate Social Media Policy," Honda, http://news.honda.com/newsandviews/AHM-Associate-Social-Media-Policy-090111.pdf (accessed June 12, 2017).

25 "American Honda Motor Co.'s Social Media Guidelines for Associates," http://news.honda.com/ newsandviews/social-media-policy.aspx (accessed June 12, 2017).

26 "The WOMMA 'Quick Guide' to Designing a Digital Social Media Policy," WOMMA, http://womma.org/main/Quick-Guide-to-Designing-a-Social-Media-Policy.pdf (accessed December 31, 2010).

27 Jeremiah Owyang, "Most Companies Organize in Hub and Spoke Format for Social Business," Web Strategist, November 9, 2010, www.web-strategist.com/blog/2010/11/09/research-most-companies-organize-in-hub-and-spoke-formation (accessed December 12, 2010).

28 Reto Felixa, Philipp Rauschnabelb, and Chris Hinsche, "Elements of Strategic Social Media Marketing: A Holistic Framework," *Journal of Business Research*, 70 (January 2017), 118–26.

Visit **https://study.sagepub.com/smm3e** for free additional online resources related to this chapter.

Tactical Planning and Execution

Learning Objectives

When you finish reading this chapter, you will be able to answer these questions:

1 What is a social media marketing tactical plan and how does it support the execution of a social media marketing strategy?

2 What is a channel plan and how is it used?

3 How does a content plan relate to experience strategies? What are the elements included in the content plan?

4 What is an editorial calendar and what should be considered in developing the calendar?

5 How do social media teams manage the roles, tasks, and schedules related to executing social media tactics?

Tactical Planning for Social Media Marketing

In the last chapter you learned how to plan a strategy for a brand's social media marketing. The social media marketing strategic plan may exist independently or may be a sub-plan of an integrated marketing communications plan. When part of a marketing communications (marcom) plan, social media marketing activities will be aligned with other marcom elements such as advertising and sales promotions to amplify the brand's message and/or to activate campaign events. Consequently, many of the tactical decisions mentioned in this chapter, such as establishing brand persona and identifying a creative strategy to guide brand communications, may already be determined. The stories that relay the brand meaning to the target audiences along with existing brand assets may be in place and ready for the social media team to use as a base. Even for new brand launches, brand identity, the pillars that will serve as the foundation for the brand's image and position, and the value proposition it promises to deliver will be defined as part of the brand's strategic marketing planning process.

  In this chapter, you will learn the process for developing a tactical plan. The **tactical plan** brings the social media marketing strategy to life. There are several practical steps required including determining the right channels, content to deliver the desired experience, rules of engagement, and schedule. As if that's not enough, we must also develop processes to create, produce, and deliver the content, conversation, and other experiential elements of our strategy.[1] In other words, we will address the why, who, where, what, when, and how of social media marketing. With this foundation for how social media marketing is accomplished from a practical perspective, you will see how the strategic decisions interplay as we cover the zones, strategies, and tactical decisions in-depth in the next section of the book.

Why: Value-Driven Social Media Marketing

Social media tactics are the actions taken to execute the social media strategy. The strategy considered the situation analysis, target audience, and objectives to guide the zones of social media that the brand can best use to reach and engage the target audience. The tactics will guide the brand's activities in the zones of social media marketing, but must do so in a way that fits with the objectives. The objectives are the why—the reasons or purpose for social media marketing. Table 5.1 reviews possible objectives, the strategy for achieving the objective, and possible tactics. As we saw in earlier chapters, there are several possible marketing objectives that brands use social media marketing to address. The table uses a few of these to demonstrate how we map strategic objectives and strategies to tactical objectives and tactics.

Who: Understanding and Honoring the Target Audience

Target audience research was a key component of the strategic social media marketing planning process. It provided the insight needed to devise an experience strategy capable of engaging the target audience in the zones of social media. **Engage** is a key word because of the culture of social media. Remember social media is about participation and sharing. The cultural expectation is that participants will interact, co-create, and share and this expectation exists for consumers as well as for brand participants. For this reason, a social media strategy should be based on an experience. The Merriam-Webster Dictionary defines

Table 5.1   Mapping Objectives for Strategies and Tactics

Strategic Objective	Strategy	Tactical Objective	Tactics
Create brand awareness	Expose target audience to brand	Build brand presence in social communities Post interesting and interactive messages Engage in conversations with fans and influencers Promote links to high-value content	Develop brand profiles in selected SNS (e.g., Facebook, Linkedin, etc.) Post daily in each network Respond to comments and questions daily Use influencer list to target conversations around campaigns
Build brand image and reputation	Communicate brand image Encourage word-of-mouth communication	Develop robust content that reinforces brand messages while being of value to target audience Publish content on owned media channels and rich media experiences in social communities	Create, produce, distribute, and post content following content calendar Include interactive elements in all content as well as links to owned media content and share tools Retain influencers to seed priority content
Differentiate brand from competition	Provide experiences that illustrate differential advantages	Create and publish content that demonstrates value Invite reviews and ratings from happy customers as credible evidence of value	Create content for blog that highlights points of differentiation Develop recommendation widget Host reviews and ratings on-site and optimize for mobile search Use email marketing to request reviews 10 days after purchase
Generate demand/ acquire customers	Create desire and deliver	Monitor social channels for prospective leads Seed influencers for persuasion and amplification Use group deals and crowdsourced lists to drive sales	Keyword monitoring generates alert for follow-up from sales team Influencer initiatives focused on specific sales goals Periodic flash sales announced on SNS
Retain customers/ build loyalty	Engage, delight, inspire, thank, and reward customers	Cluster fans and loyal customers to create brand community Build fan relationships Collaborate and cocreate Reward reviews and ratings and other WOM communications Listen and monitor Respond to questions and comments	Invite UGC tied to each campaign and SNS Thank contributors publicly and reinforce fan behavior by sharing and favoriting UGC content Positive WOM triggers delivery of coupon or other reward to fan Monitor brand mentions and respond to thank, solve problem, or alert internal teams to potential crises

experience as 1) direct observation of or participation in events as a basis of knowledge and 2) the fact or state of having been affected by or gained knowledge through direct observation or participation. The Cambridge Dictionary defines experience as the process of getting knowledge or skill that is obtained from doing, seeing, or feeling. If marketers are to be effective at engaging people, we need to understand what experiences might inspire action—inspire the audience to do, see, and/or feel. Likewise, target audience research will guide decisions of where and when. It will provide guidance on the social media networks and channels the target audience uses as well as the activities they participate in, when they participate, the devices they use, the people and brands they engage with, and more.

The persona is the character description that highlights key information about the target audience. Chapter 2 reviewed the elements of personas in-depth and that information became part of the strategic planning process covered in Chapter 4. Here we rely on personas again. It's useful to review the persona or revise it to reflect insights that will guide tactical decisions. Figure 5.1 provides a template for a persona focused on guiding social media tactics.

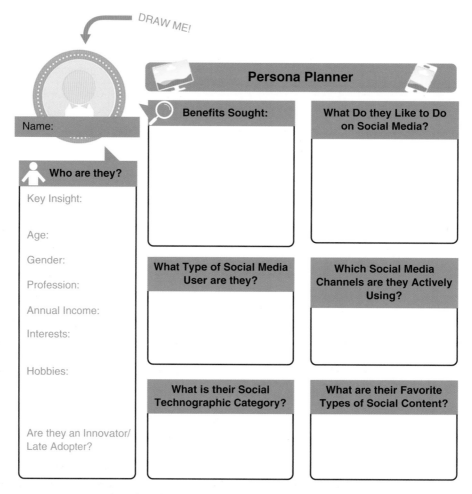

Figure 5.1   Persona Template for Planning Social Media Tactics

Where: The Channel Plan

The next decision determines where the brand will engage with the target audience. For simplicity, we are reviewing the process for tactical planning as a linear one. In reality, these decisions are considered in tandem. The culture, guidelines and rules, and functionality (as well as characteristics of the population membership) of each prospective **channel** will influence what can and should be shared, how people engage with each other, and choices about the timing and frequency of participation. In this step, each channel is evaluated for fit. Some of the questions that will facilitate channel selection include:

- Who uses this channel, what are they using it for, and how much time do they spend here?
- What are conversations like here? What kinds of content work best here?
- Will participation in this channel help us meet our objectives? Does it make sense for our business to use this channel?
- What specific goals can be pursued here given the channel's functionality? Do these goals relate to objectives in our strategic plan?
- Can we establish a unique presence and make a valuable contribution to the community? Does our brand image, voice, and tone fit with the **channel culture**?
- Are our competitors present here? If so, how are they performing?
- If we participate in this channel, what will we contribute? What will we ask fans and followers to do when they engage with us and after engagements? Share? Comment?
- Does the channel offer paid media options to ensure audience reach and the ability to target specific audience segments?

The characteristics of each channel should be considered. Remember there are several possible **social media channels**. We mention those with the largest audiences and adoption rates for marketers, but there are thousands of options available. Depending upon the target audience, the industry, and the objectives for social media, smaller, niche channels may be effective. Figure 5.2 provides an overview of the characteristics associated with several major channels.

The answers to the questions posed and the evaluation of the characteristics of the channels will facilitate the creation of a **channel plan**. Figure 5.3 illustrates a sample channel plan. It identifies the vehicles the brand will use to reach and communicate with the target audience and summarizes the tactics that are recommended for each vehicle. Channel selection influences subsequent decisions on the topics and types of content the brand will create and publish, as well as the volume of brand activity and the forms of engagement the brand will use. Keep in mind that these choices must take into account available resources. The size of the social media team and the budget available for social media marketing will influence the number of channels, the types of content, the sources of content, and the volume and frequency of distribution and promotion of content.

Some channels work for both B2B and B2C marketers, while some (like LinkedIn) are best for one more than the other. This is reflected in the channel choices made by B2B and B2C marketers, as shown in Figure 5.4. Channel plans will include any owned media options and paid media purchased on social media sites as well. Figure 5.5 shows the extent of marketers' use of paid media on social network sites.

	Facebook	Twitter	Pinterest	YouTube	LinkedIn	Instagram	Snapchat
Focus	Brand pages & paid advertisements. The largest and best social media network for brands.	Quick interaction with audience in 140 characters or less. Largely organic vs paid reach.	Very visual, so must have strong graphic ability or product imagery. Promoted pins increase paid reach.	The home for video content. Vlogging and paid advertising are great ways to create brand awareness.	Professional network with affluent audience. News and articles can go a long way in creating positioning as thought leader.	Image-based platform with a sharing community. Can gain exposure through hashtags and creating appealing photos and videos.	Send and receive snaps, or texts. Or, post a snap to your story. This can be a great way to communicate instantly with followers.
Demographic overview	Ages 25–54	Ages 18–29	Ages 18–35	All Ages	Ages 30–49	Ages 18–29	Ages 18–24
Typical use	• Building relationships • Learn about product/ service	• News articles & conversing • Keep up with activities	• Online scrapbooking • Learn about product/service	• "How to's," and entertainment • Learn about product/service	• News articles & networking • Keep up with activities	• Building relationships, conservations • Keep up with activities	• Building relationships, conservations • Learn about product/service
Best for B2B or B2C	B2C	B2B and/or B2C	B2C	B2C	B2B	B2C	B2C
Best for brands to meet these objectives	Creating brand loyalty	Public relations	Lead generation	Brand awareness	Business development	Lead generation	Brand awareness
Media used	• Video • Photos • Links	• Photos • Links	• Photos • Links	• Videos • Links	• Video • Photos • Links	• Video • Photos	• Video • Photos
Good for Zone 1 (Relationship & Community)	✓	✓			✓	✓	✓
Good for Zone 2 (Publishing Content)	✓	✓	✓	✓	✓	✓	✓
Good for Zone 3 (Entertainment)	✓			✓	✓	✓	✓
Good for Zone 4 (Commerce)	✓		✓			✓	

	Facebook	Twitter	Pinterest	YouTube	LinkedIn	Instagram	Snapchat
Best Content	Images and videos	News and articles	Images and infographics	How to videos	News and articles	Images	Images and video
Sample Tactics	• Brand fan engagement • Lead generation or customer acquisition • Share mix of relevant links, blog posts & engaging content • Promote upcoming events • Engage with influencers	• Brand engagement • Lead generation or customer acquisition • Share mix of relevant links, blog posts & engaging content • Segment influencers and create lists • Communicate issues to support team and ensure follow-up • Listen and respond to relevant conversations • Build reputation	• Brand awareness • Lead generation or customer acquisition • Share mix of relevant imagery – both brand-related • Create boards leveraging both content & company culture • Follow other businesses, thought leaders, consumers and partners	• Brand awareness & engagement • Viral sharing • Showcase company culture • Post product videos & demos	• Brand awareness & engagement • Lead generation or customer acquisition • Share mix of relevant links, blog posts & engaging content • Promote upcoming events • Engage with influencers	• Brand awareness • Engage with visual assets • Showcase products • Showcase company culture • Showcase marketing events • Link back to website, blog and other content assets	• Brand awareness • Engage with visual assets • Showcase products • Showcase company culture • Showcase marketing events • Link back to website, blog and other content assets

Figure 5.2   Channel Characteristics of Major SNS

Channel Plan

CHANNEL		PURPOSE		EDITORIAL PLAN					MEASUREMENT	
Owned	Tactic	Demographic	Benefit	Featured Topics	When/Ideal Velocity	Theme	Content Type	Tone/Rules Of Engagement	Call(s) to Actions	Engagement Indicators
Facebook	Establish brand presence, build relationships	Appeal to "Susan" and "Steven" personas	Entertain, inform, promote and support	Health and wellness, technology, life hacks, living one's best life	Post at least 2x/ day, for every company-related posting, share 3 non-promotional posts	Monday: Research data Tuesday: White papers Wednesday: Example of the week Thursday: Speakers videos Friday: Meet the team	Posts, e-books, visual content, research data	Experienced, friendly and enthusiastic Never "force" our company into other conversations unless it's highly relevant/helpful	"Subscribe to our weekly newsletter" "Download e-book" "Enroll in Training Today"	New followers, comments, likes and shares
Instagram	Increase brand awareness, engage with new client base, develop fans	Appeal to user of like brands, using comparative hashtags	Entertain, increased user base, increase product knowledge	Health and wellness, Company culture, food and nature	Post at least once per day. Share alternating company and non company items.	Monday: Product Photo Tuesday: Meme Wednesday: "Behind the Scenes" Offices Photo Thursday: Food Photo Friday: Meet the team	Product images, staff, inside the office, foodie pics	Experienced, friendly and enthusiastic Altruistic and a life to aspire to	"Subscribe to our weekly newsletter" "Download e-book" "Enroll in Training Today"	New followers, comments, regrams, tagged photos and likes
Twitter	Share relevant articles, establish brand presence and awareness, create community and engage with users	Appeal to user of like brands, using comparative hashtags	Entertain, inform, promote and support	Health and wellness, technology, life hacks, living one's best life	Post at least 2x/day, for every company-related posting, share 3 non-promotional posts	Monday: Research data Tuesday: White papers Wednesday: Example of the week Thursday: Speakers videos Friday: Meet the team	Posts, e-books, visual content, research data	Experienced, friendly and enthusiastic Never "force" our company into other conversations unless it's highly relevant/helpful	"Subscribe to our weekly newsletter" "Download e-book" "Enroll in Training Today"	New followers, comments, likes

CHANNEL		PURPOSE		EDITORIAL PLAN					MEASUREMENT	
Paid	Tactic	Demographic	Benefit	Featured Topics	When/Ideal Velocity	Theme	Content Type	Tone/Rules Of Engagement	Call(s) to Actions	Engagement Indicators
Facebook	Targeted Facebook ads and sponsored posts	Health enthusiasts, living in 30-mile radius with a household income of $75k+	Clicks leading to new training enrollment	Health and wellness, living one's best life	Run 3 months prior to event, with 50% of budget running within one month prior	Use testimonials and real past participants asked to submit UGC	Photo and video A/B variant testing, budget split 50/50	Altruistic, a life to aspire to Experienced, friendly and enthusiastic	"Enroll in Training Today"	Clicks, comments, likes and shares

Figure 5.3   A Channel Plan Example

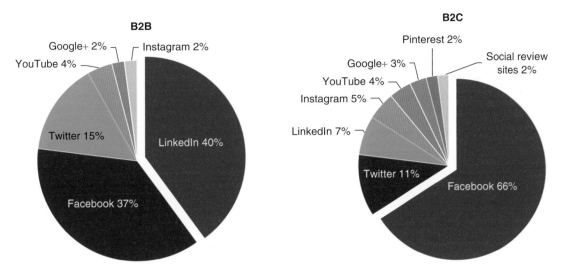

Figure 5.4   Channel Usage for B2B and B2C Marketers

Source: Michael Stelzner, *2016 Social Media Marketing Industry Report*, Social Media Examiner, www.socialmediaexaminer.com/wp-content/uploads/2016/05/SocialMediaMarketingIndustryReport2016.pdf (accessed June 16, 2017)

Reproduced with kind permission of the Social Media Examiner

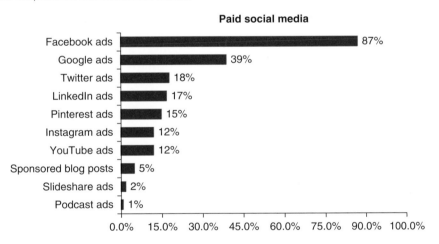

Figure 5.5   Marketer Use of Paid Media in SNS

Source: Michael Stelzner, *2016 Social Media Marketing Industry Report*, Social Media Examiner, www.socialmediaexaminer.com/wp-content/uploads/2016/05/SocialMediaMarketingIndustryReport2016.pdf (accessed June 16, 2017)

Reproduced with kind permission of the Social Media Examiner

What: Designing the Experience

What will the brand ask the target audience to do? The answer to this question is the basis for the experience the brand will offer the audience. It must not only enable participation and sharing by virtue of its design but should inspire the audience to participate and share. It must be consistent with the brand's image and be valuable to the audience. For this reason, the ideal **experience** can be thought of as one that captures the sweet spot at which the audience's passions and needs intersect with the brand's identity. Like advertising, it must be able to attract attention, break through a clutter, deliver the intended message, and aid comprehension and recall, while positively influencing brand attitudes and purchase intent. Wait, there's more! It should be **discoverable** so that the brand appears during relevant searches. It should be **authentic** and **conversational** to fit the culture of social media. Finally, it should be **scalable** and **sustainable**. That's quite a challenge! Perhaps it's no wonder that so little social media marketing efforts earn audience engagement.

Table 5.2   Characteristics of Effective Social Media Tactics

Interactive	Targeted	Value-Driven	Authentic
Participatory	Distinctive	Purpose-Driven	Conversational
Shareable	Consistent	Memorable	Discoverable
Symbolic	Functional	Experiential	Inviting

The design of the experience therefore encompasses several elements: 1) type of **tactic**, 2) **content type**, and 3) **content strategy**, including themes, topics, appeals, source, and style.

Types of Tactics

The experience the brand offers the target audience should align with the relevant zone of social media marketing. In other words, in the zone of social community, the experience should build relationships and will likely include conversation and sharing. In the zone of social publishing, the experience should be informative and/or educational. In the zone of social entertainment, the experience should be entertaining. In the zone of social commerce, the experience is related to shopping and buying. Some **tactics** are cross-zone while others are not. Table 5.3 describes the tactics marketers use to achieve experience strategies and the related zones of social media.[2] You'll learn more about these tactics as we cover each zone of social media in-depth in the next section of the book.

Table 5.3   Social Media Marketing Tactics

Tactic	Zone	Description
Branching	1	Complementing offline brand presence with a presence in social network sites (e.g., brand profile aligned to brand elements)
Contributing	All	Contributing in a valuable and meaningful way; investing in the community
Friending	1	Participating in relational activities with other members of the social community (e.g., conversations, interactions, shared activities)
Informing/ Broadcasting (i.e., friendvertising)	All	Posting one-way messages about brand and/or its offer (product, price, promotions), possibly linking to e-commerce site
Clustering	All	Building communities around shared interest (i.e., social object) whether as an embedded social community (e.g., GoPro Facebook fan page), owned branded community (e.g., MyStarbucksIdea), or brand-sponsored community (e.g., Always' BeingGirl community)

Tactic	Zone	Description
Listening/ Monitoring	All	Monitoring social media, assessing and responding, collecting data for market research purposes
Collaborating	All	Cooperating, partnering, and/or co-creating (i.e., interdependent contributors)
Crowdsourcing	All	Enlisting the efforts of many individuals to acquire resources to accomplish a task (i.e., many independent contributors)
Seeding/ Propagating	All	Increasing social word-of-mouth communication by triggering viral network effects with influencers
Educating	2	Teaching, explaining, and/or coaching others
Entertaining		Providing socially enabled entertainment and/or participating in social activities in which the social object is entertainment
Gamifying	3	Associating the brand with a game or gamifying exposure to the brand message
Incentivizing	3, 4	Offering a reward in exchange for social engagement (e.g., giving gamers credits if they view an in-game ad)
Selling	4	Facilitating sales with social apps and widgets, conducting transactions within SNS, supporting purchase decisions with social word-of-mouth communications
Serving	1	Providing customer service on social network channels

Content Types

Regardless of the type of tactic or the zone of social media in which the tactic is deployed, there will be one or more types of content employed. Tactics may require a venue for the audience to interact with the brand, such as an app, widget, bot, or game. Most commonly, tactics rely upon content as the social object with which the audience can engage. A **content type** is an information asset whose attributes distinguish it from all other kinds of content. There are a plethora of content types marketers can use. Some content types include live video, prerecorded video, photos, images, articles, quotes, infographics, announcements, news headlines, questions and answers, statements, case studies, ebooks, white papers, songs, jingles, games, performances, and more. Don't forget conversations! As Bizzuka CEO, Jon Munsell, famously said, "If content is king, conversation is queen."[3]

How do marketers choose? Marketers will consider which types of content are typical for the SNS where the content will be deployed, fit the tactic's strategic intent, most popular among the target audience (perhaps based on data on engagement rates by content type), best for relaying brand messages, and feasible given the staffing, creative, monetary, and temporal resources of the brand. Figure 5.6 presents the content marketing matrix which plots content type according to whether the information being delivered in the content type is **emotional** or **rational** and whether the target audience is in a **passive** or **active** stage of the purchase process.[4] Figure 5.7 provides assessments for the most commonly used content types in social media marketing on key selection factors such as interactivity, perceived value, source, production cost, and results. Figure 5.8 charts marketer use of several popular types of content and the perceived effectiveness for each.[5]

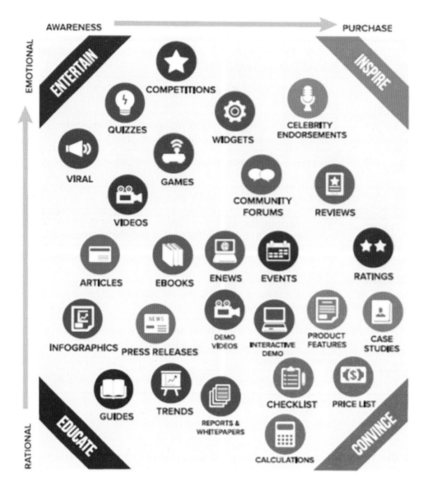

Figure 5.6   Content Marketing Matrix: Mapping Content Type to Target Audience Interest and Needs

Source: D. Bosomworth, 2014, 'The Content Marketing Matrix', *SmartInsights*, www.smartinsights.com/content-management/content-marketing-strategy/the-content-marketing-matrix-new-infographic/?utm_source=hubspot&utm_medium=pdf&utm_campaign=contentplanning. With permission of Digital Marketing advice site Smart Insights (www.smartinsights.com)

Content Strategy

The specific themes and topics for the content must be identified. Themes may be based on brand values, industry issues, target audience interests, integrated marketing communications campaigns, seasonal events, and more. The only requirement is that the themes identified fit with the brand, the target audience, and the tactics being employed. The topics will be subcategories of the themes identified. Working with the themes and topics, the team will brainstorm ideas and assign the ideas a title. Ideas deemed worthy of further development can then be assigned to a team member and tracked through the stages of development, approval, production, publication, promotion, and assessment.

Content Type	Suitable for Objective	Participatory (P)/ Shareable (S)	Publish to Channels	Promote on Channels	Desired Action	Cost/ Difficulty
Images	Brand awareness, engagement, lead generation, customer acquisition	P + S	Instagram, Facebook, Twitter and Pinterest	Instagram, Facebook, Twitter, Pinterest	Comments, likes, shares	Low
Pre-recorded Video (ODV)	Brand awareness, engagement, point of differentiation	P + S	Instagram, Facebook, Twitter, Blog, YouTube	Instagram, Facebook, Twitter, Pinterest, Blog, YouTube	Views, comments, likes, shares	High
Pre-recorded Video (repurposed)	Brand awareness, lead generation, customer acquisition, engagement	S	Facebook, Instagram, YouTube	Instagram, Facebook, Youtube, Twitter, Snapchat, Blog	Views, comments, likes, shares	Low
Blog Post	Brand awareness, engagement, event promos, influencer promos, brand equity	S	Blog, Facebook, Twitter, LinkedIn, Instagram, Pinterest	Facebook, Twitter, LinkedIn, Instagram, Pinterest, Snapchat	Views, inquiries, comments, likes, shares	Low-Moderate
Infographic	Brand awareness, engagement, lead generation, customer acquisition	P + S	Blog, Instagram, Facebook, Twitter, Pinterest	Instagram, Facebook, Twitter, Pinterest, Embed	Comments, likes, shares	Moderate
Article Page	Brand awareness, engagement, event promos, influencer promos, brand equity	S	Facebook, Instagram, Twitter	Facebook, Instagram, Twitter	Comments, likes, shares	Moderate
Case Study	Brand awareness, engagement, event promos, influencer promos, brand equity	P	Blog, Facebook, Twitter, LinkedIn, Instagram, Pinterest	Blog, Facebook, Twitter, LinkedIn, Instagram, Pinterest, Snapchat	Views, inquiries, comments, likes, shares	Moderate
Annual Report	Brand awareness, engagement, lead generation, customer acquisition, influencer engagement, brand equity	P	Blog, Facebook, Twitter, LinkedIn, Instagram, Pinterest	Blog, Facebook, Twitter, LinkedIn, Instagram, Pinterest, Snapchat	Views, inquiries, comments, likes, shares	High

Figure 5.7   Evaluation of Content Types for Social Media Marketing

Types of Content Created vs. Considered Most Effective According to US Content Marketers, Sep 2016
% of respondents

	Created	Considered most effective
Research/original data	74%	18%
infographics	74%	17%
Product reviews	74%	16%
Videos	70%	13%
Blog posts	57%	14%
Case studies	56%	6%
White papers	55%	5%
Interviews	49%	7%
Podcasts	38%	2%
Ebooks	23%	1%

Figure 5.8   Content Types by Marketer Use and Perceived Effectiveness

Note: n = 300; numbers may not add up to 100% due to rounding Source: Clutch, "2016 Content Marketing Survey" Jan 10, 2017

Source: "Types of Content Created vs. Considered Most Effective According to US Content Marketers", September 2016 (% of respondents), eMarketer, January 20, 2017, www.emarketer.com/Chart/Types-of-Content-Created-vs-Considered-Most-Effective-According-US-Content-Marketers-Sep-2016-of-respondents/203148 (www.eMarketer.com). Reproduced by permission of eMarketer Inc.

The Content Marketing Institute recommends a series of questions to answer in the discovery process for a **content strategy**:[6]

- Is the target audience actively seeking information about your brand? Is their attitude toward the brand positive? What content or information do they need? Can you help solve a "pain point" in their jobs or lives? What can you offer them that they would care about?

- What differentiating value can your brand bring? What can you develop that is truly different from and more valuable than that of the competition?

- What could we develop that will be synergistic with the brand's overall marketing efforts?

- What do we need to say? What will the target audience be receptive to?

- What content types will be used? Can the content be developed as a series to increase impact?

- Where will the content be published and distributed?

- What resources do you have already or can you acquire to develop content? Can you syndicate content from existing sources? Can you provide value through curating content from other sources? If original content, do the resources exist in-house? Who in the company has the expertise to help? What internal assets and other content do you already have? What resources (staffing, partners, vendor services) will you need?

Note that in addition to devising a creative idea and a rationale for why it should produce content that meets the criteria and will achieve the desired results, the questions include assessing what is feasible. Some social media marketing teams are a team of one; others may include several people in specialized roles. Some teams will have access to **talent** (such as web designers, copywriters, graphic designers) and **brand assets** (such as video footage, commercials, print ads, brochures, and annual reports) from other divisions in the company that can be repurposed as **source content**. Other teams will be creating from scratch.

An additional consideration is the content mix in terms of point of view (POV) or intended beneficiary. Research suggests that people are more likely to engage, and engage positively, when the content posted or shared takes the point of view of the receiver, rather than that of the sender. In other words, the messages should have more "you"-focus than "me"-focus. When brands share a post that touts the launch of a new product, the focus is on the brand and if the audience engages, it is the brand that benefits. When a brand shares an entertaining video that brings joy and amusement to the audience, the focus is on the audience and if the audience watches the video, the audience benefits. See the difference? Industry best practices suggest that the content mix should follow an 80–20 formula such that 80% of the content is audience-focused and 20% brand-focused. In other words, for every four social media posts that are **audience-centric**, the brand can share one post that is **brand-centric** or sales-oriented.

Figure 5.9 illustrates a planning template used in planning content strategy. Sample themes and topics are identified in the column on the left. The planner includes space for the title, content type, creative source, anticipated distribution channels, and production schedules.

A common dilemma for social media marketers is the desire to develop new, high-value content while staying under budget and within staffing parameters. Google's "The YouTube Creator Playbook for Brands" recommends developing a content strategy that includes three levels of content: 1) hygiene, 2) hub, and 3) hero.[7] **Hygiene content** is a constant foundation. It serves as the brand's active presence in each social community and includes archived content that is "evergreen." Evergreen content has a long shelf-life; the information is likely to remain useful and reliable over a long period of time. Day-to-day interactions and posts in social channels are also part of the brand's hygiene content. **Hub content** is published less frequently than hygiene content but is of greater value to the target audience and more likely to generate interest and engagement. It may be published on the brand's owned media such as a brand website that aggregates all of its content and links to all social media profiles or it may be published on a social community appropriate for the content type (e.g., videos on YouTube). Hub content is publicized in hygiene content posts about the hub content along with links to the content and share tools to encourage people to spread the information. Lastly, **hero content** is truly buzz-worthy content.

Style

The content developed for social media should be consistent with the brand's style and personality in other communications media. To accomplish this, the social media marketing team should be well versed in the brand's **style guide**, sometimes called a brand identity guide. The guide will ensure that the **brand standards** are followed. The voice and tone of social media communications should be consistent with the brand persona established for the brand's social media presence.

Categories & Messaging Themes	Topic Content		Voice	Media Type(s)	Destination Channels												Production Notes		
	Include a call to action for all articles		Company vs individual voice																
	Topic/ Keywords	Title	Brand, Mascot, User, Influencer	Articles/Blog – Video – Podcast – Infographic – Presentations – Newsletters – Email	Website	Wordpress Blog	Facebook page	Twitter	LinkedIn	YouTube	Google+	Slideshare	Pinterest	Snapchat	Blogger	Flickr	Due Date	Assigned To	Target Publish Date
		Primary content type: Image, Video, Case study, White Paper, Testimonial																	
Value Propositions																			
• Points of differentiation • Client needs/concerns • Defending and defining our voice • Top 3 things we want people to know • Top 3 things we want people to do • Primary calls to action																			
Any Unique Way(s) to be involved with our Company or Product																			
• How are we unique? • How to be involved • How to purchase products																			
Company																			
• Company history • Our core values • Mission statement • Vision statement • Company or product stats																			
Industry																			
• What's trending • Competitive landscape • Industry studies • Upcoming industry trade shows and events																			
FAQ's and Product & Sales Support																			
• Product comparision posts • List and "how to" posts • Client story post • Testimonial post • New product launch • Social contesting post																			
Events and/or Announcements by Month																			
January–December																			

Figure 5.9   Planning Content for a Social Media Editorial Calendar

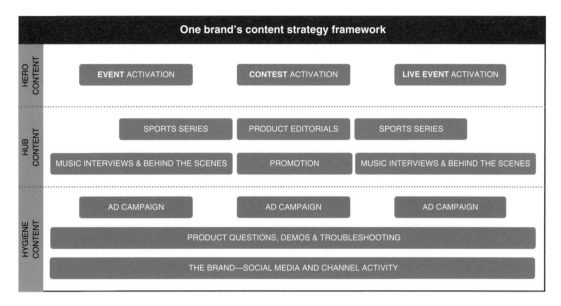

Figure 5.10   A Sample Content Strategy Framework

Source: Google, "The YouTube Creator Playbook for Brands," www.thinkwithgoogle.com/intl/en-gb/research-studies/youtube-brand-playbook.html (accessed June 16, 2017)

Reproduced with kind permission of Google

Publishing Standards

The content strategy will likely also include standards for content that ensure everything published and promoted for social media marketing is optimized for effectiveness. For instance, keywords, tags, and meta-tags that are relevant for the brand's search engine optimization (SEO) strategy should be emphasized in social media content. Hashtags used for specific brand campaigns or related to seasonal themes will be identified. The standards may include guidelines for title or headline word count, preferred headline words, types of preferred interactivity (e.g., quizzes or polls), links, thumbnails, and so on.

Content Strategy Document

The decisions will be documented in a brief content strategy document, as shown in Table 5.4.

Table 5.4   A Content Strategy Document Example

Tactical Approach	Most content will align with the primary tactics of educating and contributing and secondary tactics of friending and serving; minimal content will broadcast information about our products, pricing, and special offers (80/20).
Type	Because our brand offers a high-involvement, high-risk service, credible and detailed information is valuable for preparing the audience to choose a service provider. Videos and articles published on our company blog will be the primary content types. These will be promoted with short, conversational posts in our chosen social channels.
Content Theme	Content themes will include 1) brand slogan; 2) empowering decision makers for risky decisions; 3) stressful decisions.

(Continued)

Table 5.4   (Continued)

Content Topics	Videos will relay the stories of customers told in the form of a dramatization. The story arc will engage the viewer in an emotional and well-crafted drama that ultimately delivers a testimonial for our service. The videos will be constructed as a series with one episode for every type of situation faced by our clients. These will be supported by a downloadable how-to guide that explains how prospective customers facing similar situations can choose a solution to meet their needs. Suggested topic titles are provided in the content calendar.
Style	The brand's persona is that of trusted advisor. The brand's voice will reflect a personality that is empathetic, reassuring, reliable, and strong.
Implementation Standards	All content with have a consistent voice, tone, heading, nomenclature, and editorial style. All content will include a call to action, a link to the company website, and the brand logo.

EXHIBIT 5.1

Brita's Filtered Life Series includes #FilterYourFeed Twitter Tactic[8]

iStock.com/cmannphoto

Brita, a brand known for its ability to filter contaminants out of water, has tied its social media strategy to its core benefit—filtering! The "Filtered Life" campaign, which looks at all the bad stuff that can be removed from human consciousness as a metaphor for what filters do to water, includes the zones of social community and social publishing. The experience strategy relies on tactics based on branded video content and a Twitter app. The app, Filter Your Feed, scans users' tweets and replaces negative tweets with positive messages—like pictures of puppies! The positive messages generate earned media. These organic posts are seeds that help to spread the campaign to others. Users are incentivized to accept the positive posts with an altruistic appeal: Brita will donate $1 to the Cybersmile Foundation, an anti-cyberbullying non-profit, for every negative post deleted and positive post shared. The campaign uses owned media in the form of a microsite at www.brita.com/filtered-life, which hosts Brita's content and serves as a social media hub with links to Brita's profiles on several social media channels, including Twitter and YouTube. The app is promoted using paid ads on Twitter and YouTube.

How: Producing and Scheduling Content Posting and Promotion

The next stage of tactical planning is to establish processes for producing the content identified in the content strategy and a schedule to guide the work flow.

Producing the Content

Each content unit must be created and produced. Teams may use variations of **creative briefs** to document the required characteristics and elements of each content unit. If the content piece is part of a larger campaign, there may be a series of briefs, moving from campaign level to content type to content unit and for content projects that involve multi-media, a content element brief may even be used. The briefs will provide the information the responsible staff person needs to ensure the deliverables meet the associated requirements. The guidelines may be very specific such as number of words used in the title, inclusion of a short link, use of an image of a specific size, inclusion of campaign hashtags, use of a **call to action** (CTA), and so on.

As content is developed, it will be documented and catalogued. This ensures that content can be reused or repurposed in the future. Over time, the team will amass a database of content including posts, tweets, photos, hashtags, articles, and so on. The best ideas will produce content that can be repurposed for several related uses. This is called **atomization**—the content can be partitioned and/or repackaged in several ways while still remaining strategically aligned. Not only is atomization an efficient way to use resources, it also provides message **amplification**. Having related but distinct content on different social channels increases the likelihood that the target audience will be exposed to the message multiple times. This enhances message recall.

Scheduling with a Content Calendar

The **content calendar** captures which content is scheduled and prioritized for an organization, generally with an annual, quarterly, monthly, and sometimes weekly view. The most commonly used format is a spreadsheet, built in Microsoft Excel or Google Sheets. Companies that work with Social Media Management services (e.g., Sprout Social, Hubspot, Buffer) will use calendars integrated into the system. Content calendars help to identify, prioritize, and plan for new- and future-content creation. Calendars will typically include several sheets to accommodate planning for different time periods while maintaining perspective of how the content fits together. For instance, a content calendar may include the following views of the content and calendar:

1 Year-at-a-glance view with seasonal themes and major campaign dates.
2 Monthly view of content in production.
3 Monthly view of content scheduled for posting by social channel.
4 Weekly view of content for posting by social channel.
5 Weekly view of daily post schedule by social channel.
6 Daily view of social media activity, organized by content or by social channel.
7 Content index.

On-Going, Seasonal, and Campaign-Driven SM Activity Across Calender	Q1			Q2			Q3			Q4		
	JANUARY	FEBRUARY	MARCH	APRIL	MAY	JUNE	JULY	AUGUST	SEPTEMBER	OCTOBER	NOVEMBER	DECEMBER
Listen/Monitor/ Respond												
Maintain Brand Presence												
Increase Brand Awareness – Paid												
Encourage Customer Reviews												
Seasonal Category Elements	New Year, New Year – Resolutions	Valentine's Day	S.Party's Day	Easter	Mother's Day; Wedding Season	Graduation			Back to School	Halloween	Prepare for Holiday Parties	Christmas
Campaign Project – "Like a Pro"												
Campaign Project – "Sparkle"												
Support IMC												
Provide customer care upon alert												
Comments												

Figure 5.11 Summary of Annual Content Calendar

Blog/Video	Category	Topic	Headline/Title	URL	Publishing Site	Image/Thumbnail	KEYWORD(S)/#hashtag	Description	OFFER/CTA	Social Promotion	Paid?
Month: Week 1											
Author: Shari Moines	Educate/Build brand rep	Commuting	5 solutions for the bike commuter		YouTube		bike commuting	Video description	how to select a commuter bike (ebook)	Twitter, Pinterest, Facebook, PAID post	yes FB post boost
Due Date: 10/20/2012											
Publish Date: 10/21/2012											
Post 2											
Author:											
Due Date:											
Publish Date:											
Week 2											
Author:											
Due Date:											
Publish Date:											
Post 3											
Author:											
Due Date:											
Publish Date:											
Week 3											
Author:											
Due Date:											
Publish Date:											
Post 2											
Author:											
Due Date:											
Publish Date:											
Week 4											
Author:											
Due Date:											
Publish Date:											
Post 2											
Author:											
Due Date:											
Publish Date:											

(Continued)

Figure 5.12 (Continued)

Social Community	Category	Topic	Title/Headline	URL/link	Image	Facebook	Twitter	Snapchat	Pinterest	Instagram	#Hashtags
Month: Week 1 (Date)											
Post 1											
Type: Promotion/offer Date: 10/20/2014 aid boost: yes	Special offer New helmets				paste image here	Check out these new helmets just in. Deluxe and cute! You're stylin' now! (LINK)	You gotta get one of these #coolhelmets #womens biking (shortlink image)	Image story series	You gotta get one of these #coolhelmets #womens biking (shortlink image)	You gotta get one of these #coolhelmets #womens biking (shortlink image)	#bikehelmets #women'scycling
Post 2											
Type: Blog post Date: 10/13/2014 aid boost: no	Best ways to commute to work.			paste url here to blog post	(pulled from blog)	write post promoting blog article here					
Post 3											
Type: Tip/value add Date: aid boost: no											
Post 4											
Type: Blog Date: aid boost: no											
Post 5											
Type: Promotion/offer Date: aid boost: yes											
Post 6											
Type: Tip/value add Date: aid boost: no											
Week 2 (date)											
Post 1											
Type: Promotion/offer Date: 10/20/2014 aid boost: yes	Special offer New helmets				paste image here	Check out these new helmets just in. Deluxe and cute! You're stylin' now! (LINK)	You gotta get one of these #coolhelmets #womens biking (shortlink image) (shortlink URL)	Check out these new helmets just in. Deluxe and cute! You're stylin' now! (LINK)	You gotta get one of these #coolhelmets #womens biking (shortlink image) (shortlink URL)	You gotta get one of these #coolhelmets #womens biking (shortlink image) (shortlink URL)	#bikehelmets #women'scycling
Post 2											
Type: Blog post Date: 10/13/2014 aid boost: no	Best ways to commute to work.			paste url here to blog post	(pulled from blog)	write post promoting blog article here					
Post 3											
Type: Tip/value add Date: aid boost: no											
Post 4											
Type: Blog Date: aid boost: no											
Post 5											
Type: Promotion/offer Date: aid boost: yes											
Post 6											
Type: Tip/value add Date: aid boost: no											

Figure 5.12 Weekly Content Calendar for Blog and SNS

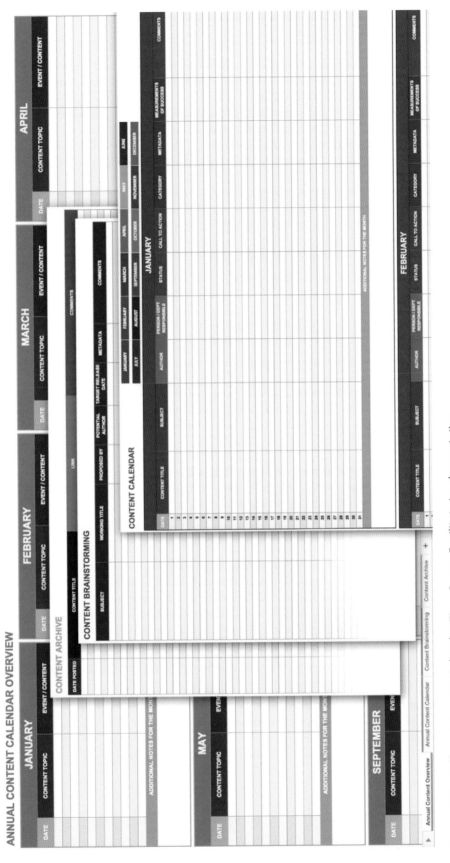

Figure 5.13   Different Content Calendar Time Spans Facilitate Implementation

Source: "Creating Your Social Media Strategy: Free Social Media Templates for Excel," SmartSheet, www.smartsheet.com/social-media-templates (accessed June 16, 2017)

Figure 5.11 depicts an example of a simple annual view. Figure 5.12 illustrates a typical weekly schedule organized by content and date. Figure 5.13 shows how various elements of the content calendar relate to each other.

There is no right or wrong way to organize a content calendar. If you Google "social media marketing content calendars" you will find several free Excel templates from social media marketing service providers.[9] Different templates will provide varying levels of detail. All are easily adapted as you gain experience and develop preferences for the calendar planning system that works best for you.

How you design, share, and access your editorial calendar will ultimately depend on your particular marketing goals and available resources. But at the most fundamental level, we recommend that your calendar include the following fields:

- The **date** the piece of content will be published.

- The **topic** or **headline** of the content piece.

- The **author** of the content.

- The **owner** of the content—i.e., who is in charge of making sure the content makes it from ideation to publication and promotion.

- The **current status** of the content (updated as it moves through your publishing cycle).

Depending on your company's specific goals, your content team's workflow, the formats, and platforms with which you plan to work, and the volume of content you will be creating, you may also want to track these elements to help you stay organized and on track over the long term:

- **The channels where the content will be published**: this can include owned channels (such as your blog, Facebook page, website, YouTube page, email newsletters, etc.), or you can expand your tracking to include paid and earned channels, as well.

- **Content formats**: is it a blog post? A video? A podcast? An infographic? An original image? To get more mileage from the content you create, consider repurposing it into other formats.

- **Visuals**: speaking of assets, it's important that you don't overlook the appeal that visuals can lend to your content, both in terms of social sharing potential and overall brand recognition. Tracking the visual elements you include in your content efforts—such as cover images, logos, illustrations, charts—will make it easier to ensure that your work has a signature look and cohesive brand identity.

- **Topic categories**: this helps make your calendars more searchable when you are looking to see about which target topics you already created a lot of content—or which you haven't covered often enough.

- **Keywords and other meta-data**, such as meta-descriptions and SEO titles (if they differ from your headlines), which will help you keep your SEO efforts aligned with your content creation.

- **URLs**: this info can be archived as an easy way to keep your online content audits updated, or to link to older pieces of content in the new content you create.

- **Calls to action**: this helps you ensure that every piece of content you create is aligning with your company's marketing goals.

The calendar will reflect the intended volume and frequency of activity for each channel in your social media plan. Studies on the effectiveness of posting schedules suggest that brands be active several times each week, spread among each day of the week, with fewer high-value content posts for blogs and video channels and more brief, conversational posts for social network sites. Ultimately though, the choice should fit with the overall strategy and objectives and the team's capacity to deliver fresh, effective content and social interactions.

Roles and Workflow

A clearly defined workflow will help your team communicate more efficiently, and it gives everyone something to be accountable for. A **social media workflow** is a sequence of connected steps that enables the organization to act efficiently with minimal overlapping tasks and resources in order to implement the social media marketing plan effectively. A solid workflow helps you and your entire team to:[10]

- understand the big vision behind daily tasks and projects

- know what each person's role and responsibilities are

- complete projects requiring different skills as a team, and

- prioritize time and resources.

Workflows can be incredibly complex, especially for large teams in global companies. Most teams have five or fewer members though so creating a workflow is manageable and worthwhile. To implement a workflow that actually works, follow these steps:

- Figure out exactly what tasks need to be completed for every piece of content you produce and the daily activities required for posting to each channel in the plan.

- Understand what role would be the best for completing each task.

- Assign those tasks to the people who fill those roles. When projects require skills from multiple people on the team, identify whether the tasks can be completed concurrently or must move forward in linear fashion.

- Assign due dates based on what needs to be done first, second, third, and so on.

- Hold everyone accountable for getting their stuff done on time.

EXHIBIT 5.2

Many Social Media Marketing Mistakes Happen Because of Poor Tactics[11]

Narasimhan M V/Shutterstock.com

Marketers make social media mistakes all too often. The most common tactical errors fall into these broad categories: 1) posting from the wrong account (personal posts on work profiles and vice versa), 2) mishandling responses when replying to comments, 3) creating content that offends the target audience, 4) posting content without checking it first, 5) promoting the competition, 6) sharing too much information, 7) auto-tweeting without monitoring for current events, 8) co-opting a trending topic for reach, and 9) responding to trolls.

MINI CASE STUDY

In a Fight for Brands, Instagram Trounces Snapchat[12]

Brands have to consider several factors when selecting the right channel mix to support social media marketing efforts. Those channels become the communities where brands relate to prospects and fans, represent the brand persona through imagery, messaging, and behavior, and accomplish the practical objectives of their social media marketing efforts. The population size, demographics, and usage rates of a channel's user base must be considered along with the channel's functionalities for content, engagement, paid impressions, social commerce, routing to owned media, and utilities like automated scheduling features and measurement dashboards. Social media marketing teams want to wow fans with fabulous social content experiences, but they have to do so facing time, staffing, and budgeting constraints.

Snapchat's growing popularity, largely attributed to its disappearing stories, baited many brands to experiment with the channel. Instagram responded with a feature of its own, Stories, that share photos and videos for 24 hours. Instagram's channel tools make it easier for social media teams to publish polished content, more aligned with their brand's image, while maintaining the authenticity of instantaneous posts. When it comes to channel choice in a showdown between the most popular SNS featuring photos and video shorts, social media marketing managers seem to agree Instagram Stories achieve greater reach than Snapchat, and have higher resource efficiency.

The resource crunch is a real one, especially for fashion brands. Kyle Wong, CEO of Pixlee, said "Content generation is hard. These brands have a limited bandwidth to manage these social platforms. Most fashion brands out there probably have one person max running social media accounts. They are spread thin between keeping multiple channels updated, rather than engaging the community on those channels."

Other channel issues? For brands targeting an audience with more disposable income, Instagram is the winner. Instagram's population base is larger than Snapchat's and its users skew significantly older: 51% of its user base is above age 35, compared to just 14% of Snapchat users. These older users, in many cases, have more disposable income than their younger Snapchat-using peers. Instagram also has a leg up in discoverability, as

Voyagerix/Shutterstock.com

Snapchat lacks a robust search function, making it difficult for consumers to find brand Snapchat accounts.

Instagram Stories are already being used by brands like Ted Baker to deliver episodic entertainment shared over a series of days and serve as the object for engagement across other channels. Not only does Instagram Stories shift the channel into the zone of social entertainment, it also makes it possible for brands to use the channel for social commerce tactics. Stories can be "shoppable" with links to purchase items featured in photos and videos. Even organic brand posts can be tagged with product information and links to e-commerce sites—a big plus for brands to drive social commerce without paid posts.

Results and Outcomes

Instagram's competitive move sounds like a win, but what do the numbers say? As a result of Instagram Stories, Snapchat's growth slowed by a whopping 82%. Instagram's audience was already larger and engagement rates suggest Stories is a welcome feature. Early results show hundreds of millions of daily views for Stories. And for individual brands? One social media strategist reported getting upwards of 90,000 views on Instagram, compared to just 3,000 on Snapchat.

CRITICAL REFLECTION

Stress and the Social Media Marketer

Being a social media marketer sounds like a dream job! You get to spend most of your waking hours doing what other people do for fun! You tweet, you snap, you pin! You show off your creative flair with clever images and witty banter. And that's really all it takes for a brand to build and maintain a successful social media program, right? Not quite. Social media has been described as a beast that requires constant feeding. Constant means always, as in 24/7, 365 days a year. The beast requires it be fed with fresh ingredients and while you are concepting and prepping, any number of developments might need your attention. The result—stress!

(Continued)

(Continued)

Figure 5.14   A Day in the Life of a Social Media Manager

Source: Karen Uyenco, "Infographic: A Day in the Life of a Social Media Manager," Meltwater, February 9, 2016, www.meltwater.com/blog/infographic-a-day-in-the-life-of-a-social-media-manager-2/ (accessed June 16, 2017)

Reproduced by kind permission of www.meltwater.com

The **Stress in America** report, published by the APA, states that 86% of adults in the US experience social media stress. Constant checkers—people who frequently check email, texts, and social media accounts—experience the highest levels of social media stress.[13] Don't worry—there are solutions to reduce social media stress! The answer is to take a "digital detox" from time to time. Unfortunately, digital detox isn't really an option for those whose livelihood requires being connected to social media—as it does if you are part of a social media marketing team. What might work for people whose jobs don't require them to be connected virtually around the clock is something social media marketers can only dream about.

REDPIXEL.PL/Shutterstock.com

 ## CHAPTER SUMMARY

What is a social media marketing tactical plan and how does it support the execution of a social media marketing strategy?

The tactical plan brings the social media marketing strategy to life and addresses the why, who, where, what, when, and how of social media marketing. There are several practical steps required including determining the right channels, content to deliver the desired experience, rules of engagement, and schedule. It also involves developing processes to create, produce, and deliver the content, conversation, and other experiential elements of our strategy.

What is a channel plan and how is it used?

The channel plan determines where the brand will engage with the target audience. In this step, each channel is evaluated for fit. It is important to ask if brand image, voice, and tone fit with the channel culture. The culture, guidelines and rules, and functionality of each prospective channel will influence what can and should be shared, how people engage with each other, and choices about the timing and frequency of participation.

How does a content plan relate to experience strategies? What are the elements included in the content plan?

Experience strategies are how social media marketers inspire the target audience to engage with the brand in social media, participate or interact with the brand, and hopefully also share the brand experience with others. The experience may be delivered using an app, game, branded entertainment, or many other formats, but most often, the experience is in the form of content. The content plan includes the tactical decisions to bring the experience strategy to life.

What is a content calendar and what should be considered in developing the calendar?

Content calendars help to identify, prioritize, and plan for new- and future-content creation. Calendars will typically include several sheets to accommodate planning for different time periods while maintaining perspective of how the content fits together. The content calendar captures which content is scheduled and prioritized for an organization, generally with an annual, quarterly, monthly, and sometimes weekly view. The calendar will reflect the intended volume and frequency of activity for each channel in your social media plan.

How do social media teams manage the roles, tasks, and schedules related to executing social media tactics?

A clearly defined workflow will help your team communicate more efficiently, and it gives everyone something to be accountable for. A **social media workflow** is a sequence of connected steps that enables the organization to act efficiently with minimal overlapping tasks and resources to implement the social media marketing plan effectively. A solid workflow helps you and your entire team understand the big vision behind daily tasks and projects, understand roles within the group, and prioritize time and resources.

REVIEW QUESTIONS

1   What are social media tactics?

2   Why should a social media strategy be based on an experience? Describe a social media brand experience that you found engaging. What characteristics of the experience made it effective?

4   Describe four tactics marketers use to achieve experience strategies and note the related zone(s) of social media.

5   Why should brands develop hygiene, hub, and hero content?

6   What are the components of a content strategy document? How is this different from a content calendar?

7   What are the benefits of a defined social media workflow?

EXERCISES

1   Find a real-world example of a brand's social media strategy that is based on an experience. Describe its target audience and effectiveness. How would you vary the experience to apply to the other zones of social media?

2   Choose a brand and evaluate its channel plan (where the brand engages with the target audience). What conclusions could you draw about the fit of the channel?

3 Analyze a brand profile on Facebook or Twitter. Identify **four** types of social media marketing tactics they have recently used.

4 Imagine you are planning an upcoming campaign for a local coffee shop. Create a content strategy document.

5 For the same coffee shop create a sample content calendar (week, month, or annual).

CHAPTER NOTES (access all weblinks listed here at: https://study.sagepub.com/smm3e)

1 Several resources contributed to the explanations, tables, and templates in this chapter. See in particular the following excellent sources (all accessed June 16, 2017): 1) *Content Strategy Alliance, Tools and Templates: A Best Practices Handbook*, Content Strategy Alliance, 2015, http://content strategyalliance.com/csa-best-practices/csa-handbook; 2) Michelle Linn, "A Blueprint to Jump-Start Your Content Marketing Strategy," Content Marketing Institute, January 1, 2015, http://content marketinginstitute.com/2015/01/blueprint-jump-start-content-marketing-strategy; 3) Jodi Harris, "The Content Marketing Book of Answers: Strategy & Planning," Content Marketing Institute, 21 June, 2016, http://contentmarketinginstitute.com/2016/06/content-marketing-strategy-planning; and 4) templates and guides by CoSchedule (www.coschedule.com), Buffer (www.buffer.com), Hubspot (www.hubspot.com), Marketo (www.marketo.com), SmartSheet (www.smartsheet.com), Curata (www.curata.com), and Sprout Social (www.sproutsocial.com).

2 The tactics listed include 11 identified and defined by Accenture; see Accenture, *Talk With Me not At Me: Playing to Win with Social Media*, 2014, www.accenture.com/t20150523T022446__w__/us-en/_acnmedia/Accenture/Conversion-Assets/DotCom/Documents/Global/PDF/Dualpub_1/Accenture-Playing-Win-Social-Media.pdf (accessed June 16, 2017).

3 Diana Shafer, "Bizzuka CEO John Munsell's Quote Heard Around the World," Bizzuka Blog, December 1, 2011, https://bizzuka.com/company-blog/bizzuka-ceo-john-munsells-quote-heard-around-the-world (accessed June 16, 2017).

4 Danyl Bosomworth, "The Content Marketing Matrix," Smart Insights, January 12, 2014, www.smartinsights.com/content-management/content-marketing-strategy/the-content-marketing-matrix-new-infographic/?utm_source=hubspot&utm_medium=pdf&utm_campaign=contentplanning (accessed June 16, 2017).

5 "Types of Content Created vs. Considered Most Effective According to US Content Marketers, Sep 2016 (% of respondents)," eMarketer, January 20, 2017, www.emarketer.com/Chart/Types-of-Content-Created-vs-Considered-Most-Effective-According-US-Content-Marketers-Sep-2016-of-respondents/203148 (accessed June 16, 2017).

6 Joe Pulizzi, "A Simple Approach to Document Your Content Marketing Strategy," Content Marketing Institute, October 10, 2016, http://contentmarketinginstitute.com/2016/10/simple-content-marketing-strategy (accessed June 16, 2017).

7 Google, "The YouTube Creator Playbook for Brands," https://think.storage.googleapis.com/docs/creator-playbook-for-brands_research-studies.pdf (accessed June 16, 2017).

8 Jack Neff, "Can Brita Filter the Negativity Out of Twitter? Here's How It's Trying," Advertising Age, April 5, 2017, http://adage.com/article/cmo-strategy/brita-filter-negativity-twitter/308581/?utm_

source=daily_email&utm_medium=newsletter&utm_campaign=adage&ttl=1492036735&utm_visit=2032908 (accessed June 16, 2017).

9 A list to several excellent templates is provided at Mitchel Hall, "Content Marketing Editorial Calendar Templates: The Ultimate List," May 8, 2017, www.curata.com/blog/content-marketing-editorial-calendar-templates-the-ultimate-list (accessed June 16, 2017).

10 "How to Use A Content Marketing Editorial Calendar to Save a Ton of Time," CoSchedule, https://coschedule.com/content-marketing-editorial-calendar (accessed June 16, 2017).

11 "#Fail: 29 of the Biggest Corporate Brand Social Media Flubs," CB Insights, March 17, 2017, www.cbinsights.com/blog/corporate-social-media-fails (accessed June 16, 2017).

12 Bethany Biron, "How Instagram Beat Out Snapchat as Fashion's 'Social Darling'," Glossy, March 28, 2017, www.glossy.co/platform-effect/how-instagram-beat-out-snapchat-as-fashions-social-darling (accessed June 16, 2017).

13 Maggie McGary, "Social Media Stress is Real," SocialFish, March 13, 2017, www.socialfish.org/2017/03/social-media-stress-is-real (accessed June 16, 2017).

Visit **https://study.sagepub.com/smm3e** for free additional online resources related to this chapter.

PART 3

The Four Zones of
Social Media

Social Community

Learning Objectives

When you finish reading this chapter, you will be able to answer these questions:

1 How do social networking communities enable user participation and sharing?

2 In what ways can brands utilize social networking communities for branding and promotion?

3 How can brands reach consumers organically using social network sites? What characteristics do brand fans exhibit?

4 What forms of paid media can be used in social communities? Why is paid media important to social media marketers?

The Social Community Zone

In this chapter we dive deeper into the zone of social community, the first zone in our model, shown in Figure 6.1. Recall that *all* zones in the social media mix are built on social networks, technologically enabled, and based on the principles of shared participation.

As we plan, we want to devise a way to encourage customers to participate and to share and to do so within the zones within which we operate. What will invite participation and sharing? That's our experience strategy. Where will they participate and share? Within the zones. Of course, we may use any of the four zones. But in this chapter our focus is on the first zone, the zone of social community. Let's think of zone 1 as the relationship zone. Social media networks provide a structure for social interactions. They focus on acquiring and maintaining relationships above all else. Conversation and collaboration are the principal activities in this zone, though we often converse and collaborate around content, whether provided by brands, users, or others. Brands encourage this participation through engagement.

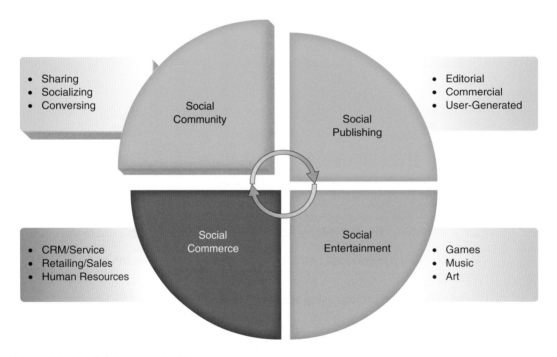

Figure 6.1   Social Community Zone

Social network sites are the community vehicles that house and enable social engagement. Facebook is the juggernaut of social networks, with the most members worldwide.

EXHIBIT 6.1

World Map of Social Networks

The map illustrates that Facebook is dominant around the world—in fact, it is the most used social vehicle in 119 countries! What if Facebook didn't exist? The map would look very different. The leading social network sites in a Facebook-free world are Instagram, Twitter, Odnoklassniki, and Reddit. Instagram would win 37 countries including most of South America. Twitter would rule in 8 countries including the United States. Odnoklassniki would win eastern Europe and the Middle East. Reddit would lead in Canada, Australia, New Zealand, Denmark, and Norway.[1]

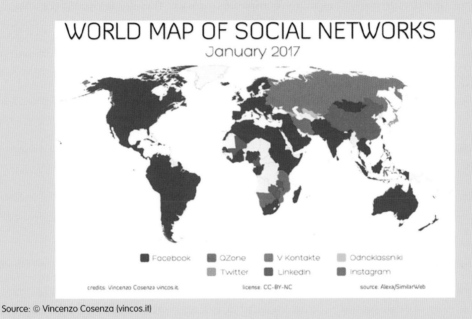

Source: © Vincenzo Cosenza (vincos.it)

Reproduced by kind permission of vincos.it

Social networks are the foundation of social media because every form of social media is based on participation from a *community* of members. Still, it is useful to compare and contrast social networks and to understand how their defining dimensions affect our ability to market brands within the social space. This is particularly relevant as we see a trend to users utilizing more social channels for specialized purposes. Social network sites all maintain the basic network structure we discussed in Chapter 3—nodes that interact with one another, flows between node members, and graphs connected to others by way of node relationships. However, social network sites vary in terms of three important dimensions:

1   Audience and degree of specialization.
2   The social objects that mediate the relationships among members.
3   Degree of openness.

Audience Specialization

Social network sites can be internal or external, general or specialized. Internal sites are those a specific organization builds for its own use and limits to members of the organization. Rather than hosting several subcultures within a larger social network site, an **internal social network** provides a method of communication and collaboration that is more dynamic and interactive. This is a lot like the *intranet* that many companies provide their employees. For instance, Nissan launched a site for its employees called N-Square. The network enables employees to post profiles, maintain a blog, participate in discussion groups, and share files.[2] Microsoft uses a network it calls TownSquare, IBM has the BeeHive, and Yahoo! employees meet in the Backyard. In contrast, an **external social network** is open to people who are not employed by the site's sponsor. That said, some external social networks are sponsored by brands.

Social networks are, of course, about networking—participating in the kinds of activities that enable members to build and maintain their relationships with other people. However, the nature of those relationships also affects the characterization of the social network. LinkedIn is a professional social network that emphasizes career experience and the need to maintain connections to those we know professionally. The primary benefit is to be able to call upon one's network when looking for a consultant, employee, job, or other career-related search. There are several professional networks held together by industry, purpose, and personal career goals. Care2 is a social network for people who want to help with social causes. Focus is a network for business and technology experts. Den provides a social network where architects and designers congregate.

Just because a social network focuses on personal relationships over professional ones doesn't necessarily mean that it has a broad target. For instance, Jdate.com is a dating social network for Jewish singles. Its mission is social, but it still targets a niche audience. There are several networks designed around specific target audiences defined by demographic characteristics including age (e.g., ClubPenguin, Webkinz), marital status (e.g., MarriedLife, MarriedPassions), income (asmallworld.net, affluence.org), and so on.

Social Objects and Passion-Centric Sites

In industry terms, sites designed around object sociality, the ability of an object to inspire social interaction, are known as **vertical networks**. The term describes the narrow, deep focus of social network sites that differentiate themselves because they emphasize some common hobby, interest, or characteristic that draws members to the site. These vertical networks do not attract the same traffic typical of general sites, but one might argue that the members are more involved because of the common interest that initially brought them to the site. They function much like so-called *niche markets* in the physical world; this term refers to marketplaces that offer a relatively small number of items to buyers who tend to be loyal to these outlets.

Openness

Social network sites can be closed, gated communities entirely controlled by the vendor that offers the platform. At the other extreme they can be accessible to any members or developers who wish to participate. Many SNS require new members to register for membership and to use login specifications to access the community. It often makes sense for a social network site to keep a record of membership even if anyone is allowed to join. This information can be invaluable for purposes of member management, product development, promoting the site, and utilizing the member data for other purposes. How might social networks utilize member data? It becomes a source for big social datasets, which we covered in Chapter 2. Because social networks have access to vast amounts of detailed data about members' preferences, friends, and activities, they can offer highly targeted ad placements for advertisers. Social network sites may eventually license that data to external marketers who could use the data to target potential customers. For now, the social community site with the most data, Facebook, isn't selling member data, but some speculate that it will.[3]

Marketing in the zone of social community doesn't have to mean marketing on Facebook. But Facebook is the most popular SNS for marketers. Why? That's where the consumers are. Of course there are other SNS and brands can build their own online brand communities (OBC), but social networking fatigue and social lock-in help Facebook maintain its dominance. Fatigue is higher when people manage multiple community accounts. The steady streams of content flowing from multiple networks, reaching us even with mobile notifications, add to this sense of fatigue. Social lock-in occurs when a user is unable to transfer social contacts and content from one social network to another.

One widely discussed solution is to develop a system of identity portability such that a single profile would provide access across social network sites with a single login and shared information. This is the goal of OpenID, an authentication protocol that works across participating sites. Unfortunately, OpenID works only on OpenID-enabled sites, limiting the portability for users. Sites can also choose to enable authentication with Facebook Connect, an option that has been more widely adopted.

Social Network Activities

Engagement is the currency of social network sites. How do we interact with others on social media platforms? We addressed this question in Chapter 2. But especially for the zone of social community, the answer has three parts: we mingle, we chat, and we share.

We can think of social networks as communication hubs; virtually all of them offer users access to a contact list and an interface that makes it easy for people to talk to one another. However, most sites offer more features than these basic ones. The new standard for social network sites is to offer tools, widgets, applications, and features that encourage social sharing; sites provide people with the tools they need to reveal elements of their digital identities. These elements include information about us or things that we create—such as our opinions, photos, videos, songs, and artworks. They may also take the form of secondary content—things that others create which we feel are worth redistributing to our social networks, such as retweets, links to a celebrity blog, or even brands we "like" on our Facebook page. Mark Zuckerberg, president and CEO of Facebook, said this about sharing: "People have really gotten comfortable not only sharing more information and different kinds, but more openly and with more people. [This is a] social norm that has evolved over time."[4]

Social media empower us because we all have the capacity to share something if we choose to do so. Some users are creators; they actively produce content in the form of video, podcasts/music, stories and articles, and blog posts. They may publish their own website.

Creators are a busy bunch—24 hours of YouTube video is posted every minute. The rest of us may not possess the technical skill or the desire to produce original content. We're happy leaving that work to others—many of whom are professionals. Still, we certainly are avid consumers of the content—YouTube videos alone get billions of views every day.

Remember that analysts estimate that lurkers—those people who consume content by reading posts and watching videos, but who do not contribute to the flow of content—make up about 90% of any online community. Although not everyone is a creator who develops artifacts such as videos and podcasts for distribution in their social network, anyone *can* join a network, update a status, post secondary content from others, and provide feedback on the content others post in their networks. The act of sharing changes this dynamic, because even lurkers can redistribute secondary content to a larger network of people. In this sense even fairly passive participants can extend their reach well beyond their own social graph. ShareThis, a provider of a widget that enables visitors to easily share content they discover online, found that though almost half of users preferred email for sharing interesting content with others, most of the remainder preferred to use a social media channel to share.[5] Applications such as ShareThis minimize the investment of time and effort necessary to share secondary content on a social network, so it's more likely that content will spread rapidly. This is one of the reasons marketers are attracted to social media as a communication channel. The viral spread of content amplifies the brand's reach, potentially delivering millions of impressions beyond what would have been possible without social sharing.

A study of social media users found that 75% of people are likely to share content via social media channels. The top three reasons people share content "socially" are because they find it interesting and/or entertaining, they think it could be helpful to others, and to get a laugh. Although the content can be virtually anything you can send in digital form, most people reported sharing family pictures and video, news about family and friends, funny videos, news articles and blog posts, and coupons and discounts.[6]

Marketing Applications in the Social Community Zone

As we discussed earlier, the social community zone focuses on relationships. Brands can leverage paid, earned, and owned media options in social network sites to meet several marketing objectives including promotion and branding, customer service and customer relationship management, and marketing research. In social network sites, brands can purchase paid space for advertising and utilize share technologies to further leverage the value of the advertising impressions. They can stimulate earned media, brand-related word-of-mouth communication, by participating and embedding the brand in social communities. Brands seeking a deeper connection to social media users can sponsor a social community or create a dedicated OBC, a form of owned media. There's an added bonus, too. Links to brand-related online content shared via social media affect the search engine rankings delivered by search engines such as Google and Yahoo! So not only can consumers be influenced by brand interactions and references to brands made by those in their network, they also can be led to branded content via search listings. That's a topic we'll cover further in Chapter 7 when we discuss search engine optimization.

Social Presence: Brands as Relationship Nodes

Brands must create a **brand profile** within the selected social networking communities in which they wish to command a presence. In this way, the brand acts as a node in the network's social graph. Doing so increases the opportunities for interactions with customers and prospects and also encourages people to talk about the brand with each other.

When a brand launches a profile on social network sites, the brand exists much as people do on the sites. Just the mere presence of a brand on a social network site results in more positive brand attitudes.[7] Friends can interact with the brands; share information, photos, and videos; and participate in two-way communication. As we discussed in Chapter 4, brands may participate as a corporate entity, as one or more people representing the brand, or as a mascot. Whichever the choice, the brand will develop a profile to represent its persona and then should interact in keeping with that profile—like a good actor, it should "stay in character." In so doing, the brand is personified. Brand personification is defined as "imbuing trademarked or otherwise proprietary-named products and services with a human form and/or human attributes, including a generally distinctive physical appearance and personality."[8] Even brand mascots, also known as spokescharacters, can achieve the benefits of personification. A **brand mascot** is a fictional persona with a distinct personality created to represent a brand; it may include animated characters (e.g., GEICO's gecko) as well as human actors portraying spokescharacters (e.g., Flo for Progressive Insurance).[9] Note that mascots differ from spokespeople, who are human beings endorsing the brand and not a brand-specific invention.

Building brand personas strengthens brand personality, differentiates brands from competitors, and sets the stage for a perceived relationship. It is a natural expansion of the trend for brands to create personalities for themselves, both through the use of creative language—including style, imagery, tone, and creative appeals—and music. Consumers perceive personified brands as active contributors in dyadic relationships.[10] We can see this in the higher engagement rates earned by brands that reinforce their persona in social media.[11] Consumers also respond positively to brand mascots, treating the brand mascots like humans (known as an anthropomorphic response) in their interactions with the brands in social communities.[12]

Assuming the brand's persona is likeable and credible, it can facilitate **message internalization** (the process by which a consumer adopts a brand belief as his or her own). When it comes to likeability, brand mascots may be a perfect fit. In addition to physical characteristics, the dimensions of spokescharacter likability include personality, humor, and consumer experiences. All are dimensions that can serve as a foundation for engaging social media participation.[13]

What does it take to devise a good brand persona? Brand personas should be consistent with the brand's style guide. Social media are still components of an integrated marketing communications program and, as such, the decisions made for the brand's style guide still apply. The "voice" of the brand in social channels will need to be consistent, whether the approach is humanized, mascot, or corporate. The social media aspects of the style guide will enable multiple people to create content and converse with fans in the role of the brand. It will ensure that brand representation is consistent. It will include indicators like brand personality traits.

EXHIBIT 6.2

Hanka Steidle/Shutterstock.com

Travelocity's Roaming Gnome Stays in Character

Consider the Travelocity Gnome and its brand profiles. The Gnome is quirky, fun, and irreverent. He speaks with an accent and likes to go places! The Gnome wants to inspire people to see the world ... and potentially use Travelocity to do it. What's his story? He was kidnapped! One day he was a bored gnome on a lawn in England; the next, he was traveling all over the world with his kidnapper. Even after he was free, the Gnome enjoyed it so much that he just kept traveling.

https://twitter.com/RoamingGnome—@Roaming Gnome

The personality and fit with the brand overall are clear in all social media communications. Brian Solis, author of *Engage!*, recommends that brand managers build the brand's social media persona on a foundation of eight decisions:[14]

1   What are the brand's core values?
2   What are the brand's pillars, or social objects that illustrate these values?
3   What has the brand promised to its customers?
4   What are the brand's aspirational attributes?
5   What traits are associated with the brand?
6   What opportunities exist?
7   How does the brand align with the company's overall culture?
8   What stories can help bring the brand's personality to life?

There is a lot of clutter and fragmentation in social media. It can be hard for a brand's voice to be heard. There are several applications that can help brands analyze their social profiles and identify strengths, weaknesses, and opportunities. Some examples include Likealyzer, Fanpage Karma, and Cscore. The social vehicles also offer insights to aid page development.

Brand Participation and Friendvertising

The most social brands in the world might already be among your "friends." Many social network users like, friend, or fan brands. The most popular brands include Starbucks and Coca-Cola. And who could resist being friends with Oreo cookies? That's a friendship that lasts a lifetime! These brands maintain a social presence in online communities as they invite people to interact and share content related to the brand.

In the early years of social media marketing, brands joined social network sites as a supplemental way to reach their target audiences. Just as you see your friends' posts in your news feed, you also see the posts of brands you "like," "friend," or "follow." Brands simply had to get people to friend the brand and—voila!—brand messages would reach those people in their news feeds. Because brands don't pay SNS for their profiles and their posts, social media was perceived as a free media channel. Facebook defines the number of people you can reach for free by posting as **organic reach**. Brand participation in social network sites enables brands to share information about brand benefits and special deals, provide customer care, and build relationships by engaging in conversations with consumers in the community. Of course, these benefits aren't truly free—social media participation requires an investment of time. Still, compared to traditional advertising costs, participating in social communities is a low-cost supplement for brands to reach consumers.

Brands earn value in social media when they engage consumers over time (relationship marketing) and when they encourage consumers to interact with the brand and share those interactions with others. Brands stand to benefit from heightened brand loyalty among engaged consumers and a more expansive reach for brand-related messages. The **earned reach** (the breadth and quality of contact with users) gained when people share positive brand opinions and branded content with others is invaluable because of the influence attributed to individual, personalized brand endorsements. Does this lead to sales? Yes—75% of social media users report buying something they heard about on social media. We're talking about the power of word-of-mouth communication, as we discussed in Chapter 3. But first, how can brands grow their network of friends/followers/fans?

At a minimum, brands want consumers to friend, follow, or like the brand's social presence. Do consumers make friends with brands? According to Sprout Social, a leading social media management company, 86% of social media users have friended a brand. Social media relationships between brands and consumers are one of many factors that may influence purchase decisions, but active engagement in social channels is related to positive brand attitudes and purchase intentions.[15] When asked, 57% say they are more likely to buy from brands they've friended. Why do people friend brands? Figure 6.2 illustrates the top reasons. Perhaps it's not surprising to see that interest in brand products and a desire to find deals and incentives top the list. But 25% of people want a two-way dialogue with the brand. In other words, they want a relationship.

Post Content and Type

While a brand's friends are open to brand communications in social communities, brands need to carefully consider what they choose to post. Studies of brand activities and firm-generated content (FGC) in social communities suggest that many brands treat social media much as they would other forms of broadcast media, posting brand information and offers. Gallaugher and Ransbotham's 3M Model of social media dialogue management is useful for conceptualizing approaches to FGC. The 3Ms are Megaphone (company broadcast posts),

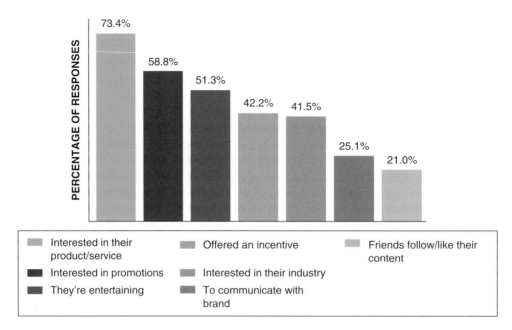

Figure 6.2   Why People Friend Brands on Social Media

Source: "Turned Off: How Brands Are Annoying Customers on Social," The Q3 2016 Sprout Social Index, Sprout Social, http://sproutsocial.com/insights/data/q3-2016/ (accessed June 18, 2017)

Reproduced by kind permission of Sprout Social, Inc.

Magnet (firm posts that invite consumer engagement), and Monitor (posts that reflect listening and responding to consumer conversations). To date, research suggests most brands use social media as a megaphone, overlooking the value of magnet and monitor posts.[16] Unfortunately, studies also clearly demonstrate that consumer engagement (in the form of likes, shares, and comments) is higher for brand posts that are interactive (e.g., posing a question) and consumer-focused, rather than brand-focused (i.e., audience-centric versus brand-centric).[17] For instance, a study of engagement effective for Facebook posts from 800 brands found that posts could be categorized as informative (e.g., product features and price offers) or persuasive (e.g., emotional or philanthropic). Informative content reduced engagement while persuasive content increased post engagement.[18] Even brand mascots are guilty! Their posts are primarily brand endorsements and shares/retweets of other user content.[19] Without persuasive messages, brands minimize the amplification effects they could generate if their audiences found the FGC worth sharing with others.[20]

Brands are using multi-media posts, especially photos and videos, to enhance post attractiveness and generate consumer engagement but media type and design aren't the only factors influencing consumer responsiveness.[21] The purpose of the FGC and its orientation (audience-centric or brand-centric) matter too.[22] The implication? Consumers don't want to see brand posts that they perceive to be simply another form of advertising. They want authentic, relevant content that relates to the community context of conversation and socialization.

Engagement is even stronger when brands incorporate experiences into their social media activity. Brands that incorporate experiential opportunities generate significantly higher levels of likes, shares, and comments.[23] This is why we emphasize the importance of identifying an experience as part of the social media strategic planning process in Chapter 4.

How are brands performing? The *State of Social Engagement Report* studied 85 brands across six social communities. According to the report, 95% of brands are stuck in "broadcast" mode, using social channels as a megaphone. Fewer than 40% of the brands studied ever asked questions of their followers or responded to their follower's comments to the brand. Only 2% of brands consistently responded to customers' posts.[24] Not only is this approach less effective, it can drive brand followers away. The top reason people give for unfollowing a brand in social media is too many promotional messages.[25]

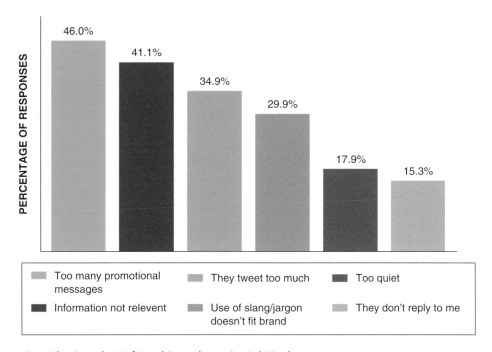

Figure 6.3   Why People Unfriend Brands on Social Media

Source: "Turned Off: How Brands Are Annoying Customers on Social," The Q3 2016 Sprout Social Index, Sprout Social, http://sproutsocial.com/insights/data/q3-2016 (accessed June 18, 2017)

Reproduced by kind permission of Sprout Social, Inc.

Brand Engagement

How do social network sites encourage participation and sharing by members? They make sharing engaging and they make it easy. Brands enhance participation by providing experiences for users that are worth participating in and telling others about. Experiences may involve any of the four zones, but the zone of social community is where conversations take place in and around the experiences.[26]

What does it mean to engage? People differ on their explanation of this. In all likelihood this is because engagement means different things. Just as being satisfied might mean being satisfied across a host of specific areas, being engaged may also mean being engaged in a variety of ways. Still, that's what we must do. Engagement is the very essence of social media. Without it, social media might as well be television. Engagement is the heart of it all.

A simple view of engagement is that of consumer response to FGC in social channels. While this is perhaps the least valuable form of engagement, even it is difficult for brands to accomplish. A study of popular brands on Facebook (including Tide, Cheerios, Honda, and others) calculated the percentage of the fan base that participated with the brand. Participation rates ranged from 1% to 7.35%, with an average participation rate of 3.70%.[27] As we learned, brands can do a better job of interacting and offering relevant FGC. Not all of the relevant factors are within a brand's control, though. Participation is also tied to privacy concerns, use of the Internet to search for information prior to purchase, use of social media for socializing and entertainment, and time spent on SNS.[28]

Engagement takes many forms. From a customer perspective, engagement means customers' behavioral manifestation toward a brand or firm, beyond purchase, resulting from motivational drivers.[29] How do customers behave when they are engaged? They may exhibit positive word-of-mouth behaviors, provide recommendations, help others make decisions. As we discussed in Chapter 3, word-of-mouth communication is critical for brands. It is perceived as trustworthy and credible, and substantially more so than advertising messages. A study of the impact of word-of-mouth communication and FGC for 60 brands found that WOM influenced brand equity, brand attitudes, and purchase intent, while FGC alone only facilitated brand attitudes.[30]

Brand engagement, of course, may encompass many levels from mild to evangelistic, and brands should seek to grow fans at the lower levels, investing in them so they become true fans. Brands can develop fans by helping them move from lower levels of engagement to higher ones. The higher the engagement the more positive outcomes for the brand in terms of positive word-of-mouth, enhanced perceptions of brand equity, and possibly sales. All of those positive benefits of engagement occur when brands are able to encourage people to become brand fans.

Brand Fans

Brands can purposefully cultivate **brand fans**. The word *fan* refers to a person who is enthusiastic about something or someone. Fans display their loyalty and affection for celebrities, sports teams, and musicians in the physical world when they buy T-shirts or other licensed products, join fan clubs, and flock to concerts or stadiums. In a social network, a similar display of loyalty may be as simple as clicking Facebook's "like" button and "joining" a sponsored page in the networking site. An online fan community is a **fandom**.

The brands with the strongest social followings around the world include:

- Coca-Cola
- Red Bull
- Converse
- Samsung Mobile
- Nike Football
- Playstation
- Starbucks
- Oreo
- Walmart

Curious how your favorite brand stacks up across the major social channels of Facebook, Twitter, YouTube? Visit www.socialbakers.com to search its free social statistics area.

For brands to truly leverage social networks as places to build relationships with customers, fan relationships should strive to mimic those found among strong fan communities such as Trekkers and Trekkies (members of the Star Trek fandom) and HOGs (fans of Harley Davidson). Random House's Figment is an example of an owned social community; it targets teens who love to read and write fan fiction. Fans who define their own individual identities at least in part by their membership in a fandom share five key characteristics:[31]

1 *Emotional engagement*: the object is meaningful in the emotional life of the fan. For example, members of Figment see fan fiction as a part of their self-concept and their membership in the social community as part of their social identity.

2 *Self-identification*: the fan personally and publicly identifies with like-minded fans. Figment members call themselves "figgies" and use #figgies when interacting on social media channels other than the Figment community platform.

3 *Cultural competence*: the fan has a critical understanding of the object, its history, and its meaning beyond its basic functionality. Figgies are fan fiction enthusiasts who know the development of the genre, the stories of successful fan fiction authors, and more.

4 *Auxiliary consumption*: the fan collects and consumes related items and experiences beyond the basic object. For figgies, items related to their favorite books, movies, and celebrities are desirable. Figgies might attend fan fiction conventions, going in costume!

5 *Production*: the fan becomes involved in the production of content related to the object. Figgies post their fan fiction stories on Figment where other fans can read, critique, and contribute to the stories.

Figment is considered one of the most successful brand communities. Despite the presence of all five fan characteristics, the weakness for Random House is that the fans are truly passionate about fan fiction—not about Random House. Brands that inspire brand love may experience more benefits than those who sponsor a community dedicated to a separate fan passion.

Are the fans being amassed by brands active in social networks true fans who define themselves by their participation in a brand community, or just brand users who are willing to acknowledge some affiliation with a brand? It's so easy to like, follow, or become a fan. Liking a brand is an easy, low-involvement step and it's one that frequently comes after exposure to an ad requesting a "like" as a call to action. Can these fans develop brand love? Maybe, but research suggests that brand fans join brand communities because they already like or love the brand, not the other way around.[32]

The **fan base** is an indicator of the brand's success in establishing a known presence within a community. But to build brand equity and lasting loyalty, brands need more than brand awareness and recognition or even brand affiliation. As brands embrace social media marketing, they acknowledge that a strong relationship exists between brand and customer when the customer has a high level of brand engagement.

We can think of engagement as a continuum. At one end, people may affiliate with a brand online simply because they want to acknowledge the brand. For example, you might affiliate with Oreos because you have a nostalgic connection to the brand based on childhood experiences. It doesn't mean that you plan to buy Oreos now or that you are otherwise engaged with the brand. At the other end, affiliates may want to interact with a brand in meaningful ways, perhaps even working with the brand to develop new products and services. Lego fans, for instance, are infamous for their high levels of brand engagement. Brands with strong fan bases even build museums for fan visits! Cadbury, Ben & Jerry's, Tabasco, Volkswagen, and Crayola have all provided a physical destination for passionate brand fans. And somewhere in between are fans who want special offers and find they benefit from branded content.

Why might people engage with brands? One possible reason is the aspirational value of brands in people's lives. Brands help people build their ideal selves and engagement with the brand online is a path to that self. In other words, the brand is a reflection of the fan's idealized self. That's just what PhaseOne Communications found in a study of 75 brands across six vertical markets. They concluded that users engage with brands based on how they wish to be perceived by their own social graph.[33] Research suggests that increasing brand knowledge and emotion increases the perceived value of the brand in the mind of the consumer. As a consumer's knowledge increases, so too does his or her emotional attachment to the brand.[34] Brands can also leverage fans to get new fans. Fan activity on social profiles can engage new fans.[35]

Level of engagement makes a big difference in terms of the buying decision process. One study specifically measured the value of being a brand's Facebook fan. It found that people spend about $72 more on a product for which they have a social network affiliation than for one they do not. Fans are also 28% more likely than non-fans to continue using a brand, and 41% more likely to recommend a fanned versus non-fanned product to a friend.[36] Fans in the study also said they felt connected to their brands.

Importantly, brands that use social media to develop a relationship with customers need to find ways to provide a **return on emotion** for the fans. Return on emotion conceptually assesses the extent to which a brand has delivered a value in exchange for the emotional attachment fans have awarded it.[37] Traditionally, the relationship between brand and consumer is asymmetric, with more effort invested by the fan. One industry study suggests that for brands to succeed as social friends to consumers, building heightened engagement and loyalty, consumers must feel that their efforts are reciprocated and the relationship is symmetric.[38] To do so, brands should socialize with fans and participate in conversations using a credible and authentic brand voice.

Ultimately, this social media marketing approach seeks to drive awareness and liking of brands while also building earned media. As we suggested earlier, brands should use social spaces to give consumers reason to share positive stories and product information. To encourage this, brands can offer branded assets such as downloads, shareable widgets and wallpapers, and invitations for consumers to co-create branded content. Brands should also be sure to provide value to the fans by using the branded page as an information hub to announce new products, company news, contests and promotions, and career opportunities. Perhaps most importantly, brands should respond to fan questions and posts. Let's take a look at three key strategies brands can use to engage consumers in their social communities: conversations, real-time marketing, and contests and requests for user-generated content.

EXHIBIT 6.3

Brand Profiles Create Presence and Opportunities for Engagement

Brands develop their profiles within the confines of the social vehicle. That's why a brand profile isn't truly owned media, which is under complete control of the brand. Still, brands can leverage the features of different social vehicles to develop a meaningful social presence. Zara is a good example. It posts often and focuses posts on fashion trends. It maintains a Lookbook app within the profile for fans to use to stay up to date on the latest styles. The interactive app includes photos and videos and is optimized for mobile.

f11photo/Shutterstock.com

The city of Philadelphia used this strategy to build its brand equity and awareness for tourism. The destination marketing organization (DMO) is called Visit Philly and its core mission is to bring more people to Philadelphia and encourage them to spend money during the visit! Visit Philly created profiles on Instagram, Twitter, Facebook, and Pinterest and linked those accounts with its owned media site at www.visitphilly.com. The presence is meant to build the brand equity of Philadelphia as a destination, increase (ad) impressions of the city to tourists, and influence tourists' desire to visit. Visit Philly focuses on the use of photography to spotlight its brand offering. As such, Instagram serves as the primary network for the brand's persona. Still, images are pushed out to Twitter, Facebook, and Pinterest too. A gallery of the best images and images provided by Philly fans organically is maintained on the website.

Visit Philly builds love on Instagram: http://instagram.com/visitphilly#

Conversations: Brands Talk

When we say "brands talk," we mean they talk! That's right. If brands want to engage consumers in conversation, they have to converse. Can this approach be effective? Apparently so. That is if the most popular brands on Twitter are any indication. Brands like Charmin, GE, and Major League Baseball delight Twitter followers with clever, witty banter and multi-thread conversations with fans.

And no one knows the power of conversation better than Taco Bell. It has used its social presence (yes, to even try to influence earned media, the brand must be present) to present itself as a hip and fun friend. While brand managers may worry that this kind of investment of resources won't result in sales, that doesn't seem to be an issue for Taco Bell, which reportedly sold 100 million Doritos Locos Tacos in the first 2½ months of sales—with, you guessed it, a launch via social media. How is Taco Bell managing this? Its social presence is humanesque and it starts conversations! These conversations could be with you, me, or any other follower, but they are entertaining and engaging! Take, for example, this exchange with @menshumor:[39]

@menshumor: "This morning I gave birth to a food baby and I think @tacobell is the father."

@tacobell: "I want a DNA test."

Real-Time Marketing (RTM)

What is real-time marketing? It's kind of like social media conversation on the fly. Brands post messages that resonate with the moment, whether that moment is planned or spontaneous. As we discussed earlier, brands can provoke conversation in social networks. With RTM, the brands leverage current events to do so. These messages have a short life-span. Heinz ketchup used its social media fan base to hijack Super Bowl advertising—garnering engagement while eschewing the $5 million ad placements during the big game. A few days before game day, Heinz launched a tongue-in-cheek campaign with the hashtag #SMUNDAY to petition for the Monday after the Super Bowl to be made a national holiday. The petition pointed out that on average 16 million people call in sick for work on the Monday after the Super Bowl. An RTM message is sometimes even shorter than the typical 30-second advert! But it works because of its timeliness and relevance.

EXHIBIT 6.4

Oreos' Tweet Sparked RTM Trend

Family Business/Shutterstock.com

What about a spontaneous example? Oreo is the king of RTM, perhaps even being the first brand to incite the use of this technique. During the 2013 Super Bowl, game play halted during an unexpected power outage. Oreo's digital agency, 360i, responded fast, tweeting a picture with the caption, "You can still dunk in the dark." Even though Oreo had no paid advertising during the broadcast, it was able to leverage the experience in real time to share its brand message.

Contests and Requests for UGC

Brands can seed many forms of content in social communities as they try to boost engagement and sharing. One of the most popular tools is the user-generated contest campaign (also known as a *UGC contest*). UGC campaigns offer a way for brands to invite consumers to engage and interact while they develop shareable content. The lexicon of online marketers includes many commonly used phrases and accompanying acronyms related to user-generated content, also known as consumer-generated media. Consumer-generated media (CGM) or UGC are the catch-all phrases for user content. User content is organic when its creation is motivated by an intrinsic intent on the part of its creator rather than incentivized or guided by the brand itself. Organic brand-oriented UGC, at least when promoting the brand in a favorable light, is valuable and suggests highly engaged customers. For example, a YouTube video espousing one's love for one's iPad is organic UGC—Apple didn't invite or incent the fan to create and post the content.

Is it effective? Studies show that user-generated social media communication positively influences brand equity and attitude toward the brand and contests are a tried and true method for generating that communication.[40] A comparison of movie ticket sales among groups who were exposed to a movie-themed microsite, a social media contest for the movie, or both, found that using both as a combined approach was most effective.[41]

A UGC campaign is sometimes called participatory advertising. Brands invite content, set mandatory guidelines and specifications, and possibly also provide participants with selected *brand assets* such as footage from prior commercials that ran on TV. Brands must pay attention to vehicle rules. Whether the campaign will run on Pinterest, Instagram, or Facebook, each vehicle has published guidelines. UGC contests encourage people in the target audience to develop and submit content related to the campaign. The content is then shared on social sites in the form of a gallery, which others can view and pass on to their respective networks.

UGC contests engage consumers and spread the message by leveraging consumer networks. It takes work to organize and oversee the process and promotion to activate these contests, but on the other hand they provide interesting content at a relatively low cost to the brand—especially compared to what professional advertisers charge to create commercials! Depending upon the contest design, UGC contests can also offer ways to engage different types of consumers—creators, joiners, conversationalists, and collectors. In addition, they provide content for journalists to include in stories about the brand, so ultimately this enhances a brand's public relations profile.

The most frequently used manifestation of UGC is the request for a personal story and/or photo. For example, in the Hanes campaign, "Undercover Color," women shared the color of their underwear on Twitter. The campaign fit with the brand's core product and also related to the target audience, because a woman's color choice is a reflection of her personality and mood. Another variation is the "create your own ad" contest, which has been used by numerous brands including Frito-Lay, Dove, and Chevy. Sponsors encourage submissions with incentives such as prize money or the chance for the winning entry to be broadcast on television.

Brand Social Communities

Ultimately, brands can develop and engage communities (called an **embedded brand community**) using existing SNS like Facebook or develop its own independent, online community (called an **online brand community** or OBC). Regardless of the approach, community management is a critical part of optimizing marketing outcomes. The *State of Social Engagement Report* scored 85 brands on the quality of their social community engagement including several categories: 1) cohesive social channel strategy, 2) active community management, 3) content mission, quality, and storytelling, 4) engagement and community relationship building, 5) collaboration with influencers, and 6) amplification efforts. Content missions were used to capture the value content provided to community members such as education, customer support, entertainment, philanthropy, special offer, or sales appeal. Community relationship building included communicating with members, responding to their posts and doing so quickly and effectively. Few brands in this study were truly engaging. In fact, 51 of the 85 brands scored ≤50% of the possible points. Only three brands scored above 80%: Spring, Pfizer's Meningitis Community, and AT&T. The bottom line? Brands can benefit from social media participation, and especially from brand communities. But brands have room for improvement to fully benefit from the organic value in the zone of social community.

Paid Media in Social Network Sites

Just as brands may advertise on websites throughout the Web, they may also choose to advertise within social communities. Marketers invest more than $32 billion per year on paid advertising in social network sites. Facebook captures nearly 70% of that ad spending.[42]

Organic brand impressions are more influential and credible than paid impressions. In a nutshell, people who see Facebook impressions organically are measurably more likely to take actions on the web.[43] So why are marketers investing in paid ads in social media? In a word—algorithms. Today, the algorithms SNS use to deliver content in member news feeds make it more difficult for brand messages to reach their fans. News feeds were once chronological, but over time, SNS began using algorithms to deliver news feed posts that are customized for each user. Facebook's algorithm is based on thousands of variables designed to assign a **relevancy score** for each piece of content that could be exposed to a user. For users, the result should be a better overall experience. You should see more of the type of content you've liked in the past from people and brands you've interacted with. Mark Zuckerberg explained: "Our goal is to build the perfect personalized newspaper for every person in the world."[44] According to Zuckerberg, the average Facebook member only sees about 100 posts a day on their news feed, even though more than a thousand posts are being contributed from our network during that time period.

This is bad news for marketers. What percentage of people will see organic posts? Studies suggest that organic reach may be as low as 2% and no higher than 16%.[45] In other words, even a brand with a million fans will only reach 20,000 of the fans with each post. Obviously, this makes it more difficult for brands to meet their reach objectives for marketing messages, but it also means less engagement—fewer likes, comments, shares and ultimately fewer conversions, leads, and customers. The situation is expected to worsen. Facebook has warned brands to expect zero organic reach in the near future.

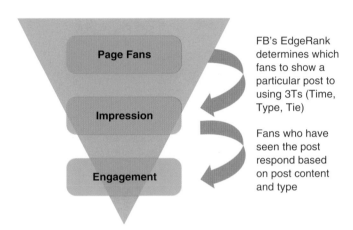

Figure 6.4   Understanding Organic Reach in SNS

That's the major reason companies are turning to paid media options in SNS. These ads may take the form of standard display or video ads, ads in mobile apps, or may be more integrated (and less intrusive) in the form of native advertising. Paid ads in social networks can be targeted using geographic segmentation, demographic segmentation, psychographics, and behavioral targeting. Remember the member profile data and behavioral data captured from social footprints? SNS use that data to provide advertisers with advanced targeting techniques. Facebook's targeting capabilities have gotten considerably better over the past few years. Marketers can reach their ideal target persona based on demographics, interests, web behavior, and more. Companies can merge email addresses from their customer databases and website visitor data to target social media users directly—an option called **custom audiences**. Facebook offers targeting of **lookalike audiences**, that match the characteristics of known customers. A popular technique is to use targeted ads to "retarget content," also called remarketing. People who have visited a company website before are served an ad for the product on Facebook. In addition to targeting, SNS provide tracking and effectiveness reports for advertisers. You'll learn more about these reports in Chapter 11.

Advertising Types

Display ads may include text, graphics, video, and sound, much like traditional print ads and commercials but they are presented on a website. Figure 6.5 presents an overview of the advertising options for the major SNS including pros and cons, cost per thousand

Social Advertising

	Facebook	Twitter	Instagram	LinkedIn	Pinterest	Snapchat	YouTube
Active Monthly Users	1.8 Billion	313 Million	600 Million	106 Million	150 Million	400 Million	150 Million
Average CPM	$7.19	$10	$5.68	$27	Based on CPC you set	$55–$100,000 campaign minimum	Varies between campaigns
Percent Millennials	41%	36%	34%	13%	67%	63%	34%
Pros	• Largest social network • Granular targeting capabilities	• People often tweet while watching TV • Advertisers can create combined TV and Twitter campaigns	• Large social network with strong millennial following • Works well for brands with strong imagery	• Ability to reach and target affluent, professional audience with accurate profile information	• Users create boards based on themes & are receptive to shopping • Can reach qualified audience while in research phase	• Users are engaged & typically must take an action to prompt an ad, or use a sponsored filter	• Pairs sight, sound and motion for a captive audience in a familiar format
Cons	• Cost of advertising is increasing • Can be hard to break through clutter	• Dose not have many targeting capabilities or ad positions	• On average, higher CPC and lower CTR than seen on Facebook	• Users do not login as frequently as they do other social networks	• Can only advertise via promoted pins	• High cost of entry • Ads are not shareable • No outbond linking	• Pre-roll can be seen as invasive • Inability to target specific videos
Options	• CPM or CPC based • Sponsored post in News Feed • Right side-rail ad positions	• Promoted tweets • Promoted accounts • Promoted trends	• Sponsored post	• Right side-rail ad position • Sponsored update in News Feed	• Promoted pins	• Sponsored stories • Sponsored filters • Post-roll ads	• Display ads • Video overlay ads • Pre-roll • Post-roll
Latest Developments	• Facebook just acquired Instagram, allowing you to buy cross-platform & run ads based on performance	• Allows targeting based on user search history outside of Twitter	• Add a blue call to action button • Sponsored posts to increase qualified traffic	• Recently launched tools that allow targeting outside of the platform	• Contemplating adding "buy" button that would allow for more seamless shopping on platform	• In-story ads are new • Recently became publicly traded, will likely see increase in advertising opportunities	• YouTube red, the new pay to play, ad-free platform • Skippable and non-skippable ads

Figure 6.5   Advertising Options for the Major SNS

(CPM), and specific options.[46] Whether the ads are text-oriented (e.g., a classified ad in a newspaper), text and graphics (e.g., a print ad in a magazine), or rich media (e.g., a television commercial), digital display ads are enhanced with a response device in that viewers can click the ads (called a clickthrough) to reach a target landing page. A landing page is the first page that a person sees when he or she clicks through an ad to reach a brand's target site. It's an important page for marketers, in that the content on the landing page will influence whether visitors stay at the site or move on to another page.

Display ads that are designed to have the look and feel of the website on which they are placed are known as native ads. eMarketer estimates that native advertising in social network sites will surpass $23 billion in 2018.[47] The Interactive Advertising Bureau (IAB) defines native advertising as "paid ads that are so cohesive with the page content, assimilated into the design, and consistent with the platform behavior that the viewer simply feels that they belong."[48] The advertising content is delivered "in-stream," as though it is organic content shared by members of the social network site. Because the ad content flows naturally alongside organic content on the social network site, it doesn't interrupt the user experience the way traditional advertising does. For this reason, native advertising is thought to be less irritating and more effective. Sponsored posts in Facebook, featured videos on YouTube, and promoted tweets in Twitter are examples. Though ad design is always evolving to leverage technological capabilities, current types of native advertising include in-feed, paid search, widgets, promoted listings, in-ad native elements, and custom.[49] Native ads can be evaluated on five characteristics using the IAB Native Advertising Evaluative Framework.[50] Each characteristic represents a continuum ranging from most to least harmonious given the context and capabilities of the website where the ad will be placed (see Table 6.1).

Table 6.1   IAB Native Advertising Evaluative Framework

Characteristic	Description	Degree of Harmony – High	Degree of Harmony – Low
Form	How does the ad fit with the overall page design? Is it in the viewer's activity stream?	In-stream ad delivery	Out-of-stream ad delivery
Function	Does the ad function the same as other types of content experienced on the site?	Matches site content	Does not match site
Integration	How well does the ad match the surrounding content in terms of behavior?	Mirrors site behaviors	Does not mirror site
Buying & Targeting	Is the ad placement targeted or run of network?	Narrowly targeted	Broadly targeted
Measurement	Is the ad designed for branding (and evaluated on engagement metrics) or direct response (evaluated on conversion metrics)?	Brand engagement metrics	Direct response metrics

Native advertising isn't unique to social media, or even digital media. Advertorials have long been a tactic used in print media to integrate paid ads with editorial content. Like advertorials, native advertising must be labelled with a disclosure that the content is an ad rather than organic content. Why? The Federal Trade Commission (FTC) Act prohibits deceptive practices, including advertising that misrepresents or omits information that is likely to mislead a consumer, acting in a reasonable situation.[51] Native ads seek to be harmonious with the context of the site in which the ad is placed. The result is essentially a disguise—the ad appears as though it is impartial content. As such, consumers may respond differently than they might if they know the content is sponsored. For this reason, the FTC developed a guide for businesses using native advertising.[52] The bottom line? Ads must be transparent. If the ad design disguises the ad's identity, a clear and prominent disclosure must be provided. A reasonable consumer should be able to distinguish what content is paid advertising and what is site content (whether editorial or organic, user-generated content). Common disclosures include labels such as "advertising, sponsored, brought to you by", and so on. Despite the use of disclosures, research suggests that most people cannot distinguish between native advertising and other site content. In one study, just 8% of participants recognized native ads, even though the ads were labelled. When participants recognized ads as such, they tended to evaluate the ad content more negatively.[53]

Enhancing Paid Ads with Sociality

Social ads are online display ads that incorporate user data in the ad or in the targeting of the ad and enable some form of **social interaction** within the ad unit or landing page. In these applications, user data are harnessed to deliver ad messages that are relevant to the recipients based on their characteristics and online behaviors. These ads often customize the ad content; they may even incorporate references to friends of the target. The ads are personalized using details from user profiles, images, relationships among users, data gathered from applications, and interactions within a user network. Like other online display ads, they incorporate a response device, enabling interested viewers to click through to a landing page (which could be the brand's social profile). Personalized social ads enhance perceived ad relevance, brand attitudes, click intention, and ad recall.[54] There are variations of social ads:[55]

1   A **social engagement ad** contains ad creative (image and text) along with an option to encourage the viewer to engage with the brand (e.g., a clickable "like" button or a link).

2   A **social context ad** includes ad creative, an engagement device, and personalized content.

3   **Organic social ads** are shared on a person's activity stream following a brand interaction (such as liking the brand). Organic social ads occur only after a brand interaction and are thought to carry enhanced credibility.

When organic social ads, also called **derivative branded content**, are triggered with social engagement or context ads, effectiveness improves. A limitation is that organic social ads occur only when community members have interacted with the brand's social ads, on the brand's own profile, or with some branded application or game. If few people choose to interact, few organic social ads will be generated.

Paid media is a valuable communication method for ensuring that target audiences are exposed to brand messages. The advertising communicates the message but the design enables social network users to engage with the ad and share the ad with their own social network. As such, the paid ad acts as a **seed**, capable of propagating additional impressions as it is shared. Of course, marketers can also seed social media marketing efforts in other ways as well.

Elements of Ad Design

Although advertising can include photos and videos, interactivity such as in-ad mini-games, links, and text, the typical Facebook ad includes six elements, as depicted in Figure 6.6.[56] The most popular type of ad on Facebook (75% of all Facebook ads) is the Page Post Link ad. The most popular words used in Facebook ads are you/your, free, now, and new.

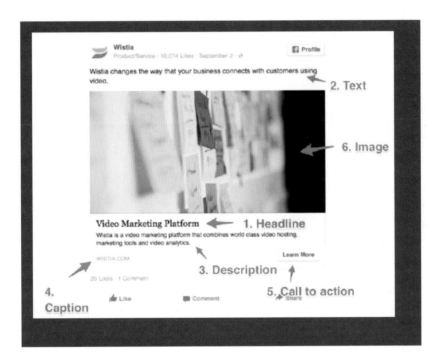

1. **Headline** – the main title of the ad, the headline must grab attention using fewer than 250 characters.
2. **Text** – a short preview description about the product or site.
3. **Description** – information about the brand, product, or offer.
4. **Caption** – a link to the brand's website URL.
5. **Call to action** (CTA) – a button showing people where they should click.
6. **Image** – an enticing picture related to the brand or product.

Figure 6.6   Elements of Facebook Ad Design

Source: Debra Garber, "How to Win at the Facebook Ads Game: Pros and Cons," DLVRIT, September 2016, https://blog.dlvrit.com/2016/09/facebook-ads (accessed June 18, 2017)

These words naturally attract audiences by emphasizing the consumer point of view, highlighting value, and suggesting urgency. Ads should include a call to action. The most popular CTAs are "Learn More," "Shop Now," and "Sign Up." The CTA invites the audience to interact with the ad, delivers interested customers to the brand's landing page, and provides a way to measure ad response.

CRITICAL REFLECTION

Guilt by Association: Facebook Live

When consumers see brand messages in social communities, several elements may influence their perceptions of the brand and the message and their response. The news feed posts near or around the brand message is one such element. For instance, the "emotional contagion" experiment, an experiment in which the news feeds of hundreds of thousands of Facebook users were systematically manipulated to increase or decrease their exposure to negative or positive messages. The results showed that user emotions and mood are affected by the sentiment expressed in the posts they see. The valence of the message influenced the sentiment users later expressed in their own posts. What effect might occur if Facebook users are exposed to a graphic crime in their news feed? Might their emotional response transfer to the brand, harming brand attitudes?

That's a risk brands will have to consider now that Facebook Live was used to live broadcast the gang rape of a young woman in Chicago.[57] As the attack streamed on Facebook, 40 users saw the post in their news feed and watched. Sadly, not one of the viewers reported the attack to the police. It's also not the first time Facebook Live has been used to publicize a crime. A few months earlier, attackers who brutally beat a disabled person streamed their crime using Facebook Live.

Media research suggests that message comprehension is influenced by the context of the vehicle and surrounding content. In fact, that's part of the logic behind using native advertising. Facebook Live is real-time streaming. With no delay to prevent inappropriate content, brands will have to consider carefully the potential impact of advertising on Facebook.

Ultimately, brands can achieve the most by including paid and earned media in their social media marketing efforts. Paid and earned media support each other and drive traffic to owned media. Figure 6.7 illustrates how paid and earned media work together in social media to promote brand messages. Recent research emphasizes the importance of brand participation in social communities as brands manage the interactions from multiple sources of brand information available to consumers. Google's ZMOT (Zero Moment of Truth) studies confirm that people may be exposed to numerous sources of information about a brand before they make a purchase. The sources include brand communications but also include information from word-of-mouth communication in social communities and news media. Advertising was once one-to-many but targeting and digital media make it possible for advertising to communicate one-to-one. At the same time, word-of-mouth has shifted from one-to-one communication to one-to-many, via social media. The interactivity and interdependence of information sources result in an **echoverse**, defined as "the entire communications environment in which a brand/firm operates, with actors contributing and being influenced by each other's actions."[58]

Feedback loops exist between all of the stakeholders in the brand's environment. As brands operate in the echoverse, they should utilize personalized social media communication to brand fans and customers.

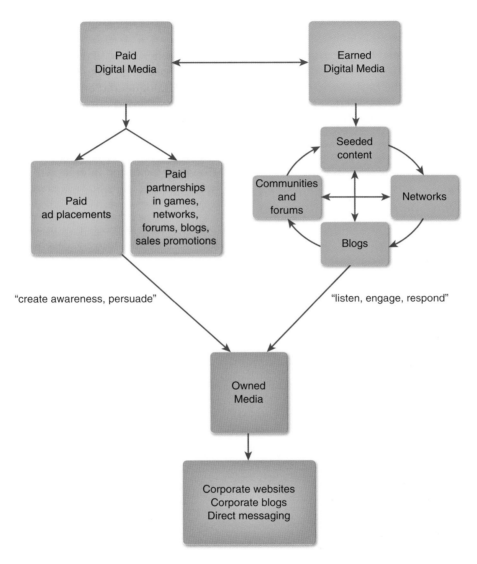

Figure 6.7   The Relationship Among Owned, Paid, and Earned Media

Is the Brand Ready for Social Relationships?

Clearly, there is a lot to be gained for brands operating in social media, and from friending customers in social networks.

Managers should ask these questions before deciding whether social relationships will work for a specific brand:

- Is the brand set up for engagement? Mark Kingdon, CEO of Organic, Inc., a digital marketing agency, said that "Brands have to allow for and anticipate dialogue, because consumers very much want to engage with brands and not all brands are set up for engagement. A lot of brands are simply set up to broadcast their message to an audience."[59] Some brands will be safer with one-way communication.

- If the traditional brand participates in social media, where should the brand be? Should the brand have its own dedicated social network space (e.g., Nike's Joga)? Or will the brand have the best chance of creating consumer dialogue and engagement by using an existing network such as Gather or Facebook? Is there a social network site that is well suited to the brand? For example, Purina is perfectly suited to advertising on Dogster, but its message may not be as effective on Glue.

- How can the brand's profiles be developed in such a way as to reflect the brand's personality? With what voice will the brand speak? How will the brand interact within the site?

- If "fan pages" exist among brand loyalists on social network sites, how can the brand leverage the fan sites to better meet its objectives?

- How can the brand integrate its social network presence into other campaign components? Integration may start with simple steps such as including a Facebook icon in other brand messages and develop into utilizing the social network for sales promotions such as coupon distribution and contest administration.

MINI CASE STUDY

Tito's Vodka Nurtures Brand Social Community

Vodka has been enjoying a rise in popularity thanks to a new generation of cocktail-oriented consumers. Riding that wave is Tito's, a mid-priced "handmade" and copper-kettle distilled vodka brand from Texas. Not long ago, Tito's was limited to bars focused on craft liquors. Now its sales surpass those of major brands like Ketel One.

Founded by Bert "Tito" Beveridge, brand awareness was built little by little as Tito visited bars and festivals, handing out samples and sharing the story of his handmade vodka. Given Tito's roots in one-to-one communication, perhaps it's not surprising that it markets its brand almost exclusively using a social community presence and engagement. The two-person team in charge of Tito's social media marketing uses Sprout Social for community management and listening. The listening enables the team to make decisions about their campaigns, including deciding on flavor profiles for its quarterly cocktail recipes.

Tito's fans are part of an embedded brand community, on Facebook, Instagram, and Twitter. The brand persona uses an image of the bottle's label and the handle @TitosVodka, but the brand's personality is clearly present in posts and replies to fans. Brand posts are designed to align with the culture of each site and norms of participation while engaging Tito's fans with conversation, interactivity, and relevant content. For instance, the "Fresh Start" campaign invites people who are searching for a new direction in life to take part in an exercise called "Line Down the Middle." On the left, participants write down what they love to do. On the right, they write what they are good at doing. Tito reminds participants that their future should be at the intersection of their passions and their talents. People are encouraged to share their exercise on social media using the hashtag #TitoMoment. Tito's stays true to its brand history too. Its "Meet the Maker" campaign on Facebook celebrates artisans of all kinds.[60]

Tito's claims to be the vodka for dog people and this brand association is reinforced with a branded playlist on Spotify featuring famous dog songs like "Hound Dog" and "Who Let the Dogs Out." Fans contribute UGC on Instagram, posting pictures of their dogs, using the hashtag "vodkafordogpeople." The only social object likely to generate more enthusiasm than dogs is babies.

ohrim/Shutterstock.com

The social media campaigns follow best practices for organic engagement. In an interview with Entrepreneur, Tito said, "Social media is a great platform for a word-of-mouth brand, because it's not just about who has the biggest megaphone." This vision is echoed by Tito's social media coordinator, Katy Gelhausen, who said, "We never viewed social media as another way to advertise ... We're on social so our customers can talk to us."[61] Dialogue and brand fan conversations are the brand's recipe for social engagement. The brand makes a promise to respond to fan comments and it is delivering! More than 80% of Tito's social media posts are replies to inbound messages from fans.

Results and Outcomes

Tito's sales and market share speak for its success using social media marketing, but engagement metrics do too. Its posts average more than 500 interactions each. The size of the brand community is growing. After Tito's launched its dialog approach to social media communication, engagement from fans increased 162% and organic impressions from fans sharing brand content rose 81%.[62] Community membership increased more than 10%. Its Facebook community is more than 70,000 members strong. On Instagram, Tito's Vodka reaches more than 40,000 followers and on Twitter, more than 50,000.

CHAPTER SUMMARY

How do social networking communities enable user participation and sharing?

People participate around experiences. Brands aid in this by providing experience strategies that relate to their marketing objectives. Social media networks provide a structure for social interactions. They focus on acquiring and maintaining relationships above all else. Conversation and collaboration are the principal activities in this zone, though we often converse and collaborate around content, whether provided by brands, users, or others. Brands encourage this participation through engagement.

In what ways can brands utilize social networking communities for branding and promotion?

Brands have three key ways of utilizing social networking communities for branding based around owned, earned, and paid media. Brands should develop a social presence in the chosen social networks.

This is not truly owned media but it is a brand's representation of itself in the social communities. They can encourage engagement especially among brand fans which may ultimately result in an embedded brand community. Brands can earn media by participating in dialogue, using real-time marketing, and creating opportunities to encourage user-generated content using techniques like contests. Brands can also create their own social community network. Lastly, brands can purchase paid advertising opportunities.

How can brands reach consumers organically using social network sites? What characteristics do brand fans exhibit?

Facebook defines the number of people you can reach for free by posting as organic reach. Brand participation in SNS enables brands to share information about brand benefits and special deals, provide customer care, and build relationships by engaging in conversations with consumers in the community. These benefits aren't truly free, as social media participation requires an investment of time, but compared to traditional advertising costs, participating in social communities is a low-cost supplement for brands to reach consumers. Brands may also encourage people to become brand fans. Brand fans are enthusiastic about something or someone. Fans display their loyalty and affection for celebrities, sports teams, and musicians in the physical world when they buy T-shirts or other licensed products, join fan clubs, and flock to concerts or stadiums. In a social network, a similar display of loyalty may be as simple as clicking Facebook's "like" button and "joining" a sponsored page in the networking site.

What forms of paid media can be used in social communities? Why is paid media important to social media marketers?

Just as brands may advertise on websites throughout the Web, they may also choose to advertise within social communities. As companies recognize the limits of organic reach and ad impressions, they are turning to paid media options in SNS. Paid media may take the form of standard display or video ads, ads in mobile apps, or may be more integrated (and less intrusive) in the form of native advertising. Paid ads in social networks can be targeted using geographic segmentation, demographic segmentation, psychographics, and behavioral targeting. SNS use member profile data and behavioral data to provide advertisers with advanced targeting techniques. Marketers can reach their ideal target persona based on demographics, interests, web behavior, and more.

REVIEW QUESTIONS

1   What social activities are the focus of participation in social communities?

2   How can brands create identities in social communities?

3   What are the types of social networks in social media?

4   What are the characteristics of social ads? How effective are social ads?

5   How can brands engage consumers in social communities?

6   What is earned media? How do brands encourage earned media with their social networking activities?

7   What are the characteristics of brand fans?

EXERCISES

1 Discussion: Should a social network own our social data? Is it an invasion of privacy for social networks to collect and use the information we leave as we deposit digital footprints in a site and around the Web?

2 Discussion: If one of your friends on a SNS shared multiple branded advertisements over the course of a day or week, would this change how you felt about that friend? Would you feel your privacy had been invaded somehow?

3 Discussion: Are Facebook friends the same as real friends? Are Facebook fans real fans? Explain.

4 Analyze a brand profile on Facebook. Consider Gallaugher & Ransbotham's 3M Model. Does the brand use social media for megaphone, magnet, and monitor posts? How engaging is each type of post?

5 Interview three people who are passionate about some interest. Document the time and resources they spend to engage with this object. Despite their passion for very different objects, what similarities or common patterns do you observe among them? Do they engage in this interest in social communities? Do you see the five characteristics of fans exhibited in their behavior?

 CHAPTER NOTES (access all weblinks listed here at: https://study.sagepub.com/smm3e)

1 For World Map of Social Maps Ranked Second, January 2017, see Vincos Blog, http://vincos.it/world-map-of-social-networks (accessed July 3, 2017).

2 "Nissan Launches 'N-Square' Internal Social Networking Site," Internal Comms Hub, November 17, 2007, www.internalcommshub.com/open/news/nissan.shtml (accessed December 20, 2010).

3 Mark Sullivan, "How Will Facebook Make Money?" *PC World*, June 15, 2010, www.pcworld.com/article/198815/how_will_facebook_make_money.html (accessed December 31, 2010).

4 Quoted in Marshall Kirkpatrick, "Facebook's Zuckerberg Says the Age of Privacy Is Over," Read Write Web, January 9, 2010, www.readwriteweb.com/archives/facebooks_zuckerberg_says_the_age_of_privacy_is_ov.php (accessed December 21, 2010).

5 Debra Aho Williamson, "Brand Interactions on Social Networks," eMarketer, June 2010, www.emarketer.com/Report.aspx?code=emarketer_2000694 (accessed December 20, 2010).

6 Josh Mendelsohn and Jeff McKenna, "Social Sharing Research Report," Chadwick Martin Bailey, September 2010, www.cmbinfo.com/cmb.../Social_Sharing_Research_Report_CMB1.pdf (accessed October 15, 2010).

7 Rebecca Walker Naylor, Cait Poynor Lamberton, and Patricia M. West, "Beyond the 'Like' Button: The Impact of Mere Virtual Presence on Brand Evaluations and Purchase Intentions in Social Media settings," *Journal of Marketing*, 76:6 (2012), 105–20.

8 Ronald J. Cohen, "Brand Personification: Introduction and Overview," *Psychology and Marketing*, 31:1 (2014), 1–30.

9   Lance Kinney and Jennifer Ireland, "Brand Spokes-Characters as Twitter Marketing Tools," *Journal of Interactive Advertising*, 15:2 (2015), 135–50.

10   Susan Fournier, "Consumers and Their Brands: Developing Relationship Theory in Consumer Research," *Journal of Consumer Research*, 24 (1998), 343–73.

11   Kuan-Ju Chen, Jhih-Syuan Lin, Jung Hwa Choi, and Jung Min Hahm, "Would You Be My Friend? An Examination of Global Marketers' Brand Personification Strategies in Social Media," *Journal of Interactive Advertising*, 15:2 (2015), 97–110.

12   Ibid.

13   Margaret Callcott and Barbara J. Phillips, "Observations: Elves Make Good Cookies: Creating Likable Spokes Character Advertising," *Journal of Advertising Research*, 35 (1996), 73–9.

14   Brian Solis, "The Social Media Style Guide," June 14, 2010, www.briansolis.com/2010/06/the-social-media-style-guide-8-steps-to-creating-a-brand-persona-2 (accessed June 30, 2010).

15   Alhabash Saleem, Anna McAlister, Chen Lou, and Amy Hagerstrom, "From Clicks to Behaviors: The Mediating Effect of Intentions to Like, Share, and Comment on the Relationship Between Message Evaluations and Offline Behavioral Intentions, *Journal of Interactive Advertising*, 15:2 (2015), 82–96.

16   Filiz Bozkurt Bekoglu, "Strategic Approach in Social Media Marketing and a Study on Successful Facebook Cases," *European Scientific Journal*, 12:7 (2016), 261–73.

17   Lisette De Vries, Sonja Gensler, and Peter S.H. Leeflang, "Popularity of Brand Posts on Brand Fan Pages: An Investigation of the Effects of Social Media Marketing," *Journal of Interactive Marketing*, 26:2 (2012), 83–91.

18   Dokyun Lee, Kartik Hosanagar, and Harikesh Nair, "The Effect of Social Media Marketing Content on Consumer Engagement: Evidence from Facebook," 2014, https://papers.ssrn.com/sol3/papers.cfm?abstract_id=2290802 (accessed June 17, 2017).

19   Kinneya and Ireland, "Brand Spokes-Characters as Twitter Marketing Tools."

20   Yu-Ting Chang, Hueiju Yu, and Hsi-Peng Lu, "Persuasive Messages, Popularity Cohesion, and Message Diffusion in Social Media Marketing," *Journal of Business Research*, 68:4 (2015), 777–82.

21   Ibid.

22   Lisa Spiller, Tracy Tuten, and Michelle Carpenter, "Social Media and its Role in Direct and Interactive IMC: Implications for Practitioners and Educators," *International Journal of Integrated Marketing Communications*, 3:1 (2011), 74–85.

23   Wondwesen Tafesse, "An Experiential Model of Consumer Engagement in Social Media," *Journal of Product & Brand Management*, 25:5 (2016), 424–34.

24   *The State of Social Engagement 2016*, Report, *Lithium*, www.lithium.com/download?p=/pdfs/whitepapers/Lithium-the-state-of-social-engagement-2016_k8IG3ISe.pdf (accessed June 18, 2017).

25   "The Social Generations: Millennials Ask, Gen X Buys & Baby Boomers Observe," The Q1 2017 Sprout Social Index, Sprout Social, http://sproutsocial.com/insights/data/q1-2017 (accessed March 15, 2017).

26   Christian Crumlish and Erin Malone, *Designing Social Interfaces* (Sebastopol, CA: O'Reilly Media, 2009).

27   Ashish Kumar, Ram Bezawada, Rishika, Ramkumar Janakiraman, and P.K. Kannan, "From Social to Sale: The Effects of Firm Generated Content in Social Media on Customer Behavior," *Journal of Marketing*, 80:1 (2016), 7–25.

28   Ibid.

29   J. Van Doorn, Kay Lemon, V. Mittal, S. Nass, D. Pick, P. Pirner, and C. Verhoef, "Customer Engagement Behavior: Theoretical Foundations and Research Directions," *Journal of Service Research*, 13:3 (2010), 253–66.

30   Bruno Schivinski and Dariusz Dabrowski, "The Effect of Social Media Communication on Consumer Perceptions of Brands," *Journal of Marketing Communications*, 22:2 (2016), 189–214.

31   Robert Kozinets, "Brand Fans: When Entertainment and Marketing Intersect on the Net," in Tracy Tuten (ed.), *Enterprise 2.0: How Technology, E-Commerce, and Web 2.0 Are Transforming Business Virtually* (Santa Barbara, CA: Praeger Publishers, 2010), pp. 145–66.

32   Leslie K. John, Oliver Emrich, Sunil Gupta, and Michael I. Norton, "Does 'Liking' Lead to Loving? The Impact of Joining a Brand's Social Network on Marketing Outcomes," *Journal of Marketing Research*, 54:1 (2017), 144–55.

33   Tom Troja, "Social Is About Aspirations: How to Get People to Aspire to Your Brand," iMedia Connection, May 8, 2012, http://blogs.imediaconnection.com/blog/2012/05/01/social-is-about-aspirations-how-to-get-people-to-aspire-to-your-brand (accessed June 15, 2013).

34   N. Sinha, V. Ahuja, and Y. Medury, "Corporate Blogs and Internet Marketing: Using Consumer Knowledge and Emotion as Strategic Variables to Develop Consumer Engagement," *Database Marketing and Customer Strategy Management*, 18:3 (2011), 185–99.

35   B. Jahn and W. Kunz, "How to Transform Consumers into Fans of Your Brand," *Journal of Service Management*, 23:3 (2012), 344–61.

36   "The Value of a Facebook Fan: An Empirical Study," Syncapse, June 2010, www.brandchannel. com/images/papers/504_061810_wp_syncapse_facebook.pdf (accessed December 20, 2010).

37   Anna Farmery, "What Is Your Return on Emotion?" The Engaging Brand Blog, July 2009, http://theengagingbrand.typepad.com/the_engaging_brand_/2009/07/what-is-your-return-on-emotion. html (accessed December 31, 2010).

38   "Fluent: The Razorfish Social Influence Marketing Report," Razorfish, 2009, http://fluent.razorfish. com/publication/?m=6540&l=1 (accessed December 21, 2010).

39   Ann Handley, "Marketing Trend for 2014: Smaller Messaging Has a Big Impact," Entrepreneur. com, www.entrepreneur.com/article/229806 (accessed August 29, 2014).

40   Schivinski and Dabrowski, "The Effect of Social Media Communication on Consumer Perceptions of Brands."

41   Emily Mabry and Lance Porter, "Movies and Myspace: The Effectiveness of Official Websites versus Online Promotional Contests," *Journal of Interactive Advertising*, 10:2 (2014), 1–15.

42   "Facebook Gets Strong Majority of World's Social Ad Spending," eMarketer, July 25, 2016, www. emarketer.com/Article/Facebook-Gets-Strong-Majority-of-Worlds-Social-Ad-Spending/1014252 (accessed June 18, 2017).

43   Jim Tobin, "New Research: Organic Facebook Impressions Lead to a 76% Increase in Brand Website Visits," *Ignite*, January 10, 2012, www.ignitesocialmedia.com/social-media-stats/new-research-organic-facebook-impressions-lead-to-increase-brand-website-visits (accessed June 18, 2017).

44   Lindsay Kolowich, "How the News Feed Algorithms Work on Facebook, Twitter & Instagram," Hubspot, April 14, 2016, https://blog.hubspot.com/marketing/how-algorithm-works-facebook-twitter-instagram#sm.0004b7ol91cduds6tlj2qb4zw13aj (accessed June 18, 2017).

45   Tobin, "New Research: Organic Facebook Impressions Lead to a 76% Increase in Brand Website Visits."

46 Based in part on Maija Palmer, "How Social Media Sites Compare as Advertising Platforms," *Financial Times*, 2015, www.ft.com/content/91a471be-ea87-11e4-96ec-00144feab7de (accessed June 18, 2017).

47 "eMarketer Unveils Estimates for Native Ad Spending," eMarketer, March 21, 2017, www.emarketer.com/article/eMarketer-Unveils-Estimates-Native-Ad-Spending/1015457 (accessed June 18, 2017).

48 Bartosz W. Wojdynski and Nathaniel J. Evans, "Going Native: Effects of Disclosure Position and Language on the Recognition and Evaluation of Online Native Advertising," *Journal of Advertising*, 45:2 (2016), 157–68.

49 Ibid.

50 "The Native Advertising Playbook," *Interactive Advertising Bureau*, December 4, 2013, www.iab.com/wp-content/uploads/2015/06/IAB-Native-Advertising-Playbook2.pdf (accessed June 18, 2017).

51 "Native Advertising: A Guide for Businesses," Federal Trade Commission, www.ftc.gov/tips-advice/business-center/guidance/native-advertising-guide-businesses (accessed June 18, 2017).

52 Ibid.

53 Wojdynski and Evans, "Going Native: Effects of Disclosure Position and Language on the Recognition and Evaluation of Online Native Advertising."

54 Freya De Keyzera, Nathalie Densb, and Patric De Pelsmacker, "Is This for Me? How Consumers Respond to Personalized Advertising in Social Network Sites," *Journal of Interactive Advertising*, 15:2 (2015), 124–34.

55 Jon Gibs and Sean Bruich, "Advertising Effectiveness: Understanding the Value of a Social Media Impression," Nielsen Company and Facebook, April 2010, http://uk.nielsen.com/site/documents/SocialMediaWhitePapercomp.pdf (accessed December 21, 2010).

56 Massimo Chieruzzi, "The Science of Successful Facebook Ads," AdEspresso, February 29, 2016, https://adespresso.com/academy/ebook/the-science-of-successful-facebook-ads (accessed June 18, 2017).

57 Aamer Madhani, "Suspected Gang Rape of Chicago Teen Streamed on Facebook Live," *USA Today*, March 21, 2017, www.usatoday.com/story/news/2017/03/21/chicago-gang-rape-teen-streamed-facebook-live/99447884 (accessed June 18, 2017).

58 Kelly Hewett, William Rand, Roland T. Rust, and Harald J. van Heerde, "Brand Buzz in the Echoverse," *Journal of Marketing*, 80:3 (2016), 1–24.

59 E. Steel, "Using Social Sites as Dialogue to Engage Consumers, Brands," *Wall Street Journal*, November 8, 2006.

60 Tanya Dua, "The Recipe for Tito's Killer Social Media Cocktail," Digiday UK, February 12, 2016, http://digiday.com/marketing/recipe-titos-killer-social-media-cocktail (accessed June 18, 2017).

61 "Tito's Handmade Vodka Establishes Brand Loyalty with an Authentic Social Strategy," Sprout Social, http://sproutsocial.com/insights/case-studies/titos (accessed February 17, 2017).

62 Ibid.

7

Social Publishing

Learning Objectives

When you finish reading this chapter, you will be able to answer these questions:

1 What are the channels of social publishing?

2 Who creates the content published in social channels? What kind of content can be published?

3 What content characteristics enhance perceived content quality and value? How can marketers plan and organize their efforts as they embrace a social publishing strategy?

4 What is the role of social publishing in social media marketing? How do social media marketers utilize search engine optimization and social media optimization to meet marketing objectives?

5 How can social content be promoted? What role do social news and social bookmarking sites play in content promotion?

The Social Publishing Zone

In this chapter, our focus shifts to the second zone of social media, as shown in Figure 7.1. Social publishing is the production and issuance of content for distribution via social publishing sites. Content is the unit of value in a social community, akin to the dollar in our economy. It provides a social object for community participation. Social publishing sites aid in the dissemination of content to an audience by providing a digital location for content while also enabling audience participation and sharing. Social publishing empowered content creators to expose their creative works (user-generated content) to the world and build an audience without the barriers present in traditional publishing models. As social media has evolved, so too has the social publishing ecosystem. Individual users range from amateur to professional. Traditional media organizations like magazines and newspapers use social publishing to promote their products and drive traffic to their owned media sites. Organizations use social publishing to disseminate information to their stakeholders. And, of course, social publishing is an essential distribution channel in brand content marketing efforts. Brands value social publishing for its ability to communicate a variety of information, reach and attract audiences, reach an extended audience through peer-to-peer sharing, capture audience feedback, identify prospective customers, and support other marketing efforts including search engine optimization.

The channels of social publishing include blogs, media sharing sites, social network sites, and social bookmarking and news sites. Blogs are websites that host regularly updated content. Media-sharing sites include video-sharing sites such as YouTube, Vimeo, and Ustream; photo-sharing sites such as Flickr and Instagram; audio-sharing sites such as Podcast Alley; and document-and presentation-sharing sites such as Scribd and SlideShare. Increasingly, social sites enable multi-media—e.g., Snapchat users can snap photos and video. You can see that some of the vehicles used for social publishing are social network sites that facilitate relationships in the zone of social community. This is particularly true for Facebook, which, as a social utility, provides functionality across all four zones of social media. The vehicle is not the defining element of social publishing; rather, it is the sharing of knowledge via content in an environment that also enables discourse and other forms of participation.

In this chapter, you'll learn some basic principles of content creation and distribution; how marketers can design content for search engine and social media optimization; and how to promote social content using social media press releases, microblogs, and social news and bookmarking sites.

Publishing Content

Content marketing has evolved as a core aspect of marketing communications. According to the Content Marketing Institute, content marketing is a "strategic marketing approach focused on creating and distributing valuable, relevant, and consistent content to attract and retain a clearly defined audience—and, ultimately, to drive profitable customer action."[1] The philosophy of content marketing emphasizes that brands should publish high-value content that pulls the audience in. The content may be published in owned, paid, or social media channels but regardless, social media should be used to activate the content and drive audience engagement, conversation, and amplification through sharing.

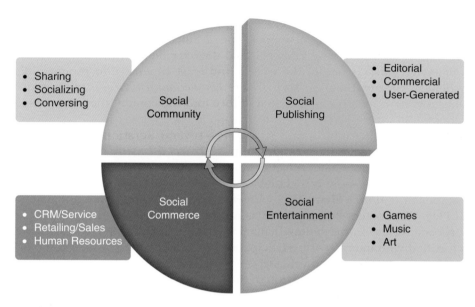

Figure 7.1   The Social Publishing Zone

Types of Content

The types of content published online, and shared via social media, include an enormous range of material. Some examples include research, instructions, opinions, essays, poetry, fiction, information, fashion photos, advice, art, or photos from that wild party last week. It may be curated or original. Social media content may begin with content published for some other purpose, such as a broadcast commercial, entertainment film, or news story that is repurposed for social publishing. Or the content may be entirely original contributions that community members produce and publish. Ideally, social media content should do more than repurpose offline content for digital display, although we often do find this kind of "secondhand content" on some sites. Note that we distinguish the meaning of content for social publication from that of content shared in the zone of social community, such as comments, photos, announcements, and other posts shared in social communities.

Content appears in a variety of different formats such as:

- blog posts and feature articles
- press releases
- white papers, case studies, and ebooks
- newsletters
- videos (prerecorded and live)
- webinars and presentations
- podcasts
- photos
- infographics.

Content can be any of these and more. Developments in technology are enhancing existing forms of content and creating new ones. For instance, virtual reality applications have resulted in "immersive video," also known as 360-degree video. Of the many forms of virtual reality, immersive video is one of the easiest and least expensive to produce, distribute, and experience. Already, the *New York Times, The Economist, National Geographic*, and other publishers have incorporated virtual reality into the content they are publishing for social media.[2]

Content is increasingly multi-layered; it offers several iterations and/or applications based on the primary piece. For instance, suppose *Travel & Leisure* magazine publishes an article on fashionable solutions to travel clothing dilemmas. The online magazine site also publishes the article, but now it includes several social features including a 360-degree video, a comment option, a Share This widget, a bookmarking option, and a game called Pack and Play. The content began its life as a piece of content in the traditional press. It was repurposed for use in the online magazine. But it didn't become social until the content was fortified with interactivity, participation, and shareability. Note too that the social components of the content added value to everyone connected to the content. The original publisher gained additional readers through the sharing option and enhanced the stickiness of the site (making the site more attractive to online advertisers) because it offered social features. The readers were able to better use the information in the article because they could share it, store it for later reference, and practice the tips offered in the Pack and Play game application.

Figure 7.2 provides a breakdown on the most popular types of content brands use for social publishing, along with key information on the best channels to use and the difficulty level to create or cost to outsource production.

Channels of Content Distribution

Content needs an audience. To reach an audience, publishers need a distribution channel strategy. Where will the content be published? Not only will the content live in this digital location, social media promotion of the content will drive people to its venue. Here we review the typical types of channels chosen. Keep in mind that different forms of content lend themselves to specific channels.

Blogs

Blogs began (in 1994!) as simple online logs posted in reverse chronological order, and developed into a widely used publishing venue for individual and corporate use. With hundreds of millions of blogs in existence, blogging is clearly a publishing venue here to stay. However, blogging has evolved: once a way to simply share opinions, activities, and experiences via text postings, today many blogs include information of all kinds expressed with multi-media. When video is prevalent, they are known as vlogs. Blogs are primarily owned media. The blogger controls the website and the blog's content. However, some social media vehicles enable a form of blogging that does not fall into the owned media category. For instance, Tumblr enables blogging within the Tumblr social network. Bloggers may be hobbyists, part-timers, corporate bloggers, or self-employed bloggers. Many of the influencers with celebrity status are bloggers. To learn more about the history of blogging, read the blog post, "A Brief Timeline of the History of Blogging" by Hubspot, a company specializing in inbound marketing and sales software (yes—a blog post about blogging!).[3]

Content Type	Description	What	Benefits	Sweet Spots	Cost to Outsource	Difficulty	Power Tips
Blogs	Most content marketers think of the blog as the cornerstone of their content marketing; a company blog allows for a subjective point of view	An online hub for opinion pieces, advice, listicles, checklists and more	Search rankings, thought leadership, community building, subscription growth	Company website	Low to moderate	Easy to start, challenging to maintain	Marry keyword strategy and storytelling, write magnetic headlines, and feature interesting images
Articles	Address issues your audience faces with an objective writing style	Helpful, informative lessons	Search rankings, thought leadership	Company website, guest posts	Low to moderate (often prices by length)	Low	Solicit ideas and drafts from subject matter experts, address common problems and feature interesting images
Infographics	Most people love infographics	Visual representation of data, lists, ideas and stories	Great potential to be shared, communicate information in a small space	Blog, Pinterest, SlideShare	High	High, requires design expertise	Secure posts with infographics, keep it simple, and offer code to embed the infographic
Videos	Videos have become a dominant force in content marketing	Styles include how-to, animation, documentary, demonstrations, and more	High engagement and conversion; appeals to mobile users	YouTube, Vimeo, blog	Usually high	Ranges from easy to demanding	Make them fun and human, ensure audio quality is high, and publish full or partial transcripts for SEO
Podcasts	Currently booming in popularity, but remain under-utilized	Audio program, like radio segments	Appeals to mobile users	Blog, iTunes and other podcast networks	Moderate to high	Time intensive	Establish a regular schedule, hire for voice skills, invest in quality recording equipment
Case Studies	Powerful sales enablement tool	True story of client success; usually text	Credibility booster	Website, blog	Moderate	Time intensive	Include specific information, conduct interviews for quotes, and repurpose other formats (i.e., podcast and video)

(Continued)

Figure 7.2   (Continued)

Content Type	Description	What	Benefits	Sweet Spots	Cost to Outsource	Difficulty	Power Tips
E-Books	Versatile, powerful and can serve many purposes over a long period of time	Multi-page documents with generous use of graphics	Thought leadership	Offers on key pages; often gated (form required);	High	Time and research intensive	Plan to extract key elements and repurpose, include research, include insights of industry leaders
White Papers	A good fit for complex product categories	Deep educational content	Thought leadership	Offers on key pages; often gated (form required);	High	Time and research intensive	Plan in advance to extract key elements and repurpose, include research, include insights of industry leaders
E-Newsletters	Package timely and topical content for prospects and customers who have granted you permission to send them email	Email with consolidated stories and links	Lead nurturing	Applicable to all devices and receptive audiences	Moderate	Easy; usually based on existing content	Promote other content, be brief
Quizzes	Proven to be popular, especially with younger demographics	Fun, interactive tests, assessments, etc.	High engagement	Blog, social media	Moderate	Can be demanding	Use simple formats, e.g. multiple choice, deliver scores/ conclusion, and make highly visual
Visual Content for Social Media	May be an illustration, photograph, or collage created or chosen to attract social media users	Images with captions, quotes and/or headlines	Highly shared by avid social media users	Pinterest, Facebook, Instagram	Low	Low	Format separately per social channel, choose images with stopping power, and experiment with writing styles

Figure 7.2   Content for Social Publication—Form, Channel, and Execution

Source: based in part on information reported in Barry Feldman, "Types of Branded Content," Feldman Creative, February 5, 2016, http://feldmancreative.com/2016/02/types-of-branded-content (accessed June 20, 2017)

Blogs offer an opportunity for individuals to express their opinions, share their expertise, make money by selling on-site advertising, and attract clients for consulting work. They also offer opportunities for organizations to establish thought leadership on a topic, increase traffic to targeted websites such as an organization's e-commerce site, build links to other corporate sites, and build brand awareness.[4] For example, Heather Armstrong's blog, *Dooce*, established her as a creative writer capable of providing her readers with insight and amusement into the life of a typical woman.[5] David

Armano's *Logic + Emotion* blog grew his reputation as a visual thinker and experience designer.[6] Blogging may be an outlet for creative expression but can also be a business! As influencers, the top bloggers in the world earn hundreds of thousands of dollars each month from on-site advertising, affiliate marketing, and brand sponsorships and endorsements. In fact, one of the best sources of information on social media marketing strategies, *Mashable*, is a blog. Its founder, Pete Cashmore, is among the top earning bloggers in the world with revenues estimated at $600,000 per month. The blog began in Cashmore's bedroom in Scotland when he was just 19.[7] Another favorite blog is *Dogshaming*. This popular blog publishes images of dogs (like the picture of Chloe shown in photo 7.1) who have misbehaved. The images are submitted by its readers and so are based on user-generated content.

Media-Sharing Sites

Like blogs, media-sharing sites enable individuals and organizations to publish content online. However, whereas blogs are typically in the realm of owned media, media-sharing sites are earned media because their environments are not directly controlled by the person or organization posting the content. Instagram, Pinterest, and YouTube are all media-sharing sites. Often, the choice of which media-sharing site to use is dictated by the type of content to be distributed. The style of content should be customized for the site's personality. Some media-sharing vehicles are serious, others quirky.

EXHIBIT 7.1

Ford Social Connects its Social Publishing Channels

Ford maintains a corporate hub for its social media content called Ford Social, but video content is shared on its YouTube channel, photos are shared on its Flickr photostream and on Instagram, fact sheets and other corporate content are shared on Scribd, and news is shared on its Twitter feed.

(Continued)

(Continued)

Reviews, covered in Chapter 9, are also a form of content that can be published using media-sharing sites. Media-sharing sites like Pinterest and Instagram may be used to drive sales as well as customer engagement.

Visit: http://social.ford.com

Chuck Wagner/Shutterstock.com

Content Producers: What Is "Authentic"?

Content can take so many forms that it's sometimes difficult to categorize. This is especially true in the online world, where the lines between what is real and what is not become increasingly blurred. For example, people often share YouTube clips of outrageous or racy commercials with their friends—but in many cases these spots were not produced by the company (sorry to disappoint you). In fact, the proliferation of untruths and exaggerations (or so-called **urban legends**) is so widespread that specialized websites do nothing but verify or refute them. The website Snopes.com is the best known of these.

This ambiguity also exists when we try to identify the sources or distributors of content. At one time, it was easy to classify a message as either journalistic, editorial, or commercial. A journalistic message reports on facts in an objective and unbiased fashion. In an editorial message, the source expresses an opinion or interpretation along with the factual information. The most obvious example is the editorial page of a newspaper, where a writer presents an argument that may criticize a government, a company, or a politician. This section of the paper is clearly marked as editorial. In contrast, a commercial message such as an advertisement makes it clear that the intent is to persuade the reader or viewer to change an attitude or behavior; the source has paid a fee to place the message in a medium. So, it's obvious in a traditional newspaper that a half-page plea, say, to pass environmental legislation or carry out sanctions against governments that permit whaling, is sponsored and paid for by an identifiable organization.

For news and educational content, traditional press organizations hire journalists to research, verify, and write credible, objective, trustworthy stories. These media outlets then deliver that content to a paying audience via newspapers, newsletters, magazines, and radio and television programs. The traditional press controlled the message and the channel, but it adhered to accepted industry guidelines and norms. Similarly, traditional entertainment companies or production houses created and distributed their own content. Broadcast networks commissioned the development of programs and movies they showed on the stations they owned. And the transition from editorial to commercial content was clear with broadcast announcements like "And now a word from our sponsors," or labelling content as "advertorial."

Increasingly these lines are blurring and, as a result, the authenticity and trustworthiness of messages published and shared through social media (and, for that matter, other forms of media as well) may not be clear to consumers. For instance, journalism today includes both the objective storytelling of the results of investigative reporting as well as the subjective storytelling of interpretive journalism. Interpretive journalism blurs the line between editorial messages and journalism in that it goes beyond the basic facts of an event or topic to provide context, analysis, and possible consequences. The development of native advertising, which we introduced in Chapter 6, blurs the line between organic posts and paid posts in social media.

Though content from traditional media sources is still valuable, today these sources struggle as consumers increasingly turn to other places to access their news and entertainment. People no longer need to subscribe to the local newspaper in order to get credible news. Instead they can read email, Twitter posts, blogs, and updates to social network sites, all from their smartphones. Some estimates suggest that more than 60% of adults get their news from social media.[8] This seismic shift has forced the closing of media providers around the world as they fail to find new ways to monetize their businesses. Major newspapers such as the *San Francisco Chronicle* have closed, while other traditional media vehicles merge with online companies—for example, the venerable print magazine *Newsweek* was acquired by *The Daily Beast*. Other traditional content providers adapt to the new media environment as they shift from delivering their messages on a printed page (or, as some new media people like to say, "dead trees") to mobile applications. *Gourmet* responded by evolving into the first mobile magazine. It closed operations due to declining subscriptions and ad revenues. *Gourmet Live* instead delivers articles to foodies on their mobile phones. But, unlike the old dead tree delivery system, this content is also social—subscribers can interact, share, and play games within the application.

In addition to a blurring of the lines between editorial and commercial messages, today we witness an explosion of user-generated content—which, as we've seen, is the lifeblood of emerging social media. In many cases, everyday people create and post this content for personal reasons rather than to receive financial reward. A proud father shoots video of his son's high school graduation and shares it with the family. An expecting young mother chronicles the story of her pregnancy and birth. A retired couple keeps a photo log of their yearly trips where they explore the world together.

What's new about this consumer-generated content? In one sense, absolutely nothing! People throughout history have written stories, commissioned portraits, kept diaries, and more recently taken photos and videos of family events. What is new is that due to the Social Media Value Chain, people can share this content with those beyond their immediate area. Today they post photos to Flickr or perhaps a less-than-flattering video from last night's raucous party on YouTube. This content is largely shared in the context of social communities (zone 1), but it is also published content, crossing into the realm of zone 2.

In terms of the content itself, UGC is perceived as authentic because it is assumed to represent the views of the creator. The subject matter of UGC may be virtually anything, including content related to brands. Brands and consumers can benefit from UGC; it may facilitate awareness, desire, and the choice to purchase or not. You may stumble upon this content while you search for specific information about a product or brand, discovering it accidentally. And, because of the power of social media, these inputs may well impact what others think or even change a firm's marketing activities. In this form of **cultural co-creation**, co-created meanings (among both producers and consumers) fold back into the culture. In fact, it is the influence of UGC on brand image that has led marketers to conclude that brand meaning is now co-created—whether brands like it or not! Some brands have embraced co-creation, finding ways to involve consumers. The prevalence of "share your story" campaigns are a manifestation of brand co-creation.

Intrinsic and Extrinsic Motives and Content Authenticity

It's useful to distinguish between UGC that people voluntarily publish and content that appears because some organization has invited contributions from users. **Organic content** is content that a person feels intrinsically motivated to prepare and share. People tend to view organic content as authentic and trustworthy. In the early days of social media, most content was organic content contributed by regular people (users). Just as crowdsourcing has been used to accomplish challenging tasks, brands can benefit from crowdsourced content. **Consumer-solicited content (CSC)** refers to invited but non-compensated **citizen advertising**, which is another way to describe marketing messages that actual consumers create. Sometimes marketers call this approach participatory advertising; brands invite submissions, set mandatory guidelines and specifications, and possibly provide partici-pants with selected brand assets such as footage of the brand in use or logos and former commercials. **Incentivized content** is encouraged by the offer of an *incentive*, such as the chance to win a contest, receive free merchandise, or even earn cold hard cash. In these cases the contribution is a response to a **call to action (CTA)**. This term refers to a direct request in a marketing message for a specific behavior. You've observed a similar technique in TV infomercials, where a host reminds you to "Call right now. Operators are standing by!" That's a call to action. In social media marketing, calls to action ensure that people participate in the social media campaign. Perhaps the most famous example is the Crash the Super Bowl contest sponsored by Doritos and Pepsi, which gave citizen advertisers the chance to win $1 million and see their ad on air. One winner, called "Time Machine," cost just $300 to make. The approach paid off for Doritos in terms of ad effectiveness, with user submissions landing among the top ten ads shown for memorability and likeability. That's pretty impressive when you remember that the Doritos spots were "homemade" and cost so little to create.

Sponsored content refers to *paid* content. People are paid for their content creations, and brands may actively seek out influencers like bloggers, videographers, and artists to participate in the campaign. For example, the company PayPerPost pays bloggers to endorse products. Sponsored bloggers are known as **spokesbloggers**. These bloggers may also participate in other paid forms of endorsement, like attending or hosting events. This is particularly common in the fashion industry where bloggers like Aimee Song (of the blog, *Song of Style*) command a great deal of respect for the influence they have with their readers. Because our cultural expectation for blogs (and other forms of content in the social media space) is that they present independent, non-funded, non-commercial content, the FTC introduced specific guidelines for social media content producers. The intent of the guidelines is to protect the public from advertising disguised as social media by ensuring that sponsorships are transparent. This is the subject of this chapter's critical reflection feature.

Counterfeit conversations occur when an organization plants content that masquerades as original material an actual consumer posted. Chick-Fil-A allegedly created a puppet account on Facebook after people flocked to its real Facebook page to complain. In response, a girl named "Abby Farle" went on Facebook to respond to the complaints with a counterargument—one that favored Chick-Fil-A. Farle was outed as a fake after someone noticed Farle's profile picture was a stock photo.[9] Such hoaxes may be user-generated too. After Target announced its children's clothing would be gender-neutral, critics took to Facebook to complain. Facebook user Mike Melgaard came to Target's defense. He created a fake Facebook account and posed as a Target customer service rep—under the name AskForHelp, with a bull's-eye profile pic—and began excoriating the haters with comically sarcastic replies. He got away with it for about 16 hours, too, commenting on about 50 posts before the fake account was shut down.[10] And on top of all this, brand fraud, scams by brand impersonators, is a growing problem, both for the brands whose reputations are harmed and for the consumers who are at risk from being a victim of a scam.

Developing Effective Branded Content

According to the Content Marketing Institute, 89% of B2C brands and 83% of B2C brands use social publishing and content marketing.[11] Branded content enables organizations to develop a strategic, well-designed message and distribute the message through social channels, resulting in additional reach, engagement, and earned media in the form of word-of-mouth communication and buzz. To be effective, brands must develop content that is aligned with their strategy and brand image, and valuable to the target audience. Table 7.1 highlights the marketing objectives B2B and B2C marketers seek to accomplish using social publishing. Table 7.2 identifies the types of content used by B2B and B2C marketers.

Table 7.1   Marketing Objectives Pursued Using Social Publishing by B2B and B2C Marketers

Marketing Objective	B2B	B2C
Brand Awareness	79%	74%
Engagement	71%	71%
Lead Generation	80%	66%
Customer Retention/Loyalty	56%	63%
Sales	62%	53%
Building an Audience via Subscription Growth	52%	50%
Customer Evangelism/Creating Brand Advocates	42%	46%
Lead Nurturing	66%	45%
Upsell/Cross-Sell	38%	30%
Cost Savings	16%	22%
Other	2%	3%

Source: Content Marketing Institute, *B2C Content Marketing: 2017 Benchmarks, Budgets, and Trends*

Table 7.2   Types of Content in the Social Publishing Strategies of B2B and B2C Marketers

Content Type	B2B	B2C
Social Media Content	83%	85%
Blogs	80%	75%
Email Newsletters	77%	75%
Ebooks/White Papers	65%	35%
Pre-Produced Video	60%	60%
Infographics	58%	48%
Webinars	58%	31%
Online Presentations	42%	31%
Illustrations/Photos	39%	45%
Interactive Tools	28%	31%
Digital Magazines	17%	15%
Mobile Apps	14%	21%
Podcasts	12%	10%
Content Hubs	10%	10%
Live Streaming	10%	16%
Virtual Conferences	8%	6%

Source: Content Marketing Institute, *B2C Content Marketing: 2017 Benchmarks, Budgets, and Trends*

As in any other media, not all content is created equal. Some is trash; some is important. Some content is fun, some inspiring, and some just titillating (anyone for "Keeping Up With the Kardashians"?). As Figure 7.3 shows, we can characterize content in terms of its originality and substance according to a **content value ladder**.[12] Let's take a closer look at this form of classification:

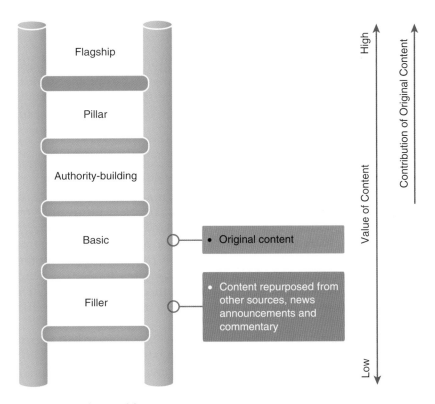

Figure 7.3   A Content Value Ladder

- At the lowest step in the ladder we find the least important type of materials. **Filler content** is simply content repurposed from other sources. A site called ArticlesBase.com is a free online article directory. It hosts articles that have been contributed by authors hoping to expand the reach of their work online. Others can use the articles posted on ArticlesBase at no charge. They just search for the topic of interest, copy and paste the article to their own site, and cite the contributing author. Filler content can also come from other content providers (blogs and posts on media-sharing sites) and syndicated sources such as PRNewsWire and the Associated Press.

- All other content on the ladder is **original content**. The first level of original content refers to contributions that originate with the poster but are not "weighty" enough to establish the creator as an authority in the topic area or serve as a reference piece for the audience.

- If that original content positions the sponsoring entity as an authority on the subject in question, then we call it **authority-building content**. Brands publish backlink-building content to establish and maintain their reputations as experts and thought leaders in their industries.

- If a source creates a solid foundation of original content, the foundation blocks are known as **pillar content**. Typically pillar content is made up of content that continues to attract viewers over time. The content's impact grows exponentially over time as other people share it through reposting, citations, and retweets. For this reason, these posts are called **compounding posts**.[13]

- **Flagship content** is original, authority-building, pillar content that becomes a seminal work in the field. It may be ground-breaking or pioneering work that helps to define a phenomenon or shape the way people think about something for a long time. Those pieces of content create a draw for years to come. Flagship content is also called **evergreen content**.

In Chapter 5, we talked about the value of developing a content mix that includes hygiene, hub, and hero content. This is similar to the content value ladder in that it recognizes that brands must offer some high value content to develop an audience, but it's unrealistic to develop only high value content. Doing so would likely result in insufficient content for maintaining a consistent publishing cadence. That said, developing high-value, original content pays off. HubSpot Research analyzed thousands of blog posts from more than 15,000 companies.[14] The results showed that only one in ten posts are compounding posts, but those posts accounted for 38% of the blog traffic across the sample. The remaining posts are decaying posts; they deliver a surge of traffic, but then decay over time. The takeaway? One compounding post is worth more than six decaying posts for driving traffic, generating leads, and influencing sales.

What are the characteristics of high-value content? The answer will depend upon the industry and target audience, but there are some common characteristics to consider. Part of the equation is based on the quality of the ingredients used; part is tied to the popularity of certain types of content and content traits. Table 7.3 highlights five popular types of content.[15] Each type addresses an audience need and presents the information in a useable format. Though how-to and list content tend to be popular regardless of the social media vehicle, keep in mind that content should be appropriate for the channel of communication. The style, tone, length, use of multi-media, and descriptive hashtags could all vary for content published on Instagram versus on a brand's blog. Brands can create variations of a single piece of content to address channel characteristics. This can help to increase share of voice and exposure to the target audience.

Content can also be categorized according to functional orientation (abstract or tactical), topic breadth (broad or narrow), and topic temporality (evergreen or terminable). Broad topics are of interest to a large audience. Tactical content helps the viewer by explaining important information, providing instructions, or giving advice. Evergreen content has a long expiration date. In contrast, general content may be interesting and relevant but can't cut through the clutter as well as content that solves a problem for the audience. Narrow topics are of interest to niche audiences; the relatively smaller size of the audience equates to fewer content views, likes, and shares. Terminable posts are time-sensitive. In other words, they have an expiration date, after which the content isn't relevant. The content may be related to current events (a technique known as "newsjacking") or announcements about limited-time offers. Terminable posts serve as filler content or original (but low value) content. Hubspot's study of posts found that most compounding posts were broad, tactical, and evergreen.

Table 7.3   Types of Pillar Content

Type	Description	Example
"How-To" Article	This form of content is the most popular type posted, according to an analysis of content shared on several news sites including Digg and StumbleUpon.	How to Make Brownies in a Crockpot
Definition Article	This type of post defines a concept. Although this is a straightforward approach, it provides a high level of utility for those interested in the concept being defined.	What Is Web 2.0?
Glossary Article	This form of article includes a series of definitions related to each other and creates a resource guide on the topic.	A Glossary of Literary Terms
Theory Article	Theory articles offer some unique insight into a topic but the content is opinion. They are equivalent to opinion-editorial pieces in your local newspaper.	Media Aren't Social
List Article	These forms of content use bullets for easy readability and consumption. They may draw on humor or education in detailing the list.	Top 10 USB Thumbdrive Tricks

Source: based on Starak, "How to Write Great Blog Content—The Pillar Article"

These principles hold true whether the content is original, branded content, sponsored content (such as when a brand sponsors an influencer to focus on the brand in his or her content), or brand-related UGC. For marketers, content should be of value to the target audience. The content will then be sought after and shared. Let's look at some examples of how brands have successfully launched social publishing strategies.

Velocity Partners used social publishing to reach its clients. A B2B marketing agency based in the UK, Velocity Partners wanted a way to emphasize its culture to prospective clients. The traits it values in customer relationships became the basis for an ebook, *The B2B Marketing Manifesto*, which it published on its website. The ebook can be downloaded (once prospects enter basic contact information, which feeds Velocity's lead generation funnel), comments are enabled on the site, and the link can be shared using Twitter, Facebook, and other social sites. Indium Corporation provides materials used to produce electronics. Are you thinking, how could a company like that use social publishing? Well, it did! It created a blog called *From One Engineer to Another*, which provided guidance and training to its target audience. The fashion company French Connection wanted a way to provide advice to its target audience the way a personal shopper would. It built a YouTube channel called YouTique that provides short videos on fashion advice. Lauren Luke started out as a part-time cosmetics salesperson in Newcastle, England. She developed a YouTube channel with instructional videos to help her sell more products. The videos have millions of views and catapulted Luke to a thought leader in the cosmetics industry. Just five years later, she has her own brand of makeup and a series of books.

Are you seeing a pattern here? Whether the marketing is B2B or B2C, the content adds value. It's relevant. It's not about selling. It's about providing something that people can participate in and share that experience with others. The core of the content may be published in owned media and made shareable or it may be published in a media-sharing site or it may have elements of both. But the content is engaging and relevant. It is content people want to share because it's just that good.

This brings us to a final point on creating high-value content for social publishing. Remember that we want the content to be viewed, but we also want it to stimulate the audience to participate and to share the content with their own social network. When creating content, ask whether what you've created is interesting enough to trigger participation and sharing.

Distributing and Promoting Content

High value content can't meet marketing objectives unless it reaches the target audience. This means that rather than rely solely on search engines and a handful of fans to drive organic reach, social publishers need to distribute and promote the content. According to research from the Content Marketing Institute and MarketingProfs, marketers use an average of six social media channels to distribute content.[16] They also use paid advertising on social network sites to get the word out to the target audience. To optimize impressions, content should be published and promoted. Table 7.4 highlights the different distribution channels used by marketers. Table 7.5 reveals the different ways marketers promote content.

Table 7.4   Social Publishing Vehicles Used by B2B and B2C Marketers

Publishing Vehicle	B2B	B2C
Facebook	76%	89%
LinkedIn	89%	66%
Twitter	77%	73%
YouTube	59%	65%
Google+	35%	37%
Instagram	26%	47%
SlideShare	26%	10%
Pinterest	30%	39%
Medium	6%	5%
Snapchat	3%	11%
Tumblr	2%	8%

Source: Content Marketing Institute, *B2C Content Marketing: 2017 Benchmarks, Budgets, and Trends*

Table 7.5   B2B and B2C Marketers Use Paid Promotions to Activate Social Content

Paid Promotion of Social Content	B2B	B2C
Social Promotion	84%	89%
Search Engine Marketing	67%	76%
Traditional Online Banner Ads	55%	60%
Native Advertising	41%	50%
Content Discovery Tools	18%	29%
Do Not Use	8%	7%
Print or Other Offline Promotion	58%	68%

Source: Content Marketing Institute, *B2C Content Marketing: 2017 Benchmarks, Budgets, and Trends*

For marketers there is a twofold goal for social publishing: (1) to increase exposure to the brand's messages and (2) to use the content to drive traffic to the brand's owned media. The social publishing process is similar to the media planning process we see for traditional advertising campaigns. In those cases the **media plan** designates how the campaign's creative content will be disseminated to the target audience using specific media vehicles such as radio or billboards. The media planner sets specific goals for what is to be accomplished through the ad placements in terms of audience reach, exposure to the message, and desired outcomes. Social publishing works much the same way except the creative content seeking exposure is not necessarily an ad (in the traditional static or rich media formats) and the distribution of that content is accomplished with inbound links or link chains to the content from search engine results, other websites, and social media communities. In other words, traditional media plans utilize paid media to achieve marketing objectives. Social publishing relies upon owned media and earned media online to reach these goals.

Just as traditional media plans vary considerably in terms of complexity and sophistication, so too do social publishing strategies. Marketers must determine what content to publish and where and then develop a strategy to maximize exposure to the content through search engine rankings and social sharing. In fact, we can identify two types of optimization that an organization can use (either individually or in combination) with on-site and off-site optimization tactics. Table 7.6 summarizes these levels.

Using **search engine optimization (SEO)**, the process of modifying content, site characteristics, and content connections to achieve improved search engine rankings, marketers develop and publish content in ways that improve the likelihood that search engines will rank the sites well in response to search queries. Whereas SEO is all about increasing the prominence of a site on search lists using on-site and off-site tactics, **social media optimization (SMO)** is a process that makes it more likely for content on a specific social media platform to be more visible and linkable in online communities.[17] If the content is valuable and engaging, other sites will link to it. And people will share it, post it, rank it, tag it, and augment it with their own stories about your brand.

All of this linking activity in turn increases the credibility of the marketer's message—exactly the goal of social publishing. SMO not only provides additional visibility for a marketer's message, it benefits search rankings because it increases the likelihood that others will link to it. Thus, SEO focuses on earning higher organic search engine rankings whereas

SMO focuses on earning organic links to content. SMO is used by search engine optimizers because those links also improve rankings. The optimization process is so important that it has created an entirely new field of specialists who help organizations to stay afloat in the growing sea of content. Let's take a closer look at each level of social publishing.

Table 7.6   Media Optimization Matrix

Type of Optimization	On-Site	Off-Site
Search engine optimization	Optimizing content value, tags, keywords, titles, URL	Publishing related content elsewhere with links to original Creating a linkwheel structure
Social media optimization	Including share tools and RSS feed options	Promoting on social news and social bookmarking sites Microblogging content headline and link Promoting social media press releases

Level 1: Social Publishing and Search Engine Optimization

The first level focuses on ways the brand can increase exposure to its online content and drive site traffic by publishing related components of the content across several social sites. These placements include links back to the targeted site. This cross-promotion to the branded content is accomplished with owned media and the placement of related content on media-sharing sites (earned media).

© iStock.com/manley099

How can a business use different elements of social publishing to multiply its exposure in an inexpensive way? Let's consider the brand SOS (SellOurStuff). SellOurStuff is an eBay reseller of luxury goods. As a promotional tool, SOS might create a branded article, an article that is written to promote SOS's expertise in the field, on "7 Ways to Spot Luxury that (re)Sells." The article is a promotional piece that educates the company's prospects on the types of items SOS could auction successfully while it encourages them to retain SOS as their auctioneer.

The article is a good piece of content—but it won't help SOS unless prospects are exposed to it. SOS publishes the piece on its main website at SOS-SellOurStuff.com, and the company also posts a teaser to the article with a link to the original content on the SOS blog. Next, SOS takes the images from the article and posts them to Flickr (again with a link to the original) and also creates a Prezi slideshow of the content to share at the Prezi site (with again, you guessed it, a link back to the original). Finally, SOS creates a badge that its top clients can post on their own personal webpages to show visitors that they have an "Eye for Luxury." That is, SOS designates these top clients as people who already know the rules for spotting luxury that resells. The SOS badge also links back to the branded content on the SOS website. In this example, SOS created content that promotes its brand message. It then shared the content on its own site and on other sites where it had some control as to what was presented and how it linked back to the branded content. Publishing in multiple places creates additional "opportunities to see" (OTS) for the target audience and brand-controlled links to the targeted site.

At this point, the brand can utilize search engine optimization to improve how its content is listed in response to search queries. These listings are crucial—as you probably know from experience, most people tend to follow up only on the first few results they get from a query. SEO is a complicated technical process, and it's also a bit of a cat-and-mouse game. For example, #1 site Google uses a secret algorithm to decide which sites will appear at the top of a search list. The company changes this formula on a regular basis, so SEO experts engage in a constant contest to figure out the algorithm and then modify their sites to keep up with Google's changes.

Consumers love their search engines. The rankings these search engines generate are crucial because they drive site traffic—and of course traffic is social media's lifeblood. No traffic, no interest. No interest, eventually no site. Sites that attract heavy traffic are valuable for two reasons:

1   A large number of visitors makes it more likely the sponsor will benefit from a higher rate of **conversion** (i.e., the person browsing actually purchases, so he or she is converted from a browser to a buyer).

2   The more "eyeballs" the site attracts, the more advertising revenue the site can generate (assuming it sells ad space to other advertisers).

SEO is the key tool used for **search engine marketing**. SEM refers to a form of online marketing that promotes websites by increasing the visibility of the site's URL in search engine results, both organic and sponsored. Incidentally, there are hundreds of search engines, and some sites that do not feature search as their primary function also offer search engine capabilities. YouTube and Facebook, for instance, are also used for search.

When someone enters a query, called a **SERP** (Search Engine Results Page), the search engine turns to its index for the best matches and then returns a search results list to the user. The results list includes the organic results, which are listings ranked in order of relevance based on the search engine's ranking algorithm, and the sponsored results, which are paid advertising links.

How Do People Use Search Results?

Let's say you've dreamed of owning a high-end designer handbag—the Hermès Birkin. Celebrities and fashionistas carry it, it's always in scarce supply, and a new one can set you back a year's tuition. A brand new Birkin is out—too expensive—but maybe you can find a used one online. You might visit Yahoo! and enter the search query, "Hermes handbags." The search results list leads off with **sponsored**, or paid, links. In this case, e-retailers such as DesignerPurseOutlets.com and Bluefly.com have paid for sponsored listings. The search results then provide a series of **organic** listings for Hermès as well as e-retailers such as eBay and The Purse Blog. These sites did not pay to be listed; they are based on the search engine's model for delivering relevant search results. However, in addition to these retailers you may see several merchants that offer counterfeit versions of the bag. Why? Those sites were listed in part because Google's algorithm indicated that the content was a good match to your search query. (We'll go into more depth on how this works in a bit.) You might now refine your search, but if it turns out you'd consider a Birkin replica, you might click through to one of the listed sites (and possibly make a purchase, or at a minimum build the site's traffic figures, which will help it earn ad revenue).

As you can imagine, it's very important for a brand or site to appear in a search list so that the shopper will at least consider clicking on the link. Although search engine marketers can buy paid listings from search engines, it's preferable to earn organic results. One reason is that these results have no **pay-per-click** fees. These are the fees a marketer pays when someone clicks on an online display ad. Organic results also tend to generate more site traffic, presumably because people view them as more credible referrals from the search engine.

Organic entries, especially the first few, garner most of the attention in a typical search. Clickthroughs taper off pretty rapidly, so few people tend to go beyond the first ten or so. Of course, pages and pages of search results could be returned for any given search—but again, for the most part these won't generate much traffic. For example, the search on Hermès handbags returned a whopping 1,900,000 listings.

We know that people tend to look at the first searches in a list rather than the entire list (few of us would make it to listing number 1,900,000 no matter how badly we wanted that Birkin bag). Still, it's helpful to understand more about which links the user is likely to follow. Researchers use **eye-tracking studies** to help identify the characteristics of a search page that determine this. They borrow this method from more traditional advertising researchers, who for many years have hooked respondents to sophisticated devices that follow the precise movements of eyeballs as they scan ads on TV or computer screens.

This method shows clearly that most search engine users view only a very limited number of search results and do so in one of a few viewing patterns. When typical respondents look at a search page, their eyes travel across the top of the search result, return to the left of the screen, and then travel down to the last item shown on the screen without scrolling. On most screens, this means that every user will view the first three search results, but they may or may not scroll down. Search engine marketers call this space on the screen where listings are virtually guaranteed to be viewed the **golden triangle**.[18] So the real value—the sweet spot—is in earning a list rank that is on the first page, and preferably one of the top three listings ranked. This pattern is still prevalent, but more recent eye-tracking studies suggest that people are scanning vertically now as well, creating an elongated "F" pattern.[19] The shifts in viewing patterns are attributed to changes in the layout of SERP pages and viewing SERPS on mobile devices. Of the patterns identified, relevant, organic, top-ranked listings still achieve the highest clickthroughs. How can a source enhance the probability that its listing will appear within one of these viewing patterns? For many organizations, this is (literally) the million dollar question! And that's exactly the point of search engine optimization.

How Search Engines Work

Search listings are produced by search engines using indexed data and an algorithm that determines a listing's relevance to the search query. Search engines use **web crawlers** (also known as *spiders* and *bots*); these are automated web programs that gather information from sites that ultimately form the search engine's entries. The programs are called crawlers because they crawl websites. They follow all the links, site after site, collecting data until the link network is exhausted. After the bots gather this information, they index (classify) it using labels the sites provide. The indexed data include tags and keywords derived from site content. Then, when someone enters a search query, the search engine applies its algorithm to determine the sites that are most relevant to the search query. This algorithm determines which sites are identified in the search listing and the ranking of the sites presented.

On-Site Optimization

You can see that optimizing content in order to improve search engine rankings is an important marketing task. How do marketers optimize? They use one of two key approaches: (1) on-site optimization or (2) off-site optimization. This is because the bots look for cues on-site, especially tags, and for off-site indicators such as links from other sites as they index data.

On-site, coders try to optimize certain site characteristics (called on-site indicators) that the search bots and the search engine index. In plain English, this means they tinker with elements of the site to make indexing more efficient and ensure that the web crawlers will classify the site the way the developers intend. The primary on-site variables are keywords embedded in the page's tags, title, URL, and content.

Keywords tell the bot what information to gather and specify the relevant topic. The bot will collect this information for the search engine to use in indexing. The keywords explain to the search engine when to deliver your site as a search result. Consequently, choosing the right keywords is critical to ensuring a site shows up in relevant searches. Once you have selected your keywords, you will work them into the areas crawled by the bots—the site's tags, title, URL, and body copy (or content).

For example, say your website sells vintage comic books. To ensure that a buyer who wants to snag a pristine copy of *Wonder Woman Issue #5*: *Battle for Womanhood*, published in 1942, will visit your online store, you might code your site with these labels:

- **Meta-tag**: code embedded in a webpage. Meta-tags are visible to site visitors but only by viewing the source code for the page. Meta-keywords should include three or four of the targeted keywords. The meta-description should include two or three sentences that summarize the page content. The description is shown with the search engine listing. The vintage comic book store might include meta-tags such as adventure comics, Wonder Woman, superheroes, and vintage.

- **Title tag**: an HTML tag that defines the page's title. The title is displayed in the browser's title bar, in search engine results, and in RSS feeds. Title tags should include no more than 12 words, with at least two keywords. For example, your website title tags might read: Comics Direct Sales Rare Comics/Vintage Comic Books—Vintage Comics offers comic book collectors vintage adventure comics.

- **Heading tag**: an HTML tag that is used to section and describe content. Heading tags should include keywords. Tags for heading levels are designated as H1, H2, H3, and so on. Within the webpage, major headings (named for keywords) will be designated with code such that the sections are recognizable to the bots. For example, the first heading on the page will be designated "<h1>This is heading 1</h1>". Keywords might include superheroes, wonder woman, vintage, comics, dc.

- **Title**: your headline—the main indicator of your page's content. It should be loaded with keywords. Writing optimized titles may seem difficult to some because the style of an optimized title is quite different from that of a story headline a journalist might write. A traditional headline may be indirect; the idea behind a traditional headline is to engage the audience without giving away the story. For instance, a print magazine article about vintage comic books and the prevalence of high-quality replicas might be titled "Vintage Comic Replicas Indistinguishable From the Real Thing." An optimized title might read "Shop Wise: 5 Tips for Ensuring That Vintage Collectible Is Real, Not Fake, Comics" to ensure that the search would index on keywords. Another difference is that the title needs to be more literal than the one we might use in an article: bots are pretty smart, but they don't understand metaphors or puns. "Cute" titles such as "You Can Experience the Adventures of Wonder Woman" or "Counterfeit Comic Books Frustrate Law-Abiding Super Heroes" just won't cut it.

- **URL**: the website address. To optimize the URL, use a static URL and include the title of the article or the keywords in the URL. Static URLs do not change and they do not include variable scripts. **Dynamic URLs** are generated from scripts and change over time, making it difficult for people to return to your content later.

Ideally, you'll have a story or topic in mind around when you devise the content. For example, SOS's owner knew that a story explaining how to determine which luxury items will sell and which will bomb would have high value to eBay hobbyists. The story itself should help to determine the keywords, but it shouldn't be the only source. You will also want to include keywords that reflect popular search terms. Before writing the story, the first step is to research the keywords that will help ensure the bots will index the site's data and the algorithm will show relevance to search queries. So, if your "story" is "Sell your luxury used goods with SOS" you may also want to include more general keywords such as "consignment" to be sure potential resellers find it when they search.

How can you generate a strong list of keywords? **Keyword research**! This process is a critical step to design the content and the site's page for successful search engine optimization. Keyword research involves answering these questions:

- What is the topic of your article? What words and phrases best describe the article?

- What terms are your competitors using as keywords? You can find this out when you analyze their article titles, meta-tags, and body copy.

- What words are suggested by **keyword generators** such as Google AdWords Keyword Tool or The Free Keyword Tool?

- What are the derivatives of your keywords? For example, SOS might pick derivatives of handbags such as bags, purses, clutches, totes, and so on. Free SEO tools such as Google Suggest will offer variations on search terms you may not have thought of.

- How much search volume does the keyword generate compared to other keywords you might use? Is it worth using given the resulting search volume? You can check Google Trends to see how much interest there is in your keywords. This useful tool will show how often the keyword was searched and from which geographic regions.

SEO marketers may want to use **long tail keywords**. This term refers to multi-phrase search queries. They are much more targeted than a general keyword because they may say exactly what the searcher wants to find. For instance, the long tail keywords for the keyword topic Hermès handbags might include "finding a gently used Hermès Birkin bag," "identifying a fake Birkin," and "best deals on designer handbags." Because the long tail keywords are actual search queries (and you can use the same tools to find these queries as you did to identify your basic keywords), they help to optimize the site.

Off-Site Optimization

Bots don't look only at site information as they index data and feed information back for the search engine's algorithm. They also use other indicators off-site to determine the value of a site's content. These off-site indicators include the number of links to a website from other sites, the credibility of those sites, the type of site promoting the link, and the link text (called **anchor text**) these sites use. Therefore, search engine optimizers will not stop at tweaking on-site characteristics like the title and meta-tags. They will also strive to earn links from high quality sites.

Links are the building blocks of social publishing. The more links to your content, the higher the ranking you will probably receive during a search engine query. There are two approaches to building links. The first approach is to publish related content and links across other sites (branded sites and social media channels). These venues are under the control of the marketer—it is simply a matter of developing the content and identifying where related content and links can be placed to promote traffic to the original site. The second approach is to encourage other, unaffiliated sites to link to the brand's content. This can be accomplished in different ways, such as using **affiliate marketing**, but we'll address how social media optimization builds unaffiliated links when we discuss level two of social publishing.

Building affiliated links to content is an extension of the first level of social publishing, in which the brand publishes related content with links back to the main site among several branded sites and social media outlets. This is exactly what SOS did in our earlier example. In addition to using links from related content, the marketer will also strategically formulate these links to form a linkwheel. **Linkwheels** increase the number of links back to a site. They are built on a hub-and-spoke system that uses web properties (i.e., link pages) as spokes to send one link to the home site and another link to the next property. Several properties are set up as spokes; the targeted page is the hub.

Figure 7.4 shows a sample linkwheel for SOS. The linkwheel system ensures that if a user comes to a site and clicks on a link, that site will connect the user to the next hub site and to the next spoke site, and so on. The spoke sites can also be used as a hub in a new linkwheel as new content is developed and published. The result of this tactic is that the main site gains links from other sites with branded content using the linkwheel. When other sites link back to the content, it's called a **backlink** or a **trackback**. The site's search ranking benefits then from the increase in the link quantity (this is called **link juice**). Further, all of the new sites used by the main site to promote it can also be indexed and ranked in searches. If done well, a search engine query could produce a results list with several links to sites owned by the same company.

Linkwheels and other SEO tactics can be used appropriately, but there is room for abuse in this system. Have you watched an episode of *Gunsmoke* on TV Land or an old western on Hulu? Cowboy with a white hat—a hero. Black hat—a villain. This western analogy applies to SEO culture. Social media insiders classify SEO marketers as white, gray, or black hats:[20]

- **White hats** play by the rules of the system, striving to provide good quality content, with the best use of keywords and tags, and earned links at reputable sites. They create site maps so that every page is linked to every other page and search engine bots can crawl every page.

- **Gray hats** take some liberties with the system. For example, they will utilize a keyword density (the number of times the keyword is used in the body of a page) that is beyond that of the typical usage of keywords, but below that of true keyword.

- **Stuffing** (the insertion of a superficially large number of keywords throughout a site's content and tags). Gray hats also duplicate content at multiple sites and create **link exchanges**, where sites agree to link with each other. They may also utilize **three-way linking**, ensuring that their own sites link to each other in sequence and then back to the original site, and **paid links**, which are considered somewhat unethical in that linking should be the realm of earned media, not paid.

- **Black hats** manipulate the system by utilizing several tactics considered unethical in the realm of search engine optimization. For example, with linkwheels, the more spokes in the wheel, the more links to the hub site. Because the search engines rank in part based on number of links, black hats simply set up a massive number of property sites linking to the hub and using the same anchor text. It works. And it's easy and inexpensive. Software can be used to automatically build thousands of links using social media properties such as Tumblr and WordPress while RSS feeds populate the content. Especially for smaller search engines, a black hat linkwheel can send a site soaring to the top in search rankings. Big search engines such as Google combat the black hats by changing the crawler criteria and the indexing algorithm. If Google sees hundreds of links to a site, it will devalue the link, assuming there's a black hat operating behind the scenes.

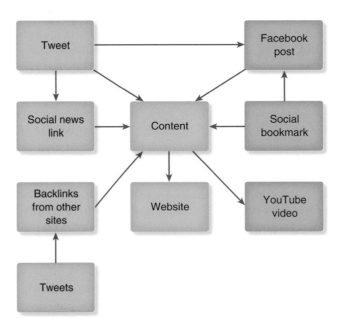

Figure 7.4   SOS Linkwheel Structure

Black hats also keyword stuff and place keywords in hidden text by making the font color of keywords the same color as the page background. They may also utilize **gateway pages** (pages that real visitors are directed past) stuffed with keywords, and **cloaking** (the display of misleading content to search engines). In addition, they utilize **link farms**—groups of websites that link to each other and pages with unrelated links solely for the purpose of creating more links to the targeted pages. Finally, black hats may spam websites with links.

Level 2: Social Media Optimization

Just as SEO tactics optimize a site to increase its exposure (through links) and search engine rankings, social media optimization employs tactics to increase the likelihood that others will share and promote content. Essentially, SMO seeks to leverage the network effect to spread endorsements of a brand with links to the brand's content. These shared links are essentially referrals—a form of testimonial from other players in the social publishing zone. Whereas brands use zone 1 to develop relationships and engage consumers to garner influence impressions, the word-of-mouth communication in zone 2 gains influence posts and referrals to the brand's content. Influence posts are word-of-mouth content from published sources like bloggers and reviewers.

What's the difference between search engine and social media optimization? Both have the same goals—to support inbound marketing and enable the target audience to find and consume the brand content. But SEO is more about finding ways to ensure search engines index the site and to calculate a good result ranking for the content, whereas SMO is about encouraging the sharing of the content.

In other words, SEO focuses on manipulating the processes controlled by the search engines (because even in this social world, Internet users rely heavily on search engines to find information online). In contrast, SMO focuses on building community. SEO efforts target machines. SMO targets people. SMO is especially valuable to marketers because it improves search engine rankings. This happens because bots prefer links, especially high-quality ones. For now at least, search engines tend to rate social media links as higher quality.

As we've seen, sharing behavior is a cultural norm in most online social communities. Content can be promoted on social networks, blogs, microblogs, and **social bookmarking** and on news sites that use **aggregators**. People can also share links to content in these channels by email. As a result, the potential impact for a piece of content can be huge. That's because as people share links to content with their network, some of those people will consume the content, and some of those will also share the content with their network, and so on.

How do we optimize for social media? As with SEO, there are on-site and off-site tactics.

On-Site Optimization Tactics

SMO is all about encouraging people who are exposed to your content to share, promote, and recommend it. To do this, the content needs to be valuable, interesting, or entertaining enough that someone wants to endorse it. We're back to the importance of good content, and you'll learn more about developing good social media content a bit later in this chapter. Aside from the issue of good content, though, we can use the title (as we did with SEO) and other site features to encourage endorsements and sharing. Search engines also consider the quality of a linking site and its type. A site will rank better in search engine results listings if independent sites link to it, and if those sites are of high quality and high relevance.

Let's return to SOS for an example of this process. SOS is a reseller of many types of luxury items. Suppose that one of its blog posts on fashion tips is picked up by fashion blogger Reese Blutstein. Reese does a post on the tips article with a link to SOS. Reese is a fashion influencer and her blog, Double3xposure, is a must-follow. Reese's style is perfect for drawing attention to SOS; she specializes in minimalist, vintage-inspired pieces styled in unexpected ways. It's not long before hundreds of other fashion blogs have linked to the SOS post too. Because each of these blogs have their own linkwheel to drive traffic, SOS has a lot of potential to further spread the original post beyond this audience. Reese, for instance, maintains a presence on Instagram, Facebook, and Twitter.

SOS has a winner here in terms of quantity of links. But are these links of high quality? The search engine would rather see links from industry-related sites. Since SOS is a luxury reseller, links from other fashion sites would hold more value in the indexing algorithm. That's true unless the linking site is a power site. This label refers to a site with enormous readership, such as CNN.com. If CNN.com runs a story on how moms increasingly focus on saving money but still wish they could feel fashionable, they might reference SOS as a great site for deals. That link is going to be worth a lot of link juice to the search engine.

Title

Our goal is to persuade people to access our content. How do users initially decide whether a site is worth checking out? The most likely candidate is simple: the title. We can enhance interest in content when we compose a catchy title. Social media pros refer to the careful crafting of a title that markets the content as linkbaiting.

To continue the fishing metaphor, let's look more closely at techniques that make linkbaiting effective. You can guess what's coming next: we choose a hook that increases the likelihood that the intended audience will share and/or click. Hooks are used to position the content for the target audience. For example, consider this blog post title: "The Marketer's Ultimate Guide to Link Bait."[21] The author could have titled the post, "The Basics of Linkbaiting," but she realized that including the qualifier "ultimate" and the keywords "marketer" and "link bait" would optimize the title and increase clickthrough rates (CTRs).

- The resource hook is a common type in social news sites. It refers to content written with the intent to be helpful to the target audience. For example, Weight Watchers might create an article titled "5 Easy Methods to Burn Calories."

- The contrary hook refutes some accepted belief. Challenging the belief incites people to read the content if only to argue the point. For instance, Weight Watchers might post an article titled "Lose Weight With Chocolate;" the company recognizes that this will spark an interest from those who believe chocolate cannot possibly be part of a weight loss plan (just too good to be true).

- The humor hook is designed to show that the content will entertain. For example, a funny post about dieting might use the title, "Obese Skunk Cuts Out Bacon Sandwiches."

- The giveaway hook promises something for free. In other words, it embeds a sales promotion, an incentive offered to encourage a specific behavior response in a specific time period, into the content. For example, our Weight Watchers' article could have been titled "Save $50 Doing What's Good for You!"

- The research hook offers a claim about something of interest. For example, our Weight Watchers' article might claim, "66% of Americans Are Overweight, But You Don't Have to Be."

Titles don't make content more valuable, but they do influence whether people choose to view the content and share the content with their social networks. Other title best practices include using relatively short titles (under ten words), including the words "how" or "why," and emphasizing the audience's point of view.

Share Tools

People are more likely to connect to our content (using that call to action we discussed earlier) if we make it easy for them to follow through. **Share tools** are **plug-ins** that appear as clickable icons on a website and enable the viewer to bookmark or share the page with many social networking, social news, and social bookmarking sites. Plug-ins are third-party applications that "plug in" to a main site to add some form of functionality. In this case, the functionality is the ability to easily share the site's content with external sites. Many social media sites offer their own site-specific plug-in (Facebook has a Like plug-in; Twitter offers a Tweet This button; Digg has a Smart Digg button) or a site may wish to utilize a multi-share tool such as Share This or Sexy Bookmarks.

Social media are about community, so reciprocity matters. Remember the Golden Rule you learned as a child: "Do unto others as you would have them do unto you." You'll want to reward those who link to you by including trackbacks, which promote those who promote your content. When someone links to your site, you'll post a trackback on your site to theirs. The trackback gives attribution to sites linking to you. It can be a method of communication between bloggers but, importantly, it provides an easy way to acknowledge those who send traffic to the brand's site by reciprocating their kindness.

RSS Feeds

Syndicate content with an RSS feed, a tool to automatically feed new published content to subscribers. Enhancing the ease of content distribution with an RSS feed makes it easy for others to consume new content as it is offered by having that content feed directly into their feed reader or email.

Off-Site Optimization Tactics

Social media suffer from an embarrassment of riches—there's way too much content available for people to process on their own. Millions of tweets are posted daily. There are hundreds of thousands of blogs. There are also corporate white papers, articles from online publishers, and other valuable content available online. Thus, the average consumer can easily be overwhelmed or simply miss valuable sources of information. That's why it's important for social media marketers to optimize their socially published content. We can optimize off-site for social media in three key ways. First, we can publish a social media press release to promote our content. Second, we can use a microblog to encourage sharing of our announcements. Third, the content can be promoted on social news and bookmarking sites.

The Social Media Press Release

A press release is an announcement public relations professionals issue to the news media to let the public know of company developments. For social media marketers, a release is also a key tool, but a **social media press release** is structured a bit differently. It should have an optimized title, good keywords and tags, links to the main site landing page, RSS feed options, share buttons, and embeddable multi-media content that can be shared on several networks, in addition to the typical press release content. That's right—a press release is social when it has been prepared in a way that ensures the content is shareable. Figure 7.5 provides a template for a social media press release.

An organization can publish a social media press release on distribution sites such as PRWeb and Pressit, both social media news release services. In addition, organizations with a corporate blog should also post the social media press release on the blog so that it can be indexed easily by search engines.

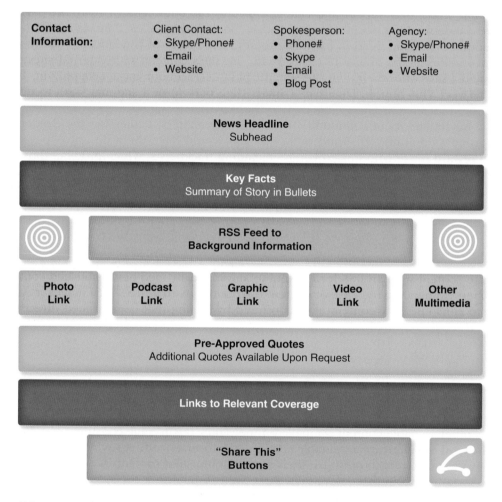

Figure 7.5   A Template for a Social Media Press Release

Microblogs

Whereas blogs share a story, microblogs share headlines. That's probably one reason that Twitter, the leading microblog service, defines itself as a real-time information network. Microblog posts can be useful for reminder communications and ensuring top-of-mind awareness, but they can also provide valuable links, direct traffic, and build credibility and reputation.

Brands can post their own links, but social media optimization comes into play when brands figure out ways to encourage others to retweet the message. This may be as simple as offering content valuable enough that others wish to retweet it or asking followers to retweet. Or it may mean offering an incentive to share the links.

Social News and Bookmarking Sites

Have you read current news on Digg or bookmarked online articles for research using Diigo? Digg and Reddit are two leading social news communities. Social news communities share and promote online news. Diigo is a social bookmarking site. Social bookmarking sites save your bookmarks online so they are always available wherever you have online access. They are social because these bookmarks can be shared and the collective intelligence can promote a bookmark to other interested members. They are very similar, with social news focused more on content distribution and social bookmarks more intent upon the organization of content.

Social news and bookmarking communities play an invaluable role, because they filter vast amounts of information into sets that individuals can manage. In many cases this process is as simple as if a trusted friend told you she personally visited ten ski resorts, and then she suggested the three she was sure you would like. You still might pick and choose among the three, but there's no way you could have considered the original ten anyway, so you're happy to take her word for it. Imagine how much happier you'd be if five other friends gave you the same recommendations!

Social news websites are social communities that allow their users to submit news stories, articles, and multi-media files including videos and pictures so the submissions can be shared with other users and the general public. Submissions receive enhanced attention and visibility if they get a lot of votes from users. Social bookmarking communities are similar to social news communities in that users can share material from around the Internet with each other, and the size and influence of a user's network affect the ultimate influence of the resource in question. However, those who use social news sites put a priority on message promotion, whereas those who use social bookmarking sites place a priority on organizing the links they want to save and store. Users store and organize bookmarks (using tags) to online source materials within the social bookmarking site (instead of storing bookmarks with one's Web browser) to make the information easily sortable, retrievable, and accessible.

These communities uphold the principles of media democratization. Individuals determine what material is disseminated throughout the community, as well as the value ratings associated with the material. Users act as editors; they identify what material should be pushed to the featured areas of the site. The process supports the wisdom of crowds perspective we discussed in Chapter 1, in that individual users recommend and vote on submissions. The site then uses algorithms to filter content and determine the popularity of a story. The algorithms include number of votes received as well as other factors such as the richness of the discussion related to the story. The system ensures each individual has a voice, if he or she chooses to use it, but it also enables some voices to be heard louder than others. The most active and respected participants, the influencers or opinion leaders, come to hold positions of high authority in the community.

Although there's always the potential to manipulate the voting system (like ballot box stuffing in the physical world), the algorithms minimize this threat by seeking to identify **voting campaigns** (in which voters are incentivized to vote for a story). In addition, some social news websites have editorial staff who review stories and award featured positions for relevant, newsworthy stories (though bookmarking sites generally do not). There are more than 100 such sites. Buzzfeed and Reddit are two of the major players.

Planning a Social News Campaign

Choosing the communities to seed and target can be difficult. There are several social news sites and social bookmarking sites, just as there are several social networks. Depending on the campaign's objectives and target audience, it may make sense to focus on the leading sites or alternatively to find a niche site that attracts a smaller number of passionate participants. The community should also be evaluated for quality and engagement. Inactive or weak communities will not offer the social support necessary to propel a successful social news marketing campaign. Consider this list of community characteristics when evaluating the desirability of a community target:

1 What is the community's focus (general news, specific topics)?

2 How many active users are involved in the community? What kind of traffic does the site receive?

3 How active are the top users on the site?

4 How many comments on average are generated for each new submission?

5 How many votes are required to earn front page status on the site?

6 Are stories on the site's front page recent? How rapid is story turnover?

7 Are there limitations for branded content in the community's Terms of Service?

8 What have others (such as bloggers) said about the social news site?

Just as journalists receive pitches for content from public relations specialists who pitch stories that promote specific brands, influential social news users may receive pitches for branded content. The influencer's referral is valuable because he or she provides an unbiased, third-party word-of-mouth endorsement of the content. The process of influencing the influencers follows the traditional public relations model that gets information to be distributed into the hands of those in a position to distribute it to a large number of people. The key to success is to ensure that the content pitched is relevant to the people it targets.

As most people do not appreciate hearing from a friend only when she needs a favor, influencers as a group are unlikely to respond well to obvious pitches from social media marketers. Just like a good salesperson in the physical world, the effective social media marketer understands that it's important to build a relationship with the other person *before* he or she offers a sales proposition. Some care must be taken to introduce oneself, acknowledge the contributions the influencer makes to the community, and flatter the influencer's judgment and expertise in making high-quality content submissions. The influencer will be helping the brand by virtue of the content submission and vote, so it can be useful to help the influencer by offering other content that will be perceived as desirable prior to pitching the branded content. And don't simply send along your social media press release. Instead, a more personal pitch that emphasizes knowledge of the influencer's recommendation patterns and the marketer's relationship to the branded content is likely to be effective.

MINI CASE STUDY

Social Publishing: The Heart of GoPro's Strategy

GoPro is a camera company that has become famous for its portable action cameras. The devices are ideal for capturing customer experiences, whether they are snow-boarding or commuting to work. In fact, that was the motivation behind the creation of the first GoPro camera. Founder Nick Woodman was frustrated that he couldn't capture his experiences during a surfing trip to Australia because the professional equipment required was too expensive and complex for personal use. Today, GoPro uses several elements of marketing communications in its integrated strategy, all built upon the theme of "personal heroism." GoPro's name and its slogan "be a hero" encourage personal heroism by encouraging customers to believe they can capture experiences just as professionals do.

iStock.com/Wetframes

Social media marketing, and especially social publishing, is a dominant element of GoPro's marketing communications.[22] It creates original content, using GoPro equipment, sponsors professional influencers, and also embraces UGC. Naturally, the content is visual, including photos and video. GoPro stays current with technological advances. It was one of the first brands to create 360-degree video. One of its most engaging videos used a six-camera spherical rig to capture surfing inside the waves of Tahiti. It generated 160,000 reactions and more than 140,000 shares. GoPro's cameras are designed to capture the unfiltered first-person perspective that social media users crave. Why? In a word—authenticity.

To encourage and incentivize UGC, GoPro developed its GoPro Awards campaign. To participate, users submit their photos and videos to GoPro's webpage. If their content is selected, they can win prizes. In addition to the financial award, winners are also given exposure—sharing their work with millions of GoPro fans. To showcase the professional-grade functions of their cameras, GoPro also builds content from "featured photographers." These images are accompanied by rich descriptions from the photographer's point of view, consistent with revealing pro tips for GoPro's everyday users.

Content is distributed via Facebook, Instagram, YouTube, and Periscope and promoted with microposts on Twitter. GoPro's Facebook community is more than 10 million members strong and growing at an average of 80,000 new fans per month. It is also diverse—only 35% of its Facebook fans are in the United States. Its YouTube channel has more than 4 million subscribers. GoPro has masterfully developed a social publishing strategy that includes original, branded content, influencer content, and UGC distributed through social channels in a manner that keeps fans and followers engaged with fresh and authentic content.

Results and Outcomes

GoPro's social publishing strategy is impressive, but is it effective? In a word—yes! It has millions of members on each vehicle with several thousand more members added each month. According to the Total Social rankings from Engagement Labs, GoPro was the #1 brand of consumer electronics on Instagram and #6 on Twitter in measures of social media engagement, impact, and follower growth.[23] In terms of individual content, video and photos across all social vehicles commonly earn hundreds of thousands of likes, hearts, and shares.

CRITICAL REFLECTION

Disclosure in Social Publishing

As we've seen, social media marketers can benefit from incorporating influencers into their strategy in each of the four zones of social media. In social publishing, brands pay influencers to create high-value content that endorses the brand. Brands benefit from the content, access to the influencer's audience, and the power of persuasion associated with the influencer's likeability, authority, trustworthiness, and authenticity. As influencers became a more prevalent tactic among social media marketers, the Federal Trade Commission developed guidelines for appropriate disclosures. The FTC already protects consumers from deceptive advertising practices, but the new guides clarify what is considered deceptive in the context of social media influencer endorsements and the expectations for disclosure under the law. If there's a connection between an endorser and an advertiser that consumers wouldn't expect and it would affect how they evaluate the endorsement, the connection should be disclosed. But that's not all the law requires. A sponsorship statement or any other disclosure necessary to prevent deception must be clear and conspicuous. A "disclosure" that consumers aren't likely to read isn't really a disclosure at all. The FTC reiterated that point in its online guide, *How to Make Effective Disclosures in Digital Advertising*, stating: "Simply making the disclosure available somewhere in the ad, where some consumers might find it, does not meet the clear and conspicuous standard."[24]

As social media users, do we need this protection? Apparently so—at least if Warner Bros Home Entertainment is indicative of the lengths brands may go to utilize influencers. The FTC charged Warner Bros. for failing to disclose that it had paid prominent YouTubers thousands of dollars to create, distribute, and promote content highlighting one of its video games, Middle Earth: Shadow of Mordor.[25] The endorsement deal influencers agreed to include several requirements. Influencers' videos, which became the property of Warner Bros., were subject to pre-approval before posting. The videos were required to feature gameplay, include positive messaging about the game, exclude any bugs or glitches in the game, and include a verbal call to action for viewers to go to the game's website. Influencers were also required to promote the sponsored content with a minimum of one Facebook post or tweet on Twitter.

Those requirements aren't illegal. The legal complaint arose from specific instructions from Warner Bros. that any disclosures be hidden deep in the video description, in an area known as "below the fold" because it is only visible if someone clicks to "show more." Some of the influencers involved in the complaint disclosed in the obscure location, but others didn't disclose at all. For instance, one influencer wrote: "This video sponsored by Warner Bros." followed by this telling statement: "No one reads this far into the description ... what are you doing snooping around." Another stated, "This has been one of my favorite sponsored games, so thanks that I could play it for free!!"—failing to mention that in addition to free play, Warner Bros. was paying them thousands of dollars. In a statement, a FTC representative said: "Consumers have the right to know if reviewers are providing their own opinions or paid sales pitches. Companies like Warner Brothers need to be straight with consumers in their online ad campaigns." To help brands and influencers, the FTC offers several guides covering the characteristics of deceptive advertising in social media and suggestions for effective disclosure.[26]

CHAPTER SUMMARY

What are the channels of social publishing?

The channels of social publishing include blogs, media-sharing sites, microsharing sites, social book-marking sites, and social news sites, as well as owned media sites with social components.

Who creates the content published in social channels? What kind of content can be published?

Anyone can create the content published in social channels. Content can be editorial, commercial, or user-generated. Content appears in a variety of different formats such as blog posts and feature articles, microblog posts, press releases, white papers, case studies, ebooks, newsletters, videos, webinars and presentations, podcasts, and photos.

What content characteristics enhance perceived content quality and value? How can marketers plan and organize their efforts as they embrace a social publishing strategy?

As Figure 7.3 shows, we can characterize content in terms of its originality and substance. The higher the level of originality and substance, the higher readers will perceive the content's quality and value to be. The lowest level of quality and value is associated with filler content, which is content resourced from elsewhere. Original content is of higher value than filler content, but can range from basic original content to the highest quality level, called flagship content.

What is the role of social publishing in social media marketing? How do social media marketers utilize search engine optimization and social media optimization to meet marketing objectives?

Social publishing enables marketers to distribute branded content. Also called content marketing, this approach helps to bring consumers to the brand's sites. Because consumers utilize search engines to find information online, using search engine optimization to improve search engine rankings is an important marketing task. Thus, when we publish content, the content should be optimized for search engines. We also want people to link to our site—a form of referral. This is the goal of social media optimization.

How can social content be promoted? What role do social news and social bookmarking sites play in content promotion?

Social content can be promoted with social media press releases, microblog posts, and social news and social bookmarking sites. The press release and microblog posts encourage sharing among interested people and provide links to the original content. Social news sites enable a way to share links to the content and to promote the content through community rankings. Social bookmarks also enable shared links and a form of content quality ranking.

REVIEW QUESTIONS

1   What is social publishing? What kinds of content can be published socially?
2   How can social publishing, along with SEO and SMO, help to meet marketing objectives?
3   How can a site be optimized for search engines?
4   Why is it important to achieve a top three ranking in a list of search engine results?
5   Explain the concept of the linkwheel.
6   What are the different types of tags that are used by search engine optimizers to influence search engine indexing?
7   What role does social media optimization play in search engine optimization? How are the two concepts related?
8   Explain the five types of linkbait and why linkbaiting is important.
9   Is there a difference between social news sites and social bookmarking sites? Explain.

EXERCISES

1   Visit a website of your choice.

    a   Go through the website to identify the components that were strategically optimized using SEO and SMO techniques. What could have been done to optimize the site further? Print out a screen image and label the page for in-class discussion.

    b   Identify the keywords you think would be good tags for the site.

    c   Run a search query using the keywords. Does the site show up in the first page of rankings? In the top three? Why do you think the site was successful (or not)?

    d   While you're on the search results page, take a look at the sponsored and organic results listings. How do they differ? Which would be most influential if you had been conducting a real search?

2   Visit Blogger or WordPress and sign up for a free blogging account. Complete your profile and add the standard blog components to your blog layout.

    a   Now write your first post (your instructor may assign a topic or you can start with one of the review questions).

    b   Optimize your post using the techniques described in the chapter.

    c   Create your own social media linkwheel with the pages you have in your digital footprint.

    d   Try to get your content to spread through the network effect by seeding the content and drawing upon the influencers already in your network.

3   Register for a social bookmarking site and a social news site. You can choose which ones you wish to use. Once you've completed your profiles on the two sites, be sure to add your new activity to your digital footprint.

4   Visit the social bookmarking site you joined and look up a topic of interest for you. Select ten headlines that have been saved by other users. Classify the headlines according to the type of linkbait used in their title. Anecdotally, does it seem like there is a relationship between the number of users who have bookmarked the content and the type of linkbait used? Explain.

5   Visit Google's free SEO tools, listed below. Enter several search terms to see how they present information to you on keywords, trends, and phrases.

    a   Google Suggest

    b   Google Keywords

    c   Google Trends

6   Read the FTC "Guides Concerning the Use of Endorsements and Testimonials for Advertising" at www.ftc.gov/os/2009/10/091005revisedendorsementguides.pdf. How will the guides affect your own brand mentions in social spaces?

CHAPTER NOTES (access all weblinks listed here at: https://study.sagepub.com/smm3e)

1   Content Marketing Institute, *B2C Content Marketing: 2017 Benchmarks, Budgets, and Trends*, http://contentmarketinginstitute.com/wp-content/uploads/2016/10/2017_B2C_Research_Final-rev-10-26-16.pdf (accessed March 17, 2017).

2 "Facebook Adds VR to the Timeline", eMarketer, www.emarketer.com/Article/Facebook-Adds-VR-Timeline/1015392?ecid=NL1001 (accessed March 17, 2017).

3 "A Brief Timeline of the History of Blogging", Blogspot, https://blog.hubspot.com/marketing/history-of-blogging#sm.0004b7ol91cduds6tlj2qb4zw13aj (accessed March 17, 2017).

4 "Who's Blogging What: Better Business Blogging in 2011," HubSpot, www.hubspot.com/ebooks/better-business-blogging-in-2011 (accessed December 19, 2010).

5 Heather Armstrong, *Dooce*, www.dooce.com (accessed January 1, 2011).

6 David Armano, *Logic + Emotion*, http://darmano.typepad.com (accessed January 1, 2011).

7 Annika Darling, "The 10 Top Earning Bloggers in the World," The Richest, February 2, 2014, www.therichest.com/rich-list/world/worlds-10-top-earning-bloggers (accessed March 5, 2014).

8 "News Use Among Social Media Platforms 2016," Pew Research Center, www.journalism.org/2016/05/26/news-use-across-social-media-platforms-2016/#fn-55250-1 (accessed March 17, 2017).

9 Todd Wasserman, "Chick-Fil-A Accused of Setting Up Fake Facebook Account," *Mashable*, July 25, 2012, http://mashable.com/2012/07/25/chick-fil-a-accused-of-setting-up-fake-facebook-account/#f18lCF3XZqq3 (accessed June 18, 2017).

10 Tim Nudd, "Man Poses as Target on Facebook, Trolls Haters of Its Gender-Neutral Move With Epic Replies," AdWeek, August 13, 2015, www.adweek.com/creativity/man-poses-target-facebook-trolls-haters-its-gender-neutral-move-epic-replies-166364 (accessed March 17, 2017).

11 Content Marketing Institute, *B2C Content Marketing: 2017 Benchmarks, Budgets, and Trends.*

12 Chris Garrett, "Diggbait, Linkbait, Flagship Content and Authority," chrisg.com, February 11, 2008, www.chrisg.com/diggbait-linkbait-flagship-content-and-authority (accessed December 25, 2010).

13 Mimi An, "Compounding Blog Posts: What They Are and Why They Matter," Hubspot, January 28, 2016, https://research.hubspot.com/reports/compounding-blog-posts-what-they-are-and-why-they-matter (accessed March 17, 2017).

14 Ibid.

15 Yaro Starak, "How to Write Great Blog Content: The Pillar Article", www.entrepreneurs-journey.com/845/pillar-article (accessed March 17, 2017). See also: "What Type of Content Is Most Popular on Digg, Reddit, Propeller, Delicious, and StumbleUpon," Social Media Trader, December 29, 2007, http://socialmediatrader.com/analysis-what-type-of-content-is-most-popular-on-digg-reddit-propellerdelicious-and-stumbleupon (accessed June 24, 2010).

16 Content Marketing Institute, *B2C Content Marketing: 2017 Benchmarks, Budgets, and Trends.*

17 Rohit Bargava, "5 Rules of Social Media Optimization (SMO)," Influential Marketing Blog, August 5, 2006, http://rohitbhargava.typepad.com/weblog/2006/08/5_rules_of_soci.html (accessed January 1, 2011).

18 Chris Sherman, "A New F-Word for Google Search Results," Search Engine Watch, March 7, 2005, http://searchenginewatch.com/3488076 (accessed June 29, 2010).

19 Rebecca Maynes and Ian Everdell, "The Evolution of Google Search Results Pages and Their Effect on User Behavior," White paper, Mediative, www.mediative.com/SERP (accessed July 4, 2017).

20 Linking Strategies, www.webhostingtalk.com/wiki/Linking_strategies#Three-way_linking (accessed December 25, 2010).

21 Pamela Vaughan, "The Marketer's Ultimate Guide to Link Bait," HubSpot, July 18, 2012, https://blog.hubspot.com/blog/tabid/6307/bid/33393/The-Marketer-s-Ultimate-Guide-to-Link-Bait.aspx (accessed July 4, 2017).

22 "GoPro: Creating an Authentic Brand Through User-Generated Content: Case Study," Social Bakers, www.socialbakers.com/social-media-content/studies/go-pro (accessed June 18, 2017).

23 Engagement Labs, "GoPro, Fitbit, Lenovo and Beats by Dre Plug into Social Media, While Tech-Giants Apple, Samsung and Sony Charge Offline Conversation," January 14, 2016, www.engagementlabs.com/press/gopro-fitbit-lenovo-and-beats-by-dre-plug-into-social-media-while-tech-giants-apple-samsung-and-sony-charge-offline-conversation (accessed June 18, 2017).

30 "Warner Bros. Settles FTC Charges It Failed to Adequately Disclose It Paid Online Influencers to Post Gameplay Videos: Influencers Were Paid Thousands of Dollars to Promote 'Shadow of Mordor'," Federal Trade Commission, July 1, 2016, www.ftc.gov/news-events/press-releases/2016/07/warner-bros-settles-ftc-charges-it-failed-adequately-disclose-it (accessed June 18, 2017).

25 Ibid.

26 ".com Disclosures: How to Make Effective Disclosures in Digital Advertising", Federal Trade Commission, March 2013, www.ftc.gov/tips-advice/business-center/guidance/com-disclosures-how-make-effective-disclosures-digital (accessed June 18, 2017).

Visit **https://study.sagepub.com/smm3e** for free additional online resources related to this chapter.

8

Social Entertainment

Learning Objectives

When you finish reading this chapter, you will be able to answer these questions:

1 What is social entertainment? What is branded entertainment? How is it distinguished from content marketing used in social publishing?

2 How can social media marketers use social entertainment to meet branding objectives? Why is social entertainment an effective approach for engaging target audiences?

3 What are the characteristics of social games and gamer segments? How can marketers effectively use social games? How are alternate reality games different from other social games?

4 How are brands using original digital video as a social entertainment tactic?

5 In what ways are marketers using social music, social video and television, and social celebrity to share brand messaging?

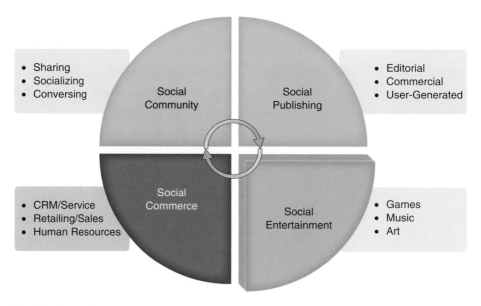

- Sharing
- Socializing
- Conversing

Social Community

- Editorial
- Commercial
- User-Generated

Social Publishing

- CRM/Service
- Retailing/Sales
- Human Resources

Social Commerce

Social Entertainment

- Games
- Music
- Art

Figure 8.1   The Social Entertainment Zone

The Social Entertainment Zone

Have you played Criminal Case? Felt addicted to Pet Rescue Saga? Maybe you get your music fix on Spotify and watch and chat about your favorite television shows on Telfie. The third zone of social media is social entertainment. The zone of **social entertainment** encompasses events, performances, and activities, which are experienced and shared using social media, and designed to provide the audience with pleasure and enjoyment. Within this zone, users can experience entertainment and share the experience with others. The distinction between the zones of social publishing and social entertainment is the orientation: knowledge-sharing versus entertainment-sharing. Broadly, social entertainment encompasses the digital and social forms of media that are otherwise addressed by the entertainment industry. By that, we mean that social entertainment channels are digitally connected, participatory, and shareable. As such, social entertainment includes social games, socially enabled video games, alternate reality games, social music, and social television and video.

Marketers can use aspects of social entertainment in several ways, along a continuum from low to high brand presence. The level of brand presence influences the ease and complexity of execution, with low levels requiring relatively little time, effort, and money and high levels requiring more substantial brand investments. As paid media, marketers can buy advertising space in and around the source of entertainment. In this way, marketers can reach a desired audience through existing social entertainment properties. Brand integration, also known as product placements, within social entertainment vehicles can also be arranged. Brands can sponsor entertainment content in social channels. Lastly, brands can create *owned* vehicles of social entertainment by creating branded content whether it be games, music, or video. This option is known as **branded entertainment**. We will focus on *social* branded entertainment but keep in mind that branded entertainment also exists in traditional media.

Branded entertainment is a subset of content marketing. Content marketing is also the basis for social publishing strategies utilizing relevant, high-value information desired by the target audience, as we discussed in Chapter 7. However, for branded entertainment, the content seeks to capture attention and retain that attention for a prolonged period of time (at least compared to the standard 30-second ads) and to do so by entertaining the audience. Social branded entertainment goes a step farther to encourage the audience to interact with the content and to share the content and their interactive experience with the content with their social networks. As in other social media settings, influencers can also play a role.[1]

This brings us to the need to distinguish between social publishing and social entertainment. Both utilize the principles of content marketing to some extent (but not entirely). Just as advertising has been associated with the goals of informing and/or entertaining, so too is content marketing. The content marketing aspects of social publishing are focused on the goal of informing. The content marketing aspects of social entertainment are focused on the goal of entertaining. As a review, remember that social publishing is most akin to traditional media in that any one (whether brand, news organization, or individual) can publish content in online channels. These channels may be part of a media-sharing site or owned media such as a blog. Across socially published content, the primary goal is to express a POV via information. For brands, this POV is an opportunity to build reputation, encourage positive WOM about the brand, and share relevant information. Social entertainment is most akin to the entertainment industry, which provides amusement, distraction, and escape to audiences. In the marketing context, brands add value by producing social entertainment venues or leveraging popular social entertainment venues to reach an audience. Both social publishing content and social entertainment content can be distributed via social channels and vehicles, such as YouTube. While some vehicles may specialize in a specific zone, most social network sites have cross-zone functionality. This is certainly the case for YouTube. Likewise, Facebook defines itself as a social utility because of the depth and breadth of its service capabilities across all four zones of social media.

Social Entertainment as Play

Entertainment can be thought of in the context of play and brands that utilize entertainment as a channel (whether via paid or owned media) are ingratiating themselves into the consumers' realm of play.[2] Individuals voluntarily choose to actively participate in entertainment media just as they may other enjoyable activities—they play! Play and the motivations for individuals to participate include power, identity, fantasy, and frivolity. These four aspects of play are present in social entertainment. Social entertainment that builds on the 'play as power' concept provides participants with a competitive task. Play as identity provides symbolic benefits to the participant in that the form of entertainment is self-expressive, reveals affinities and interests, and provides for a sense of affiliation. Social music and social film are largely thought to be most relevant to those who are motivated by play as identity. Play as fantasy encourages participants to engage in creative, imaginative experiences. Play as frivolity provides for fun, plain and simple. The goal is not challenging but relaxing. These four aspects of play are easily identifiable in all components of social entertainment. To the extent that we can understand why consumers engage in social entertainment, as marketers, we can then find ways to provide value for those target audiences that are consistent with our brand message and marketing objectives.

Social Entertainment and Marketing Objectives

Why are brands turning to social entertainment? Social entertainment can reach audiences where and when they are spending time, in a context that enables frequent engagement with the brand message. What's more, while traditional advertising is sometimes thought of as irritating, people find value in brand integrations with entertainment. Sprout Social's Social Index report found that among millennials, 38% follow brands on social media for entertainment value.[3] Edelman's Brand Engagement in the Era of Social Entertainment Survey found that 34% of people and 52% of those between 18 and 34 years old perceive value in online branded entertainment.[4] It is because of this perception of value that people seek out social entertainment and choose to engage with it. All forms of social entertainment, whether branded or not, provide for a more immersive and longer-lasting experience with the brand. In this chapter, we'll explore how brands can use social games, social music, and social video and television to meet branding objectives. Our coverage is categorized by content type, but organized to reflect the brand presence continuum, from low (utilizing existing social entertainment properties) to high (developing original, branded, social entertainment content).

Social Games

Social games make up the largest active area of social entertainment. At their core, they are games but, importantly, they are social—that is to say, they are digital, interactive, and shareable online with one's network. The context of a social game revolves around goal-oriented activity with defined rules of engagement and online connectivity among a community of players. According to the International Social Games Association, 750 million people play social games. Smartphones are credited with the surge in popularity; 84% of social games are played using apps on mobile devices. Social game revenues worldwide are estimated to reach more than $2 billion by 2020.[5]

What makes a game social is largely what makes *any* form of social media social—the existence of and participation in a community and sharing within the community. Games are social when players share their game play with others. This means that by definition social games are multi-player games. The social components of the game will be enhanced if there is communication among the players, tools to share activities and achievements, and methods to encourage others to join in the play. Therefore, we define a social game as a multi-player, competitive, goal-oriented activity with defined rules of engagement and online connectivity enabling conversation among a community of players. Most social games include a few key elements:

- *Leaderboards*: a listing of the leaders in the game competition.
- *Achievement badges*: symbols awarded to show game levels achieved and shared with the community.
- *Friend (buddy) lists*: a list of contacts with whom one plays and the ability to communicate within the game.

The characteristics that appeal to serious gamers—the sense of competition and immersion within a dedicated community of players—can be heightened with the addition of social elements. And, people who once felt games were nothing more than a waste of time for teenage boys who huddle in basements among discarded pizza boxes, now find casual, social games an enjoyable way to chase away boredom, spend time online with friends, and, quite simply, play.

Gamer Segments

At one time, we could easily categorize gamers based on the centrality of gaming in their lives. Gamers were either **casual** or **hardcore**, and the games they played reflected this division within the gaming community. Casual gamers played **casual games** and hardcore gamers played **core games**. Casual games are distinguished by low barriers to entry. They require only a small amount of time per session, are easy to learn, and are readily available online. For example, someone who wants to play Pet Rescue Saga can just hop online and start matching gemstones for whatever brief time he or she has available. Most casual, social games can be played using a mobile app, the most popular game variant. eMarketer estimates that 80% of smartphone owners game on their device.[6] Studies of how people spend time on smartphones suggest that game play is the second most frequent smartphone activity (communication and social networking is first), accounting for an average of 537 minutes per month.

In contrast, a core game such as Call of Duty: Ghost requires a much larger time investment. Core games typically require extended lengths of time per game-play session (90 minutes to several hours), are highly immersive, and demand advanced skills for ongoing play. They may be available online, or may have specific hardware and software requirements. Hardcore gamers value realism in the game's contextual clues and challenge in the game's activities; casual gamers value ease of use and immediate gratification. Although the stereotypes of casual versus hardcore gamers still hold some truth, social games are blurring the distinctions between these two types, and indeed they are bringing new gamers (and crossover games) into the mix.

Gaming is not limited to male teens, as most of us assume. Jason Allaire, co-director of the Gains Theory Gaming Lab said, "There is no longer a 'stereotypical game player,' but instead a game player could be your grandparent, your boss, or even your professor."[7] Let's take a look at the demographic characteristics of gamers.[8] Today a staggering 65% of American households play computer and video games. The gender mix of gamers no longer skews male—at least not when it comes to casual social games. There are gender differences in the types of games preferred. Women tend to show a preference for puzzle and trivia games. The number of female gamers aged 50 and older is a fast-growing segment that is expected to continue growing as seniors recognize the value of gaming as a social entertainment experience. Historically, casual gamers trend older and female whereas hardcore gamers skew younger and male. Table 8.1 summarizes the differences between social games and core games.

Millions of gamers are active daily and the most popular social games top 10 million players daily. Still, most social games have relatively low reach (percentage of social media users who play the game). Games by Zynga, King, and Electronic Arts (EA) are most effective with reach estimates around 15%.[9] There are differences in the dedication of gamers to their respective games, but overall games exhibit a high degree of stickiness. As a reminder, stickiness describes the ability of a medium to attract an audience and keep that audience. In this context, stickiness is measured as a ratio of daily to monthly game players. In other words, the stickier the game, the more often players will play. Estimates suggest that the stickiest

Table 8.1   The Differences Between Social Games and Core Games

Casual/Social Games	✓ Short, snackable games. Primarily 2D environments
	✓ Mainly played on web, social sites and mobile/tablets
	✓ Demographic skews female
	✓ 146 million US players
	✓ Highly fragmented due to low cost to produce
Core Games	✓ Immersive and/or realistic games that require long time periods to complete. Primarily 3D environments
	✓ Mainly played on console and PC. Mobile/tablet growing with better hardware
	✓ Demographic skews male
	✓ 119 million US players
	✓ Low fragmentation due to higher cost to produce

Source: *IAB Games Advertising Report, 2015*, Interactive Advertising Bureau, www.iab.com/wp-content/uploads/2015/09/IAB-Games-PSR-Update_0913.pdf (accessed March 18, 2017)

games are MyVegas Slots (84%), Words with Friends (54%), and Candy Crush (61%).[10] Game designers attribute stickiness to design: games are designed with a compulsion loop such that every action you experience produces a response that makes you want to do it again.[11] When we feel pleasure, a substance called dopamine is released in our brains. Common addictions including sex, nicotine, and gambling all stimulate dopamine production. This form of reinforcement is thought to explain the prevalence of gaming as an online activity, and the growth in social game play (whether mobile or stationary) across demographic groups. Casual gamers do spend less time on games each week than do core gamers, but even in these cases eMarketer estimates that 34% of gamers spend more than four hours a week playing games, 8% spend about three hours, 17% spend about two hours, and 9% spend one hour. For example, more than 43.7 million people play Zynga's Words with Friends each month. They average six hours of game time each month over an average of 113 sessions of game play, lasting about three minutes per session. That's a lot of game time—and a lot of opportunities for brands to interact with prospective customers.[12]

Gaming involves more than an investment of time, however. These activities require attention and active involvement. Unlike many other forms of media consumption, players are not likely to be multi-tasking during a game or consuming multiple forms of media simultaneously. Gamers aren't texting, talking, or using the remote to channel surf when they're engrossed in killing orcs or acquiring farmland. This heightened attention and focus is among the benefits gaming offers to marketers. While other media channels suffer from attention fragmentation due to the simultaneous use of multiple media devices (called media multi-tasking), gaming commands singular focus. Games meet all of the criteria for viable market segmentation:

- The market is substantial, reachable, and measurable.
- The gaming demographic has broadened so that games are now considered viable vehicles to reach women and older consumers as well as young males.
- Gamers spend sufficient, dedicated time with games to achieve valuable ad impressions.

How We Categorize Social Games

Game design is built upon several layers, including platform, mode, milieu, and genre.[13] In fact, any platform can potentially support a social game environment. If the game can operate as multi-player and includes online connectivity for communication and sharing among the players, it is social. Let's take a closer look at the dimensions we use to characterize games.

Game Platforms

A **game platform** refers to the hardware systems on which the game is played. Game platforms include **game consoles** (consoles are interactive, electronic devices used to display video games such as Sony's PlayStation, Microsoft's Xbox, and Nintendo's Wii), computers (including both online games and those that require software installation on the player's computer hard drive), and portable devices that may include smartphones or devices specifically for game play such as the Sony PSP or Nintendo DS.[14] However, it's important to keep in mind that social games often appear on multiple platforms: gamers have a strong tendency to use two or more platforms, so marketers can reach them as they move back and forth.

Mode and Milieu

Mode refers to the way the game world is experienced. It includes aspects such as whether a player's activities are highly structured, whether the game is single player or multi-player, whether the game is played in close physical proximity to other players (or by virtual proximity), and whether the game is real-time or turn-based.[15] **Milieu** describes the visual nature of the game, such as science fiction, fantasy, horror, and retro.

Genres

The **genre** of a game refers to the method of play. Popular genres include simulation, strategy, action, and role-playing. Each of these genres is represented in the game market whether the games are casual, core, or social games.

- **Simulation games** attempt to depict real-world situations as accurately as possible. There are several subgenres including racing simulators, flight simulators, and "Sim" games that enable the players to simulate the development of an environment. Among social games, simulations include FarmVille, Pet Resort, and FishVille. Gamers trace most of the innovations in today's simulation games to the pioneering Sim City game.

- **Action games** consist of two major subgenres: **first-person shooters (FPS)**, where you "see" the game as your avatar sees it, and *third-person games*. Contextually there is little difference in these subgenres given the extent to which gamers identify with their avatars. The avatar acts as a virtual prosthetic connecting the player and the environment. Action games are **performative** in that the player chooses an action that the game then executes. The actions may revolve around battles, sports, gambling, and so on. Examples of social action games are Epic Goal (a live-action soccer game), Paradise Paintball (a first-person shooter social game), and Texas Hold'Em (a social gambling game).

- **Role-playing games (RPGs)**, games in which the players play a character role with the goal of completing some mission, are closely tied to the milieu of fantasy. Perhaps the best-known RPG started its life as a tabletop game—Dungeons and Dragons. Players adopt the identity of a character in the game story and go about completing tasks and collecting points and items as they strive to accomplish the intended goal. **MMORPGs**—*massive multi-player online role-playing games*—are a type of RPG that truly encompasses the social aspects of gaming. For years, World of Warcraft was the largest of these with millions of paid subscribers. However, in recent years, the entry of "free to play" games and the popularity of League of Legends has resulted in a decline in popularity for the once juggernaut game.

- **Strategy games** are those that involve expert play to organize and value variables in the game system. These games may involve contextualizing information available from secondary sources outside the game itself, including previous experience with game play. Later in this chapter we will discuss alternate reality games as a game form for marketing. Although these games stand apart from other social games due to their complexity, they are also strategy games that involve the solving of puzzles and the systematic evaluation of new information and choices to be made to continue in the game. **Puzzle games**, a common variant in the realm of social games, are also a type of strategy game. Social strategy games include Kingdoms of Camelot, Highborn, KDice, Word Cube, and Lexulous. Of course, there is quite a bit of blurring between the genres; you can play other games strategically even though they may best be categorized as sims, action, or role plays.

Game-Based Marketing

Brands can utilize social games for marketing in several ways—and they should! Games offer a targeted audience, large reach, a high level of engagement, low intrusion methods of promotion, and a way to interact with brand fans.

The *Global Games Market Report* predicts that worldwide revenues will reach $118 billion by 2019, with $52.5 billion attributed to mobile games.[16] While some users are content to pay $2 to download Angry Birds from iTunes, or purchase in-game upgrades, the reality is that only 5% of social gamers actually pay for games. The remaining 97% (500 million + users) worldwide play the free versions, using a system of social currency to unlock features, levels, and virtual goods within the game. This social currency takes the form of game credits, which are earned by viewing ads and interstitial videos, and completing lead generation offers while inside the game environment. Ad revenues represent just a portion of these revenues as game producers also earn revenues from the sale of virtual goods in games and game purchase or subscription fees. Brands have many choices when it comes to marketing with social games. They may choose to promote a brand's message in an existing game property. In these cases the brand can advertise in and around the game using display advertising and product placements, sponsor aspects of the game, and integrate the brand into game play. In addition, a brand can take an even bigger step and develop its own **advergame**, a game that delivers a branded message. We'll review each approach.

Around-Game and In-Game Advertising

Around-game advertising is shown while the game loads, during natural breaks in gameplay between levels or rounds, or throughout the game but as a placement above or below the game environment. **In-game advertising** is promotion within a game that another company develops and sells. Ads delivered in social games (online and mobile) have higher click-through rates, higher completion rates, and higher engagement rates than do other online ads.[17] The cost of in-game advertising varies but starts around $35 CPM (cost per thousand impressions). Around-game advertising is much less expensive (typically starting around $2 CPM), but also is less effective. Marketers can choose from among four general methods for around- and in-game advertising:[18]

1 **Display ads** are integrated into a game's environment as billboards, movie posters, and storefronts (depending of course on the game's context), or simply as ad space within the game screen. The display advertising may be static or dynamic and include text, images, or rich media (i.e., video). Rich media advertising can run pre-roll (before the game begins), interlevel (between stages of the game), or post-roll (at the game's conclusion), though interlevel is the most common placement.

2 **Static ads** are hard-coded into the game and ensure that all players view the advertising.

3 **Game ads** (sometimes called mini-games) are ads that launch a branded mini-game. In other words, the ads are a game within the game. Game ads are short so as not to interrupt the game experience for players, but interactive to enhance player engagement with the brand. These are a relatively new development in the industry but early research on their effectiveness suggests a lot of promise.[19]

4 **Dynamic ads** are variable; they change based on specified criteria. This technique is managed by networks such as MediaSpike and Massive, which offer insertion technology to place ads across multiple games. The networks contract with game publishers to place advertising in their games. By combining games from several publishers, networks create a large portfolio of in-game media opportunities for advertisers. The network works with publishers to strategically embed advertising, sell the placement to advertisers, serve the ads into the games in the network, and manage the billing and accounting for the process.

Dynamic advertising is valuable because of the high degree of control and real-time measurement it offers. In addition, this approach makes it possible to develop an ad network within game families. It makes it possible to aggregate numerous games, platforms, and genres into the ad network. Massive Inc. conducted a series of research tests to gauge the impact of dynamic in-game advertising. It found that in games using dynamic advertising, brand familiarity, brand ratings, purchase consideration, ad recall, and ad ratings all increased significantly compared to a control group. The study, which involved more than 1,000 gamers across North America, included tests of several advertising categories, including automotive, consumer packaged goods, and fast food.[20]

In-game ads are often connected to **value-exchange offers**, which are perceived as a form of currency among game players. Players are incentivized with an offer in exchange for interacting with the in-game ad. The offers can be for virtual goods (which players can use in the game or offer as gifts to friends), currency (used to advance in the game), or codes (used to unlock prizes and limited-access player experiences). Players are rewarded with the virtual goods, currencies, or codes if they take certain actions such as interact with the brand in the game, make a purchase, "like" the brand on Facebook, watch a commercial, or answer a survey. Value-exchange offers are a form of **transactional advertising**. The technique can be enhanced by branding the virtual good offered to players. This technique is part product placement, part direct response advertising, and part sales promotion. When the virtual goods are branded, it's a win-win. Players actually prefer branded virtual goods to generic ones. A study by AdNectar found that in games where players have a choice between comparable branded and unbranded virtual items, the branded items were preferred 10 to 1.[21]

Electronic Arts (EA), one of the most successful social and mobile game developers, identified four types of advertising it offers for marketers who wish to place their brands in EA games: (1) traffic drivers, (2) quests, (3) store tabs, and (4) media integrations. All are forms of transactional in-game advertising. Traffic drivers seek to drive players to a brand's Facebook page in exchange for a free virtual good. For instance, in EA's The Sims Social, players could download Dove Hair Spa virtual goods with a visit to the Facebook page. Quests involve multiple tasks in-game during which the player interacts with the brand. Toyota used a quest integration for players to earn a virtual Prius. Store Tabs are virtual stores in-game that are totally dedicated to the brand. Media integrations require players to watch a short video advert to unlock a virtual good. Some of the brands that have used one or more of these tactics in EA games include Dunkin Donuts and Wendy's.

MINI CASE STUDY

Burger King Complements MARCOM with #AngriestWhopper Social Game

Burger King worked with Gamewheel to develop a social game to integrate with its #AngriestWhopper campaign.[22] The campaign needed to drive traffic to Burger King restaurants and to trial of the Angriest Whopper, a Whopper loaded with fiery jalapenos. The social game was designed to reinforce the product message and incentivize restaurant visits and purchases. The principle of the game is simple yet addictive: players were challenged to collect 20 jalapeños in under 20 seconds to unlock discount coupons redeemable at Burger King restaurants. The game provided a novel way for end-users to interact with an industry giant, both online and offline. The game not only boosted online app engagement, but it also directly correlated to increased store sales.

iStock.com/ThomasVogel

Results and Outcomes

Was the game a success? Absolutely—in just two months, players participated in more than a million game sessions. That was a lot of coupons won. Did the game also drive restaurant traffic? It did. More than 100,000 game coupons were redeemed, suggesting that the game not only scored for brand engagement, but also resulted in sales.

If that's not enough evidence, read on for more on the measurable benefits of social game advertising.

- Ads in social games achieve an average CTR of 3.8% online or 3.2% mobile, while the average online ad earns just 0.2% or less and a Facebook sponsored ad between 0.3% and 3.2%.[23]
- A rich media ad placed in a social game earns an average CTR of 11.5% online or 10.0% on mobile, while the rate for the average online rich media ad is just 3.3%.[24]
- Do you finish watching video ads served to you online? You aren't alone. Video completion rates for ads online is under 58%. But video ads delivered in social games are completed 89% of the time.
- And the rate for "value-exchange ads" (those are the ads that offer you game-related goods)? These are opened 100% of the time online and 91.4% for mobile play. Ninety percent of players say they pay active attention to the brand message when interacting with incentives and brand liking improves after ad engagement.

Users exposed to an incentivized advertisement or video inside a social gaming environment are 161% more likely to visit the brand's website and 36% more likely to shop for the brand at the store location after the engagement.[25]

Product Placement

A **product placement** is simply the placement of a branded item in an entertainment property such as a television program, movie, or game. Sponsored placements are hard coded into the game environment and generally cost between $350,000 and $750,000 depending on the type of placement and the popularity of the game. A placement can be very simple—involving nothing more than having a brand visible in a scene—or it can be heavily integrated into the story and context.[26]

Screen placements that visually incorporate the brand into the scenery are the most common form of product placement. The placement may be as simple as a brand of soda present in the background or branded attire on in-game characters. For example in *FIFA*, players may wear Adidas shoes.

Script placements take the process one step farther: they include verbal mentions of the brand's name and attributes in the plot. In the Japanese version of Metal Gear Solid: Peace Walker, the character could drink Mountain Dew, eat Doritos, and spray himself with Axe to recover or develop additional strength for game play. Gamers note that product placements that are realistic enhance the game's realism and make the game more enjoyable.

Brand Integration

In-game immersive advertising opportunities include interactive product placements, branded in-game experiences, and game integration between the game and the brand. In the film industry this is known as a **plot placement**. Plot placements involve situations in which the brand is actually incorporated into the story itself in a substantive manner. Brands need to be cautious when integrating the brand message into social games. Research on the effectiveness of brand integration suggests that brand recall and recognition are positive, but the attitude toward the brand and the game can vary.[27] Players appreciate realistic brand integrations that are consistent with the game plot. They also seem to recognize and appreciate that brand sponsorships may make a game free to the player.[28] However, when brand integrations are not perceived as valuable, player attitudes are negative.[29]

CRITICAL REFLECTION

Social Game Advertising Puts Children At Risk

When it comes to marketing, children are a vulnerable target market. They may lack media literacy skills that help them distinguish between what is or isn't advertising and they may be more easily influenced by persuasive communications. As social gaming and related advertising became more prevalent, the European Commission decided to investigate. The study was extensive including focus groups and interviews in eight countries, content analysis of popular social games, and experiments to examine the relative influence of social game advertising. The report, entitled *Study on the Impact of Marketing Through Social Media, Online Games and Mobile Applications on Children's Behaviour,* found that the top 25 most popular social games all included some form of advertising (either contextual ads and/or product placements embedded in the game).[30] Further, the advertising influenced children's behavior subliminally (without the children's awareness) and drove brand desire and in-app purchases. Parents are typically thought to be the first line of defense to protect children from manipulative advertising practices. But the study found that while most parents were aware that the games included advertising, they did not consider the advertising a risk to their children. Are the parents right? Perhaps there is more risk than parents might imagine. Consider the social advergame, Bolt, sponsored by Gatorade.

While Gatorade is known to provide benefits to hydrating athletes in extreme situations like marathons or professional play, for most of us, water is the better choice. Gatorade learned that one of its key target audiences—teenage athletes—tended to choose water during practice because they believed it provided the hydration they needed. Gatorade responded by integrating the brand and an anti-water message into its social advergame![31] Bolt, developed by Rock Live, Inc., features athlete Usain Bolt, a Gatorade-sponsored athlete. The brand integration explained that Gatorade helped Bolt (already identified as the fastest man in the world) have even better performance but that water was the enemy, hurting performance. In the game, players make choices that affect how fast Bolt's character moves through the course. Gatorade resulted in faster times and higher scores while water slowed Bolt down. The game was downloaded more than 2 million times, played as many as 87 million times, and resulted in 4 million new online fans. Overall, 820 brand impressions were served, reinforcing the message that Gatorade is better than water at enhancing athletic performance. The game integration was a Bronze winner in the Interactive Advertising Bureau's MIXX awards. Seventy-three percent of players were 13 to 24 years old, consistent with the brand's key demographic. Gatorade's in-game advertising successfully delivered the misleading message that water is the enemy to its teenage target audience. The case study video submission was posted on the IAB MIXX website with other winners until it was removed shortly after, following outcries about the ethics of the tactic from nutritional bloggers and journalists.

Advergames

With advergaming, the game itself is a form of branded entertainment. It is designed by the brand to reflect the brand's positioning statement. As such, advergames are engaging vehicles for branding. They are almost exclusively available online rather than in hard media because of the desire to have a cost-effective method of distributing the game to a large audience. Likewise, they tend to be casual rather than core games because of the costs associated with creating and promoting core games. When they include social components like friend lists, chat, sharing of experiences and results, and badges, they are known as social advergames. For example, the global, fast-casual restaurant brand

Chipotle created a social advergame called the Scarecrow. The campaign won a Grand Prix and two Gold Lions at Cannes, possibly the most prestigious award for creativity. In addition to being well integrated with other elements of Chipotle's integrated marketing communications campaign, the game also included an element to activate store visits and sales. Players achieving average to high marks in the game earned coupons for redemption at Chipotle locations.

Social advergames aren't just for B2C marketers. IBM developed its CityOne social advergame to target city managers and urban planners. Players are tasked with solving a city's most pressing problems in the areas of banking, retail, energy, and water with technology.[32] The game has an underlying goal of teaching city planners about new technologies and examining the consequences of possible choices they make in addressing common urban issues. Thousands of people in more than 100 countries have played since the game launched. Oracle used a mini-advergame on Facebook to promote its Oracle Cloud services and events to IT specialists. The game, called Cloud Stacker, visualized how easy it is to stack Oracle Cloud services and ended with an invitation to register for an Oracle event. On average, players played the game twice. Compared to Oracle ads, the mini-advergame had an increased CTR of 85%.[33]

Industry and academic research supports the use of social games for branding purposes. Though there are many factors involved in whether this approach will be successful, studies suggest that brands affiliating with social games are more memorable, talked about more often and more positively, and are better liked than if a social game were not used.[34]

Still, the effectiveness of social advergames is not guaranteed. Social design is not the only dimension which influences the player experience, and consequently, attitudes toward the brand message. Others include tactical, sensorial, and affective design dimensions.[35] Tactical design influences player experience by posing intellectual challenges that surprise, intrigue, and trigger response. Sensorial design elements relate to the five senses (sight, hearing, taste, smell, and touch), with the objective of triggering sensory experiences with visual and cinematic elements, sounds, and language. Affective design influences the emotions players experience. All of these dimensions have the potential to influence player attitudes toward the brand associated with the game. The extent to which these dimensions are operationalized to create a game in which the brand's role is central to game play, and the brand category and image are congruent with the context of the game's story, can impact game enjoyment, brand memory recall, attitude toward the brand, and intent to play in the future.[36]

Brand recall is best when the brand is in harmony with the game story. However, players tend to report higher game enjoyment, intent to play in the future, and attitude toward the brand when the brand is treated more as a game sponsor than as a central element of the game story. Effectiveness can also be influenced by individual factors of the players.[37] The bottom line? Social advergames have the potential to achieve valuable brand objectives, but more study is warranted to understand gamer response to other design dimensions.

Jane Chen of Ya Ya Media, a video game developer, had this to say of advergaming's potential: "It is one of the few advertising mediums that effectively reaches target audiences in all day-parts—including hard-to-reach at-work hours … The most effective advergames push deeper down the purchase funnel and can serve to qualify buyers and incentivize consumers to visit retail outlets or even purchase directly online. The natural interactivity of games provides the perfect stimulus and ongoing communication channel between brands and their customers."[38]

The Bottom Line: Why Do Social Games Work for Marketers?

Social games have the potential to be a major weapon in a marketer's arsenal. As gaming continues to explode as a consumer activity, we expect to see many more of these vehicles—and you should too. Players tend to be in a receptive mood when gaming and branding efforts result in more positive brand attitudes. And, it's relatively inexpensive to use this medium, brand exclusivity is available (where a sponsor is the sole advertiser in a gaming environment), and metrics are available to measure just how well the game works to attract players. Game advertising is also one of the few forms of digital advertising that is not subject to ad-blocking software.

Of course, like any advertising medium games do have some negatives that the industry has to deal with. One is game clutter; like the pervasive problem of *advertising clutter* in other formats, this means that there are way too many games out there that compete for players' attention. Facebook alone offers hundreds of social games, and this number multiplies when you consider the massive inventory available on games offered on game networks (such as Pogo.com), microsites, and via consoles and software. Unlike advertising clutter, however, the problem is compounded by the time investment involved in playing a game. You can either look at or not look at a popup ad on a website and move on, but if you choose to play a game you need to devote time to learning the rules and mastering its tricks. Even for avid game geeks, there are only so many hours in a day (OK, a few more if you skip class to play your favorites). Another issue is available inventory for advertising in-game. Granted there are numerous game titles and genres, but the inventory of space available for display advertising, product placement, and brand integration is still in limited supply.

Let's summarize some key characteristics of games—in addition to cost and ease of targeting—that make this domain especially attractive to marketers going forward:

1 *Gamers are open to advertising content in games.* It's not that they're "adverholics"—just that they crave realism and many real-world venues (for better or worse) like stadiums are saturated with marketing messages.

2 *Brands benefit when they associate with a successful game.* When players love a game, some of these positive feelings rub off on the brands they encounter within it; we call this spillover a transference effect. This is the same thing that tends to happen with event sponsorships. Brands often try to link to sports and music events like the Olympics or a Rihanna concert to gain residual benefits from the brand–event association.

Not only do brands benefit from association with the game, but they can also achieve outcomes similar to when they use celebrity endorsers. Famous people whom the target audience admires also create a transference effect. That's why companies pay millions to movie stars; they hope that the knowledge that an admired person likes the brand will in turn encourage the star's fans to like it as well. Internalization occurs when members of the target market accept the beliefs of an endorser as their own. In a game context, the characters in the game's story and setting can act as brand endorsers.

The meaning transfer model states that consumers associate meaning with the endorser and then transfer the meaning to the brand in question.[39] The consumer first chooses to assign the meaning associated with the endorser to the product or brand.

Thus, meanings attributed to the endorser become associated with the brand in the consumer's mind. For game advertisers, the meaning transfer model suggests that a character's attributes can be transferred to a brand a character uses in the game as part of an in-game product placement. The key to using character endorsers successfully parallels the choice of celebrity endorsers. The character endorser should have the appropriate set of characteristics the brand desires.

3 *Players identify with the brands their characters use, and this increases their brand involvement.* Players may be particularly invested in their characters because they spend weeks, months, and even years on building their character identity and developing the attributes that will enable the character to compete at the highest possible level of the game. Even the name of the RPG genre itself, "role-playing," implies just how involved players are with their characters. When brands are embedded using immersive techniques such as enabling players in a racing game to choose their brand of race car, the players can actively interact with brands during the game experience. This "bonding" results in a heightened sense of brand identification.

4 *Branding within a game's story is an unobtrusive way to share a brand's core message.* In many ways, games approximate the immersive experience of watching a movie. Games, like movies, are capable of transcending barriers of class and culture. However, games offer more than stories told through film and literature, in that they allow the audience to actually participate in the story. When spectators become actors, they are less likely to sit back and think of reasons why the advertising message on the screen doesn't apply to them (psychologists call this common process **counterarguing**). **Narrative transportation theory** explains how even imagined interactivity can build positive brand attitudes. This theory proposes that mental stimulation through narrative storytelling encourages players to become lost in the story. Once immersed in the plot, players are distracted from advertising embedded in the game. They do not counterargue against these messages, and as a result they are more likely to form attitudes toward the brand simply based on the positive feelings the story evokes.[40]

5 *Targeting is possible for most in-game ads using gaming ad networks.* Social games were already a high value for effective reach based on game/player fit, but ad networks can tailor and customize product placements dynamically to deliver different ads based on geographic location and other segmentation variables.

6 *Marketers can measure a game's promotional value.* For both game advertising and advergaming, the game environment creates a higher impression value for the ad compared to that earned from traditional media placements. This is attributed to the frequency of exposure, the potential for interactivity with the brand's message, and the entertainment value of the platform. Millions of advertising impressions can be delivered in just a few weeks of game play at a cost as low as 25 cents per impression. In addition to the low cost, there is little advertising clutter in games, particularly when compared to other media choices. But what's equally or even more important is that marketers know how well a game works to deliver these impressions. Unlike many other forms of advertising, a sponsor can measure who saw the message and in some cases even link these exposures to sales of its product. We'll talk more about the vital issue of measuring marketing results in Chapter 11.

Alternate Reality Games: A Transmedia Genre

So far in this chapter we've focused on social games. But in addition to all the Mafia Wars and World of Warcraft players out there, other people are getting into an even newer genre that's even more immersive—one that vividly demonstrates the stunning potential of digital media. We refer to **alternate reality games (ARGs)**. Unfiction.com, a leading website for the ARG community, defines an alternate reality game as "a cross-media genre of interactive fiction using multiple delivery and communications media, including television, radio, newspapers, Internet, email, SMS, telephone, voicemail, and postal service."[41] ARGs are still social games, with a community of geographically dispersed players who compete and collaborate to solve a complex puzzle. These games are like others of the strategy genre—but on steroids. When a sponsoring brand develops an ARG it also resembles an advergame. And, because ARGs involve two or more different media, they are **transmedia social games**.

The Marketing Value of ARGs

Brands such as Levi Strauss, McDonald's, Nine Inch Nails, and Audi have used ARGs for marketing. In fact, to date, the most successful ARGs in terms of participation are brand-sponsored. Most ARGs are tied to entertainment properties such as movies, books, and video games (yes, games to promote games!). For instance, the movie *The Dark Knight* was promoted with an ARG called Why So Serious? that was played by more than 11 million people in 75 countries. It's natural that story-oriented products would promote themselves using a story-based promotional tool, but other brands can benefit from ARGs too. The key, just as with other forms of social games, is to ensure a high level of congruence between the game and the brand.

The movie launch of *A.I. (Artificial Intelligence)* in 2001 started it all with the ARG game The Beast, which a Microsoft team created. This ground-breaking promotional vehicle was set in the year 2142, 50 years after the events in the movie. This game offered three rabbit holes:

1   A clue hidden among the credits for *A.I.*

2   A trailer for the movie that invited players to call a phone number in order to receive a clue by email.

3   A promotional poster the producers sent to technology and media outlets that contained another clue.

The prevalence of brand-initiated ARGs is at least in part due to the funding necessary to build an intricate, multi-media, multi-channel narrative with characters and clues spread online and offline. Take, for instance, the Art of the Heist ARG that Audi used to promote its A3 model. ARG-related expenses ran to about $5 million.[42] Compared to television advertising, the cost of an ARG is minimal. Still, the resources required are substantial enough to warrant the need for a brand sponsor. However, this investment can pay off handsomely. For instance, Audi claims that 500,000 consumers, in its target audience of 25- to 35-year-old, upper-income males, participated in its Art of the Heist ARG, with an average exposure of four to ten minutes spent on numerous websites and pages used to embed game clues.[43] Hits to Audi's website increased 140% during the game, with the most hits originating from game sites. Its dealers earned 10,000 qualified sales leads, and 3,500 test drives could be attributed to the game.[44]

Although an ARG benefits from a sponsor's deep pockets, many of the games do not identify who is behind the effort. Instead, players play until the mystery is solved (or the sponsorship is inadvertently discovered and leaked to the community) and the brand sponsor is revealed. This type of branded ARG is known as a **dark play ARG**; it's one of the ways that brands can use **dark marketing**, which refers to a promotion that disguises the sponsoring brand. Some say it's an ethical question whether brands should acknowledge their role in an ARG (or other dark marketing promotional stunts), but thus far, both brands and players seem to recognize that the game is best left as pure play space. In the end, players have a sense of gratitude toward the brand for the game experience that translates into more positive brand attitudes, along with potentially stronger brand knowledge because participants stick with the game for days, weeks, or even months before they solve the mystery. Table 8.2 summarizes the pros and cons of the ARG strategy. All of this sounds pretty complicated, so let's first review the characteristics and vocabulary of ARGs.

Characteristics of ARGs

ARGs begin with a scripted scenario. However, over time an ARG will also become a form of consumer-fortified media as the network of gamers participates in the game by discovering clues, sharing information with others, and literally changing the structure and plot of the game with their responses. In an ARG, players not only share tips, clues, and accomplishments with the player community, they also help to direct how the story underlying the game develops. In fact, that's why sometimes ARGs are referred to as **immersive fiction**. For branded ARGs, marketers have an unmatched opportunity to share a brand story with the audience.

The games unfold over multiple forms of media and utilize many types of game elements, each tailored to specific media platforms. ARGs may utilize websites (story sites and social network sites), telephone, email, outdoor signage, T-shirts, television, radio play, and more to reveal story clues, compose scenes, and unite gamers.

ARGs are ideally suited to social media because it would be impossible to solve the puzzle alone. Among players, the term "**collective detective**" acknowledges the need for a team approach to solve the mystery. Because players from around the world participate, online communication is a necessary component to play. Many ARGs use other media channels including live events, television, radio, and so on, but social media ensure a hub of communication for the players. We summarize the basic characteristics of ARGs as follows:

- ARGs are based on a fictional story. Game characters, events, places, and plot are imagined and explored by the game writers, known as **puppet masters**.
- ARGs are strategy/puzzle games. The story unfolds as a mystery that invites players to solve clues before more of the narrative is revealed.
- Because they are transmedia social games, ARGs offer clues on multiple platforms that range from traditional media like television and newspapers to text messages and messages hidden in code in movie trailers or even concert T-shirts.

- The story is fictional as are the game characters, but the game space is not. The players are real people and the clues are revealed in real time. Consequently, *real life is itself a medium*. This characteristic has led to the ARG "TINAG" credo—"This is not a game!" Telephone numbers, websites, and locations revealed in-game are all real and functioning. Oh—and if you meet an ARG enthusiast, beware. He or she won't take kindly to references to ARGs as games (even though they are).

- Players collaborate to unravel the meanings of the clues offered but they also compete to be the first to solve layers of the mystery. Players are geographically dispersed, sometimes worldwide.

- The story unfolds, but typically not in a linear fashion. The speed of disclosure is influenced by the players' success and speed in solving clues and sharing them with the player population.

- ARGs are organic; the story may not unfold as initially conceived. Because players interact with the game, and player response can dictate the next scene in the story, stories are fluid and unpredictable.

- Players rely on the Internet, and especially social communities including forums, as the hub of communication.

- The desire for players to share information with each other and even for the story to be followed by observers attests to the viral nature of ARGs.

The Vocabulary of ARGs

ARGs have their own vernacular—understanding the lingo is the first step to understanding the culture of alternate reality gaming. The website Unfiction.com is a major clearinghouse for ARG fans. The site summarizes the basic lexicon of alternate reality gamers:[45]

- *Puppet masters*: the authors, architects, and managers of the story and its scenarios and puzzles.
- *Curtain*: the invisible line separating the players from the puppet masters.
- *Rabbit hole*: the clue or site that initiates the game.
- *Collective detective:* a term that captures the notion of collaboration among a team of geographically dispersed players who work together to flesh out the story.
- *Lurkers* and *rubberneckers*: lurkers follow the game but do not actively participate, whereas rubberneckers participate in forums but do not actively play. Consider this common line from brand-sponsored sweepstakes: "You don't have to play to win." From a branding perspective, lurkers and rubberneckers are just as critical to the success of an ARG as are the active players. Unfiction.com estimates that the ratio of lurkers to active players can range from 5:1 to 20:1, depending upon the game.
- *Steganography*: the tactic of hiding messages within another medium; the message is undetectable for those who do not know to look for it.
- *Trail*: a reference index of the game including relevant sites, puzzles, in-game characters, and other information. Trails are useful for new players coming late into a game and to veteran players who eagerly try to piece together the narrative.

Table 8.2   Pros and Cons of Using an ARG as a Social Entertainment Branding Channel

Pros	Cons
Reach can be substantial. In addition to active players, lurkers and rubberneckers may also see the messages.	ARGs require a lot of effort from initial conception through planning and execution. And, because the storyline can change depending upon the response from players, ARGs require constant monitoring and input from the game architects through and even beyond (as players are debriefed) the game's end.
The games attract media attention, resulting in earned media in the form of publicity.	Because the game can evolve in ways the architects did not originally plan, there is a risk involved. As fans drive the plot, the game can progress in ways the sponsor didn't anticipate.
Exposures earned last longer than do those for traditional media.	Hardcore brand loyalists may resent the influx of new people who express interest in the game.
ARGs are high-engagement messages. The games pull enthusiasts (players, lurkers, and rubberneckers) into the story and encourage them to seek out new information as it is presented in the game.	ARGs are unlikely to reach the same number of prospects as a brand could attract if it used mass media.
Players welcome brand-sponsored ARGs because they do not invade people's space with a brand message.	

Evaluating the Effectiveness of a Brand-Sponsored ARG

How can we measure the effectiveness of ARGs as a branding tool? ARG effectiveness measures are similar to those used for other social media approaches with a focus on site traffic and participation. We'll discuss these in greater depth in Chapter 11. The most common indicators for ARGs include:

- number of active players
- number of lurkers and rubberneckers
- rate of player registration from launch or from specific game event
- number of player messages generated
- traffic at sites affiliated with the ARG
- number of forum postings (at sites like Unfiction.com)
- average play time
- media impressions made through publicity generated about the ARG.

Original Digital Video (ODV) and Branded Video

Gaming isn't the only social entertainment option. Social media users also turn to social channels for video entertainment. As with the other forms of social entertainment, opportunities for marketing with social video and film follow the same continuum of low to high brand presence, ranging from around- and in-video advertising to product placements and brand integrations to original, branded video content.

Product placements enable brands to appeal to the audiences of popular influencers on video channels including YouTube, Instagram, Snapchat, and others. Influencers not only have relatively large audiences, they also have—well, influence—with their fans. As we discussed in Chapter 3, the opinions of influencers are trusted above many other information sources because of their perceived authenticity and transparency. This also represents a challenge for brands and influencers though. Influencers grew their fan base as an independent voice. When video content is sponsored by a brand, fans may question the validity of the influencer's brand-related content. The Federal Trade Commission requires social media influencers to prominently disclose brand deals.

According to YouTube, over 70% of people who regularly go online watch and engage with YouTube gaming, lifestyle, community, and culture content.[46] There are influencers in all of these categories but gaming is a powerhouse and consequently commands much of the brand sponsorships. More than 20 of the top 100 YouTube channels with the most subscribers worldwide are gaming related. The top video formats in the gaming category include Walkthroughs (which help gamers improve their skills), Let's Play (video coverage of a gamer in gameplay, along with commentary), Reactions (emotional responses to gaming experiences), Reviews (reviews of products), and Challenges (videos of the creator completing a challenge dare). A Google survey on viewer attitudes toward Let's Play channels reported that viewers find the YouTube creators' reactions and commentary to be a critical piece of the entertainment value of these videos. Conan O'Brien's Clueless Gamer series is a great example of this. He may not play games well, but his commentary, observations, and reactions add value and a lot of laughs. Who's the most popular Let's Play creator? That would be PewDiePie. His loyal following now outnumbers the population of Canada, making him a powerful influencer in the social entertainment community and YouTube's top earner at more than $12 million per year. To give you some perspective, Google Trends shows that searches for PewDiePie on YouTube are on a par with stars such as Eminem and Katy Perry. He's even had a cameo on the animated series *South Park*. Competitive gaming, also called **eSports**, is the fastest growing genre in the gaming category. Following the culture of professional sports teams, it has iconic players, fans, team uniforms, playoffs, and more.

A content analysis of sponsored brand content (3,700 individual content pieces including product placements, unboxing videos, reviews, and more) collected from the top 200 YouTube influencer channels found that nearly 60% of all brand-sponsored videos took place on gaming channels.[47] Figure 8.2 illustrates the distribution of brand sponsored content across YouTube categories. The study also found that 25% of sponsored content on gaming channels was placed by brands in industries unrelated to gaming. For example, BarkBox, a monthly subscription service delivering dog treats and toys, partnered with YouTuber, UberHaxorNova, to create a video featuring UberHaxorNova's Corgi, Ein, and BarkBox. The brand placement gave BarkBox access to the gamer's three million subscribers and the video scored more than 400,000 views. In a simpler version of a product placement, Smosh Games ate NatureBox snacks during one of their Let's Play videos. Given Smosh Games' subscriber base of nearly seven million, the reach was relatively small—just 500,000 views and 12,000 likes.

EXHIBIT 8.1

Dream Weaver: Casper Nurtures People with Entertainment Design to Improve the Sleep Experience

Yuganov Konstantin/Shutterstock.com

Casper is a company known for its "one model sleeps all bed in a box." While competing mattress brands have spent years educating consumers on the value of choosing a mattress as personalized to their needs and sleep habits as possible, Casper claims its scientific design results in one perfect mattress. The brand seeks a lofty goal—to be the Nike of sleep! The company didn't stop at promising the best night's sleep for people. It also sells a dog bed so pet parents can relax knowing their pup is in peaceful slumber too. With target audiences in the US and Canada, UK, and throughout the EU, Casper uses social entertainment to share its promise of restful sleep.

Its social entertainment initiative includes three tactics: 1) a bot called Insomnobot3000 that people can message when they can't sleep, 2) a series of original bedtime stories delivered via podcast, and 3) an original talk show called *In Your Dreams* in which hosts take listener calls and then analyze the meaning of their dreams.[48] The social entertainment approach is engaging while reinforcing Casper's philosophy that sleep is a major lifestyle component that affects all areas of our waking life from productivity to overall health, without the use of boring doom and gloom posts about sleep statistics and health impact. Who wouldn't like a friend to talk to during a bout of insomnia or the nurturing of a bedtime story? Casper's experience strategy in the zone of social entertainment makes participation relevant and utterly shareable.

Brands can create their own original digital video content. The stories provide an opportunity to feature the brand less obtrusively than an advertisement while providing value to the viewer in the form of entertainment. Original branded films are sometimes part of a multi-part series. Videos can be long-form but many are under 30 minutes, making them an attractive alternative to traditional television programming. The episodes run on video-streaming social sites like YouTube and Hulu. For example, Marriott, the global hotel brand, has invested heavily in original film. Its *Two Bellmen* series (on YouTube) has featured Marriott's JW Marriot brand in Los Angeles, Dubai, and Korea. Each story is based in and around the hotel. The most recent episode developed a storyline around a young Korean wedding couple to attract the highly lucrative Asian weddings and romance market. Each film costs around $200,000 to produce. Each episode has garnered several million views and more than 80% of viewers watch the entire episode. To improve audience reach, Marriott runs paid ads for the series on a variety of social networks. The company leverages film fans with special travel packages themed to the storyline.[49]

Kimberly-Clark produces a series called *Carmilla* to reach the young female audience targeted by its feminine-hygiene product, U by Kotex. While Marriott's *Two Bellmen* series highlights the hotel, the brand integration is more subtle in *Carmilla*. The story is based on a vampire-focused novella and could easily be mistaken for a drama on the CW network. The episodes are short-form—most about five minutes long—making them ideal for mobile consumption using YouTube's app. The series has been a hit! Millions of views and positive fan word-of-mouth communication about the series reinforced Kimberly-Clark's decision to renew the series for multiple seasons. Producing a full season of *Carmilla* costs between $500,000 and $1 million, or about a quarter of the cost of an average episode on a cable TV program. A survey of viewers found that 31% claimed they bought the U by Kotex brand because of the show and 93% were aware that the brand backed the series.[50]

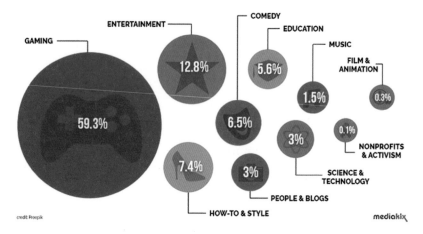

Figure 8.2   The Top YouTube Categories with Brand-Sponsored Content

Source: "Case Study: Advertising on YouTube with Top Influencers & Gaming Channels," MediaKix, May 27, 2016, http://mediakix. com/2016/05/advertising-on-youtube-case-study-influencers-sponsored (accessed June 20, 2017)

Social TV

ClickZ defined **social TV** as "technology that supports communication and social interaction in either the context of watching television, or related to TV content."[51] Both social video and social TV focus on the social object of video content, but the channels of distribution and social interaction vary. Social video is broadcast via a social channel that also facilitates audience interaction and sharing. With social TV, the viewer interaction and communication typically take place on a social network site, separate from the video broadcast channel.

For social TV to be social media marketing, it not only needs to be designed to meet marketing objectives, but also must be participatory and shareable. We say this because we believe that most examples of social TV to date leverage social community. They are engaging in conversations around the social object of the show or the characters. In this regard, they belong in zone 1—social community. However, we will cover this area of social media here due to its close affiliation with social entertainment. We also recognize that the development of technologies could rapidly create a situation that enables the true socialization of entertainment programming.

Primarily, social TV means that technology has enhanced the experience of watching video programming through the use of social media. This is to be expected given the prevalence of media multi-tasking. Surely you've done it! That means to consume one medium while engaged in one or more other media. With mobile and tablet penetration and use continuing to rise, consumers' time on the devices is bound to overlap with other frequently used medias—TV included. It's especially powerful because television was built on theatre, something that was once a shared experience but now may not be. Still, we glean more from what we see and hear if we share it with others. That is clear from the organic development of Twitter communities around programming like *The Walking Dead*.

That's pure social media, but marketers can leverage that power. How? Advertisers today often factor social media into the TV buying and planning process by evaluating affinities between programs and brands and considering the impact of TV campaigns on earned media. For marketers, the goal may be maximizing earned media impact around their campaigns. Brands can look at program characteristics to identify programs that regularly generate social media conversations around airtime—think reality competition programs, celebrity-filled award shows, and plot-twisting dramas. In addition to people who engage in social media conversation about programs, there are also people who tend to chat about the brands advertising during programs. In a recent study, Nielsen Social analyzed the overlap between these two populations—people who tweet about TV and people who tweet about brands—to understand the value of social TV audiences to brands. The study produced some interesting findings.

First, this population of social brand ambassadors—people who tweet about TV and brands—is large. The study found that in an average month, 64% of people who tweet about brands also tweet about TV. So if a brand is looking to engage people who are likely to share their brand message, connecting with social TV authors is a good place to start. Second, the study found that people who tweet about both brands and TV account for an outsized portion of all tweets about brands. The 64% of people who tweeted about brands and TV sent 78% of all brand tweets. Third, the study found that people who posted tweets about TV and brands sent three times as many brand tweets as those Twitter authors who only posted tweets about brands.[52]

Social TV data can also support marketers looking to track campaign effectiveness. Following a recent full season integration of one household brand in a reality dating show, Nielsen Social analyzed the effectiveness of the campaign by measuring the brand-related conversation among the population exposed to the TV program. Comparing the amount of brand-related tweets sent during the 70-day period before the premiere of the program to the amount sent during the 70-day program season, the brand saw an 84% increase in brand-related tweets from the audience exposed to program airings. Comparatively, the population that was not exposed to the program sent 21% fewer tweets about the brand during the program season compared to the period before the season began.[53]

There is still more to learn about the possible impact of social TV on brand communications. While Nielsen's studies suggest that brands can leverage social TV as an engagement device, it is also possible that the distracting nature of the context (watching a show, using multiple devices, and conversing with others online) harms ad message processing, reducing unaided recall.[54]

Social Music

Just as marketers can use social games as vehicles for in-game ads, integrated placements, or fully branded games, similar options are available for **social music**. This category of social entertainment has developed substantially in recent years with the entry of social, streaming music providers like Pandora, Spotify, and Shazam. It's important to reiterate that there is a difference between advertising around social entertainment spaces and truly utilizing social entertainment as a social media marketing opportunity. Technically speaking, advertising in and around social entertainment spaces is digital advertising—online or mobile. It is not in and of itself social, even if the site is social. Despite this, we will cover these options briefly.

In-Network Advertising

Social music is primarily based around cloud services providing streamed sound. Though podcast sites have long provided streamed audio, we classify podcasts as a form of media-sharing site used primarily for social publishing. iTunes, Google Play, and Amazon Music are retailers of music that may also be cloud-stored and streamed and, though these providers have some social features such as ratings and rankings, we consider these more consistent with social commerce. What then are we referring to when we suggest that marketers consider using social music for promotions? Brands can include many types of ads on social music sites, including audio ads, display ads, billboard ads (which serve as a screensaver that appears when a listener has gone inactive), and homepage takeovers (which ensure all site visitors are exposed to the ad). More integrated forms of advertising with social music include the use of branded playlists and the use of microsites within the social music vehicle.

Why should marketers consider social music sites as possible ad vehicles? Like games, these social sites offer targeting and reach capabilities. Advertisers can target using age, gender, preferred music genre, and location. Ad impressions are charged on a CPM basis. A benefit with social music is that production may be provided by the site (at least for Pandora and Spotify at the time of this writing). As noted, simply posting an ad in the social media space is not social media marketing. That action offers the benefit of reach and frequency but not that of truly engaging.

Immersive Branding

Brands that want a more integrated option need to find ways that the brand itself can add value to the content that the target audience values. Recent examples include branded playlists and branded microsites that focus around artists or styles of music that target market value. This enables the brand to truly leverage the social community aspects of the vehicle in question. The key here is for brands to find ways to add value to music that people are already passionate about. This is not unlike what sponsorship marketing has been doing … except now we are doing it among social media communities. Coca-Cola's Placelists campaign provides a good example. Placelists is a social music app hosted by Spotify. Visit www.coca-cola.com/placelists to experience it for yourself. The concept is based on existing music and existing places. Do you have a place that you love? Is there a sound that always brings you back to that place? That's how one of us feels about the Gypsy Kings. Wherever she is, whatever she is doing, if she hears a song by the Gypsy Kings, she is transported to Europe, sitting at a café watching people go by. That's just what Coca-Cola Placelists seeks to do. Or even more! Do you wish to know what people are listening to now in Argentina? Placelists can do that too and let you feel that you are a part of that experience. It's all part of a Coca-Cola Spotify app. The app uses folksonomies too—with people tagging songs to geographic memories. Are you worried your favorite locale doesn't have a Placelist? Not to worry! Coca-Cola has activated the campaign by seeding the app with 30 locations, 40 songs per location. Coca-Cola wants every place in the world to have its own Placelist. Importantly, as a social media campaign, you and others can influence Placelists.

Another example? BMW—clearly a leader in the development of digital, branded content, it too sought to inspire fans with music. With the campaign objective of increasing awareness and consideration of the BMW 320i, it created a branded app on Spotify that enabled a music set based on iconic American road trips. Each road trip generated a custom playlist curated for that location. What's your favorite road trip? The drive down U.S. Route 1 viewing the Pacific Coast is a favorite. Of course, the brand is never far from reach and the playlist is shareable.

These are Spotify examples, but Pandora has done well too! Toyota has created Toyota Sessions, a custom station featuring emerging artists. In this regard, Toyota has aligned itself with the culture of Pandora, providing a discovery engine for worthwhile artists.

Brands that recognize the passion people have for music are investing even more heavily. Converse created several recording studios that it makes available to artists for free. The program is called Converse Rubber Tracks. The site provides free audio clips produced at the studio and visitors are encouraged to use the clips in their own social media content (but remember to use the hashtag #rubbertracks when sharing!).[55] These examples suggest the ways brands can truly integrate with the passion fans feel for music and provide something meaningful. To our knowledge, no brand has fully adopted social music to the extent of developing branded music. But this area is new and developing … we'll see!

CHAPTER SUMMARY

How can social media marketers use social entertainment to meet branding objectives? What are the types of social entertainment? Why is social entertainment an effective approach for engaging target audiences?

Social entertainment provides opportunities for marketers to reach people with content that is welcomed and with which people want to spend time. By developing marketing messages in, around, and integrated with social entertainment, marketers can ensure the target audience spends more time with brand messages. Social entertainment includes social games, social music, and social TV.

What is branded entertainment? How is it distinguished from content marketing used in social publishing?

Branded entertainment is entertaining content that is produced by a brand rather than by a third party. Original digital video is a growing form. The Marriott-developed *Two Bellmen* series is an example. It is a type of content marketing. Content marketing is also used in social publishing strategies for social media marketers, though social publishing strategies focus primarily on content that provides opportunities for thought leadership. Also, social publishing can be utilized by users (to publish user-generated content).

What are the characteristics of social games and gamer segments? How can marketers effectively use social games? How are alternate reality games different from other social games?

A social game is a multi-player, competitive, goal-oriented activity with defined rules of engagement and online connectivity among a community of players. Most social games include a few key elements such as leaderboards, achievement badges, or buddy lists that allow players to compare their progress with other players. Traditionally we distinguished gamers as either casual or hardcore, depending on how much time they spent playing and how important the games were to them. This distinction is blurring as more "mainstream" players get involved. Today there are many women and older people who are avid gamers in addition to the base of young, male players.

An organization may choose to promote its message in an existing game property. In these cases the brand can advertise in and around the game using display advertising and product placements, sponsor aspects of the game, and integrate the brand into game play. In addition, a brand can take an even bigger step and develop its own customized advergame that delivers a more focused and pervasive branded message.

Players tend to be in a receptive mood when gaming and branding efforts result in more positive brand attitudes. In addition, it's possible to finely target users because most games attract a fairly distinct type of player. And, it's relatively inexpensive to use this medium, brand exclusivity is available (where a sponsor is the sole advertiser in a gaming environment), and metrics are available to measure just how well the game works to attract players.

ARGs are a type of social game. They begin with a scripted scenario. However, the game changes as the network of gamers participates in the game by discovering clues, sharing information with others, and literally changing the structure and plot of the game with their responses. The games unfold over multiple forms of media and utilize many types of game elements, each tailored to specific media platforms. ARGs may utilize websites (story sites and social network sites), telephones, email, outdoor signage, T-shirts, television, radio play, and more to reveal story clues, compose scenes, and unite gamers. ARGs are best suited to brands that want to reach people who are willing to invest the time to engage in this kind of activity.

How are brands using social music, social television, and social celebrity for brand messaging?

Brands add value by curating content for fans, engaging content around conversations about social television, and affiliating with social celebrities. The brand is not the main focus in these activities but they add value by understanding why fans are participating in the respective form of social entertainment.

REVIEW QUESTIONS

1 What is social entertainment? What are the types of social entertainment?

2 How do casual gamers differ from hardcore gamers? Are social gamers casual, a hybrid of casual and hardcore, or a new segment of gamer all together?

3 What are the four major game genres? Provide examples of each. What is the distinguishing characteristic associated with each genre?

4 What makes a game social? Explain the characteristics of social games.

5 Explain the differences between pre-roll, post-roll, and interlevel in-game advertising.

6 What is an advergame? How do we distinguish it from other social games?

7 How is brand integration and immersive in-game advertising different from other forms of branding in social games?

8 Why is brand sponsorship of video influencers so effective?

9 What is the advantage of using original branded video content for marketing rather than advertising in other content?

10 What is social music?

11 How can entertainment brands leverage social TV?

EXERCISES

1   Are branded offers in social games ethical? Choose a side and debate this issue with a classmate. Then post your opinions and find out what your social graph thinks of this common practice.

2   Choose a social game to play. As you interact with the game, keep a journal of your experience. In particular, note the advertising and branded components and your reactions to them. How does your experience affect your attitude toward the brands?

3   Choose three people you know who watch YouTube videos. Interview them about whether they notice sponsorships of their favourite celebrities and channels. Have they responded to branded offers? Write a blog post on their brand experience in watching YouTube videos and their resulting perceptions of the brand.

4   Visit Unfiction.com or argn.com to see what ARGs are playing now. Explore one of the current games. Is it associated with a brand (or is it a dark play ARG, with the brand yet to be identified)? Make a list of non-entertainment brands that could use an ARG to tell their story and immerse their brand fans.

CHAPTER NOTES (access all weblinks listed here at: https://study.sagepub.com/smm3e)

1   Sami Main, "Fullscreen's Research Finds Gen Z Enjoys Branded Content More than Millennials," AdWeek, May 23, 2017, www.adweek.com/digital/fullscreens-research-finds-gen-z-enjoys-branded-content-more-than-millennials (accessed July 3, 2017).

2   Jie Zhang, Youngjun Sung, and Wei-Na Lee, "To Play or Not to Play: An Exploratory Content Analysis of Branded Entertainment in Facebook," *American Journal of Business*, 25:1 (2010), 53–64.

3   "The Social Generations: Millennials Ask, Gen X Buys & Baby Boomers Observe," The Q1 2017 Sprout Social Index, Sprout Social, 2017, http://sproutsocial.com/insights/data/q1-2017 (accessed March 15, 2017).

4   "Brand Engagement in an Era of Social Entertainment," Edelman Insights, 2012, www.edelman.com/insights/intellectual-property/matter-brand-engagement (accessed November 14, 2013).

5   "Essential Facts About the Computer and Video Game Industry," Entertainment Software Association, April 2016, http://essentialfacts.theesa.com/Essential-Facts-2016.pdf (accessed June 20, 2017).

6   "Gaming on Mobile Leads All Other Platforms," eMarketer, August 12, 2013, www.emarketer.com/Article/Gaming-on-Mobile-Leads-All-Other-Online-Platforms/1010125 (accessed March 18, 2017).

7   Steve Hicks, "Does the Video Game Industry Hold the Keys to the Future of Advertising? Engage Consumers via Brain Chemistry," Adweek, February 16, 2014, www.adweek.com/news/advertising-branding/engage-consumers-brain-chemistry-155531 (accessed June 25, 2014).

8   Alison Murdock, "Consumers Spend More than 1 Billion Hours a Month Playing Mobile Games," Verto Analytics, May 17, 2016, www.vertoanalytics.com/consumers-spend-1-billion-hours-month-playing-mobile-games (accessed March 18, 2017).

9   "Verto Index: Mobile Games," Verto Analytics, June 23, 2016, www.vertoanalytics.com/verto-index-mobile-games-2 (accessed March 18, 2017).

10 Ibid.

11 Hicks, "Does the Video Game Industry Hold the Keys to the Future of Advertising?"

12 "Verto Index: Mobile Games."

13 Thomas Apperley, "Genre and Game Studies: Toward a Critical Approach to Video Game Genres," *Simulation & Gaming*, 37:1 (2006), 6–23.

14 *IAB Games Advertising Report, 2015*, Interactive Advertising Bureau, www.iab.com/wp-content/uploads/2015/09/IAB-Games-PSR-Update_0913.pdf (accessed March 18, 2017).

15 Apperley, "Genre and Game Studies: Toward a Critical Approach to Video Game Genres."

16 *2016 Global Games Market Report*, Newzoo, April 2016, https://newzoo.com/insights/articles/global-games-market-reaches-99-6-billion-2016-mobile-generating-37 (accessed March 18, 2017).

17 Michelle R. Nelson, "Recall of Brand Placements in Computer/Video Games," *Journal of Advertising Research*, 42:2 (2002), 80–92.

18 *IAB Games Advertising Report, 2015*.

19 "Game Ads—The Next Big Thing After Video Ads?" Gamewheel, April 3, 2016, www.gamewheel.com/game-ads-next-big-thing-after-video-ads (accessed March 18, 2017).

20 "In-Game Advertising Research Proves Effectiveness for Brands Across Categories and Game Titles," June 3, 2008, https://news.microsoft.com/2008/06/03/in-game-advertising-research-proves-effectiveness-for-brands-across-categories-and-game-titles/#F40TZm8fSfcu9O4f.97 (accessed June 20, 2017).

21 "AdNectar: Users Prefer Branded Virtual Goods 10 to 1", Engage Digital, www.engagedigital.com/blog/2009/08/07/adnectar-users-prefer-branded-virtual-goods-10-to-1 (accessed March 18, 2017).

22 "Burger King: Angriest Whopper Case Study," Gamewheel, 2016, www.gamewheel.com/stories/burger-king (accessed March 18, 2017).

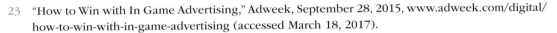

23 "How to Win with In Game Advertising," Adweek, September 28, 2015, www.adweek.com/digital/how-to-win-with-in-game-advertising (accessed March 18, 2017).

24 Nicole Sorochan, "Social Gaming and the Enormous Advertising Opportunity Within," OneNet Marketing, October 27, 2016, http://onenetmarketing.com/blog-posts/social-gaming-and-the-enormous-advertising-opportunity-within (accessed March 18, 2017).

25 Gigi Devault, "Social Media Research—RockYou and Interpret Perfect Social Gaming," The Balance, October 15, 2016, www.thebalance.com/social-media-research-rockyou-and-interpret-2296767 (accessed June 20, 2017).

26 Cristel Russell, "Toward a Framework of Product Placement," in J.W. Alba and J.W. Hutchinson (eds), *Advances in Consumer Research* (special issue), 25 (1998), 357–62.

27 Michelle R. Nelson, "Recall of Brand Placements in Computer/Video Games," *Journal of Advertising Research*, 42:2 (2002), 80–92.

28 Ralf Terlutter and Michael Capella, "The Gamification of Advertising: Analysis and Research Directions of In-Game Advertising, Advergames, and Advertising in Social Network Games," *Journal of Advertising*, 42 (2013), 95–112.

29 Brian Kinard and K. Hartman, "Are You Entertained? The Impact of Brand Integration and Brand Experience in Television-Related Advergames," *Journal of Advertising*, 42 (2013), 196–203.

30 European Commission, *Study on the Impact of Marketing Through Social Media, Online Games and Mobile Applications on Children's Behaviour*, March 2016, http://ec.europa.eu/consumers/consumer_evidence/behavioural_research/docs/final_report_impact_marketing_children_final_version_approved_en.pdf (accessed June 17, 2017).

31 Nancy Huehnergarth, "Water Is the Enemy, Gatorade Mobile Game Tells Youth," *Huffington Post*, January 8, 2014, www.huffingtonpost.com/nancy-huehnergarth/water-is-the-enemy_b_4557456.html (accessed July 12, 2014).

32 CityOne Game, IBM, August 10, 2010, www-01.ibm.com/software/solutions/soa/innov8/cityone/index.jsp (accessed June 17, 2014).

33 Oracle Cloud Stacker Case Study, Gamewheel, www.gamewheel.com/stories/oracle (accessed March 18, 2017).

34 Tracy Tuten and Christy Ashley, "Do Social Advergames Affect Brand Attitudes and Advocacy?" *Journal of Marketing Communications*, 22:3 (2013), 236–55, www.tandfonline.com/doi/abs/10.1080/13527266.2013.848821#.U8UVUpRdWSp (accessed June 20, 2017).

35 Teresa de la Hera Conde-Pumpido, "A Conceptual Model for the Study of Persuasive Games," *Proceedings of the 2013 DiGRA International Conference: DeFragging Game Studies* (2014), www.digra.org/wp-content/uploads/digital-library/paper_13.pdf (accessed March 18, 2017).

36 Tuten and Ashley, "Do Social Advergames Affect Brand Attitudes and Advocacy?"

37 Sara Peters and Glenn Leshner, "Get in the Game: The Effects of Game-Product Congruity and Product Placement Proximity on Game Players' Processing of Brands Embedded in Advergames", *Journal of Advertising*, 42:2–3 (2013), 113–30.

38 Joseph Jaffe, "Advergaming Equals Attention," iMedia Connection, May 7, 2003, www.imediaconnection.com/articles/ported-articles/red-dot-articles/2003/may/advergaming-equals-attention (accessed July 3, 2017).

39 Grant McCracken, "Who Is the Celebrity Endorser? Cultural Foundations of the Endorsement Process," *Journal of Consumer Research*, 16:3 (1989), 310–21.

40 Ibid.

41 "Glossary", Unfiction, www.unfiction.com/glossary (accessed July 18, 2010).

42 David Kiley, "Advertising of, by and for the People," *BusinessWeek*, July 25, 2005.

43 Ibid.

44 Ibid.

45 "Glossary", Unfiction.

46 "Case Study: Advertising on YouTube with Top Influencers & Gaming Channels," Mediakix, May 27, 2016, http://mediakix.com/2016/05/advertising-on-youtube-case-study-influencers-sponsored/ (accessed June 20, 2017).

47 Ibid.

48 Jonathan Ringen, "How Cult Mattress Company Casper Plans to Get You into Bed," *Fast Company*, February 13, 2017, www.fastcompany.com/3067484/how-cult-mattress-company-casper-plans-to-get-you-into-bed (accessed July 3, 2017).

49 "Marriott's New Two Bellmen Film Is Squarely Targeted at Asian Consumers," Skift, January 18, 2017, https://skift.com/2017/01/18/marriotts-new-two-bellmen-film-is-targeted-squarely-at-asian-consumers (accessed March 18, 2017).

50 Mike Shields, "Kimberly Clark Scores Hit Video Series with 'Carmilla'", *Wall Street Journal*, August 29, 2016, www.wsj.com/articles/kimberly-clark-scores-hit-video-series-with-carmilla-1472464800 (accessed March 18, 2017).

51 Marko Muellner, "2014: The Year of Social TV," ClickZ, October 15, 2013, www.clickz.com/clickz/column/2300252/2014-the-year-of-social-tv (accessed July 13, 2014).

52 "Stirring Up Buzz: How TV Ads Are Driving Earned Media for Brands," Nielsen, February 22, 2016, www.nielsen.com/us/en/insights/news/2016/stirring-up-buzz-how-tv-ads-are-driving-earned-media-for-brands.html (accessed March 18, 2017).

53 "Fast Friends: How Brands Are Capturing the Attention of Social TV Audiences," Nielsen, September 15, 2014, www.nielsen.com/us/en/insights/news/2014/fast-friends-how-brands-are-capturing-the-attention-of-social-tv-audiences.html (accessed March 18, 2017).

54 Steven Bellman, Jennifer A. Robinson, Brooke Wooley, and Duane Varan, "The Effects of Social TV on Television Advertising Effectiveness," *Journal of Marketing Communications*, 23:1 (2017), 73–91.

55 Converse Rubber Tracks, Converse Music, www.converse-music.com/rubbertracks/?_ga=1.21382 2036.1520383848.1472562584 (accessed March 18, 2017).

Visit **https://study.sagepub.com/smm3e** for free additional online resources related to this chapter.

9

Social Commerce

Learning Objectives

When you finish reading this chapter, you will be able to answer these questions:

1 What is the relationship between social commerce and e-commerce? How are mobile devices and software applications influencing the development of social commerce?

2 How do social shoppers use social media as they move through the consumer decision-making process? Which social commerce elements should marketers employ to meet social shoppers' needs?

3 How do ratings and reviews provide value for consumers and marketers?

4 What are the psychological factors that influence social shopping?

The Zone of Social Commerce

When was the last time you went shopping? Yesterday? Last weekend? Were you online or in your local mall? Did you go alone or with someone else, or maybe even with a group? Shopping is at its heart a social activity. Doing it with others makes the activity more enjoyable—even when your shopping buddies don't agree with your choices. Our shopping companions, known among marketers as **purchase pals**, help us to think through our alternatives and make a decision. They validate the choices we make. When we don't have a purchase pal with us, we might turn to surrogate pals like sales associates and other shoppers. Shopping together can be a shared activity that strengthens our relationships with others, but it also reduces the risks we associate with making purchase decisions. Perhaps this has been one reason for the prevalence of in-store shopping over online shopping. E-commerce may finally have a solution for those who hate to shop alone but who would still rather browse online while they hang out at home in their pajamas: **social commerce**.

Social commerce is a subset of e-commerce (i.e., the practice of buying and selling products and services via the Internet). It uses social media applications to enable online shoppers to interact and collaborate during the shopping experience, buyers to complete the stages of the purchase decision process, and to assist marketers in selling to customers.[1] Social commerce encompasses social shopping, social marketplaces, and hybrid channels and tools that enable shared participation in a buying decision. Thus, social commerce enables people, both networks of buyers and sellers, to participate actively in the marketing and selling of products and services in online marketplaces and communities.[2] The social commerce elements covered in this chapter include ratings and reviews, curated merchandise, shopping apps including mobile chatbots, social marketplaces, social-network-driven sales, and group buys (Figure 9.1).

Historically, wired shoppers have relied heavily on the Internet as an information source during the decision process—but many then turn to offline stores to complete the purchase.

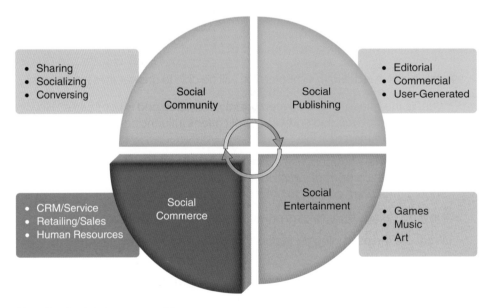

Figure 9.1   The Social Commerce Zone

Increasingly though, shoppers are also completing their purchases online. According to comScore, shoppers now make more purchases online than offline.[3] The comScore study also found that 44% of smartphone users made purchases through their devices. eMarketer estimates that 91% of Internet users are **digital shoppers**, defined as Internet users who have browsed, researched or compared products digitally via any device whether or not they bought digitally.[4] Of those, 88.5% shopped online using their smartphone. Online shopping offers many benefits to shoppers, such as the ability to comparison shop easily and efficiently, convenience, enhanced selection, and cost savings. When e-commerce is facilitated by social media channels and social software applications, the result is social commerce. Though most online shopping is performed using a desktop or laptop computer, mobile devices are driving much of the growth of social commerce.

Compared to other sources of e-commerce traffic, social media is still a minor channel, driving just 1.2% of e-commerce traffic in the US and most of that from Facebook. Most e-commerce traffic is attributed to organic search results, paid search results, and email marketing.[5] In Southeast Asia, though, 30% of all online sales occurred through social networks, like Facebook and Instagram. Additionally, 80% of shoppers in Southeast Asia used social media to research items and contact sellers.[6]

Social shopping is the active participation and influence of others on a consumer's decision-making process, typically in the form of opinions, recommendations, and experiences shared via social media.[7] In other words, social shopping is the term used to capture consumers' behavior as they use social media in their purchase decisions. In contrast, social commerce is the commercial application of social media to drive the acquisition and retention of customers.

The Social Media Value Chain and characteristics of social communities covered in Chapter 1 are reflected in social commerce. Social network sites like Facebook, Instagram, and Pinterest serve as channels for users and brands to share information, experiences, and offers—whether peer-to-peer or consumer-brand. Social marketplaces like Etsy and eBay are also channels for social commerce, as are social shopping malls like Wanelo. E-commerce sites can also get in on social commerce by socially enabling the site with functionality for customers to share, comment on, and review products. In each channel, users participate and engage in word-of-mouth communication that can influence purchase decisions and sales. Likewise, influencers will exist in each channel. Social software including algorithms, apps, and bots will personalize user experiences and provide functionality for participating in social commerce, whether by searching for product reviews, viewing recommended lists, or using voice commands to shop. People participate in social commerce using a connected device. Most online shopping is by desktop or laptop computer, but mobile commerce is increasing rapidly. It's not a big leap to see that mobile social media use can easily integrate with mobile commerce behaviors. Plus, there are other devices enabled for social shopping, especially those with voice commands like Amazon's Echo or Google's Home.

Social commerce lets consumers share product information electronically; easily post opinions and access the opinions of others; and communicate with friends, family, and associates about shopping decisions without regard to place or time. Whenever consumers navigate product information online using social commerce tools, such as bookmarking their favorite products, emailing product summaries, and subscribing to RSS feeds of other users' favorite product lists, they are social shopping. Social shopping provides utility to our shopping experience because it lowers our perceived risk.[8] We can feel more certain, by using social shopping tools, that we got the best price, made the best choice, and know whether our friends will approve of our decision. It's the digital answer to our desire as consumers to shop with others—but with the added convenience and power of online technologies.

Social Commerce: The Social Shopping Experience

It's a cold day in mid-December, and David is spending some time on Facebook reading about his friends' recent activities. A social ad for 1-800-Flowers appears on the side of his news feed that promotes flowers as a Christmas gift and provides an endorsement that

Tsyhun/Shutterstock.com

thousands of people like 1-800-Flowers. Remembering that he hasn't yet sent a Christmas gift to his grandmother in Texas, David gets a brainstorm—he really doesn't have the time to spend hours at the mall looking for something for Grammy. He clicks the ad to reach 1-800-Flowers' Facebook page. There he sees a promotion for 20% off his order if he "likes" the page and a "Shop Now" call to action. With a click of the Shop Now button on the Shop tab of 1-800-Flowers' page, David can browse flower selections and price points. Not sure whether 1-800-Flowers is the best choice, David first visits 1-800-Flowers'

Wall. Comments from past customers fill the page, and David can read the posts from satisfied and dissatisfied customers along with the responses from company service representatives. He chooses three arrangements he likes, but then he uses Facebook Messenger to ask his two sisters to help him decide which is best. They both respond within ten minutes (and as usual, they both pick the same one!). Now David is confident he's got a winner! He could use the Buy button in Facebook to complete his transaction, but he's running late for a class. He uses 1-800-Flowers' chatbot on Facebook Messenger to place the order. The bot, named GWYN, makes a few additional gift suggestions and places the order. Share technologies post to David's Wall: "David bought a holiday arrangement at 1-800-Flowers" and "David likes 1-800-Flowers." Once the flowers arrive and David knows how well Grammy liked them, he plans to return to the page to share a review on 1-800-Flowers' Wall. From there, the cycle begins again as another individual sees shared posts about the brand and/or social ads. Figure 9.2 illustrates how David's actions map to the consumer decision-making process—and he went through the whole process using social media!

We all know some people who shop simply for the sport of it, and others (like David) whom we have to drag to a mall. Shopping is how we acquire needed products and services, but social motives for shopping also are important. Shopping is an activity that we can perform for either utilitarian (functional or tangible) or hedonic (pleasurable or intangible) reasons.[9]

A shopper's motivation influences the type of shopping environment that will be attractive or annoying; for example, a person who wants to locate and buy something quickly may find loud music, bright colors, or complex layouts distracting, whereas someone who is there to browse may enjoy the sensory stimulation.[10] How such environments translate to social commerce shopping experiences is still unknown. But we can still see where these motives may play a role in social shopping. Hedonic shopping motives include social experiences (the social venue as a community gathering place), opportunities to share common interests with like-minded others, the sense of importance we experience when others wait on us, and the thrill of the hunt.[11] After all, the role of hunter/gatherer has long been ingrained in the human psyche.

Surely, too, there are utilitarian motives at play for social shoppers. E-commerce enabled shoppers to find alternatives and a wealth of pricing information with the click of a mouse. Consumers benefit from the convenience and ease of shopping with more choices and better information. Social commerce further enables shoppers to access opinions, recommendations, and referrals from others within and outside of their own social graphs, again potentially improving the ability for consumers to make the most rational and efficient decisions. But there's one more benefit offered by social commerce that was missing from e-commerce—the social aspect of shopping that people got when they shopped in person with their purchase pals and interacted with salespeople. Social commerce provides that missing ingredient to the e-commerce equation. For example, David trusted the reviews he read about 1-800-Flowers and his sisters' judgment when choosing a gift for Grammy (though he would probably consult other purchase pals before he buys a new gaming console). Interacting with 1-800-Flowers' gift concierge, GWYN (an acronym for "Gifts When You Need"), helped David make the purchase using his smartphone and the Facebook Messenger app.

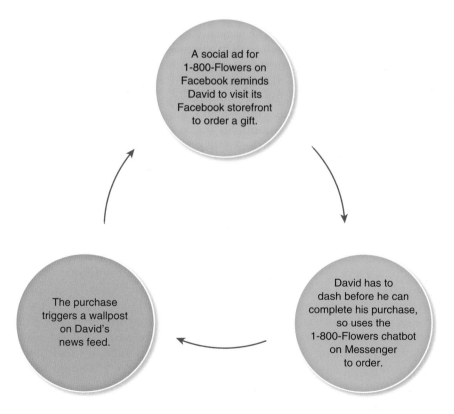

Figure 9.2   Social Commerce and the Customer Decision-Making Process

It was only a few years ago that retailers scrambled to figure out how to present their store offerings online and worried as to the effect of e-commerce on their traditional business models. Now, things are changing again as they assess the influence of consumer desires to shop online socially.

Social Commerce and the Shopping Process

At the end of the day, *shopping online is still shopping.* Sure, the way we locate and purchase products may not look the same—but the successful marketer understands that our basic shopping orientations (e.g., to obtain a needed product or service, to connect with others, to stimulate our senses) are the same as our ancient ancestors possessed.

Furthermore, it's helpful to break down the process of shopping in terms of the stages of consumer decision-making. Though we may make some simple decisions in fewer steps, important decisions require five steps:

- problem recognition
- information search
- alternative evaluation
- purchase
- post-purchase evaluation.

When we look at these stages we realize that what seems at first to be an "obvious" and quick decision ("throw something in the cart") is in fact a lot more complicated. On the bright side, many current social media applications are out there to help consumers make it through each of these stages. Table 9.1 summarizes the decision-making stages and illustrates some of these social media and social commerce tools that already are changing how we shop (but not why we shop!). So social commerce is a part of e-commerce, and it leverages social media to aid in the exchange process between buyers and sellers. That seems straightforward enough, but social media are sufficiently complex and broad to influence e-commerce in all five of the consumer decision-making stages. **Problem recognition** may be triggered by discovering information about a product on social media, whether by user comments, influencer content, or advertising. A recent study found that 81% of consumers have bought something they saw shared on social media, but less than 2% said their purchases were influenced by traditional advertising.[12] Some SNS position the network as a discovery tool. That's the case with Pinterest, a visual curation network. A study of Pinterest users by research firm, Millward Brown, found that 96% of Pinterest users gathered information and purchase research on the site.[13] Nearly half of the pinners surveyed were using Pinterest to plan for purchases related to a major live event—getting married, buying a home, or having a baby. Michael Yamartino, Head of Commerce at Pinterest, explained: "Pinterest is a discovery platform, in the same category as Google. For brands, it's about repurposing content from their site and publishing their entire product catalogue as you might a site map for Google to aid discovery."[14] People in the problem recognition phase may also engage in **participatory commerce**, a subset of social commerce in which people participate in the design, selection, and/or funding of a product innovation. Sites like Threadless and Kickstarter facilitate the collaboration between prospective customers and innovators.

EXHIBIT 9.1

Betabrand Embraces Participatory Commerce

iStock.com/Dragonimages

Online clothing company Betabrand crowdsources the design and selection of all the products it manufactures and sells. Have an idea for apparel that meets an unmet need? Pitch it at Betabrand's website. Once your design is submitted, Betabrand's community will vote on the design and make suggestions for improving it. One of Betabrand's big success stories? Dress yoga pants! That's right—pants that are stylish and formal enough for work, but with the comfort and stretch needed for yoga class. They make taking advantage of that lunchtime yoga class feasible and it all happened through social commerce.

The next stage, information search, is the primary driver of social commerce and social shopping behaviors. We noted earlier that even for offline purchases, wired consumers tend to search online for information prior to making an actual purchase. In a book sponsored by Google, Jim Lecinski explains the process, coining the term, ZMOT—Zero Moment of Truth.[15] The concept is based on a related concept long understood by retailers, and particularly those in the consumer-packaged goods industry. It draws from the notions of First Moment of Truth (FMOT), the moment a consumer chooses a product from the store shelf, and the Second Moment of Truth (SMOT), the moment the consumer uses the product and feels satisfaction or dissatisfaction. ZMOT emphasizes that consumers today may be influenced in several moments online prior to making a purchase decision. Though the number of sources and types of sources vary by region and product category, on average consumers will use more than ten sources of information before a purchase. These sources may be owned media content vetted by the brands in question, paid media in the form of an ad, or word-of-mouth content posted by users in social media channels. There are several sources of information available via social media, but the most influential are reviews and ratings. Savvy brands will strive to be involved in this part of the purchase process, cultivating positive word-of-mouth and other forms of influence impressions, leveraging the content by encouraging its spread online, and facilitating the development of the content.

Table 9.1   Social Commerce Tools for Purchase Decision Stages

Decision Stage	Social Commerce Tools
Problem Recognition	Social ads on social networking sites
	Shared endorsements from friends posted in activity streams
	Curated images and lists on sites like Pinterest
	Location-based promotions (e.g., Yelp)
	Participatory commerce (e.g., Kickstarter)
Information Search	Comments (influence impressions) throughout social channels (opinions posted on a brand's Wall, tweets about an experience, etc.)
	Queries and responses within social networks (e.g., LinkedIn and Facebook)
	Ratings and reviews posted on sites (e.g., Yelp, Zagat, Citysearch)
	Product and pricing information tagged to image posts
	Social search queries on SNS
	Wish lists, gift registries
	Conversational commerce (chatbot services)
Evaluation of Alternatives	Bar code scanning/price comparisons
	Recommendations, testimonials, recommendation agents, and popularity filters ("ask your network" apps, video testimonials such as VideoGenie, and top lists from retailers such as Amazon)
	Ratings and reviews
	Referrals
Purchase	Shop within network options (e.g., Facebook Buy, InstaShop, Snapchat Deeplinks)
	Social shopping malls (e.g., Wanelo)
	Peer-to-peer marketplaces (e.g., Etsy)
	Group buys (e.g., LivingSocial, Groupon)
	Conversational commerce (chatbot services)
Post-Purchase	Comments posted on SNS
	Request for help or comment to brand on SNS
	Participation in loyalty program with social benefits
	Ratings and reviews on review sites and retailer website
	Reviews and product experiences posted on blogs

ZMOT information may or may not be social, but much of it is—whether a Pinterest board of favorites at Macys.com or a review of pizza places on Yelp. This information, particularly that provided by **reviews** and **ratings**, influences consumers at multiple stages in the buying process. Reviews are assessments with detailed comments about the object in question. Ratings are simply scores generated by users that reflect assessments of attributes like perceived quality, satisfaction, or popularity on a scale. Estimates vary from study to study, but research consistently shows that the vast majority of Internet-connected shoppers globally search for product information online first.[16]

What makes a review or rating valuable? Ratings are a **heuristic**; a mental shortcut consumers use to help them with decision-making. For instance, if you want to choose a restaurant near the amphitheatre where you are attending a concert this weekend, you might pull up all the restaurants in the area and then choose the one with the highest average rating. Reviews provide more detailed information for those who want to evaluate the choice at a deeper level. Consequently, a good review should include product information such as features and specifications, an overall impression of the product with a positive or negative judgment, a list of pros and cons, experience with the product, and a final recommendation.[17] With these components, the review will have sufficient information for the readers to judge relevance and credibility and apply the content to their purchase situation.

Where people search varies but most start with a search engine and consequently can find all kinds of online content, including user-generated and brand-generated content on social channels. Search engines like Google are an obvious starting point for an online information search, but searches also occur on Facebook, YouTube, TripAdvisor, and elsewhere. In fact, research suggests that Amazon—not Google—is the first source of online information search for more than 50% of Internet users![18] Shoppers may not always complete their purchases online, instead they carry out webrooming—the term for researching purchases online but going to a brick-and-mortar store to complete the purchase. Consider these statistics on the use of ratings and reviews:[19]

- 95% of consumers report having read reviews prior to making a purchase decision.
- Two-thirds of consumers read between one and ten reviews before making a purchase.
- 70% of mobile shoppers are more likely to purchase if the mobile site or app includes reviews.
- 82% seek out negative reviews as an indicator of authenticity.
- 60% have viewed a review on their smartphone while shopping in-store.

In other words, this isn't a casual behavior. Shoppers are intensely studying reviews to improve their purchase decisions. Researching products online makes sense—it can save time, increase confidence, and reduce risk that might be associated with the purchase. It also ensures better, more credible information. Besides using opinions early in the decision process, consumers may also use ratings and reviews as a form of validation just prior to purchase. This is called **verification**.[20] That's right—today buyers seek out information online early in the purchase process, and then many return to validate the decision. Many later also write reviews and rate products in the post-purchase stage (the Second Moment of Truth—SMOT). Because reviews are so influential, retailers are inviting customers to rate their experience and write a review soon after products are delivered.

Recommendations from friends and family are all around us, and the prevalence of social media in the lives of wired consumers heightens our ability to share these opinions. The average consumer mentions specific brands in conversations with others more than 60 times a week.[21] Just imagine how those influence impressions can travel when shared via social networks. This number could increase as people use social media to seek out recommendations. A study from researchers at Penn State found that 20% of Twitter posts were from people asking for or providing product information.[22]

Recommendations and referrals can be simple or integrated in their execution. Facebook's "like" button, now available on millions of external webpages, is a form of recommendation. When you click it, you publicly announce that you recommend the content on the page. While others can see the total number of "likes," anyone in your network can also see that you personally made a recommendation.

This information also influences the consumer's **alternative evaluation stage**, with shoppers reporting that they read reviews to evaluate options both for products and retailers, compared prices and checked for deals, and considered the opinions of others. Whereas ratings and reviews are visible to everyone who wishes to see them, recommendations and referrals originate from the recipient's social graph. This makes them more influential than reviews and ratings because they leverage the social capital of the referrer. In fact, a Harris Interactive poll found that 71% of respondents said recommendations from family and friends have substantial influence on their purchase decisions.[23] And while we tend to trust reviews from strangers, we are more trusting of recommendations from people we know; 90% in the survey said they trust an online recommendation from someone in their network.[24]

What influences the credibility and authenticity of the reviews and ratings shoppers view? Several factors are at play. People consider the source of the review (a user or product expert), the volume of ratings, and the valence (positive or negative).[25] When a high volume of reviews and ratings is available, people tend to favor reviews from other typical people. In fact, volume of reviews has a stronger impact on sales than the presence of negative reviews![26] When the review volume is low, opinions from experts such as bloggers or professional critics is preferred. People look for cues to judge their similarity to the reviewer and the reviewer's purchase context.[27] Similarity increases trust in the review. Even the congruence between the shopper's opinion and those reflected in the reviews plays a role. In other words, even when searching for information to guide a decision, people are prone to **confirmation bias**. Reviews that focus on benefits to the consumer are more influential than those that focus on product attributes.[28]

Even with 25% of online shoppers noting that they don't always consider online reviews to be fair or trustworthy, shoppers read the content and judge for themselves whether they feel a review is useful.[29] Consumers trust information provided by other consumers via social media more than television, magazine, radio, or Internet advertising, more than sponsorships, and more than recommendations from salespeople or paid endorsers. The only source more trusted is that of recommendations from friends or family.[30] The opinions of other typical users have far more influence on purchase decisions and brand attitudes than content shared by the brand itself.[31] What about the microcelebrity influencers? A third of consumers say they are more likely to purchase a product endorsed by a non-celebrity blogger than a celebrity.[32]

By the time the shopper reaches the purchase point, he or she has used an average of ten sources of information with about half being a source delivered via social media. Social media users rely on social commerce in every stage of the decision-making process, but the least in the **purchase** stage. This may change as marketers improve the social shopping experience and new technologies like conversational commerce using chatbots in social messaging apps.

The Second Moment of Truth (SMOT), the experience using the product, is just as relevant as it always was. The product has to deliver on the brand promise. This marks the beginning of the **post-purchase evaluation** phase in the decision-making process, where the consumer evaluates the purchase and experiences satisfaction or dissatisfaction. The customer may write reviews and post comments for others to use. Forrester Research points out that this is a point in the customer journey during which social media users may post questions and comments directly to brands on SNS. Social media is the most preferred communication channel for reaching company customer service representatives. It's preferred by more people than live chat on the company website, email, telephone, or in-store assistance. Brands using social media for customer care will be alert for these posts and respond. Marcus Miller of SearchEngineLand calls this the Third Moment of Truth (TMOT), the moment of advocacy.[33] Why? It's the critical juncture between a customer becoming a brand ambassador (if the communication was positive) or a customer becoming a hater. Sprout Social measured expectations for brand responses to social media customer service requests.[34] Most social media users expect a response from a business in under four hours and 42% expect a response within one hour! Brands that respond quickly and effectively can turn complaints into positive experiences and compliments into delight. Sadly, most brands don't. Though as much as half of the social media posts directed to brands requested a response, less than 15% of those messages got a response from the brand in question. For those that did get a response, the average response time was more than eight hours. Being ignored is an insult in the conversational realm of social media. And customers respond in-kind: 36% of shunned customers say they will try to shame the company online, 29% intend to switch to a competitor for future purchases, and 14% say they write negative reviews. When the customer being shunned was happy and showing brand love, future use and brand loyalty are both damaged.

The Marketing Value of Social Commerce

Marketers will be influenced by social commerce activities whether they choose to engage or not. That's because the reputation economy in which we live ensures that there is a publishing platform for individuals. We see content creation increase with access to social channels and communities, social software, and digital devices. Regardless of whether a brand is active, this content will be generated and will be accessible by a search online. For instance, one study of Yelp reviews looked at over 4,000 small businesses with reviews on its site. None of the businesses were also engaging in advertising on Yelp. Fortunately for them, they still benefited. The study revealed that the unsolicited, organic Yelp reviews were associated with increases in revenue of $8,000 annually on average. What's more is that brands that facilitated a presence on Yelp saw an average uptick of $23,000.[35] Another study found that for independent restaurants, a one-star rating increase on Yelp was associated with an annual increase in revenues of 5% to 9%.[36]

Product opinions affect shoppers, but that isn't the only way they impact the marketing process. Online reviews generate increased sales by bringing in new customers. Further, people who write reviews tend to shop more frequently and to spend more online than those who do not write reviews. Those who review products make up just a quarter of online shoppers, but they account for a third of online sales.[37] And consumers are willing to pay a price premium for products with higher ratings.[38] For e-retailers, this means that it makes good business sense to host rating and review features. Ratings and reviews also enhance organic search traffic to the website. Organic search results improve because reviewers tend to use the same keywords (tags) in their product descriptions that searchers will use. Petco, a pet supplies retailer, found that having customer reviews on its website generated five times as many site visits as any previous advertising campaign. Those who browsed Petco's Top Rated Products had a 49% higher conversion rate than the site average, and an average order amount that was 63% higher than the site average.[39]

Reviews result in better site stickiness—customers reading reviews will stay at a retail site longer than they would otherwise. They can also enhance the effectiveness of offline promotional strategies. For example, Rubbermaid added review comments from its website to the content included in its freestanding inserts. When reviews were included, coupon utilization increased 10%.[40] Lastly, the reviews and opinion posts become a source of research data for the business, highlighting consumer opinions in a frank yet unobtrusive fashion. Some businesses believe the data resulting from online reviews to be more valuable than data from focus group research. Businesses can learn whether consumers like a competitor's brand better and why, how consumers react to positive or negative press, what stories are being spread about the brand, and which customers are being evangelical and which ones are acting as "brand terrorists." In Chapter 10, our focus will be on how marketers can use social media content as a source of consumer insight.

Best Practices to Leveraging Social Reviews and Ratings

Ultimately, it's important to remember that users are reading online reviews because they want to know what people like themselves think of a product. They must be able to trust those reviews; if they can't, the reviews won't be effective. In general, people trust reviews shared on social media, but brands must be stewards of that trust. Increasingly, reviews are questioned. Why? Deception. Estimates suggest that as much as 30% of online reviews is fraudulent. Reviews likely to be deceptive tend to include information that is not related to product use and to lack verified purchase information. These reviews may be provided by marketers (on their own products or for competing brands) or by customers who have not actually bought the product in question. Researchers estimate that legitimate reviews may come from as few as 1.5% of reviewers.[41] Research by the Chartered Institute of Marketing on brand transparency prevails upon brands to be honest on social media, reporting:[42]

- 25% have seen reviews they believe to be fake
- 21% have seen customers be paid or incentivized to post a positive review, and
- 81% find it difficult to distinguish between authentic user content and native advertising.

Amazon has taken steps to maintain the integrity of its customer review system, which millions of consumers rely on to make smart purchase decisions and avoid faulty or substandard products. In some cases, Amazon has even sued individuals who offered incentivized reviews, which are reviews of a product that was received for free or at a discount in exchange for the review. A study of 65 million reviews across 32,000 product categories on Amazon by ReviewMeta found that incentivized reviewers were significantly less likely than non-incentivized reviewers to give a 1-star rating and four times less likely to be critical in the review. Incentivized reviewers also review hundreds of products on average, potentially inflating sales performance for otherwise mediocre quality products. In response, Amazon updated its community guidelines to prohibit incentivized reviews.[43]

What other steps should marketers take? To make the most of the opportunity, marketers should develop a social commerce approach with these characteristics:

- *Authenticity*: accept organic word-of-mouth, whether positive or negative.
- *Transparency*: acknowledge opinions that were invited, incentivized, or facilitated by the brand.
- *Advocacy*: enable consumers to rate the value of opinions offered on the site.
- *Participation*: encourage consumers to contribute posts.
- *Reciprocity*: acknowledge the value of the opinions customers offer.
- *Infectiousness*: make it easy for users to share reviews on blogs and social networking platforms.
- *Sustainability*: online opinions are so influential because they live on in perpetuity. If a consumer tells a friend about a satisfying brand experience on the phone, the story once told is no longer retrievable or trackable.

What does this mean for marketers? First, marketers must ensure high standards when it comes to product quality and service if they wish to survive in the world of social reviews. It is so easy for anyone to tell everyone about his or her brand experiences, whether good or bad. That means those experiences had better be good—very good! Those that fail will have their sordid story broadcast to the social world as customers submit reviews and those reviews are shared via social networks. Second, brands should embrace, not hide—because really, online there is no place to hide—from consumer opinions. Instead, organizations can engage in word-of-mouth marketing by actively giving people reasons to talk about the brand while facilitating the conversations. There are five actions brands can take to build valuable online reviews:

- educating people about your products and services
- identifying people most likely to share their opinions
- providing tools that make it easier to share information
- studying how, where, and when opinions are being shared
- listening and responding to supporters, detractors, and neutrals.

In other words, marketers should encourage the conversation by informing consumers about the brand, offering consumers a forum for expressing opinions about the brand, and responding (making the communication two-way) to comments consumers make on the forum and elsewhere. Customers can be invited to offer reviews, resulting in more engagement and the propagation of positive word-of-mouth communication about the brand. Perhaps most important is the final component of word-of-mouth marketing—listening. There is valuable information about the need for product improvements like product features and service quality embedded in ratings and reviews.

Why Don't All E-Retailers Offer Reviews and Ratings on Their Sites?

Aside from the problem that marketers and advertisers have overlooked their value and influence, the most commonly cited reason given for not allowing online reviews on sites is the fear that dissatisfied customers will use the review feature as a venue to *flame* a brand.

Given the old adage that negative word-of-mouth communication is more damaging than positive word-of-mouth communication is beneficial, some retailers have erred on the side of caution when it comes to offering a review feature. The ratio of negative to positive reviews found on various sites suggests that this fear is unfounded. Bazaarvoice, a firm that provides a customer review and rating service for e-retailers, reports that 80% of its user-generated reviews are positive.[44]

In reality, retailers can benefit from negative reviews and should welcome them. Consumers want to see negative reviews to be able to accurately assess the degree of product risk they face when purchasing. They seek to minimize perceived performance and financial risk associated with purchases. Negative reviews give them the information they need to assess risk. The negative reviews also enhance credibility. Consumers often assume that if the reviews seem too good to be true, they probably are. Lastly, negative reviews give valuable information to the retailer on products that should be improved, augmented, or discontinued.

Social Commerce Strategies

The first level of social commerce strategy is to utilize user-generated content, encourage it, and facilitate it with social sharing and shopping functionalities customers want—providing tools that make content creation and sharing of word-of-mouth communication via social media easy and rewarding. At the simplest level, an online retailer can include **share tools** on its website. These tools may enable visitors to tweet an item, pin a picture to Pinterest, or save an item to their Wanola. More engaging tools include those that enable site visitors to create **social video testimonials** using their mobile phones (with social software apps like VideoGenie) or "share stories" in an on-site gallery. eMarketer estimates that 94% of major online retailers now include such social sharing tools on their websites.[45]

Online retailers can also enable other features that, while not user-generated, are based on user behavior and still represent a kind of social recommendation. These social commerce tools can encourage sales, brand loyalty, and advocacy. Wish lists, gift lists, and similarity recommendations (e.g., "others who bought this also bought") are examples.

Here's a summary of the opportunities marketers can provide to encourage social commerce sharing that may facilitate sales:

- *Share tools*: social software plug-ins that enable easy sharing of products sold on a retailer's website to social networks. The most popular plug-in today for retailers is Pinterest. This sharing is a form of recommendation in that others in the user's social graph can treat the pin as an endorsement.

- *Recommendation indicators*: simple buttons that provide an on-site endorsement of a product. The most common options are Facebook's "like" and Google's +! buttons.

- *Reviews and ratings*: on-site reviews and ratings with tools for writing and rating.

- *Testimonials*: a form of recommendation that enables users to share a more personal story about their experience, possibly as a video endorsement.

- *User galleries*: virtual galleries where users can share their creations, shopping lists, and wish lists. This approach is sometimes called **user-curated shopping** and may occur on-site or off-site with a community like Wanelo.

- *Pick lists*: lists that help shoppers share what they want on-site, typically in the form of a wish list.

- *Popularity filters*: filters that enable the shopper to show products by most popular, most viewed, most favorite, or most commented on.
- *User forums*: groups of people who meet online to communicate about products and help each other solve related problems.

EXHIBIT 9.2

HauteLook: The Couture Social Commerce Experience

iStock.com/Rawpixel Ltd

HauteLook, a Nordstrom subsidiary, uses social commerce to share content and engage end-users in purchases of couture clothing and other luxury products. Shoppers often have a two-pronged agenda: find a great deal on a product with perceived high value and then validate their savviness and fashion flair by sharing that experience with others. Membership in HauteLook implies exclusivity and scarcity to the target audience of purchasers of high-end, brand name luxury products discounted during flash sales.

HauteLook engages consumers at each stage of the decision-making process while simultaneously focusing on creating an exceptional social shopping experience. The "Share with Friends" section of the HauteLook online store has direct customized links to specific products and allows HauteLook to glean exposure from members sharing their purchases. The experience is also gamified in that purchases are awarded points and members can then share their "score" with friends and family, while undecided shoppers can seek input. This leverages the power of social proof to influence purchase. Social proof serves to increase desire and affirm purchase decisions. When

(Continued)

(Continued)

customers share their purchases in the SNS, the announcement serves as a testimonial. Members are incentivized to invite their friends with referral bonuses of $20 off a future purchase for each friend who joins. Using flash sales for discounting creates a sense of scarcity and urgency without lowering the perceived value of the products themselves.

HauteLook attracts new members using paid ads on Facebook and Twitter. The ads use well-designed headlines, thumbnail product images, and purchase links. Purposefully, HauteLook does not provide pricing information on the initial thumbnail image and purchase link. Consumers must click a link to obtain pricing. The clickthrough action enables HauteLook to capture lead generation data for prospects that are farther in the purchase decision funnel and which can be used for retargeting.

Its social commerce initiative also includes social media monitoring to alert the social media team when consumer posts request a response, and a fast and thorough response. This system enables the company to provide customer care and customer relationship management using social media channels.

Social Promotions and Partnerships

In addition to leveraging user-generated content both through on-site tools and cross-platform partnerships, marketers can also facilitate sales using sales promotions offered through social deal partners and shopping carts in social vehicles like Facebook and Twitter. The most extensive format would be to truly socialize the shopping function on the retailer's website. A few adventurous retailers gave this a shot (most notably, Levi's) but thus far, full implementation has not gained momentum. Amazon is perhaps the world's most friendly retailer for social shopping but synchronous, shared online shopping experiences are still not featured.

Another form is to provide for shopping from within the SNS. Facebook offers shopping from brand profile pages with its ShopNow button. Purchases are also enabled through Pinterest's Rich Pins, Instagram shoppable Stories, and Snapchat's Deep Links. Facebook has experienced the greatest success, with 86% of retailers identifying it as their most important social network for promoting specific products. Shopify reported that Facebook drove two thirds of the visits to Shopify-operated stores with an average order value worldwide of $55.00. Pinterest had an average order value of $58.95 but drove fewer visits. The best vehicle with which to partner also depends upon the type of retailer. Pinterest generated 74% of social orders in the antiques and collectibles industry at Shopify-operated stores.[46]

Marketers can also partner with other sites like **social shopping portals**. Wanelo enables users to share products they "want, need, love," which are linked to the product's page on the retailer's website. This enables conversion from browsing to truly buying. Wanelo thinks of itself as a digital mall where users can post favorite items, and comment and share with friends. Users link their favorites to specific retailer websites so that sales can be driven from Wanelo to the retailer's own site. It can be described as a multi-retailer catalog built as a social network. Products are listed with a "buy" button that connects to the retailer.

CRITICAL REFLECTION

Victims of Social Commerce Fraud: Both Consumers and Brands at Risk

Social media has become a breeding ground for cybercrime-related activity, attracting fraudsters from around the world who take advantage of these platforms because they are free, easy-to-use, and offer a global reach.[47] One of the most frequent tactics is to pose as a legitimate brand on social media. The fraudsters then scam customers while undermining the brand's reputation and creating negative brand sentiment. A study to discover the extent of social media brand fraud analyzed nearly 5,000 brand profiles on Twitter, Facebook, YouTube, and Instagram. It found that nearly 20% of social media brand profiles were fake accounts.[48] The fraudulent accounts were used to offer

Sam72/Shutterstock.com

counterfeit products and services, phish for personally identifiable information (PII), infect victims with malware, and maliciously attack brands. Some fraudulent pages are created solely to generate ad revenue. Enterprising fraudsters use the brand identity to trick followers into visiting junk websites. These sites then spam customers with ads or download adware onto their computers. Advertising fraud accounted for more than two-thirds of the fraudulent accounts identified in the study.

The report explained: "fraudsters prey on customers who try to engage with your brand. They target customers using fake customer service accounts, phony sweepstakes, and more. Some are motivated by a political agenda and create fraudulent accounts to attack a brand's image. Most often, they closely imitate the brand to make fun of the company or its customers. These protest accounts diminish brand value and create a negative or even hostile experience for customers." Social media fraudsters target users with the same "bait" they use in other cyber attacks. This includes legitimate-looking content with offers that appear too good to pass up. Fake accounts so closely resemble the real corporate account that telling them apart can be difficult for novice users. They often retain the company's look and feel, including official logos.

Why are social shoppers susceptible to social commerce fraud? There are several possible reasons. In social commerce, almost anyone can become an online seller because they do not have to invest in a website or pay into online marketplaces. The anonymity afforded by online social media can bring out non-genuine sellers or scammers to rip off innocent shoppers. People also tend to trust online reviews and recommendations, even though we don't know the people who provided the review. Social commerce fraudsters use trust appeals to leverage this norm, even faking reviews and celebrity endorsements. Fraudulent accounts can also inflate the likes and followers for the account to suggest that the accounts are real and endorsed by others.

To summarize, these more integrated approaches e-retailers can take for social commerce include offering sales promotions and social shopping opportunities, often with a partnering company. Marketers can use social commerce in several ways. The most simple approach is to encourage social sharing of the brand's offerings by providing share tools on the site. Some of these tools will result in recommendations and referrals. Other content can be encouraged by enabling a space for reviews and ratings or by developing a campaign that encourages fans to develop user-curated shopping lists. Conversion can be enhanced with social deals and campaigns planned with partners and with in-network shopping functionalities.

Psychology of Influence

Social media marketers who want to win customers find it helpful to understand what we know more generally about the **psychology of influence**—the factors that make it more or less likely that people will change their attitudes or behavior based on a persuasive message. In particular, some social shopping tools play to our **cognitive biases**. This term refers to the "shortcuts" our brains take when we process information. Unlike computers that impassively process data and produce the same result each time (when they work!), humans aren't so rational. Two people can perceive the same event and interpret it quite differently based on their individual histories, gender, and cultural biases. For example, our reactions to colors are partially "colored" by our society, so a North American might interpret a woman in a white dress as an "innocent bride" while an Asian might assume the same woman is going to a funeral since white is the color of death in some eastern cultures.

Cognitive biases are important when we look at purchase decisions, especially because they influence what we may pay attention to and how we interpret it. Even though consumers have access to more information than ever before when it comes to purchase decisions, they are also faced with the limitations of **bounded rationality**. Bounded rationality captures the quandary we face as humans when we have choices to make but are limited by our own cognitive capacity.[49] As consumers, we typically approach an identified need with an information search followed by alternative evaluation. In a world of search engines and social media, though, our information search could potentially be limitless. With thousands of online retailers carrying products, millions of product reviews to sort through, and hundreds of "friends" to ask for recommendations, online commerce is fraught with **information overload**; there's simply too much data for us to handle.

When consumers are confronted with more complexity than they can manage comfortably, bounded rationality kicks in. We adjust to the overload by finding ways to make decisions without considering all the information for an optimal choice. Instead, we often **satisfice**—this means we expend just enough effort to make a decision that's acceptable but not necessarily the one that's "best." We call the shortcuts we use to simplify the process heuristics. This term describes "rules of thumb" such as "buy the familiar brand name" and "if it's more expensive it must be better."

This process of using heuristics to simplify the decision-making process is sometimes referred to as **thinslicing**, where we peel off just enough information to make a choice.[50] When we thinslice we ignore most of the available information; instead we "slice off" a few salient cues and use a mental rule of thumb to make intuitive decisions.

Research on the psychology of influence identifies six major factors that help to determine how we will decide.[51] Let's review them and illustrate how social shopping applications and tools harness these heuristics.

Social Proof

We arrive at many decisions by observing what those around us do in similar situations. When a lot of people select one option (e.g., a clothing style or a restaurant), we interpret this popularity as social proof that the choice is the right one. There are several ways that marketers use social proof. For instance, identifying brands as the #1 choice, market leader, and so on, all point to evidence of social proof. In social commerce applications, tools can enable shoppers to see the social proof related to the product. As more people jump on the bandwagon a **herding effect** can occur.[52] Herd behavior occurs when people follow the behavior of others.[53]

Although in every age there certainly are those who "march to their own drummers," most people tend to follow society's expectations regarding how they should act and look (with a little improvisation here and there, of course). **Conformity** is a change in beliefs or actions as a reaction to real or imagined group pressure. In order for a society to function, its members develop norms, or informal rules that govern behavior. Without these rules, we would have chaos. Imagine the confusion if a simple norm such as stopping for a red traffic light did not exist.

We conform in many small ways every day—even though we don't always realize it. Unspoken rules govern many aspects of consumption. In addition to norms regarding appropriate use of clothing and other personal items, we conform to rules that include gift-giving (we expect birthday presents from loved ones and get upset if they don't materialize), sex roles (men often pick up the check on a first date), and personal hygiene (our friends expect us to shower regularly).

We don't mimic others' behaviors all the time, so what makes it more likely we'll conform? These are some common culprits:[54]

- *Cultural pressures*: different cultures encourage conformity to a greater or lesser degree. The American slogan "Do your own thing" in the 1960s reflected a movement away from conformity and toward individualism. In contrast, Japanese society emphasizes collective well-being and group loyalty over individuals' needs.

- *Fear of deviance*: the individual may have reason to believe that the group will apply *sanctions* to punish nonconforming behaviors. It's not unusual to observe adolescents who shun a peer who is "different," or a corporation or university that passes over a person for promotion because she or he is not a "team player."

- *Commitment*: the more people are dedicated to a group and value their membership in it, the greater their motivation to conform to the group's wishes. Rock groupies and followers of TV evangelists may do anything their idols ask of them, and terrorists can be willing to die for their cause. According to the **principle of least interest**, the person who is *least* committed to staying in a relationship has the most power because that party doesn't care as much if the other person rejects him or her.[55] Remember that on your next date.

- *Group unanimity, size, and expertise*: as groups gain in power, compliance increases. It is often harder to resist the demands of a large number of people than only a few— especially when a "mob mentality" rules.

- *Susceptibility to interpersonal influence*: this trait refers to an individual's need to have others think highly of him or her. Consumers who don't possess this trait are *role-relaxed*; they tend to be older, affluent, and have high self-confidence. Subaru created a communications strategy to reach role-relaxed consumers. In one of its commercials, a man proclaims, "I want a car ... Don't tell me about wood paneling, about winning the respect of my neighbors. They're my neighbors. They're not my heroes."[56]

In Table 9.2 you can see that several of the social shopping tools we covered earlier influence shoppers with social proof. Any content that we can share with others includes a social proof component. When you choose items for an online wish list and then share that list with your network of friends, you've given your friends social proof that the items listed are desirable. Testimonials have long been a source of social proof that a product is the right one to choose. Social tools such as VideoGenie make it possible for customers to share their stories with video clips they record with their mobile phones or web cams. At one time, testimonials were limited to those of typical person endorsers, celebrity endorsers, or word-of-mouth communication. Now, users can share testimonials with a written story, comments, or a video.

Authority

The second source of influence is authority. Authority persuades with the opinion or recommendation of an expert in the field. Whenever someone has expertise, whether that expertise comes from specialist knowledge and/or personal experience with the product or problem, we will tend to follow that person's advice. We can save time and energy on the decision by simply following the expert's recommendation. In advertising, we see the use of authority in ads for pain relievers that state "9 out of 10 doctors recommend." A doctor should know which medicine is best for pain, and the copy in the advertisement delivers this advice.

However, the use of authority is also in play when we see ads from someone who has experience with choosing a product for a specific functional need. For example, when Mia Hamm or Peyton Manning endorses Gatorade products, it's based not on credentials in the area of nutrition, but rather on their personal experience with needing a beverage that can rehydrate them efficiently. We listen to them because, as elite athletes, they ought to know which product is best. In the realm of social media, authority can be activated in several ways, including referral programs, reviews (from experts as well as from existing customers who can speak with the voice of experience), branded services, and user forums.

Although citizen endorsers are not paid agents representing a brand, they do hold a position of authority in the minds of other consumers. Professional experts and reviewers, whether book critics, movie critics, doctors, or lawyers, have authority in specific, relevant product categories but so do citizen endorsers who have actually used the product. In other words, one's experience with the product serves as the source of authority.

Affinity

Affinity, sometimes called "liking," means that people tend to follow and emulate those people whom they find attractive or otherwise desirable. If we like someone, we are more likely to say yes to their requests or to internalize their beliefs and actions as our own. We talked about how advertising often uses endorsers as a source of authority. They can also be used as a source of affinity. While Peyton Manning is an expert when it comes to whether Gatorade is the best choice for hydration during times of physical exertion, he is simply a likable celebrity when he endorses Timex watches. With social media, affinity is almost always present because the social shopping is tied to your social graph—to your friendships. Some tools that leverage affinity as a source of influence are "ask your network" tools that enable shoppers to request real-time recommendations from their friends, deal feeds (where friends share deals), shopping opportunities posted in friends' news feeds, pick lists, referral programs, sharing tools, and shop together tools.

Table 9.2   Social Shopping Tools and Sources of Influence

Social Shopping Tool	Social Proof	Authority	Scarcity	Affinity	Consistency	Reciprocity
"Ask your network"				*	*	
Brand butler services					*	*
Deal directories			*			
Deal feeds			*	*		*
Filters	*					
Group buy			*			*
Lists	*			*	*	
Recommendations	*	*		*	*	
Referral programs	*	*	*	*		*
Reviews	*	*			*	
Share tools	*			*		
Shop together				*		
Storefronts				*		
Testimonials	*	*				
User forums	*	*				*
User galleries	*			*		*
Geo-location promotions			*		*	

Scarcity

We tend to instinctively want things more if we think we can't have them. That's the **principle of scarcity** at work. Whenever we perceive something as scarce, we increase our efforts to acquire it—even if that means we have to pay a premium for the item and buy it before we would otherwise have wanted. Marketing promotions that use scarcity as an influence tool might focus on deals that are time-sensitive, limited-edition products, or products that are limited in supply. In social commerce, scarcity applications include deal feeds, news feeds with special offers, group buy tools, referral programs, and deal directories.

Reciprocity

The **rule of reciprocity** basically says that we have an embedded urge to repay debts and favors, whether or not we requested the help. Reciprocity is a common norm of behavior across cultures. We reciprocate kindnesses in part because we feel it is the fair and right thing to do (a social contract we have with others) and in part because reciprocation is important to well-functioning relationships. Reciprocity influences daily interactions all around us. It may be as simple as choosing a birthday present for someone for whom you wouldn't normally buy a present, but you do because they gave you a gift on your birthday. Marketers activate the rule of reciprocity to encourage consumers to choose a specific brand and to show loyalty to the brand over time. The key is to initiate an offer of some kindness, gift, or favor to the target audience. The targeted consumers will then feel compelled to respond in kind.

This is the basic principle behind the sales promotion technique of sampling; where a marketer offers a free trial of a product to consumers. The free trial illustrates the relative advantage of the product, but it also creates the perception of having received a gift in the minds of consumers. Consequently, sales of sampled products are higher than those of products that are not sampled. Some retailers send birthday and holiday cards to their top clients. Even something as simple as a greeting card can be perceived as a kindness that should be reciprocated. In social commerce, several tools can be perceived as a favor or kindness offered by the brand. These include deal feeds, group buy, referral programs, and user forums.

Consistency

People strive to be consistent with their beliefs and attitudes and with past behaviors. When we fail to behave in ways that are consistent with our attitudes and past behaviors, we feel **cognitive dissonance**, a state of psychological discomfort caused when things we know and do contradict one another. For example, a person may believe it's wrong or wasteful to gamble, yet be drawn to an online gambling site. To avoid this discomfort, we strive for consistency by changing one or more elements in the situation. Thus, our gambler may decide that he or she is betting the house only due to "intellectual curiosity" rather than due to the thrill of betting. The need for consistency is a fairly broad source of influence because it can be activated around any attitude or behavior. Marketers may instigate the need for consistency with image ads, free trial periods, automated renewals, and membership offers. Some of the social shopping tools that include a consistency component include ask your network tools, social games, pick lists, share tools, shop together tools, reviews, forums, and galleries.

MINI CASE STUDY

MantraBand Leverages User-Generated Reviews to Drive Sales

When Aysel Gunar was a student in business school, she created her first bracelet. Jewelry-making is a popular hobby for creative adults and many have launched profitable businesses featuring original and handmade jewelry. That's not what Aysel had in mind. The founder and CEO of MantraBand said she was simply, "Looking for a way to be more present and mindful in my day-to-day life."[57] With that in mind, she created her first bracelet with the words "Live in the Moment." Fast forward a few years and that simple concept is the foundation of a successful online company. MantraBand uses Shopify to commercialize its Facebook page. With Shopify, customers can shop directly from Facebook. The social commerce functionality is further enhanced with Yotpo, a social commerce app that optimizes user-generated content across multiple SNS. Yotpo automates requests for customer reviews post-purchase and incentivizes users to submit photos too. The content can then be shared on MantraBand's Facebook page as well as to Instagram Stories and Rich Pins on Pinterest, all such that the UGC itself is in essence a shoppable ad for MantraBand. The app also curates organic UGC about MantraBand from Instagram, Facebook, and Twitter so the company can analyze customer feedback and repurpose the UGC across its social media channels. Aysel attributes the open dialogue MantraBand has with customers to the social commerce app, emphasizing the trust and social proof reviews provide.

iStock.com/m-gucci

Results and Outcomes

The results? MantraBand earned 36,000 5-star reviews. Customer retention was driven with coupons delivered through the app to stimulate another purchase. The proof is in the conversion rate—a 550% lift in conversions! Check out MantraBand's engagement on its Facebook page—in addition to thousands of reviews, fans have contributed hundreds of photos and comments: www.facebook.com/mantrabands.

Benefits of Social Commerce

So far we've talked about the ways that marketers can approach social commerce. But what benefits does social commerce offer to marketers?

1   It enables the marketer to monetize the social media investment by boosting site and store traffic, converting browsers to buyers, and increasing average order value.

2   It solves the dilemma of social media return on investment. ROI is a metric for understanding how much value was created by an investment. We'll explore this concept in depth in Chapter 10. Some criticize social media for their lack of accountability, but linking sales to social media eliminates this criticism.

3   Social commerce applications result in more data about customer behavior as it relates to the brand.

4   Social shopping applications enhance the customer experience. They make online shopping fun and functional, which should mean higher levels of customer loyalty and better long-term customer lifetime value.

5   Social shopping makes sharing brand impressions easy. The brands earn referral value with these easy-to-use word-of-mouth tools.

6   Brands can keep up with the competition, and maybe differentiate themselves from others in the e-commerce space.

CHAPTER SUMMARY

What is the relationship between social commerce and e-commerce? How are mobile devices and software applications influencing the development of social commerce?

Social commerce is a subset of e-commerce (i.e., the practice of buying and selling products and services via the Internet). It uses social media and social media applications to enable online shoppers to interact and collaborate during the shopping experience and to assist retailers and customers during the process. Encompassing online ratings and reviews, applications, numerous shopping related apps, deal sites and deal aggregators, and social shopping malls and storefronts, social commerce is the last zone of social media. Though most online shopping is performed using a desktop or laptop computer, mobile devices are driving much of the growth of social commerce. Consumers are increasingly completing their purchases online, with a comScore study suggesting 44% of smartphone users had made purchases using their device rather than completing a transaction offline.

How do social shoppers use social media as they move through the consumer decision-making process? Which social commerce elements should marketers employ to meet social shoppers' needs?

Social media users rely on social commerce in every stage of the decision-making process. Social commerce is a part of e-commerce, and it leverages social media to aid in the exchange process between buyers and sellers. Social media are sufficiently complex and broad to influence e-commerce in all five of the consumer decision-making stages. Table 9.1 indicates which social shopping applications primarily affect each stage of the consumer decision-making process. Social media users rely on social commerce the least in the purchase stage. This may change as marketers improve the social shopping experience and new technologies like conversational commerce using chatbots in social messaging apps.

How do ratings and reviews provide value for consumers and e-retailers?

Ratings are simply scores people, acting in the role of critic, assign to something as an indicator. The rating may reflect perceived quality, satisfaction with the purchase, popularity, or some other variable. Reviews are assessments with detailed comments about the object in question. They explain and justify the critic's assigned rating and provide added content to those viewing the content. Both serve as a source of research during the information search and evaluation of alternatives stages of the buying process and as a tool for verifying a decision before purchase. For retailers, positive reviews generate increased sales by bringing in new customers. Further, people who write reviews tend to shop more frequently and to spend more online than those who do not write reviews. Consumers are willing to pay a price premium for products with higher ratings, too. Ratings and reviews also enhance organic search traffic to the website.

Describe the psychological factors that influence social shopping.

Research on the psychology of influence identifies six major factors that help to determine how we will decide; these can be applied to social commerce. These sources of influence are social proof, authority, affinity, scarcity, consistency, and reciprocity. Social proof occurs when we can see what others would choose or have chosen. Authority persuades with the opinion or recommendation of an expert in the field. Professional experts and reviewers, whether book critics, movie critics, doctors, or lawyers, have authority in specific, relevant product categories but so do citizen endorsers who have actually used the product. Affinity, sometimes called "liking," means that people tend to follow and emulate those people for whom they have an affinity. With social media, affinity is almost always present because social shopping is tied to your social graph—to your friendships. We tend to instinctively want things more if we think we can't have them—that's the principle of scarcity at work. In social commerce, scarcity applications include deal feeds, news feeds with special offers, group buy tools, referral programs, and deal directories. The rule of reciprocity basically says that we have an embedded urge to repay debts and favors, whether or not we requested the help. In social commerce, several tools can be perceived as a favor or kindness offered by the brand. These include deal feeds, group buys, referral programs, and user forums. The final source of influence is our tendency to be consistent. People strive to be consistent with their beliefs and attitudes and with past behaviors. Some of the social shopping tools that include a consistency component include ask your network tools, social games, pick lists, share tools, shop together tools, reviews, forums, and galleries.

REVIEW QUESTIONS

1   Explain the concept of purchase pals. Do you pull your offline and online purchase pals from the same pool of friends and family, or are they different somehow?

2   How is social commerce related to e-commerce? In the future, will e-commerce be able to exist without social applications? Why or why not?

3   What are the benefits that accrue to businesses implementing social shopping applications?

4   What is the distinction between social shopping and social commerce?

5   How are reviews different from recommendations? Why are ratings an important cue to include with a review site?

6   Explain the concept of bounded rationality as it relates to social shopping.

7   Which stage of the decision-making process is most affected by the dimensions of social commerce? Explain.

8   What is thinslicing?

9   Explain the six sources of influence prevalent in social commerce applications.

EXERCISES

1   Search Wanelo for brands you like. Can you buy the products you find? Is a recommendation tool included in the page? Can you add products to your shopping cart and check out from within the page? In your opinion, what could make the site more effective?

2   Which are more influential—reviews from experts or reviews from customers? Explain.

3   Review the list of social shopping applications presented in the chapter and visit some of the sites that use these applications. Social shopping applications provide functionality for customers, such as enhanced organization, price comparisons, risk reduction, and access to product information, but they also make the shopping experience more fun. Tag the list of applications based on the benefit the application provides—utility or fun. Which aspect of social shopping is most important to shoppers?

4   How do you feel about reviews that are incentivized? Do you still trust them? How do you decide?

5   Of the tools of influence that can affect social commerce behavior, are some more influential than others? Explain. How can marketers leverage each influence tool in social media marketing?

CHAPTER NOTES (access all weblinks listed here at: https://study.sagepub.com/smm3e)

1   Adapted from Paul Marsden, "Simple Definition of Social Commerce (With Word Cloud & Definitive Definition List)," *Digital Intelligence Today*, November 17, 2009, updated January 2010, http://digitalintelligencetoday.com/social-commerce-definition-word-cloud-definitive-definition-list (accessed June 21, 2017).

2   Amir Afrasiabi Rad and Morad Benyoucef, "A Model for Understanding Social Commerce," *Journal of Information Systems Applied Research*, 4:2 (2011), 63.

3   Madeline Farber, "Consumers Are Now Doing Most of Their Shopping Online," *Fortune*, June 8, 2016, http://fortune.com/2016/06/08/online-shopping-increases (access March 02, 2017).

4   "EMarketer US Retail Commerce StatPack," eMarketer, 2017, www.emarketer.com/public_media/docs/eMarketer_US_Retail_Ecommerce_StatPack_2017.pdf (accessed March 15, 2017).

5   Ibid.

6   "Singapore, Thailand Love Instagram, eCommerce," PYMNTS.com, December 8, 2016, www.pymnts.com/news/mobile-commerce/2016/singapore-thailand-love-instagram-ecommerce (accessed June 21, 2017).

7   Catherine Baethge, Julia Klier, and Mathias Klier, "Social Commerce—State-of-the-Art and Future Research Directions," *Electronic Markets*, 26 (2016), 269–90.

8   J. Shen, "Social Comparison, Social Presence, and Enjoyment in the Acceptance of Social Shopping Websites," *Journal of Electronic Commerce Research*, 13:3 (2012), 198–212; cf. J. Shen and L. Eder, "An Examination of Factors Associated With User Acceptance of Social Shopping Websites," *International Journal of Technology and Human Interaction*, 7:1 (2011), 19–36; J. Shen, L. Eder, and J.D. Procaccino, "Social Comparison and Trust in the Acceptance of Social Shopping Websites," *International Journal of Electronic Business*, 8:4 (2010), 360–75.

9   For a scale to assess these dimensions of the shopping experience, see Barry J. Babin, William R. Darden, and Mitch Griffin, "Work and/or Fun: Measuring Hedonic and Utilitarian Shopping Value," *Journal of Consumer Research*, 20 (March 1994), 644–56.

10 Velitchka Kaltcheva and Barton Weitz, "When Should a Retailer Create an Exciting Store Environment?" *Journal of Marketing*, 70 (2005), 107–18.

11 Mark J. Arnold and Kristy Reynolds, "Hedonic Shopping Motives," *Journal of Retailing*, 79:2 (2003), 77–95.

12 "Social Media Impacts More People's Shopping Decisions than TV," *BizReport*, July 21, 2016, www.bizreport.com/2016/07/social-media-impacts-more-peoples-shopping-decisions-than-tv.html (accessed June 21, 2017).

13 Rachel Eisenberg, "Pinterest and the Power of Future Intent," MillwardBrown Digital, May 12, 2015, www.millwardbrowndigital.com/pinterest-and-the-power-of-future-intent (accessed June 21, 2017).

14 Ed Terpening and Aubrey Littleton, "The 2016 State of Social Business," Altimeter, November 15, 2016, www.altimetergroup.com/pdf/reports/2016-State-of-Social-Business-Altimeter.pdf (accessed July 3, 2017).

15 Jim Lecinski, *ZMOT Handbook*, Think with Google, 2011, www.thinkwithgoogle.com/marketing-resources/micro-moments/2011-winning-zmot-ebook (accessed July 3, 2017).

16 Yubo Chen, Scott Fay, and Qi Wang, "The Role of Marketing in Social Media: How Online Consumer Reviews Evolve," *Journal of Interactive Marketing*, 25:2 (2011), 85–94.

17 Yuhua (Jake) Liang, Brianna N. DeAngelis, David D. Clare, Sam M. Dorros, and Timothy R. Levine, "Message Characteristics in Online Product Reviews and Consumer Ratings of Helpfulness," *Southern Communication Journal*, 70:5 (2014), 468–83.

18 Graham Charlton, "More Online Product Searches Start on Amazon than Google," SearchEngineWatch, September 27, 2016, https://searchenginewatch.com/2016/09/27/more-online-product-searches-start-on-amazon-than-google (accessed June 21, 2017).

19 "5 Social Shopping Trends Shaping the Future of Ecommerce," Power Reviews and the eTailing Group, 2010, www.e-tailing.com/content/wp-content/uploads/2010/06/social_shopping_webinar.ppt (accessed July 3, 2017).

20 "New Research Reveals Best Approach to Harness the Power of Online Influence on Purchase Behavior," *Cone*, July 14, 2010, www.prnewswire.com/news-releases/new-research-reveals-best-approach-to-harness-the-power-of-online-influence-on-purchase-behavior-98441074.html (accessed July 29, 2010).

21 Alan Vantoai, "50 Peer-To-Peer Marketing Statistics That Every Marketer Should Know," Crew Fire Blog, June 27, 2017, www.crewfire.com/50-peer-to-peer-marketing-statistics (accessed July 4, 2017).

22 Dirk Singer, "20% of Tweets About Brands," Social Media Today, September 14, 2009, www.social mediatoday.com/SMC/123878 (accessed July 30, 2010).

23 Quoted in "Social Commerce Statistics," Bazaarvoice, www.bazaarvoice.com/resources/stats (accessed July 30, 2010).

24 Jake Hird, "Online Consumers Trust Real People, Not Companies," eConsultancy, July 8, 2009, http://econsultancy.com/blog/4175-online-consumers-trust-real-people-not-companies (accessed July 30, 2010).

25 Andrew J. Flanagin and Miriam J. Metzger, "Trusting Expert- Versus User-Generated Ratings Online: The Role of Information Volume, Valence, and Consumer Characteristics," *Computers in Human Behavior*, 29:4 (2013), 1626–34.

26 Ana Babić Rosario, Francesca Sotgiu, Kristine De Valck, and Tammo H.A. Bijmolt, "The Effect of Electronic Word of Mouth on Sales: A Meta-Analytic Review of Platform, Product, and Metric Factors," *Journal of Marketing Research*, 53:3 (2016), 297–318.

27 Ibid.

28 Chen, Fay, and Wang, "The Role of Marketing in Social Media: How Online Consumer Reviews Evolve."

29 Ayaz Nanji, "Do Consumers Trust Online Reviews," MarketingProfs.com, September 5, 2013, www.marketingprofs.com/charts/2013/11563/do-consumers-trust-online-reviews (accessed July 13, 2014).

30 *Global Trust in Advertising*, Nielsen, September 2015, www.nielsen.com/content/dam/nielsen global/apac/docs/reports/2015/nielsen-global-trust-in-advertising-report-september-2015.pdf (accessed February 20, 2017).

31 Khim-Yong Goh, Cheng-Suang Heng, and Zhijie Lin, "Social Media Brand Community and Consumer Behavior: Quantifying the Relative Impact of User- and Marketer-Generated Content," *Information Systems Research*, 24:1 (2013), 88–107.

32 Eileen Brown, "Study Shows Non-Celebrity Influencers Are 10 Times More Likely to Drive In-Store Purchases," ZDNet.com, April 27, 2016, www.zdnet.com/article/study-shows-non-celebrity-influencers-are-10-times-more-likely-to-drive-in-store-purchases (accessed June 21, 2017).

33 Marcus Miller, "SEO & The Zero Moment of Truth," *Search Engine Land*, February 29, 2016, http://searchengineland.com/seo-zero-moment-truth-242692 (accessed June 21, 2017).

34 "The Social Generations: Millennials Ask, Gen X Buys & Baby Boomers Observe," The Q1 2017 Sprout Social Index, Sprout Social, http://sproutsocial.com/insights/data/q1-2017 (accessed March 15, 2017).

35 Sebastian DiGrande, David Knox, Kate Manfred, and John Rose, "Unlocking the Digital-Marketing Potential of Small Businesses," BCG Perspectives, March 19, 2013, www.bcgperspectives.com/content/articles/digital_economy_marketing_sales_unlocking_digital_marketing_small_businesses (accessed July 20, 2014).

36 Michael Luca, "Reviews, Reputation, and Revenue: The Case of Yelp.com," Harvard Business School Working Paper Series, 2011, www.hbs.edu/faculty/Pages/item.aspx?num=41233 (accessed June 12, 2012).

37 "The BazaarVoice CGC Index," Bazaarvoice, www.bazaarvoice.com/cgcindex (accessed July 4, 2017).

38 "Online Consumer-Generated Reviews Have Significant Impact on Offline Purchase Behavior," comScore, November 29, 2007, www.comscore.com/Press_Events/Press_Releases/2007/11/Online_Consumer_Reviews_Impact_Offline_Purchasing_Behavior (accessed July 30, 2010).

39 Don Davis, "Customer Reviews Help Cut Product Return Rate at Petco," Internet Retailer, June 26, 2007, www.internetretailer.com/2007/06/26/customer-reviews-help-cut-product-return-rate-at-petco (accessed July 30, 2010).

40 "Rubbermaid Products with Reviews Show Increased Revenues," Bazaarvoice Case Study, January 2010, www.bazaarvoice.com/case-studies/Rubbermaid-RR-case-study.html (accessed July 3, 2017).

41 Eric Anderson and Duncan Simester, "Reviews Without a Purchase: Low Ratings, Loyal Customers, and Deception," *Journal of Marketing Research*, 51:3 (2014), 249–69, http://web.mit.edu/simester/Public/Papers/Deceptive_Reviews.pdf (accessed July 20, 2014).

42 "Brand Transparency on Social Media," Chartered Institute of Marketing, June 9, 2016, https://exchange.cim.co.uk/infographic/brand-transparency-on-social-media (accessed February 15, 2017).

43 Nick Statt, "Amazon Is Cracking Down on Biased Customer Reviews," *The Verge*, October 3, 2016, www.theverge.com/2016/10/3/13155578/amazon-incentivized-reviews-ban-vine-program-product-bias (accessed June 21, 2017).

44 "Leading Retail Analyst Shows Retailers Can Gain Market Share Through Consumer-Generated Product Ratings and Reviews," *Business Wire*, August 15, 2006.

45 "Social Commerce Roundup," eMarketer, July 2014, http://on.emarketer.com/Roundup-07012014-SocialCommerceRoundup.html (accessed July 20, 2014).

46 Ibid.

47 Heidi Bleau, "Cybercrime in Social Media Grows 70% in Six Months," RSA, December 6, 2016, http://blogs.rsa.com/cybercrime-social-media-grows-70-six-months (accessed June 21, 2017).

48 *Social Media Protection: Brand Fraud Report*, Proofpoint, 2016, https://go.proofpoint.com/rs/309-RHV-619/images/Social%20Media%20Protection%20Brand%20Fraud%20Report%20v2.pdf (accessed June 21, 2017).

49 Gerd Gigerenzer and Reinhard Selten, *Bounded Rationality: The Adaptive Toolbox* (Cambridge, MA: MIT Press, 2002).

50 Paul Marsden, "How Social Commerce Works: The Social Psychology of Social Shopping," *Digital Intelligence Today*, December 6, 2009, http://digitalintelligencetoday.com/how-social-commerce-works-the-social-psychology-of-social-shopping (accessed July 4, 2017).

51 Robert Cialdini, *Influence: The Psychology of Persuasion* (New York: Collins, 1998).

52 J.H. Huang and Y.F. Chen, "Herding in Online Product Choice," *Psychology & Marketing*, 23:5 (2006), 413–28.

53 Wenjing Duan, Bin Gu, and Andrew Whinston, "Analysis of Herding on the Internet—An Empirical Investigation of Online Software Download," *Proceedings of the Eleventh Americas Conference on Information Systems*, Omaha, NE, USA, August 11–14, 2005, https://pdfs.semanticscholar.org/ad37/7e2f5e0b890e86d43b08ab03e4c84a80a8e4.pdf (accessed June 21, 2017).

54 For a study that measures individual differences in proclivity to conformity, see William O. Bearden, Richard G. Netemeyer, and Jesse E. Teel, "Measurement of Consumer Susceptibility to Interpersonal Influence," *Journal of Consumer Research*, 15 (March 1989), 473–81.

55 John W. Thibaut and Harold H. Kelley, *The Social Psychology of Groups* (New York: Wiley, 1959); W.W. Waller and R. Hill, *The Family: A Dynamic Interpretation* (New York: Dryden, 1951).

56 Bearden, Netemeyer, and Teel, "Measurement of Consumer Susceptibility to Interpersonal Influence"; Lynn R. Kahle, "Observations: Role-Relaxed Consumers: A Trend of the Nineties," *Journal of Advertising Research* (March–April 1995), 66–71; Lynn R. Kahle and Aviv Shoham, "Observations: Role-Relaxed Consumers: Empirical Evidence," *Journal of Advertising Research* (May–June 1995), 59–62.

57 "MantraBand Creates Social Proof with Yotpo: Case Study," Yotpo, www.yotpo.com/case-study/mantraband (accessed June 21, 2017).

Visit **https://study.sagepub.com/smm3e** for free additional online resources related to this chapter.

PART 4

Social Media Data Management and Measurement

Social Media Analytics

Learning Objectives

When you finish reading this chapter, you will be able to answer these questions:

1. How do companies utilize social media data and research to inform marketing decisions? What are the primary approaches to social media research?

2. What is the research process for collecting, processing, and analyzing residual social media data used in social listening and monitoring?

3. What are the common errors and biases associated with social media research?

4. How do brands develop social intelligence systems?

5. What is the process for netnographic research in social media communities?

The Role of Social Media in Research

To plan a social media marketing strategy that will meet objectives, marketers need to understand their target audiences and their environment. They need to know the answers to questions about consumer personalities and past experiences, motives and fears, brand loyalties, and media usage. They may need to listen to consumer complaints and identify potential public relations crises. They may need to assess the effectiveness of a marketing campaign. Why? Because every decision we make as marketers is based on what we know about the target audience and the marketing environment. From the product benefits to the brand image to the creative strategies used in the campaign to the media placement of the message, we make decisions based on what we know. And, we make better decisions when we understand the environment within which we compete. Gathering market insight and competitive intelligence are critical steps to develop strategy. Relying upon research—market, competitive, and consumer—to make more informed marketing decisions is standard practice for marketers.

Marketers rely on several variants of marketing research to make decisions. Our options include both secondary and primary research. **Secondary research** is information already collected and available for use. It may be internal, published publicly, or available via syndicated sources. Secondary data might include background on the market, industry, competitors, and the brand's history. In contrast, **primary research** collects data for the research purposes at hand. Primary data can help marketers to understand consumers in the market, including psychological makeup, spending and media consumption patterns, and responsiveness to message appeals and offers. We conduct primary research via exploratory, qualitative methods such as observation, focus groups, and in-depth interviews; descriptive techniques such as surveys; or with experimental techniques such as simulations and test markets. Social media provides new sources of data and information that were once difficult to collect or altogether unavailable. Social media have expanded the outlets for consumer expression; they have shifted the importance of utilizing user-generated content to a higher level. Content is shared by many users across many forms of social media communities. The content includes opinions, experiences, and facts expressed in text, audio, and video. Conversations are built around the content. As conversation has increased in quantity, quality, location, and format, it has also become more useful and significant to marketers. Every piece of content shared socially online is data. As we discussed in Chapter 2, the residual data can be collected and analyzed to help marketers provide customer service and service recovery (social customer care solutions), insight for developing marketing strategies, and assessments of the effectiveness of past marketing choices in meeting marketing objectives. What's more, the data can be combined with other data sources to create an even more powerful dataset.

In this chapter, we discuss the developing area of social media research and how social media marketers can utilize social content as a valuable source of marketing information. **Social media research** is the application of scientific marketing research principles to the collection and analysis of social media data such that valid and reliable results are produced.[1] The term social media research encompasses any form of research that uses data derived from social media sources. The most prevalent among marketers is the data mining and subsequent analysis of naturally occurring data across social media channels. But social media research can also encompass research on the activity and content of social media itself through ethnographic (called netnography) and other qualitative methods. In addition, we can utilize social media channels and communities as modes for data collection in primary research studies, conducting interviews, focus groups, surveys, and experiments. We're not going to go into detail about the foundations of marketing research in this chapter (are you relieved?). However, we will highlight the basic process for social media listening as well as some of the tools that improve an organization's ability to understand what its customers want and how they relate to its offerings.

Companies can utilize these social data by strategically using social listening and monitoring. Social monitoring and listening go hand in hand. **Social monitoring** is the process of tracking mentions of specific words or phrases on social media sites. Monitoring enables companies to be notified when a social mention warrants a reaction. The monitoring process acts like a trigger. **Social listening** also identifies and collects information shared on social media sites, but for listening applications, the data collected is analyzed for insights to inform strategic marketing decisions. Though both activities mine social data, monitoring is reactive while listening is proactive. Dan Neely, CEO of Networked Insights, described the difference like this: "Monitoring sees trees; listening sees the forest."[2]

What are the top applications for social monitoring and listening? According to Forrester's study on *Global Enterprise Social Listening*, social listening is used for brand monitoring, measuring the effectiveness of specific campaigns, understanding customers, providing customer service, gathering ideas for future campaigns, identifying risks that could lead to public relations crises, gathering competitive intelligence, and identifying ideas for new product development or product improvements.[3] Let's take a closer look.

Social Customer Care

Brand mentions can be used to identify service satisfaction issues. In this way, listening to social media conversations is a key activity for marketers involved in social CRM tactics. For instance, customer service teams can monitor social media to detect posts by people who write to vent about a "disservice" experience they had with a company. A study by J.D. Powers found that 67% of social media users had used a company's social media channels for customer support.[4] Of those, 84% expect a response and expect that response to occur within the first 24 hours.[5] If an organization learns about complaints quickly, it can respond quickly as well. It may have a chance to salvage a customer relationship it would have lost if the wound had been allowed to fester. Not only do brands benefit by retaining customers, these customers may also become more valuable and more loyal. Customers spend 20% to 40% more with companies who engage with their customer service requests over social media. They are also likely to become brand advocates: 71% of customers who experience a quick and effective brand response to their support requests on social media are likely to recommend that brand to others, compared to just 19% of those that don't receive any response.[6]

Despite customer expectations and the benefits of listening for customer care, this is a weakness for many organizations. The Sprout Social Index report found that only one in every ten customer care requests made on social media get a response.[7] The study measured which industries get the most customer service requests via social media, the percentage of those requests that were addressed, and the average response time, shown in Table 10.1. What really stands out? Across these industries, there is a lot of room for improvement when it comes to social listening for customer care.

Table 10.1   Brand and Consumer Index Spotlight by Industry

Industry	Avg. Response Rate	Avg. Response Time (Hours)	Avg. % Messages Needing Response	Avg. Posts per Replies	Brand Engagement Ranking	Consumer Engagement Ranking
Automotive	11%	12.6	37%	16	#12	#16
Banking/Finance	14%	9.6	31%	17	#3	#8
Consumer Goods	16%	14.5	37%	122	#5	#5
Education	8%	9.1	34%	21	#13	#7
Government	9%	10.7	38%	16	#14	#2
Healthcare	11%	11.7	41%	17	#11	#10
Internet/Technology	12%	11.8	35%	32	#6	#13
Marketing/Advertising	12%	12.4	35%	366	#10	#14
Media/Entertainment	7%	10.0	37%	55	#16	#11
Nonprofit	9%	11.0	36%	19	#15	#9
Professional Services	10%	9.8	32%	25	#7	#3
Real Estate	11%	11.5	43%	20	#8	#1
Retail	19%	9.8	42%	18	#2	#4
Travel/Hospitality	16%	10.7	38%	11	#4	#12
Utilities	17%	8.2	36%	13	#1	#6

Source: Sprout Social, The Q2 2017 Sprout Social Index, HYPERLINK "http://sproutsocial.com/insights/data/q4-2016/" \t "_blank" http://sproutsocial.com/insights/data/q2-2017 (accessed July 21, 2017). Reproduced by kind permission of Sprout Social, Inc.

Fortunately, some brands are better than others! Which global brands are the most responsive to customer posts? SocialBakers, as social media analytics provider, monitors social customer care performance and maintains a list of the top brands in a variety of industries around the world. Companies that respond to 65% or more of the queries they receive on social media earn the designation Socially Devoted. Halo BCA has been the world's leader, with an average response time of two minutes. ASOS, the British fashion retailer, averages nine minutes and Amazon Help 48 minutes.[8] You can see how other brands scored at www.socially-devoted.com.

Market Research

Social media research can inform many decisions facing the marketing strategist. These might range from ideas for new product development to target audience insight to concepts for new campaigns. For example, Krispy Kreme monitors social conversations to identify new product concepts like doughnut sushi and to test interest in new products before a global rollout.[9] Infegy, a social intelligence software provider, used social listening for consumer insight research to guide the banking industry. Among the findings? While men focused on interest rates and bank fees, women worried about budgeting and raising financially savvy kids. No need for bank marketing to be boring and stodgy anymore. Infegy also learned that people use humor to deflect money concerns—like this tweet: "I wish my bank account refilled as fast as my laundry basket."[10] Social listening can also alert marketers to impending trouble for crisis communications that might be marked by a shift in the velocity of brand mentions or assess the impact of a public relations crisis. It can also track brand mentions on competitors' brand names. Tracking brand mentions of key competitors and comparing those points to those for the brand enable marketing managers to learn how the brand is positioned in the marketplace.

Campaign Assessment

Social media research can be useful for providing feedback on how a campaign or other brand communication was received by others. H&M has long used celebrities in its marketing campaigns. Using social listening, Brandwatch, a social intelligence agency, assessed the relative effectiveness of H&M's celebrity endorsers. The differences in response to David Beckham and Beyoncé were enlightening. Beckham generated more social mentions overall, but more comments mentioning Beyoncé also included an intent to purchase (e.g., I'm definitely going to buy that bag!). Beckham generated more brand visibility for H&M, but Beyoncé likely drove more sales.[11]

Social Media Listening: The Research Process

Observational research involves recording behavior or the residual evidence of behavior. Researchers in offline contexts have done this for years; they watch people as they shop in stores, or perhaps count the number and type of candy wrappers people throw out after a party to see what they're eating. Online this kind of residual data exists in abundance. Not all of it is available to social media researchers. Some is privacy-protected. But much of these data are not. Social listening tools can draw from anything that's publicly available in the social media space. That means marketers can utilize content shared across all four zones of social media including conversations in social networks and forums, blog posts and comments, product reviews, photos shared in sites such as Instagram, videos shared on sites such as YouTube, social bookmarks and comments, and microblog posts. This content can be very useful, because it offers insight marketers can use in segmentation, needs analysis, and customer profiling. Conversations that include influence impressions provide information about brand awareness, attitude toward a brand, competitive advantage, and more because these brand mentions are explained in the context of an online discussion. Companies may approach the collection and analysis of these social data in different ways, but before we discuss the degrees of social media listening, let's review the basic process.

An Overview of Social Media Listening and Monitoring

Social media monitoring and listening literally means to monitor conversations and content in social media channels by "listening." This listening works with the aid of software that systematically searches key words it finds in social spaces such as blogs, social networks, and forums. The data are collected along with related variables like profile indicators. By carefully choosing and searching the appropriate key words and the relevant social communities, the researcher can gather insight into customer decision-making, perceptions of the brand, perceptions of competitors, and more. An automated monitoring service may be retained to crawl the web (much as search engine bots do), collecting conversations according to established criteria (called **scraping**) for inclusion in a database. From that database, conversation volume, source, and sentiment can be gauged. At this point, analysts have access to both quantitative and qualitative data.

Monitoring explains what was said, when, by whom, and how many times. Thus, this process answers four basic questions:

1   How many times was the search term found?
2   When was the search term found?
3   Where was the search term found?
4   Who mentioned the search term?

The content of the data collected is of great use to marketers. Positive comments can turn into customer testimonials for use in retailing and promotions. Comments about competitors serve as competitive intelligence. Conversations among like-minded groups of friends and connections provide consumer insight that's useful for targeting and positioning. But it gets even better: monitoring results in the development of a detailed database that analysts can use to create more insights as they synthesize the comments of thousands of people. In well-designed systems, these data can be merged with data from other channels. For instance, a brand using SocialStudio could merge the data from social monitoring with data collected from its salesforce.

Unlike a lot of traditional survey research, which is quantitative (i.e., in numerical form), much of the data collected are qualitative. Typical types of data include **verbatims** (the actual comments people post in English or other languages) as well as other identifying information such as the time the item was posted and the site on which it appeared. Multimedia posts including images and video can also be analyzed.

The approach requires the specification of a formal **research design** before any data are collected. The research design specifies a plan to collect and utilize data so that desired information can be obtained with sufficient precision and/or so that hypotheses can be tested properly. It includes decisions on the study approach (exploratory, descriptive, or experimental), the sampling plan to be used and procedures for data collection, and data analysis decisions. This in turn gives the researchers more confidence if they wish to generalize their findings to a larger population (e.g., many or all of their customers). When we apply a scientific approach to gathering data for social media research, we plan a research design to maximize the reliability and validity of our study. In addition to collecting data systematically using software that can collect and scrub relevant content, we pay special attention to the minimizing sources of error that could create bias in our results. We do so as we consider our research design decisions and set data collection protocols. Next we discuss some of these specific approaches, such as text mining, sentiment analysis, and content analysis.

Sentiment Analysis

Sentiment refers to how people think or feel (especially feel) about an object such as a brand or a political candidate. Sentiment is heavier on emotion than reason but it captures an opinion about something. In that regard, collecting and analyzing sentiment data can provide an alternative to attitudinal surveys of consumers—if, and it's a big if, people are talking about what you need to know in social spaces.

How can marketers use sentiment analysis? They can analyze product reviews to obtain insight into the mix of features people want, and the product's strengths and weaknesses. News mentions of a company can be analyzed to indicate perceptions of the company in terms of product quality, service quality, performance, and value. Customers can use sentiment analysis to systematically utilize reviews when they make purchase decisions.

Sentiment analysis is at its core attitudinal research. In fact, sometimes it is called **opinion mining**. In the context of social media conversations, it means at a very basic level to analyze content to determine the attitude of the writer. When we employ social media research to assess attitudes toward a brand, we essentially seek to determine whether the relevant conversations are positive or negative. Certain emotions are strongly related to specific words. When people feel a particular way they are likely to choose certain words that tend to relate to the emotion. From these words, the researcher will create a **word-phrase dictionary** (sometimes called a *library*) to code the data. The program will scan the text to identify whether the words in the dictionary appear. The words and

Table 10.2 Steps to Conduct Sentiment Analysis

Step 1:	Fetch, crawl, and cleanse. Data from the sources are collected using web crawlers. These simple applications move through the designated websites and collect and store the content they find. These are the same types of programs search engines use to catalog webpages. Using the word-phrase dictionary, the crawlers select only the content that appears to be relevant based on matches with the dictionary. This process is called **fetching** or **web scraping**. The scraped data need to be cleansed to eliminate any unnecessary formatting prior to moving forward. A text classifier (from the dictionary) is then applied to the data to filter any irrelevant content that made it into the data set.
Step 2:	Extract entities of interest. From this filtered set of content, relevant posts are extracted. Remember, a blog post might contain information on several brands, not just the ones of interest in the study. The data are filtered again using rules to tag the entities of interest and further narrow the data set.
Step 3:	Extract sentiment. From there, the analyst can begin sentiment extraction using sentiment indicators. These are words or other cues used to indicate positive or negative sentiment. In what proximity to the brand mention must they be to serve as an indicator? Accuracy is best when proximity is close. That's one reason why sentiment analysis of tweets tends to be more accurate than that of blogs; the message intent is easier to interpret when the data per content piece are smaller. A **sentiment dictionary** specifies sentiment indicators and rules to be used in the analysis. For instance, if the word "high" is in close proximity to the word "price," the sentiment may be scored as negative. The rules are in place in part to deal with sentence structure patterns. For instance, negation words such as "no," "not," or "never" can totally transform the meaning of a sentence; the analysis will need to be programmed to properly extract the sentiment intended.
Step 4:	Aggregate raw sentiment data into a summary. Raw sentiments are then aggregated creating a sentiment summary.

Source: Richard N. Landers, Robert C. Brusso, Katelyn J. Cavanaugh, and Andrew B. Collmus, "A Primer on Theory-Driven Web Scraping: Automatic Extraction of Big Data from the Internet for Use in Psychological Research," *Psychological Methods*, 21:4 (2016), 475–92

phrases in the dictionary are also used as **text classifiers**, in that once data are retained for further analysis, the data can also be classified according to the words and phrases in the dictionary. That might sound simplistic, but it doesn't mean it's easy to analyze sentiment. It's incredibly labor-intensive when analyzed by human coders and complex when analyzed with text mining software.

Consider this example based on Canon's PowerShot A540. A review on Epinions, a product review site, included this statement: "The Canon PowerShot A540 had good aperture and excellent resolution." A **sentiment analysis** would extract the entities of interest from the sentence, identifying the product as the Canon PowerShot A540 and the relevant dimensions as aperture and resolution. The sentiment would then be extracted for each dimension; the sentiment for aperture is "good" while that for resolution is "excellent." Of course, at this level, the coding is probably managed by text mining software. Many users post assessments; the individual sentiments are obtained and stored in a database for further analysis and reporting. Let's review the steps to conduct a sentiment analysis (Table 10.2).[12]

However, as with any technique there are challenges associated with sentiment analysis:

- First and foremost is accuracy in gauging sentiment with automated tools. The sheer volume of conversation creates an information overload issue for most brands wanting to use social media monitoring and research. The solution is the use of an automated system, but these systems still struggle with accuracy in the coding of meaning. Systems that use a mix of human analysis, keyword meaning, and natural language processing tend to provide the best accuracy scores.

- Cultural factors, linguistic nuances, and differing contexts all make it difficult to code text into negative, neutral, or positive categories. Consider this example: Perhaps we want to know the attitudes toward the movie *Chef.* We could scrape the social Web for comments about *Chef.* But could a machine accurately code those comments? For example, the word "hunger" might be denoted as a negative term. But since this movie is about the restaurant industry, a comment about hunger could be positive. A person could understand that this statement was positive for the movie, but the software program couldn't. Linguistic nuances make it difficult for mining software to achieve better accuracy levels. A chocolate torte described as wickedly sinful would be coded as negative, when it fact the descriptor is positive.

- Defining the sentiment dictionary can also be a challenge, ultimately affecting whether the right words are extracted. Words can have many meanings. Take the situation Ionis Pharmaceuticals faced. The multi-billion dollar biotech firm's name was ISIS Pharmaceuticals (and identified with the stock ticker ISIS). In addition to the negative associations the brand experienced as the Islamic State of Iraq and Syria (ISIS) grew in public recognition, social media research on brand meaning was challenged by the difficulty in extracting relevant data.

- Accuracy in the categorical data needed to make better use of data is also an issue. It's difficult to gauge who is making comments (which segments they represent) in terms of demographic and geographic descriptors. Conversation origin may be identifiable using the URL, the IP address, or the language used, but all of these methods have flaws. The URL and IP address are not always helpful (take Facebook, for instance, with users around the world). Language indicators likewise leave a lot to be desired.

Content Analysis

Sentiment analysis is a form of **text mining**: the gathering and analysis of text data from relevant sources. Sentiment analysis uses a bottom-up approach to extract patterns from text. Human coders identify the sentiment indicators and interpret patterns, but the emphasis is on software manipulation of the data based on extraction rules.

In contrast, **content analysis**, an analysis approach used to identify the presence of concepts and themes within qualitative data sets, uses a top-down approach that applies theory or empirical evidence to the coding process. For example, a researcher might test a hypothesis that TV commercials reinforce traditional sex-role attitudes by sampling a large number of ads that aired during a certain period of time and comparing the occupations that male versus female actors portrayed.

Both sentiment analysis and content analysis can include quantitative analysis, but the intent is to enable the researcher to make inferences about messages in the content relevant to the research questions. Because content analysis is used to study the meanings relayed through content, the content used as sources is broadly defined. It is most often text-based but may include multi-media. The content could originate from books, essays, interviews, newspaper headlines and articles, speeches, advertising, and so on. For social media researchers most content originates from social conversations and user-generated content posted online. The primary *unit of analysis* is the word. As images and video become more prevalent in social media, multi-media content analysis like that studied by researchers at the Visual Social Media Lab is needed.

To conduct a content analysis, the text is coded, or broken down, into manageable categories on a variety of levels—word, word sense, phrase, sentence, and theme—and then examined further for interpretation. Using **codes**, labels that classify and assign meanings to pieces of information, analysts can use the comments to determine any themes that are reflected in the comments. Table 10.3 summarizes major coding categories researchers use and provides examples to illustrate each.[13]

Table 10.3   Coding Categories for Content Analysis

Type of Code	Purpose
Context codes	Provide information on the source of the comment
Respondent perspective codes	Capture the general viewpoint revealed in the comment
Process codes	Indicate when over the course of the campaign a comment occurred
Relationship codes	Indicate alliances within social communities
Event codes	Indicate unique issues in the data
Activity codes	Identify comments that require response

Caution! Research Errors and Biases

When we look at research results, it's tempting to jump to quick conclusions about what is going on "out there." However, we need to be very careful about doing so because a variety of potential other explanations for the results exist. Numerous biases and errors may complicate the story. Every study has a certain amount of error that we cannot precisely specify; our goal as researchers is to minimize that error. Ultimately we want our research to provide as close an estimation of the truth as it is possible.

Let's briefly review several types of errors that are particularly dangerous for social media research. Market researchers should remain vigilant against potential sources of bias that could interfere with the reliability and validity of the research outcomes. Though numerous errors are possible at every stage of research, our focus is on minimizing coverage error, sampling error, measurement error, and nonresponse error. Interpretation error is also an issue for social media research, but we will address that error in the section on analysis.

Coverage and Sampling Errors

One of the first decisions we must make (after we identify the need for research information and our research approach) is to establish the population from which we need to collect data. If we were collecting primary data using survey research or interviews, we would specify the units of interest, likely the people or families to which we wish to generalize the study results. This is known as defining the **population**. That's because we want to select participants for our study who represent the people in our population. If we were to study the whole of the population rather than a subset (known as a **sample**), this would be called a **census** (like the one the US government conducts every decade). We would then define a **sample frame**, an available list that approximates the population and from which we draw a sample to represent the population.

Alas, in social media research it generally isn't possible to identify unique people as units in a defined population, though we still want to ensure that our content is representative. It also isn't possible for us to scour the entire Internet every day for every single brand mention to conduct a census of brand mentions. Instead, we define the population as the social communities to which our audience belongs. We create a sampling frame of selected social communities and websites based on their descriptions; these include membership demographics, purpose, location, and activity. In other words, rather than identifying a population of consumer units that matches our target audience and then defining a sampling frame that provides a list from which to draw access to that population, we define a population of relevant communities for those consumer units.

The sample refers to the units of content we draw from the frame for inclusion in data analysis. In this case the sampling plan should also include specifications on identifying relevant content and the time period in which content is drawn. For example, let's say we want to understand how our new video game product fares in relation to other games that are similar. We define our population as members of gaming sites such as GamesForum and Gaming Bay. Our sampling frame could be all members who post on these two forums over a four-week period, including two weeks prior to and two weeks post video game launch.

The first source of potential error we need to address is **coverage error**. This occurs when there is a failure to cover all components of a population being studied. It represents a gap between the sampling frame we use and the population we define. For social media research, the researcher must ask, "Which social media platforms and sites should be (and can be) included in data collection?" We are limited in coverage by the need to access publicly posted commentary. For instance, tweets are largely public content, so Twitter is one platform researchers commonly include in social media research studies. But Twitter represents a relatively small portion of the population of social media users. It would be hard to justify using Twitter to study hard-core gamers when a preferred vehicle for gamers is the *GamersTalk* forum. The risk of coverage error in social media research was demonstrated by researchers who modelled both sentiment expressed and vehicle source.[14] The results show that the inferences marketing researchers obtain from monitoring social media are dependent on where they "listen." Though it is typical for social media research to mine data from a single social vehicle and/or to aggregate data from several sources, both approaches can lead to faulty and misleading results due to coverage error. **Sampling** refers to the process a researcher uses to select specific cases from a sampling frame for inclusion in a study. It is almost always used in research because in most cases it is financially or logistically impossible to use a census. That's especially true for social media that literally include several platforms, thousands of sites, millions of pages and profiles, and zillions of individual pieces of content that could serve as data. A well-devised sampling plan helps ensure that a small portion of the data in the sampling universe can provide as accurate a depiction of the truth as we could get if we actually took a census of the entire population. The issue is, what is the truth? **Sampling error** is the result of collecting data from only a subset, rather than all, of the members of the sampling frame; it heightens the chance that the results are wrong. In our example, we would commit a major sampling error if we somehow sampled only female gamers who are in their fifties.

In survey research, sampling error is associated with how we draw our sample, using either a probability or non-probability method. For social media research, we will utilize these guidelines in collecting data, but two situations create additional concerns in the area of sampling error for social media researchers: (1) the echo effect and (2) the participation effect. The **participation effect** is when only some people are participating, and some participate at a high rate, effectively inflating the number of conversations that relate to the research. The actual number of conversations may not always be what it seems.

The **echo effect**, also called **online echo**, refers to the duplication in conversation volume that tends to occur in social media spaces. Online echo exists because people who share content online tend to share it in more than one community, and people in the sharer's network may then also share the same content. In Twitter, this is called *retweeting*, but sharing another person's content is common (and encouraged) throughout social media. Thus, the question is how should retweets and reposts be counted in a study?

There are also other forms of irrelevant content that can create sampling error. Spam is increasingly common in social communities but it does not represent real conversations we should include in the data set. Further, some marketers pay bloggers and other social media influencers to discuss their respective brands. These paid brand mentions could also be collected during the sampling process, but again, they do not reflect real conversations. To make it even more complicated, organic conversations could grow around these paid brand mentions. Some content is also duplicate content that is simply retweeted automatically by bots programmed to spread messages with specific keywords.

How should researchers handle these issues in the collection of data? The solution to these issues is not as simple as creating a rule to not include duplicate content. If a comment is shared by other people, the extent of sharing is an indicator of increased exposure of the message and sentiment in that someone felt the message worthy of passing along, even if the sharing didn't express an original thought. How we handle different types of mentions and duplicates is something that we must agree to before we start the study.

Nonresponse Bias

There is the potential for nonresponse error in social media research due to the participation effect. In survey research, **nonresponse error** is the potential that those units that were not included in the final sample are significantly different from those that were. If there are relevant differences, the results based on participating units may not accurately reflect the population of interest. For example, people who are willing to take a 30-minute phone survey may be different than those who aren't. This can result in **nonresponse bias**, a skewing of the results of a survey.

In social media research, we can sample from any public content posted on the sites we specify in our sampling frame. So why are we concerned about nonresponse bias? Because we've specified our population based on the communities where our customers are likely to be, but our ultimate interest is the attitudes and behaviors of people, not sites. Our specification of social media communities served as a proxy for access to the people. But not all people who are members of social communities participate actively or at the same level. Some people consume content, some join and lurk, and some are not active in social communities at all. That means there are people who may use a brand but who are not represented in the social media research analysis.

It is important to keep in mind that searches of social content may not be systematic or exhaustive. They may not be representative of the possible sites where relevant content is posted. In research terms, this form of search is akin to a *convenience sample*; the information we get is suggestive, but it's difficult to generalize it to the broader population. Though there are vast amounts of content available for analysis, we must also remember that many conversations about consumer needs and brands are still held offline—some estimate that as much as 90% of word-of-mouth conversations potentially of interest to marketers is conducted offline.[15]

What consumers talk about online in social channels and offline may vary considerably. One study of offline and online conversations of 700 brands in ten product categories over a three-year period found that online conversations gravitated heavily to media and entertainment products, technology products and services, and cars.[16] In contrast, offline conversations included heavier coverage for beverages, food and dining, cars, and technology but with no specific areas dominating the discussions. Table 10.4 illustrates the percentage of discussions by category offline and online.

Also, the content people share varies for different forms of social sites. Those who post tweets on Twitter are far more vocal than those who share feedback to videos they see on YouTube, but both sites may be included in our sampling frame. This issue must be addressed and can be managed after data collection by using weighting. **Sampling weights** are adjustment factors applied to adjust for differences in probability of selection between cases in a sample. For example, less than 14% of all Internet users are on Twitter, but Twitter generates up to 60% of content that social media monitoring tools monitor. This means that to get a more accurate picture of all users we might want to sample relatively fewer tweets than other kinds of posts. Without weighting, the data will be skewed based on the sites we choose for data collection.

Table 10.4   Word-of-Mouth Conversations Online and Offline

CATEGORY DISTRIBUTION OF OFFLINE AND ONLINE WORD-OF-MOUTH

	% OF OFFLINE	% OF ONLINE
Beauty products	5%	1%
Beverages	13%	3%
Cars	10%	17%
Children's products	2%	0%
Clothing products	7%	3%
Department stores	5%	4%
Financial services	4%	2%
Food and dining	12%	4%
Health products and services	3%	1%
Home design and decoration	1%	1%
Household products	2%	0%
Media and entertainment	9%	32%
Sports and hobbies	3%	8%
Technology products and stores	13%	17%
Telecommunications	9%	7%
Travel services	3%	1%

In a study of online and offline conversations of 700 of the most discussed brands, researchers found that what is talked about varies considerably. Offline, there are product categories that make up a large percentage of the overall conversation, but no one category dominates the discussions. Online, however, things are a bit different. A third of all conversations relate to media and entertainment brands, and cars and technology make up another third. There is very little conversation about the other product categories.

Source: Mitchell Lovett, Renana Peres, and Ron Shachar, "On Brands and Word of Mouth," *Journal of Marketing Research*, 2013 (August), 50 (4), 427–444

CRITICAL REFLECTION

Is It Ethical to Mine Social Conversations?

Social media research is a hotbed of discussion among researchers. Ethical guidelines for the treatment of human subjects are well developed for direct forms of observation. But in social media research, much of the data are public.

When researchers conduct research with human subjects, they operate under a policy of **informed consent**. Participants are made aware of the research and its benefits and implications, and they are

(Continued)

(Continued)

given the opportunity to withdraw or move forward. In social media environments, monitoring is akin to data mining of residual traces of consumer behavior, except the traces include opinions, stories, photographs, and videos. Researchers using public social media posts rely upon the fact that the posters could have chosen to protect their post to justify the lack of informed consent for their research. This view puts the onus on the social media user—by publically posting on social media, these users are waiving their rights and implying consent to any subsequent uses of their data. Organizations like the National Science Foundation and ESOMAR, however, remind us that when individuals can be personally identified in the data, the risk of potential harm warrants additional consideration. In other words, in such cases, the individual unwillingly and unknowingly becomes a documented subject in a research study.

That's just what happened when Danish researchers used data scraping software to collect data from the social network dating site OkCupid. They published the resulting database, which included the online profiles of nearly 70,000 OkCupid users, complete with usernames, political leanings, drug usage, and intimate sexual details, on Open Science Framework, a site that encourages open source science research and collaboration.[17] Online commenters, OkCupid users, the site's operators, and academics and other experts on data intelligence attacked the researchers for making user information public. In a now-famous public tweet, the lead researcher said that no effort had been made to anonymize the data because the "data is already public." Clearly, there are potential ethical concerns when scraping and mining social media data—even if the data is public.

How then should researchers manage the balance between efficiently accessing valuable data and effectively protecting individuals? For academic researchers, particularly when the research is funded by government sources like the National Science Foundation, the preliminary reviews conducted by university Institutional Review Boards (IRB) should provide for the identification of possible risks and solutions prior to the execution of the research. However, the interpretation of the risk of harm to human subjects in research (whether in data mining situations or traditional research) varies from IRB to IRB. This is illustrated by the respective IRB approvals for a study of Facebook profiles, which resulted in identifiable data by Harvard University researchers and a study of emotional manipulation among Facebook users by Cornell researchers.[18] Further, commercial research is outside the bounds of IRB review.

As a start toward developing ethical guidelines for social media researchers, one blogger has proposed a set of rules he adapted from the guidelines that a major marketing research organization (ESOMAR) applies to members who collect observational (or passive) data in the physical world:[19]

- If content has been posted to a truly public domain (i.e., there is no gate to viewing data such as registration), it can be used by the researcher.

- If content is posted in a "gated community" to be available to members only, researchers should announce their presence and request cooperation. Researchers should never pretend to be something or someone they are not when they interact in social communities.

- Assess whether the data to be collected will include personally identifiable and/or sensitive information. If they do, take steps to comply with relevant policies and protect the interests of the affected individuals. Processing of personally identifiable data should require informed consent, or at a minimum the implication of deemed consent.

- Prior to reporting and sharing of data, analysis, or results, all data should be made anonymous.

- Take steps to ensure that no harm is done due to researcher behavior or research uses.

Social Intelligence

Organizations can approach social media listening anecdotally or more systematically. At the early stages of maturity, many organizations essentially just listen to what users say in cyberspace. Analysts collect content haphazardly and inconsistently as they try to track the comments people post about their brand. For instance, they may compile a list of comments people make on a brand's Facebook fan page or the company blog. At times, they may run searches using tools such as Google Alerts, Twitter Search, and Blog Pulse to get a sense of how many times their brand is mentioned in posts. Deep Sherchan, CMO and co-founder of *Simplify360*, criticized this approach, succinctly stating, "Doing Google is not listening. That's like saying, I listen to my customers when I want to."[20] Still, the social web is rich in tools for searching social conversations. The following list highlights the top tools for free and simple social media listening:

- TweetDeck
- BackType
- Twitter Search
- Hootsuite
- HowSociable
- Topsy
- Google Alerts
- Google Trends
- Social Mention

Try this simple exercise: visit Twitter and search the term "Starbucks." How many hits did you get? Hundreds of mentions even within the past hour, most likely. For a brand like Starbucks, listening is a challenge. There are simply too many conversations going on to monitor them on an individual basis—to do so would probably require hundreds of employees who would need to drink a lot of lattés to keep up with the torrent of comments. The challenge comes in accessing that data and transforming it into something that is usable and actionable. There are many potential data uses (some of which we will cover further in the next chapter on metrics). Of course there is value in monitoring for customer care and risk management.

Listening is useful for gathering product ideas, assessing brand reputation, and learning market attitudes and perceptions that can inform decisions across the marketing mix. But there is more value still when organizations invest in social intelligence by building a system to store, classify, and manage social data for use in predictive analytics and modeling. Perhaps this explains the findings from a study of marketing executives. Though many of the executives reported using social listening, 39% maintained that the data were not actionable.[21] The data collected and analyzed should produce recommendations for marketing action that facilitate the brand's performance. Social intelligence systems make this feasible. Forrester Research defines **social intelligence** as "capturing, managing, and analyzing social data to identify and apply insights to business goals."[22]

SAS defines **predictive analytics** as "the use of data, statistical algorithms and machine learning techniques to identify the likelihood of future outcomes based on historical data."[23]

The goal is to go beyond knowing what has happened to providing a best assessment of what will happen in the future.

What kinds of decisions can be aided with predictive analytics of social data (in conjunction with other relevant data)? There are several possibilities.[24] Cluster analysis for segmentation can identify segments meeting complex criteria, including the identification of influencers. Propensity models can then be applied to predict the likelihood of engagement, purchase conversion, and referral behaviors. This is useful for prioritizing prospects, estimating the optimal investment for customer acquisition, and the value of loyalty programs. Filtering models can be applied to produce product recommendations, deliver personalized ads, and trigger coupons and other special offers. This is why big data is such an important topic for marketers.

A Social Intelligence Model

Brandwatch, an enterprise social intelligence provider, conceptualizes the social intelligence system as four layers: 1) social listening, 2) data management, 3) data analytics, and 4) distribution.[25] Social listening is the foundation of social intelligence because it sources data. In the data management stage, data are classified and organized according to relevant categories such as specific campaigns or product lines. Automated rules can also flag important data such as purchase intent or complaints and route the alert to the appropriate person or department for response. Data can then be used for advanced analytics and predictive modeling. Lastly, the distribution layer deals with how information is then translated into easily digestible insights, delivered as needed to the appropriate departments, and/or incorporated into other data needs. Distribution tools typically include dashboards and command centers. A **social media command center** is a central hub for visually monitoring social data related to the brand's marketing objectives. Stations in the center focus on specific data such as brand mentions by influencers and customer complaints. Walmart e-Labs, for instance, acquired the social media listening service, Kosmix, to fully integrate these capabilities into its command center.

Organizations can also partner with an enterprise social intelligence vendor rather than develop these resources in-house. Importantly, the leading vendors for **enterprise social listening** have the capability to pull global data from across the Internet, integrate these data with other important data sources to enable multi-channel analysis, provide an easy-to-use dashboard, and aid in the interpretation of data and in devising strategy based on the results. Forrester Research evaluated the top vendors on several criteria, including quality and extent of data sources, data processing ability, dashboard functionality, support services, analytic capabilities, reporting, customer retention, and market presence.[26] Brandwatch, Synthesio, NetBase, Sprinklr, Crimson Hexagon, Clarabridge, Networked Insights, Salesforce, and Cision earned top marks.

An In-Depth Look at Social Listening Analysis

SocialStudio, part of the Salesforce suite, allows organizations to track, monitor, and react to customer comments. The system enables real-time insights to guide decisions, drawing from over 650 million sources on Twitter, Facebook, YouTube, blogs, news, and more.

The system enables brand managers to see what people are saying about the campaign, understand who is saying what, and possibly why … because themes may appear. We can see the results in word clouds and in sentiment analysis. The analyst can access information from the campaign and company, but also about the competitors and their campaigns. A simple word cloud, drawn from comments in social sources, can provide insights for marketing managers.

Let's take Uber and New York City's taxi industry as an example. Uber is a ride-sharing service. People with the Uber application on their smartphone can post a message requesting a ride. The driver closest to the prospective passenger has up to 15 seconds to accept the request. The drivers charge a fee, but no money changes hands. Fees are exchanged through the app using the passenger's credit card information. Anyone can provide a ride. This means that Uber drivers compete with taxi services in metro areas.

In an area of high demand, like New York City, Uber may want to assess how its service (and independent drivers) compete with New York City taxi drivers. The analysis reveals social conversations about taxi fares in the city. The analysis also reveals momentum around a current event that relates to our industry. We can evaluate the commentary and choose to act if relevant … or not.

The analysis provides a social snapshot of our campaign. We can isolate the social conversations to see topics of interest, themes, advocates, and specific social channels and do so in a way that provides a comparison to competitors. That's not all. We can also do this by segmentation bases.

Using SocialStudio, we can accurately analyze how a product, campaign, or services compare against the competition and industry. For Uber, we can view when conversations spike in time and whether spikes are associated with campaign messaging or negative feedback.

UberX Social Listening for Consumer Intelligence
What are people talking about, where, and why?

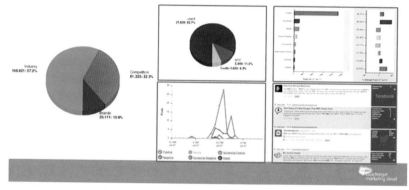

We can also assess which social vehicles are being used. What's more, we can do this in real time. The data provide us with insights and intelligence about our prospects as well as how they feel about the brand, macro views by country and language, micro views by top influencers, and more.

SocialStudio easily isolates the best conversations to understand what people are saying, to help ensure we are using the same terms to drive SEO and website traffic. These charts are totally interactive, so we can easily look at questions, complaints, or which social channel each theme is happening on. We can look at who is influencing the conversation from trending hashtags, to who is being influenced by whom. Sentiment analysis helps determine any sudden change of feeling (good or bad) that our community has toward our company, campaign, or products. Conversations can be ranked by influence and sentiment—but also classified for quick action into areas like service cases, complaints, sales leads, or general questions.

A social media marketers' dream? Imagine a world of just-in-time marketing, imagine knowing who you are reaching, the interests that each demographic from gender to location to specific age groups are rallying around, so that you are always relevant with your content, your promotion or the method in which you engage. SocialStudio gives that level of detail with a click of a button. It illustrates how each audience talks and feels about your company or brand. Are the 18- to 25-year-olds more active on Twitter than the 46- to 55-year-olds? What are the popular hashtags and why? Whatever the questions are, knowing is better than not knowing.

Primary Social Media Research

Thus far in this chapter, we've introduced two approaches to marketing research using the residual data that people leave behind as they interact in social channels. These sources of data are valuable because they provide marketers with insights into consumer opinions, interactions, and behaviors. Importantly, as secondary data, these traces are readily available and inexpensive for organizations that choose to mine the social Web. However, using residual data is not the only approach marketers can take to social media research. Organizations can collect primary data in social spaces, too. The possible approaches include the use of consumer diaries, interviews and focus groups, surveys, and experiments—all conducted within channels of social media.

For instance, Firefly MB, a global qualitative research company, conducted a global study of consumer views of social media and social media marketing.[27] Participants from 15 countries were recruited using message boards, Facebook, Twitter, and Craig's List. Firefly's research design included asynchronous one-to-one interviews conducted via consumer blogs, focus groups conducted within Facebook groups, and a hybrid approach using a proprietary online community, IDEABlog, to engage participants in a multi-day forum. The company's report, *The Language of Love in Social Media*, touts the benefits of the Firefly approach (not surprisingly). Though the participants were queried on specific topics, Firefly notes several advantages to hosting the process in social channels:

- The participants were comfortable being in an environment they frequent regularly, and the community setting led to a feeling of trust and camaraderie during the group sessions. While it can be a challenge to encourage respondents in traditional research studies to open up, the context of social media is already framed with the expectation of sharing.
- Traditional market research is sometimes criticized for its reliance on so-called professional respondents, and this approach filters out these people.
- It's easier to reach people in niche groups. Recruiting can often be a challenge, but the many specialty communities and groups in social media make finding participants with specific characteristics easier.

Twitter chats have been used in lieu of traditional focus groups.[28] Tweetchat focus groups enable input from diverse and geographically dispersed participants. However, researchers should be aware that the speed at which tweetchat conversations occur, coupled with following multiple streams of conversation in real time, make this form of data collection particularly challenging.

Ethnographic approaches, called netnography when executed in digital settings, are also possible. When marketing researchers want to understand how "real" consumers use their products, they may conduct field research where they visit people's homes and offices to observe them as they go about their everyday lives. For example, a team of researchers that wanted to learn about how teenage girls actually talk about beauty care products sponsored a series of sleepovers where they sent (female) employees to hang out overnight and record what they learned when conversation turned to cosmetics, skin treatments, and the like. Now, some social scientists adapt these methods to rigorously study online communities.[29] **Netnography** is a research methodology that adapts ethnographic research techniques to study the communities that emerge through computer-mediated communications. Like monitoring, the approach uses information available through online forums such as chat rooms, message boards, and social networking groups to study the attitudes and behaviors of the market involved. The primary difference is based on how the study takes place. In monitoring, data are collected passively. Web crawlers scour the sites designated in the sampling frame to collect the relevant content and save it to our database.

Netnography is an unobtrusive approach to research with a key benefit of observing what is likely to be credible information, unaffected by the research process. Many marketers already use a very informal and unsystematic form of netnography by simply exploring relevant online communities. However, to minimize the limitations of netnography, researchers should be careful in their evaluations by employing triangulation to confirm findings whenever possible.

How can we use netnography? One researcher recommends the following steps:[30]

- Identify online venues that could provide information related to the research questions.

- Select online communities that are focused on a particular topic or segment, have a high "traffic" of postings, have a relatively large number of active posters, and appear to have detailed posts.

- Learn about the group's culture, including its characteristics, behaviors, and language.

- Select material for analysis and classify material as social or informational and off topic or on topic.

- Categorize the types of participants involved in the discussions to be analyzed.

- Keep a journal of observations and reflections about the data collection and analysis process.

- Be straightforward with those in the online community about your purpose for participation by fully disclosing the researcher's presence in the community as well as his or her intent.

- Utilize "member checks" following content analysis of the discourse to ensure that members feel their attitudes and behaviors have been accurately interpreted.

MINI CASE STUDY

Volkswagen's #DieselGate Damages Brand

Most would agree, Volkswagen has been a strong brand in the automotive industry. That is, until #Dieselgate. In September 2015 the Environmental Protection Agency found that many Volkswagen cars sold in the United States were equipped with software that could falsely improve the performance of diesel engines on emissions tests. This cheating was subsequently acknowledged by the car maker.[31] Among the many issues at stake for the company was one of public perception and potential harm to the brand's image and equity.

iStock.com/Smeel Photography

Social listening and sentiment analysis are useful as an early warning detection system for potential crises, but they are also useful in gauging the extent of damage and response to corporate efforts to recover. As #Dieselgate dominated the news landscape, researchers used social listening tactics to study the impact of the crisis on the brand.

Early estimates of the brand damage were discouraging. The YouGov BrandIndex, which tracks daily consumer perception, found that Volkswagen's score in the US hit its lowest point in six years following the announcement—dropping from 10 to –2. In Germany, the effect was more pronounced, with the score dropping from 20 to –8.[32]

From the time that the news broke through the first two weeks of the scandal, more than two million tweets related to Volkswagen were shared. The hashtag, #dieselgate, was used by an influencer on Twitter and grew in use as news of the crisis spread. Not surprisingly, sentiment analysis of tweets related to Volkswagen during this period revealed an increase in negative sentiment. Estimates suggested that sentiment swung from an overall score of +17% to –7%.

Mentions of the scandal crossed social media vehicles including Twitter, Tumblr, Facebook, Instagram, YouTube, blogs, and news forums. Targeted analysis showed that news articles were the primary source of information about the scandal but the reach was driven by reshares on social sites. This suggested that Volkswagen should direct apologies and other corporate recovery efforts directly to the public via social media.

Results and Outcomes

Using social listening and sentiment analysis, Volkswagen could measure the damage to its brand. Its sentiment score dropped from +17 to –7%. Fortunately for Volkswagen, the sentiment score began to slowly rise over time, illustrating that the company's efforts to apologize to the public and make amends were influencing sentiment.

CHAPTER SUMMARY

How do companies utilize social media research? What are the primary approaches to social media research?

Companies use social media research to answer the same kinds of questions traditional marketing research can answer. The advantage is that there is an enormous amount of data available in social media channels. Brands use these data to inform social customer care initiatives, marketing research that guides marketing mix decisions, and the evaluation of campaign effectiveness. Most social media research uses some form of social media listening/monitoring but it is also possible to conduct surveys, focus groups, and interviews in social communities.

What is the research process for collecting, processing, and analyzing residual social media data used in social listening and monitoring?

Social media monitoring uses software to systematically search key words it finds in social spaces such as blogs, social networks, and forums. By carefully choosing and searching the appropriate key words and the relevant social communities, the researcher can gather insight into customer decision-making, perceptions of the brand, perceptions of competitors, and more. These data are scraped and then analyzed using keyword analysis, natural language processing, and human analysis of content.

Sentiment analysis is a similar approach that emphasizes how people think or feel about an object such as a brand or a political candidate. Content analysis identifies the prevalence of concepts and themes within data sets; it uses a top-down approach that applies theory or empirical evidence to the coding process. Analysts assign codes to classify pieces of information they gather so they can determine any themes that are reflected in a lot of users' comments.

What are the common errors and biases associated with social media research?

Social media research is prone to coverage error, sampling error, and nonresponse error. Coverage error occurs when there is a failure to cover all components of a population being studied. Sampling error is the result of collecting data from only a subset, rather than all, of the members of the sampling frame. Nonresponse error is the potential for those who did not participate to differ significantly from those who did.

How do brands develop social intelligence systems?

Social intelligence systems are capable of capturing, managing, and analyzing social data to identify and apply insights to business goals. According to Brandwatch, a social intelligence system should include four layers: 1) social listening, 2) data management, 3) analytics, and 4) distribution. Distribution includes dashboards and command centers. Brands may develop in-house capabilities or may partner with a vendor providing enterprise social listening.

What is netnographic research in social media communities?

Brands can also use social media in ways that do not incorporate social listening. One of the most useful approaches is known as netnography. In this approach, the researcher embeds herself or himself in the social community and observes behavior. This approach enables the researcher to draw conclusions related to the culture of the community.

REVIEW QUESTIONS

1   What is social media research?
2   Why is social media research valuable for marketers? How do marketers use it?
3   What are the sources of data for social media researchers?
4   What sources of error are common in social media research?
5   Explain the steps in sentiment analysis.
6   When should a researcher use content analysis versus sentiment analysis?
7   What are the components of a social intelligence system?
8   How can researchers use netnography?

EXERCISES

1   Visit Social Mention (www.socialmention.com) and run an analysis on a brand of interest to you. Do you agree with the analysis? Read the information provided from Social Mention on the sites from which it pulls data. Should you be concerned about coverage or sampling error in the analysis revealed?

2   Identify five videos on YouTube that include mentions of a single brand. The videos should include at least one corporate piece but the others may be user-generated. View the videos and read the accompanying comments; then conduct a content analysis of the material you find. What insights are you able to glean?

3   Visit www.brandwatch.com/case-studies and view one of its videos on social intelligence. What insights were provided?

CHAPTER NOTES (access all weblinks listed here at: https://study.sagepub.com/smm3e)

1   ESOMAR Guideline on Social Media Research, 2011, ESOMAR, www.esomar.org/uploads/public/knowledge-and-standards/codes-and-guidelines/ESOMAR-Guideline-on-Social-Media-Research.pdf (accessed July 3, 2017).

2   See Jennifer Beese, "What Is Social Listening and Why Is It Important?" Sprout Social, November 18, 2015, http://sproutsocial.com/insights/social-listening (accessed June 22, 2017).

3   Allison Smith, Mary Pilecki, Rebecca McAdams, Emily Miller, and Matthew Izzi, "Leverage Social Data to Elevate Customer Intelligence," Forrester Research, July 21, 2015.

4   See Spencer Lanoue, "The Complete Guide to Using Social Media for Customer Support," Groove, June 28, 2016, www.groovehq.com/support/complete-guide-to-social-media-customer-support (accessed June 22, 2017).

5   "The Social Generations: Millennials Ask, Gen X Buys & Baby Boomers Observe," The Q1 2017 Sprout Social Index, Sprout Social, http://sproutsocial.com/insights/data/q1-2017 (accessed March 15, 2017).

6   Lanoue, "The Complete Guide to Using Social Media for Customer Support."

7   "The Social Generations: Millennials Ask, Gen X Buys & Baby Boomers Observe," The Q1 2017 Sprout Social Index.

8   "The Newest Data on Social Customer Care by Socialbakers," Socially Devoted, 2017, www.socialbakers.com/free-social-tools/socially-devoted/q1-2017 (accessed September 22, 2017).

9   "Krispy Kreme's Social Listening Offers Nuanced Views of Different Cultures," eMarketer, October 19, 2016, www.emarketer.com/Article/Krispy-Kremes-Social-Listening-Offers-Nuanced-Views-of-Different-Cultures/1014609 (accessed June 22, 2017).

10   "Banking Behaviors Report," Infegy, infegy.com/files/InfegyBankingBehaviorsReport.pdf?utm_source=JB&utm_medium=email&utm_campaign=banking_report_2016&utm_content=drip_1 (accessed June 22, 2017).

11   "Social Listening in Practice: Campaign Measurement," Brandwatch Report, www.brandwatch.com/guides/campaign-measurement (accessed June 22, 2017).

12   "Turning Conversations Into Insights: A Comparison of Social Media Monitoring Tools," FreshMinds, May 14, 2010, http://shared.freshminds.co.uk/smm10/ whitepaper.pdf (accessed August 19, 2010).

13   R.B. Bogdan and S.K. Biklin, *Qualitative Research for Education: An Introduction to Theory and Methods*, 3rd ed. (Needham Heights, MA: Allyn and Bacon, 1998).

14   David A. Schweidel and Wendy W. Moe, "Listening in on Social Media: A Joint Model of Sentiment and Venue Format Choice," *Journal of Marketing Research*, 51:4 (2014), 387–402.

15   Ed Keller, "Wharton Study Shines New Light on Online vs. Offline Word of Mouth," MediaBizBloggers.com, December 16, 2010, www.mediabizbloggers.com/media-biz-bloggers/111949889.html (accessed December 27, 2010).

16   Mitchell Lovett, Renana Peres, and Ron Shachar, "On Brands and Word of Mouth," *Journal of Marketing Research*, 50:4 (August 2013), 427–44.

17   Robert Hackett, "Researchers Caused an Uproar by Publishing Data from 70,000 OkCupid Users," *Fortune*, May 18, 2016, http://fortune.com/2016/05/18/okcupid-data-research (accessed June 22, 2017).

18   Kalev Leetaru, "Are Research Ethics Obsolete in the Era of Big Data?" *Forbes*, June 17, 2016, www.forbes.com/sites/kalevleetaru/2016/06/17/are-research-ethics-obsolete-in-the-era-of-big-data/#52713ca27aa3 (accessed June 22, 2017).

19   "Guidelines for Social Media Monitoring," adapted from Ray Poynter, "What Are the Ethical Guidelines for Blog and Buzz Mining?" The Future Place Blog, http://thefutureplace.typepad.com/the_future_place/2010/01/what-are-the-ethical-guidelines-for-blog-and-buzz-mining.html (accessed August 7, 2011).

20   Deep Sherchan, "Why Brands Fail When It Comes to Social Media Listening," Simplify360, February 14, 2014, http://simplify360.com/blog/brands-fail-comes-social-media-listening (accessed June 5, 2014).

21   "Social Listening Can Help Brands Derive Actionable Insights," eMarketer, February 24, 2016, www.emarketer.com/Article/Social-Listening-Help-Brands-Derive-Actionable-Insights/1013625 (accessed June 22, 2017).

22 Samantha Ngo, Mary Pilecki, Carlton A. Doty, Clement Teo, Nick Hayes, and Emily Miller, "The Forrester Wave™: Enterprise Social Listening Platforms, Q1 2016: The 12 Providers that Matter Most and How They Stack Up," Forrester Research, March 2, 2016, www.forrester.com/report/ The+Forrester+Wave+Enterprise+Social+Listening+Platforms+Q1+2016/-/E-RES122523 (accessed June 22, 2017).

23 Daniel Faggella, "Predictive Analytics for Marketing—What's Possible and How it Works," TechEmergence, October 18, 2016, http://techemergence.com/predictive-analytics-for-marketing (accessed June 22, 2017).

24 Ibid.

25 James Lovejoy, "What Is Social Media Intelligence?" Brandwatch, February 24, 2015, www.brand watch.com/blog/marketing-understanding-social-media-intelligence-stack (accessed June 22, 2017).

26 Ngo et al., "The Forrester Wave™: Enterprise Social Listening Platforms, Q1 2016."

27 "The Language of Love in Social Media," Firefly MB, 2010, personal communication, COO Cheryl Stallworth-Hooper and presented at Ad Tech 2010, New York, November 3, 2010.

28 Peter R. Chai, Megan L. Ranney, Rochelle K. Rosen, Dana M. Lewis, Edward W. Boyer, "Crowd-Sourced Focus Groups on Twitter: 140 Characters of Research Insight," Proceedings of the 50th Hawaii International Conference on System Sciences, 2017, https://scholarspace.manoa.hawaii. edu/bitstream/10125/41611/1/paper0462.pdf (accessed June 22, 2017).

29 Robert V. Kozinets, *Netnography: Doing Ethnographic Research Online* (London: Sage, 2010); Robert V. Kozinets, "The Field Behind the Screen: Using Netnography for Marketing Research in Online Communities," *Journal of Marketing Research*, 39:1 (2002), 61–72.

30 Robert Kozinets, "E-Tribalized Marketing? The Strategic Implications of Virtual Communities of Consumption," *European Management Journal*, 17:3 (1999), 252–64.

31 Sameer Shah, "#Dieselgate: The Impact of Corporate Deception on Social Perception," Pulsar, December 14, 2005, www.pulsarplatform.com/blog/2015/dieselgate-the-impact-of-corporate-deception-on-social-perception (accessed June 22, 2017); Vanitha Swaminathan and Suyun Mah, "What 100,000 Tweets About the Volkswagen Scandal Tell Us About Angry Customers," *Harvard Business Review*, September 2, 2018, https://hbr.org/2016/09/what-100000-tweets-about-the-volkswagen-scandal-tell-us-about-angry-customers (accessed June 22, 2017).

32 Ibid.

Visit **https://study.sagepub.com/smm3e** for free additional online resources related to this chapter.

Social Media Metrics

Learning Objectives

When you finish reading this chapter, you will be able to answer these questions:

1. What is the role of metrics in social media marketing programs? How should metrics vary according to the level of decision-making in the organization?

2. How can the marketing funnel, customer journey, and levels of engagement guide marketing objectives and the appropriate choice of KPIs?

3. What are the steps in the DATA approach to measurement? What are the three types of metrics?

4. How do we calculate social media ROI?

5. How is A/B testing used to assess the costs and value of social media tactics?

6. How do we track social media results?

THE NUMBERS JUST DON'T ADD UP

A funny thing happened on the way to the CMO's office.

Between the realization of an eye-opening, game-changing insight gleaned from advertising test results and Web behavior data, the report you're gleefully ferrying to the C-Suite wilted, turns brown at the edges, and starts to dribble a slimy substance with a conspicuous stench.

The CMO immediately develops a nose squint. The VP of Corporate Communications has that "Oooo, you're in for it!" look in her eye and the VP of Advertising nudges the Director of Direct Marketing and says *sotto-voce*, "The golden boy is about to find out his day in the sun has turned him to toast."

The CMO points to (but does not touch):

- a traffic report from comScore
- a traffic report from Hitwise
- a chart from Compete.com
- an ad banner report from Atlas
- a traffic report from Omniture and
- another from Google Analytics

"It's like the old joke," she said with no humor at all. "If you take all the economists in the world and line them up end-to-end, they all point different directions. What the hell is going on with these numbers? Are we getting thirty two and a half million people on our website or forty-four million?"

The first time you ran into this nest of nettles, you hopped over to the white board and cheerfully explained all about:

- cookie deletion
- cookie blocking
- multiple machine browsing
- multiple browser browsing
- multiple people on the same cookie
- non-human traffic
- dynamic IP addressing
- page caching
- javascript loading
- called pixel placement

You didn't even get to the good stuff about comparing miles to gallons and about:

- different tools using
- different date cut-off routines and
- different methods to capture
- different types of data to store in
- different kinds of databases with a
- different method of data cleansing and
- different slicing and dicing segmentation to produce
- different kinds of reports that ended up in
- different feeds for integration into
- different data warehouses

... before you were thanked for your help and shown the door—permanently.

You don't fall for it this time.

This time you explain that the world of online marketing has been suffering from a delusion of precision and an expectation of exactitude.

You tell them that we live in a world of statistics and probabilities. We can't count all the stars in the sky, so we don't try. We don't try to get an actual count of

- television watchers
- radio listeners
- magazine readers
- billboard readers
- bus poster readers
- floor sticker readers
- airline ticket jacket readers
- sandwich board readers

Instead, we count some and estimate the rest.

You share the good news that we can do this better than any of the above—and we've got some astonishing tools and techniques for dynamically targeting the audience and optimizing each one's experience.

You say, "We get 36.3 million people coming to our website."

The CMO lowers her half-glasses and gives you the look you last saw when caught using the office copy machine for party invitations. So you add, "With a 4% margin of error and it's a benchmark we can compare month over month from now on."

"So somewhere between 34 and a half and 38 million," she says.

"Pretty much right between them, in fact."

Disparagingly, she asks, "You really can't give me a more accurate number of how many people saw this digital marketing masterpiece that costs me tens of millions a year?"

"I can tell you whether our digital visitors are more engaged with our brand, come back more often, buy from us and discuss our products with their friends. How many people buy our products who saw our ads on CNN and 'Oprah' that cost you hundreds of millions a year?"

The VP of Advertising makes himself visibly smaller.

"I came here to show you a way that could save four million dollars of search marketing while boosting online sales by 6 to 8%," you say.

The scowl leaves the CMO's face. The odor of dubious data dissipates. Her eyes narrow as she leans forward and says, "Show me."

The numbers don't have to be precise—just compelling.

Source: Jim Sterne, "The Numbers Just Don't Add Up," *Media Post*, October 2, 2009, www.mediapost.com/publications/article/114723/the-numbers-just-dont-add-up.html (accessed June 22, 2017). Used by permission of Jim Sterne, founder of the eMetrics Marketing Optimization Summit and Chairman of the Web Analytics Association

What Matters Is Measured

We've shown you throughout this book that brands can benefit when they participate in the social media space. With social media, brands can engage consumers, enhance brand reputation and image, build positive brand attitudes, improve organic search rankings, service customers, and drive traffic to brand locations, both online and offline. But no social media marketing campaign will conclude unless objectives are set and effectiveness has been assessed. The challenge is to identify the right measures to use. It's harder than it sounds—in fact, marketers continue to wrestle with these decisions as they seek concrete ways to illustrate the value of these techniques to others in their organizations who hold the purse strings. Nearly 90% of marketers report wishing they had better financial measures for assessing the effectiveness of social media expenditures and strategies.

Not that long ago, social media marketers felt that there were no standard metrics we could apply to social media marketing campaigns. Some believed that applying metrics to something as organic as social media was "mission impossible"—the metrics were bound to be meaningless at best because social media were not about quantitative monetary accomplishments. Many still feel this way! This sentiment is at the heart of an article touting the death of social media ROI.[1] Why? Social media are meant to be about participation and relationships between brands and consumers. In a short period of time, we've developed a host of valuable metrics, but these also come with an important caveat. The metrics we use must be appropriate for the objectives we set for the campaign. Counting followers and fans, retweets, and blog comments is relevant only if those behaviors relate to the goals of the brand's social media activity. We need to be choosy about just what measures we collect and which ones are important. **Key performance indicators** (KPIs) are those metrics that are tied to organizational objectives.[2] But, there's a catch: in order for KPIs to be valuable, we first must be sure the objectives they're supposed to measure are well defined. As the old geek saying goes, "Garbage in, garbage out." Smart social media marketers are focusing on assessing the extent to which objectives were met using KPIs.

A First Date or a Marriage?

Some metrics, such as number of unique visitors, page views, frequency of visits, average visit length, and clickthrough rates, may be irrelevant or simply fail to capture information appropriate to the reasons we use them. When we want to demonstrate the value of what we're doing, we love to count—we count impressions, visitors, friends, posts, players, even how often we count! There's no doubt that numbers are important. For instance, knowing the number of community members involved in a brand-related conversation can serve as an indicator of exposure, and the number of message threads and lines of text within a thread can serve as proxies of conversation depth. However, the *Social Media Marketing Industry Report* highlighted that only 41% of marketers agreed they're able to measure their social activities; 86% said they needed to learn more about how to measure the impact of social media marketing.[3] Perhaps the reason marketers are struggling to measure social media's impact is tied to their use of social media metrics. Table 11.1 reports the percentage of marketers using each metric to assess social media marketing, according to the *CMO Survey Report*.[4] The most commonly used metric is simply the number of impressions per social media content. Use of brand sentiment, influence, viral spread, and buzz were clearly underutilized.

The Strategic Options for Social Media Measurement model, shown in Figure 11.1, suggests an explanation for the struggle marketers report facing when it comes to social media metrics.[5] It explains that social media marketers may approach measurement along a continuum of fuzzy to quantifiable and may see effectiveness along a continuum of failing to succeeding. The result is a simple matrix indicating that social media marketers may see social media as a dead end (fuzzy measures, ineffective), in need of measurement and adjustment (quantified measures, ineffective strategies), naively optimistic (fuzzy measures, effective strategies), or as an iterative process (quantified measures, effective strategies).

Table 11.1   Marketer Use of Social Media Metrics

Metric	% Using Metric
Views/Impressions	60.3%
Site traffic	51.2%
Clickthrough rates	47.9%
Number of fans, friends, followers	47.1%
Sales conversion rates	28.8%
Social influence	23.7%
Buzz and share of voice	21.4%
Viral spread	19.1%
Brand sentiment	16.7%
Ratings	10.0%

Source: *CMO Survey Report: Highlights and Insights*, CMO Survey, https://cmosurvey.org/wp-content/uploads/sites/11/2015/09/The_CMO_Survey-Highlights_and_Insights-Aug-2015.pdf (accessed June 22, 2017)

Every manager's goal should be to move away from fuzzy measurement and towards quantifiable metrics. That way, a manager can understand what's working and what's not—and revise the approach accordingly.

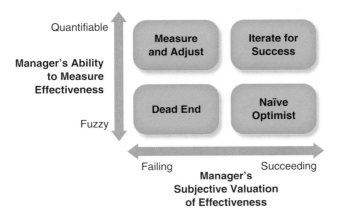

Figure 11.1   Strategic Options for Social Media Measurement

Source: Donna Hoffman and Marek Fodor, "Can You Measure the ROI of Your Social Media Marketing?" *MIT Sloan Management Review*, 52:1 (Fall 2010), 41–9, p. 47

Tying Key Performance Indicators to Meaningful Information

In many ways, social media marketing mimics online advertising in terms of the viable metrics available to measure how effective these messages are. Advertisers can measure reach (the number of people exposed to the message) and frequency (the average number of times someone is exposed), and analyze site stickiness (the ability of a site to draw repeat visits and to keep people on a site) and the relative pull (a comparison of how well different creative executions generate a response) of creative advertising. Brands can monitor clickthroughs (the number of people exposed to an online ad or link who actually click on it), sales conversions (the number of people who click through who go on to purchase

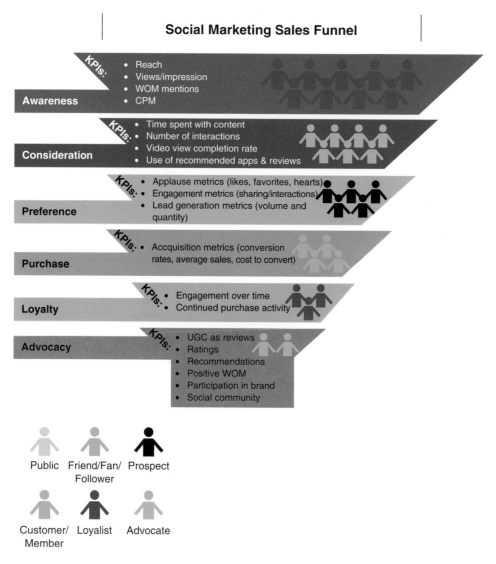

Figure 11.2   Mapping KPIs to the Marketing Funnel and Customer Journey

the product), and viewthroughs (the number of people who are exposed and do not click through, but who later visit the brand's website).

Simply counting the quantity of interactions consumers have with a brand doesn't tell us much. We also need to know the degree of engagement people feel during and after their participation, the interaction with the brand, and how these experiences influenced their feelings about the brand. We need to know whether our social media activities helped drive prospects forward in their journey (and deeper in our sales funnel). For this reason we also try to collect other numbers that are a bit more diagnostic, such as measures of brand likeability, brand image, brand awareness, brand loyalty, brand affiliation, congruency, and purchase intent. For instance, Facebook's Twitter account has more than 14 million followers, but only 11% of those fans engage with Facebook. MTV has about the same number of followers, but 26% engage. As one analyst observed, "Four thousand two hundred and thirty-one is a measurement. Without context, it is merely a number. When compared with your personal best, company expectations, or your competitors' efforts, that number becomes a metric. It is now indicative of value, importance or a change in results."[6] Figure 11.2 illustrates the relationship between the stages in the customer journey and the marketing funnel and identifies the KPIs that are relevant at each stage.

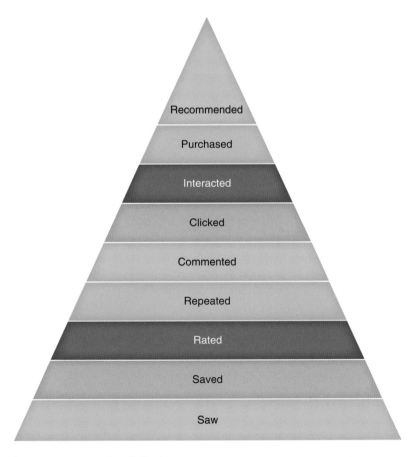

Figure 11.3   The Engagement Food Chain

Part of the challenge for social media analytics is the complexity of the constructs we wish to assess. Engagement is one of the most challenging concepts! The term is ubiquitous among marketers, so much so that its meaning is easily obscured. One way to address this concern is to apply an engagement version of the marketing funnel, as illustrated in Figure 11.3. The Engagement Food Chain shows each specific engagement action we seek as the target audience moves through the customer journey.

Forrester Research encourages marketers to measure engagement in a way that captures emotion and potential influence in addition to behavior. Its interpretation of engagement incorporates four dimensions: 1) involvement, 2) interaction, 3) intimacy, and 4) influence.[7] Using multiple dimensions aids in capturing the construct in a more meaningful way. The dimensions and the metrics used to capture each dimension are shown in Table 11.2.

Table 11.2   The Dimensions of Engagement

Engagement Dimension	Explanation	Metrics
Involvement	The presence of a person at each social touch point	Page or profile visits; content views
Interaction	The actions people take while present at the social touch point	Likes, shares, completion rates (e.g., watching entire video); average time spent per interaction (e.g., time spent playing a social advergame); comments; downloads
Intimacy	The affection or aversion a person holds for the brand	Sentiment, complaints posted in social channels, compliments posted, contribution quality, emotion expressed in UGC, brand perception, brand attitudes
Influence	The likelihood that a person will advocate for the brand	Quantity, frequency, and score of reviews and ratings; number of recommendations in social word-of-mouth communication and impressions reached due to influencer network size; referrals

To review where we are so far:

- Measurements within a defined context are metrics.
- Measurements require context to provide useful feedback.
- Metrics that are tied to objectives are key performance indicators.
- Objectives must be well defined before we can identify key performance indicators.

The Evaluation and Measurement Process: DATA

When it comes to social media marketing—or any form of marketing, for that matter—measurement isn't optional. It's a necessity for organizations that are serious about adjusting their strategies and tactics to better meet their objectives. Some may feel intimidated about specifying what it is they want to see happen when it comes to their social media activities; perhaps they believe this sets them up to fail because they're not sure they can actually define or attain specific goals. Others may still be in the early stage of the social media maturity life cycle we discussed in Chapter 4; because they're still "playing" with social media, they don't yet feel the need to define what results they would like to see. But ultimately social media will have to answer to the same masters as other kinds of traditional media—the bean counters who need to see value for their money. The investment in social media marketing will require justification. Strategists will want to understand what's working and what isn't in order to decide if a campaign needs fixing or if it's worth continuing at all. Welcome to the cold cruel world of budgets!

In reality, devising a measurement plan is a relatively straightforward process (at least on paper!). We organize our plan according to a four-step process known as the **DATA approach**:[8]

1 *Define*: define the results that the program is designed to promote.
2 *Assess*: assess the costs of the program and the potential value of the results.
3 *Track*: track the actual results and link those results to the program.
4 *Adjust*: adjust the program based on results to optimize future outcomes.

Let's dive deeper into each of these four steps.

Define

Our first—and arguably most critical—task is to define just what we want to occur and what we need to measure. Quite simply we have to define the objectives of the social media marketing campaign. After all, if we don't have clear objectives, how do we know when we've reached them? The specific objectives we might identify can vary dramatically from brand to brand but it's likely they will include three overarching issues:

1 *Motivating* some behavior from the target audience (such as visits to a website or purchases of the product).
2 *Influencing* brand knowledge and attitudes (particularly among those who are likely to spread the message to their own networks).
3 *Accomplishing* the first two objectives with fewer resources than might be required with other methods.

For instance, if we use Twitter to identify customer complaints early on and resolve those complaints online, we can potentially influence attitude toward the brand, inspire the customer to share the experience with others, and do so online at a cost far less than it normally takes a call center to resolve. Remember that organizational objectives will tie directly to the applications it has selected. At different levels of the organization, the nature of decisions varies and therefore the metrics must vary as well. Altimeter's Social Media ROI Pyramid, shown in Figure 11.4, explains how objectives vary at each business level, how executives at those levels use social media metrics, and the types of metrics that are most appropriate.[9] This framework is important for capturing the necessary insights needed to guide business priorities and resource allocations across the organization, marketing strategy decisions, and granular decisions about social media tactics.

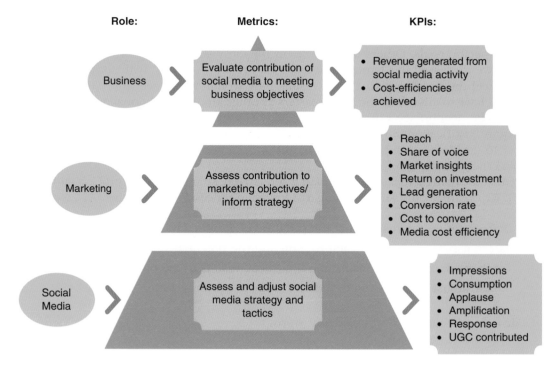

Figure 11.4   Social Media ROI Pyramid

Source: Adapted from Jeremiah Owyang, "Framework: The Social Media ROI Pyramid", Web Strategist, December 13, 2010, www.web-strategist.com/blog/2010/12/13/framework-the-social-media-roi-pyramid. Reproduced by permission of Altimeter, a Prophet company.

From a philosophical perspective, defining what's important may mean changing the way we think about marketing. Historically, marketers have addressed measurement from the perspective of company investments in customers and the extent to which those investments generated positive results. However, because social media are largely customer driven, we may need to view measurement from the perspective of the customers' investments in the company.[10] How much time are customers investing in our socially published content? How much social capital are customers putting at risk to recommend our brand?

Are Your Objectives SMART?

How can we be sure our objectives are clear enough that we can adequately measure them? The key is to state them so they have SMART characteristics:

- Specific
- Measurable
- Appropriate
- Realistic
- Time-oriented

To understand how objectives can be SMART or not, consider the following two examples:

"We will tell everyone we can about our new Facebook page and see if they like it so much they'll buy more of our product."

"We will promote our new Facebook page in display advertisements we will place on the websites for *Rolling Stone, Sports Illustrated,* and *Maxim*. On July 15 we will count the number of Facebook users who 'like' our brand and compare sales to the same period last year."

The second objective is SMART; the first, not so much. However, defining objectives in a specific manner is not as easy as it sounds. Even the most desirable of outcomes (brand engagement and cost-efficiency, for instance) must be clearly defined if they are to be useful in assessment. Examples of SMART objectives for some of the most common benefits sought for social media marketing and related metrics are provided in Table 11.3.

Table 11.3   SMART Objectives and Related Metrics

Objective	Sample of SMART Specification	Metrics
Increase brand awareness	To generate impressions equivalent to or greater than reach goals in media plan	Views, impressions, mentions, interactions
Increase share of voice (SOV)	Among all of the neutral/positive conversations about our industry in the next week/month/year, brand will feature in 15% or more of the conversations	Ratio of neutral/ positive brand mentions to mentions of set of competitors
Maintain or increase brand sentiment	To maintain positive sentiment score of 86% or higher for the brand name during the campaign schedule	Sentiment
Meet customer service needs	Respond to 90% of all mentions on social media within 4 hours/minutes	Response rates, average response time

It may seem difficult to shift from thinking about the benefits we can derive from social media marketing to ways we can measure those values. The benefits may seem intangible ("create lots of buzz!"), so an early step is to find a way to quantify results that may not lend themselves to numerical measurement. Here are some examples:

- One benefit of hosting a blog is that the target audience may use it to educate themselves about the company's product line. It is difficult to measure the value of consumer education, but there are tangible benefits we should see due to greater knowledge about a brand. Assuming that people like what they see, these efforts should move blog visitors to the e-commerce site and from there to transactions. Thus, the benefit of consumer education is valuable if it results in increases in site traffic and sales.

- Another common goal of social media marketing is search engine optimization, as we discussed in Chapter 7. We can see whether our site is optimized when we test the search rankings we achieve. In addition, better search results should lead to higher traffic to the site. Aha! Something we can measure.

- Reaching a specific audience with our brand message is a valuable outcome. Here we may need to measure impressions, but we can also compare the cost of reaching the target audience with social media to the cost of doing so using traditional media.

Social media are valuable for showing responsiveness to consumer concerns, but what is the value of the increased responsiveness? We can track customer satisfaction and retention to assess this value.

Metrics

The next step is to decide on the metric, or specific standard of measurement, we will use to measure the objective. When we specify our metrics, we need to match these to the results we are concerned about—whether attitude shifts and behavioral responses from our target audience or efficiency and profitability measures resulting from cost savings and/or increased sales. Table 11.4 lists some of the most commonly used metrics.

Table 11.4   Commonly Used Social Media Metrics

1	WOM/Buzz volume
	a Number (volume) of posts, comments, retweets/shares
	b Frequency, momentum, recency, seasonality
2	Asset popularity, virality
	a Sharing, viewing, bookmarking, downloads, installs, embedding of branded assets such as videos, pictures, links, articles
	b Changes over time
3	Media mentions (earned media)
4	Brand liking
	a Fans, followers, friends
	b Growth in fans, followers, friends
	c Likes, favorites, ratings, linkbacks
5	Reach and second degree reach (influence impressions from others)
	a Readers, viewers
	b Subscriptions
	c Mentions, links
6	Engagement
	a Comment volume
	b UGC submissions, contest participation
	c Subscriptions (RSS, podcasts, video series, document series)
	d Time spent with social pages
	e Interactions, applause, amplification
7	Rating scores, review volume and valence
8	Influence
9	Search engine optimization

10	Website effectiveness (traffic, clicks, conversions, viewthroughs, bounce rate)
11	Share of voice
12	Economic value
13	Sentiment
	a Nature of comments, tag attributes
	b Attitudes
14	Customer value
	a Sales changes online, offline
	b Customer lifetime value shifts, customer retention, lower customer acquisition costs

Source: Based on sources including David Berkowitz, "100 Ways to Measure Social Media," *Media Post Social Media Insider*, November 17, 2009; Angela Jeffrey, "Social Media Measurement: A Step-by-Step Approach," Institute for Public Relations, June 2013; Chris Murdough, "Social Media Measurement," *Journal of Interactive Advertising*, 10:1 (2009), 94–9

A Social Media Marketing Metrics Matrix

The list of possible measures applicable to social media can be overwhelming. Applying a framework to manage the types of measures is useful. The matrix shown in Table 11.5 illustrates the types and characteristics of social media metrics. The three types of metrics are activity metrics, interaction metrics, and return metrics:

- **Activity metrics** measure the actions the organization commits to social media. They capture inputs. Activity metrics are important because they are used to assess campaign effectiveness by tactic. These metrics allow for performance testing across every possible design element. For instance, by knowing the mix of paid and organic activity in social media, we can track impressions, clickthroughs, time spent with content, engagement, and virality to later assess whether paid media is performing better than organic brand activity. Every tactical element can be assessed in this way.

- **Interaction metrics** focus on how the target market engages with the social media platform and activities. Interaction measures include the number of followers and fans, comments, "likes," recommendations and reviews, and the amount of shared content. Interactions are essentially made up of all the ways in which users can participate in a social media relationship with the brand.

- **Return metrics** focus on the outcomes (financial or otherwise) that directly or indirectly support the success of the brand. They include return on investment measures, cost reduction measures, and other performance metrics. In addition to these categories, social media data can be characterized as qualitative or quantitative. Using both forms provides the hard numbers that CFOs (chief financial officers) require to fund investments in social media strategy while also valuing the soft benefits of social media such as stories, buzz, and image.

A common metric to gauge success is **return on investment (ROI)**. ROI is a measure of profitability. It captures how effective a company is at using capital to generate profits. To determine ROI we assign a financial value to the resources we use to execute a strategy, measure financial outcomes, and calculate the ratio between inputs and outcomes. Return on investment answers the question, "How much income was generated from investments in the activities?" When we apply this concept to a brand's investment in social media marketing, we call the measure social media return on investment (SMROI). SMROI answers the question, "How much income did our investments in social media marketing generate?"

Table 11.5   A Social Media Metrics Framework

Category/ Characteristic	Quantitative Measures	Qualitative Measures
Activity (input)	Number, frequency, and recency of:	Creative messaging and positioning strategy
	Posts by type, channel (blog posts, updates/posts, comments/reply comments, video, photo by SNS)	Resonance/fit of campaign appeal
	Content design:	Social media involvement
	CTA used, type of headline and number of words, average word count of post, interactive design element (e.g., poll, quiz, invitation for UGC), hashtag use	Content alignment to brand image and voice
	Summary views such as:	Relative value/audience-centricity of content
	Post rates	
	Content type mix	
	Response rate	
	Average response time	
Interaction (responses)	Number, frequency, and recency of:	Sentiment
	Impressions/reach	Engagement
	Registrations	Influence effects
	Bookmarks/favorites/likes/ratings	Recommendations
	Comments/posts/mentions/tags	Buzz/virality
	Links/trackbacks/clickbacks	
	Downloads/installs/embeds	
	Subscriptions	
	Fans/followers/friends	
	Share/forward/invite/refer	
	Reviews/testimonials	
	Traffic/visits/views	
	Time spent with post/site	
	UGC contributed	
	Discount/deal redemption rate	
	Echo effect/virality	

Category/Characteristic	Quantitative Measures	Qualitative Measures
Performance (outcome)	Engagement	Attitude toward the brand
	Cost/prospects	Brand loyalty
	Lead conversion rate	Customer satisfaction
	Average new revenue per customer	Service quality perceptions
	Cost efficiencies across marketing functions	
	Customer lifetime value	
	Earned media values	
	Shifts in average sales/site traffic/search engine ratings	
	Share of voice	
	Return on investment	

Source: Based on sources including Mike Brown, "Social Media Metrics You Should Be Tracking," Social Media Today, July 14, 2010; Angela Jeffrey, "Social Media Measurement: A Step-by-Step Approach," Institute for Public Relations, June 2013; Chris Murdough, "Social Media Measurement," *Journal of Interactive Advertising*, 10:1 (2009), 94–9

It's natural to want to quantify the value of a corporate activity and to use that value as justification to continue and expand the activity. The challenge when it comes to social media is the qualitative, viral, pervasive nature of the outcomes of social media advertising. Investments in social media generate goodwill, brand engagement, and momentum, and analysts must define how those constructs will be assessed.

Analysts have proposed several ways to estimate the financial benefits of social media. Those estimates make it possible to calculate SMROI much as we would for any other ROI estimate. Let's review some common approaches: 1) return on impressions, 2) return on social media impact, 3) return on target influence, and 4) return on earned media.[11]

- The **return on impressions model** demonstrates how many media impressions were generated by the social media tactics employed. An impression is simply an "opportunity to see" for the target audience. When a brand buys advertising space, it purchases opportunities for the target market to be exposed to the ad. Social media also provide impressions but the media space is not purchased. The costs are different. The opportunity for exposure to the brand message might be delivered as part of a virtual world event, on a social networking profile site, and with consumer-generated ads, product reviews, and so on. Impressions are valuable, according to this model, because we assume that impressions lead to changes in awareness, followed by changes in comprehension, changes in attitude, and ultimately changes in behavior (sales). Using the percentage of people reached who ultimately purchase as a way to calculate sales value, we can then determine a return on impressions by taking the gross revenue estimated minus the cost of the social media advertising program divided by the cost of the program. For example, if we estimate that Dunkin' Donuts earns $500,000 in gross revenue due to its Twitter presence, at a cost of $100,000 in time investment, the ROI for the microblogging activity is 400%.

- The **return on social media impact model** attempts to track coverage across media and in different markets against sales over time. It requires the statistical technique of *advanced multiple regression analysis* to analyze variables that may affect sales, including the mix of advertising and promotional tools used at each time and place. This approach offers the greatest potential for social media marketers, because it can include lagged measurements that control for time order of events taking place online (e.g., the timing of an event in a social world, the point at which a profile was activated, the timing of a contest conclusion, and the subsequent posting of consumer-generated ads). Return on social media impact promises to determine how sales can be attributed to each element in a marketing mix and to tactics within the social media advertising strategy. Content generation and consumption are tracked and assigned algorithm scores to dictate the weight of relative influence. Sales are also tracked at the same intervals, and then statistical analysis is used to determine how sales trends shifted according to the timing of the social media marketing.

- The **return on target influence model** relies upon survey data to assess the effectiveness of social media marketing. Surveys assess whether participants were exposed to the social media tactics and what perceptions they formed as a result of exposure. The model then calls for calculating the change in the probability of purchase based on the exposure.

- The final approach is that of **return on earned media model.** This approach uses a metric called **advertising equivalency value** (AEV) to equate publicity in news media outlets to its paid advertising equivalent. In other words, if a brand had paid for a mention in a specific space, what would it have cost? For social media advertising, an AEV would attempt to equate the following with paid advertising value: source authority, source prominence, depth of brand mention, and recommendation. To calculate advertising equivalency, the cost to purchase a display ad on a site would be used to assign a dollar value to the impressions achieved socially. For example, if we spent $50,000 on social display ads on Facebook, we could assign an earned media value of $50,000 to a thousand page views of our brand profile on Facebook. The value can also be adjusted by the subjective importance of the earned media in question. For example, one might believe that profile visits are more valuable than a display ad rotation because it suggests that visitors sought out the brand interaction. The earned media value can be adjusted to account for variables such as the popularity of the location, the relative influence of the source, and so on. The ROI calculation is then based on the difference between the AEV and the cost of the social media advertising program divided by the cost of the program. If the AEV for the Facebook profile is $50,000 but it cost $5,000 in time for its development and maintenance, the incremental gain is $45,000. The gain divided by the cost of the program expressed as a percentage reveals an ROI of 900%. This measure may be among the easiest to execute for those social media spaces that also sell display advertising. However, it is not truly a return on investment measure so much as it is a measure of effective resource utilization.

Assess

As you've begun to see from the discussion of returns, we need to know something about costs and values in order to calculate outcome measures. This is the second step in the measurement planning process—to assess the value generated from social media activities and gather feedback to use when making adjustments to strategies and tactics. Assessment is directly tied to the Social Media ROI Pyramid shown in Figure 11.4. The valuations we make must be relevant for the decisions made at each level of the organization. Consequently, assessment will include financial assessments like the return on investment models reviewed previously, cost efficiency estimates, and performance indicators for each strategic and tactical design element in the social media marketing plan.

What does it take to participate effectively in social media marketing and what is it worth? What is the value of a customer or of a lead? What does it cost to gain a lead or a customer? What does it cost to maintain a blog, develop an app, or create branded entertainment? To promote and manage a social game? To maintain an active Twitter presence? What is the value of an impression? What is the value of a Facebook fan? Is paid advertising more effective than organic brand activity? These are the kinds of questions an organization must answer. Here are some of the assessments we may conduct:

- **Performance effectiveness by design element (A/B testing)**: A/B testing is a strategy in which two versions of a message, version A and version B, are tested against each other. This is not to be taken literally, as you could have more than just two versions of the "same" message running against each other. The goal is to identify how changes to the message affect performance. A/B testing is experimentation. Controlling for all other variables, including audience targeting, one variable will be tested. The goal is to determine what design choices trigger the best performance on the KPIs. Variables to focus on include channel (e.g., Facebook, Instagram), content type (e.g., infographic, photo, list article), call to action (e.g., read now, join here), headline hook (e.g., humor hook, resource hook), use of words in headline (e.g., best, now, top), and hashtag use (e.g., number of hashtags, campaign hashtags or general hashtags used on channel). Does A/B testing pay off? Absolutely. Simply changing a single word can result in a major uptick in results. The post and ad campaign planner programs for each SNS make A/B testing easy to set up and execute.

- **Cost efficiency**: for the impressions/traffic/fans generated, which source was more cost-efficient? This calculation enables marketers to compare the cost of different tactics. To calculate, the amount of impressions/traffic/fans is tracked and the cost of each tactic is determined. Divide the total cost by the number of impressions to determine the cost per impression. Divide cost per impression from tactic 1 by cost per impression of tactic 2. Outcomes higher than 1.0 indicate that tactic 2 performed better. Outcomes below 1.0 indicate that tactic 1 performed better.

- **Opportunity cost**: what else could employees or volunteers have done if they weren't spending time contributing to the brand's social media activity? For example, what's the time value of the person tasked with creating content for the corporate blog or posting responses to irritated customers on Facebook when without these tasks he or she could have spent time on other revenue-generated tasks?

- **Service quality**: how well did the brand address customer needs using social media relative to other customer care methods? This assessment may include average comments requesting a response, response rate, response speed, and resolution rate.

- **Message/crisis control**: brands accept a risk that the brand's message will be shared or manipulated in ways that the brand would rather not have happen. But if we want to capitalize on the value of virality for message diffusion, then we also have to be willing to sacrifice some control. Still, we can assess the influence of negative communications and crises using KPIs and also gauge the successfulness of risk mitigation efforts.

EXHIBIT 11.1

A/B Testing of CTA and Other Elements

One of the most important design elements for paid advertising in SNS is the call to action. Choosing the right CTA can make a huge difference in ROI. In one case study, AdEspresso discovered that the clickthrough rate of a "Learn More" CTA outperformed "Sign Up" by 22.5%! Knowing which CTA performs best can be used to optimize future tactics. How do we decide which one is "the right" one? AdEspresso did some A/B testing to find out.[12] First, the AdEspresso team analyzed a sample of more than 35,000 Facebook ads and coded the CTA to determine the most popular CTAs. The top most frequently used CTAs are "Learn More," "Sign Up," "Shop Now," and "Download." Figure 11.5 illustrates the mix of CTAs identified in the study. They then tested the top three to see how they compared on KPIs (clickthrough rate, cost per click (CPC), cost per lead).

AdEspresso designed three ads to promote an eBook it offers as part of its social publishing strategy. To get the eBook, people had to exchange their email address. This is a typical format for a lead-generation ad. People who download the eBook become prospects. Interest in the eBook suggests they may have a need for AdEspresso services. The three ads were identical in design and target audience with the exception of one variable: the CTA. The ads ran over a 14-day period. The results? All three CTAs achieved roughly the same percentage of initial clickthroughs (see Figure 11.6). However, the percentage of people who provided their email and downloaded the eBook was higher for the "Download" CTA (50.6% vs just 40% for the other CTAs) and the cost per lead was lower ($0.802 compared to $1.208 for "Learn More" and $1.126 for "Sign Up"). The results suggest that when we run a similar offer using a Facebook ad, we should use the "Download" CTA in order to optimize ad performance.

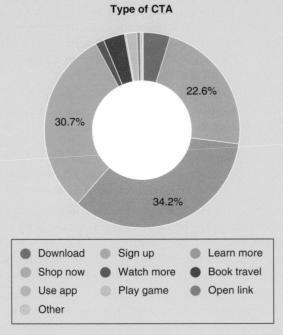

Type of CTA

22.6%
30.7%
34.2%

- ● Download   ● Sign up   ● Learn more
- ● Shop now   ● Watch more   ● Book travel
- ● Use app   ● Play game   ● Open link
- ● Other

Figure 11.5   CTA Use in Facebook Advertising

Source: Karola Karlson, "Learn More vs. Sign Up vs. Download? What's the Best Call-to-action?", AdEspresso, February 24, 2017, https://adespresso.com/academy/blog/learn-vs-sign-vs-download-whats-best-call-action. Reproduced by kind permission of AdEspresso, Inc. (accessed June 22, 2017)

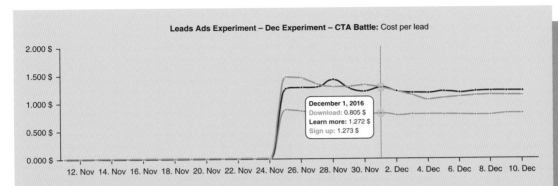

Figure 11.6   Cost Per Lead Performance by CTA

Source: Karola Karlson, "Learn More vs. Sign Up vs. Download? What's the Best Call-to-action?", AdEspresso, February 24, 2017, https://adespresso.com/academy/blog/learn-vs-sign-vs-download-whats-best-call-action. Reproduced by kind permission of AdEspresso, Inc. (accessed June 22, 2017)

Why did the "Download" CTA outperform all others regarding the lead conversion? It described exactly what a user should expect upon clicking. When people clicked on ads with the "Learn More" CTA, they might have been expecting to find out more before sharing their contact information. The general rule is that the CTA should match the ad's goal. If you want someone to sign up, use the "Sign Up" call to action; if you want people to buy your product, use the "Shop Now" CTA.

Sometimes the best approach for assessment is simply to develop a cost-benefit analysis table. Table 11.6 illustrates an example of a cost-benefit analysis to start and maintain a corporate blog.[13] The analyst needed to make several assumptions about value, and he or she researched costs to complete the assessment. The possible value associated with the corporate blog has been included and financial figures have been estimated for those benefits. If the assumptions are correct, the brand should pursue the corporate blog because the benefits outweigh the costs to maintain it.

The brand could also calculate the return on investment for maintaining the blog using the figures in the table or it could calculate the blog's **Blog Value Index (BVI)**.[14] The BVI is a simple equation that enables a company to assess whether the blog adds more value than it costs. If the BVI is under 1, the blog costs money, but if it is greater than 1, the blog yields a profit. The cost of software and hosting is assumed to be zero because presumably the organization is already covering the cost of website hosting and additional costs for the blog would be negligible.

BVIa = [adh (aay/1,000)] ÷ [abt × ehw]

where

adh = average daily hits

aay = average advertising yield

abt = average number of hours spent per day blogging

ehw = employee hourly wage of the blogger

The equation itself is straightforward, but sometimes our input figures are difficult to assess in social media. For instance, it can be a challenge to identify how many unique blog readers one has. RSS feeds report how many people are subscribed to the blog via an automated feed. But readers can also view blog content via a news filter site or blog search engine, which can limit the accuracy of the reach figures.

Table 11.6   Cost-Benefit Analysis of a Corporate Blog

Estimated Costs	
Start-up costs	
Planning and development	$25,000
Training for blogger	10,000
Ongoing costs (annual)	
Blogging platform	25,000
Brand-monitoring service	50,000
IT support	3,000
Content production	150,000
Review and redirection	**20,000**
Total costs (Year One)	**$283,000**
Estimated Benefits	
Advertising value (visibility/traffic based on 7,500 daily)	$7,000
PR value (24 stories at 10,000 each)	240,000
WOM value (370 posts at $100 each)	37,000
Support value (50 calls daily avoided at cost of $5.50/call)	69,000
Research value (5 focus group equivalent at $8,000 each)	40,000
Total benefits (Year One)	**$393,000**
Net value for Year One	**$110,000**

Track

In the tracking stage we collect and organize the data we will use to determine our results. The tracking step in the DATA process involves the following components:

- identify tracking mechanisms
- establish baseline comparisons
- create activity timelines
- capture/calculate data
- measure precursors and activity indicators
- look for patterns.

There are four main sources of information in marketers' social media data ecosystem: 1) owned site analytics (e.g., Google Analytics on owned sites), 2) SNS analytics (e.g., Facebook Insights), 3) enterprise social listening and/or analytics platforms (e.g., Brandwatch, Infegy), and 4) niche analytic solutions and platform API tools (e.g., Keyhole, Trackur).[15] Enterprise platforms may specialize in social analytics, social advertising campaigns, or social listening, but there are typically aspects of listening in analytics platforms and vice versa. Each SNS provides analytics for users. Facebook offers Facebook Insights, Twitter offers Twitter Analytics, and YouTube offers YouTube Analytics. There are also niche services that focus on specific forms of measurement. For example, Keyhole enables the tracking of the spread and reach of a hashtag. Bit.ly enables the tracking of shortened URLs. Some social media management systems like Hootsuite and Sprout Social include analytic features.

Tracking is not only concerned with determining how we will collect the data we need for making assessments. It is also concerned with organizing the data in a way that enhances their utility. There are three approaches to tracking that reflect different ways to do this: (1) forward tracking, (2) coincident tracking, and (3) reverse tracking:[16]

1   **Forward tracking** means that the tracking mechanisms are developed prior to launching the activity or campaign. Forward tracking is the most accurate approach because it enables the account team to develop a mechanism for tracking exactly the data desired. Ideally, then, the measurement plan will be created as part of the strategic social media campaign plan and the tracking mechanisms identified up front. If the organization has set SMART objectives, forward tracking should already be in place.

2   **Coincident tracking** begins during the activity or campaign. Coincident tracking can be effective in that it relies on residual data (which become the data scraped for social media research) left at the point of interaction or point of sale. It doesn't necessarily require that a unique tracking mechanism be developed. Moreover, it is interaction or outcome oriented because tracking occurs only when people leave traces of their activity or opinions. This is an imperfect approach. Searches won't necessarily reveal relevant information unless the consumer who posted used keywords or hashtags.

3   **Reverse tracking** is conducted after an activity or campaign has concluded. Reverse tracking also uses residual data and may include primary data collection such as surveys to assess the effects of the campaign. For instance, it would be simple to count the number of pieces of content uploaded to a microsite. However, without forward tracking in place, the microsite would have been missing key share technologies, making it more difficult to track the shared content originating from the site.

Given the volume of data, the multiple social channels to track, tactics, and numerous metrics, social media analytics is facilitated by the use of a **social media performance dashboard**. The dashboard is an insight tool, built to provide intuitive navigation through the KPIs and visualization of data. A summary area provides general observations and performance diagnostics. A variety of views and comparisons with competitors, industry benchmarks, and historical performance are also available. Enterprise platforms include dashboards. Each social network site presents analytics data in a dashboard too, but performance measures are limited to the respective site. Other analytics services provide a report tied to its specialization. An excellent list of several free social media analytic tools, SNS analytic capabilities, and several enterprise platforms is available at https://blog.bufferapp.com/social-media-analytics-tools.[17] The list provides a description of the metrics and analyses provided and images of the dashboards for each tool. Marketers can also select a third-party dashboard that can accommodate multiple data sources. This is recommended when the social media team needs to incorporate data sources that are not included in the enterprise platform. Klipfolio is an example of a third-party dashboard system. Figure 11.7 illustrates a screen shot of its social media analytics dashboard:[18]

Figure 11.7   Social Media Performance Dashboard

Source: "Social Media—Overview," Klipfolio, www.klipfolio.com/gallery/dashboards/social-media-overview (accessed June 22, 2017)

If you are curious about social media performance metrics for the world's most popular brands, check out Infegy's Top 50 Brands Dashboard at top50.infegy.com. Infegy, an enterprise platform, maintains the Top 50 Brands Dashboard using its Infegy Atlas service, which analyzes billions of online conversations to discover which brands are talked about the most, the overall valence of conversations about the brands, the passion expressed in comments, and the topics people mention most when talking about the brands.[19]

CRITICAL REFLECTION

Dark Social Proves There Literally Is a Dark Side of Social Media

One dirty secret of web analytics is that the information we get is limited.[20] If you want to see how someone came to your site, it's usually pretty easy. When someone follows a link from one website to another, a little piece of meta-data hitches a ride that tells the servers the source. This is called a **referral**. Referrals are categorized by source: organic search, paid search, social, direct, and so on. Direct refers to people who reached your site by typing the link into their web browser. Knowing what percentage of referrals come from specific sources informs our marketing actions, by pointing to the sites we should prioritize. The information is especially useful when making decisions about budget allocations and staff resources across social network sites. It also measures social media marketing campaign effectiveness in that it captures a behavior in the form of a clickthrough and suggests movement along the customer journey to purchase.

There's just one problem. Most referral traffic is coming from sources that can't be tracked. The phenomenon is known as "**dark social**." Though we see evidence of sharing on Facebook and Twitter and other SNS using the network's insights tool, that's just the tip of the iceberg. The vast amount of sharing is actually conducted through email, texting, and social messaging apps like Facebook, WhatsApp, and WeChat. If

iStock.com/scyther5

someone shares a link using a messaging app rather than the share tool in Facebook, the referral is not captured. Most social traffic is essentially invisible to analytics programs. In fact, a study by RadiumOne of more than 10 million shares found that 84% of social shares are relayed using dark social.[21] Just 16% of the content shared from social media is shared directly from Facebook, Twitter, Instagram, or other SNS.

The term, dark social, was first coined by Alexis C. Madrigal, an editor at *The Atlantic*, to refer to web traffic that comes from outside sources that web analytics are not able to track. She noted the analogy of dark social to dark energy, writing, "You can't see it, dude, but it's what keeps the universe expanding. No dark social, no Internet universe, man! Just a big crunch."[22] You've probably shared content via dark social yourself!

Most social content is shared via dark social, but what's more, 32% of those who share online content will *only* share using dark social channels.[23] For others, the content category plays a role in the choice of sharing channel. The content categories with the highest percentage of dark social sharing include entertainment, careers, and travel. For instance, when browsing movie reviews on an entertainment website, people are far more likely to share the reviews of movies they want to see with an intimate social network of friends via email or instant messaging than via Facebook. It appears that people consider whether the shared information will be used for collaborative decision-making with family and friends, and when it will, dark social is the preferred sharing channel. Sharing behavior is an important indicator of prospect value. This is because those who share content are nine times more likely to make a purchase than non-sharers. People also share with themselves, by texting or emailing information to themselves to act on later, a phenomenon known as **self-sharing**. Self-sharers are 16 times more likely to convert than non-sharers. As you might imagine, much of dark social happens on mobile devices. This is even more pronounced downline. When a recipient of shared content clicks the shared link, **clickback** data are generated. Two-thirds of dark social clickback traffic is from mobile devices.

From an analytics perspective, dark social creates serious issues. First, on the operational side, social media marketers should be optimizing social content, as we discussed in Chapter 7. But there isn't a way to optimize for dark social sharing. There's no way to game email or people's instant messages. There are no power influencers you can contact to drive dark social spread. There are no algorithms to understand. This is pure social, uncut. Second, in terms of basing channel selection and budget allocations by channel for future campaigns on channel effectiveness as a traffic source, dark social skews the data. Analytics may suggest that the social content we used didn't propagate well when, in fact, it may have been shared, but via dark social. Or that a channel like Facebook is not

(Continued)

(Continued)

performing well as a referral source, with the implication that we spend less ad dollars there. But what if Facebook was the originating exposure source, but the audience chose to share via dark social? Third, identifying the people who shared content would allow additional marketing communications to be targeted. Since sharers are far more likely to purchase, targeting sharers could speed up the conversion rate and possibly drive referral sales as well. Unfortunately, the causal chain is broken when it comes to dark social sharing. It's difficult if not impossible to link data about who was exposed to social content, who then shared it, and who subsequently clicked the link. The key takeaway? Some social media metrics are compromised in their ability to capture valid information. We've long known that some variables, like the value of a brand Facebook fan, are difficult to assess. The prevalence of dark social as the preferred channel for social sharing obscures our ability to assess the effectiveness of social media marketing efforts.

MINI CASE STUDY

Tourism Ireland's Approach to Social Media Measurement

Tourism Ireland is the national tourism body that markets the island of Ireland all over the world. In 2010, the organization initiated a major commitment to social media marketing.[24] Its plan included brand presence and activity on Facebook (zone 1), blogging (zone 2), a social advergame on Facebook (zone 3), and customer service via Twitter and cultivation of reviews on TripAdvisor and LonelyPlanet (zone 4).

© Tourism Ireland Limited

Source: www.tourismirelandindustryopportunities.com/how-we-can-help/social-media

Tourism Ireland realigned its brand presence and began posting activity on a consistent basis. It encouraged engagement by requesting UGC videos and photos and using polling posts from time to time. Data about the participating fans were fed into the organization's CRM system for advanced analytics. The social advergame was set in a fictitious town, Ireland Town, and mimicked the addictive gameplay style of Farmville. More than 200,000 users installed the app and more than 50% of the users played weekly. The game drove nearly 150,000 new fans to the Facebook page. The customer service initiative on Twitter produced high engagement among people who were actively planning a trip to Ireland. The blog provided a place to tell the stories of the area including history, food, architecture, and culture. Because of the decentralized nature of the regions of Ireland, the social media marketing initiative also had to incorporate eight languages and materials to support social media efforts for the regional tourism offices. How did the social media marketing efforts perform?

Results and Outcomes

The raw numbers looked impressive—the fan base grew over 1000% to more than a million Facebook fans. But, Tourism Ireland felt it lacked a metric that could measure the gestalt of its social media activities and estimate the financial value necessary to calculate return on investment. Audience engagements with a brand are varied and numerous, including brand page views, post views, page likes, content likes, comments and shares, and views of video, images and audio. The organization created a measure called **Social Equivalent Advertising Value (SEAV)** to accommodate the varied engagement indicators.[25] SEAV is based on two established measures: impressions valued on a CPM basis and clickthroughs valued on a CPC basis. By distilling the range of possible interactions that a user can have with brands on social media channels to align with impressions and clickthroughs, Tourism Ireland was able to classify most social media engagements into one of four categories, each representing a deeper level of engagement:

1   Post impressions: views of brand posts.
2   Page impressions: views of a brand page.
3   Personal response: clicking to view brand content.
4   Public response: endorsing by liking or commenting and/or sharing content.

Next, Tourism Ireland identified non-social marketing activities that were roughly equivalent to generating each engagement and used those equivalents to estimate costs. An Excel plug-in was used to extract engagement data from Facebook and Twitter Insights. From there, it was a simple process to calculate SEAV. The process resulted in cost/values for each engagement level (in Euros): 1) .007, 2) .033, 3) .200, and 4) .200. Any organization can use this model to calculate its SEAV. They just have to keep in mind that the cost/values will vary depending upon the equivalency values selected to approximate costs in their industry. For Tourism Ireland, the SEAV figure suggested that its social media engagement had a financial value of more than $2 million. Calculating SEAV enables marketers to place a tangible value on its organic social media marketing activities which can then be used to assess return on investment.

Baselines

One useful way to track a campaign's effectiveness is to construct a baseline. This is a metric (often expressed visually) that allows a marketer to compare its performance on some dimension to other things, such as how competitors are doing or how its own efforts fluctuate over time. Comparing performance to that of competitors for the same timeline is a useful activity for gauging the relative effectiveness of the brands' respective social media activities. Likewise, it is useful to make comparisons between the brand's baseline performance and that of the industry as well as regional social media performance. Figure 11.8 provides a simple baseline comparison between a marketer's efforts pre-social media campaign and post-campaign. SocialBakers, an enterprise analytics platform provider, publishes social media performance reports by industry and country monthly.[26]

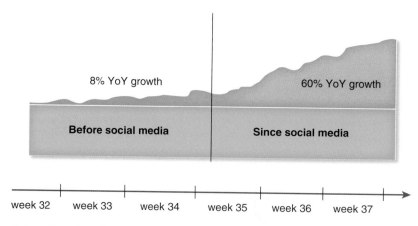

Figure 11.8   A Baseline Graphic

Note: YoY = Year over Year

Adjust

The final step in the process is adjusting. There is little value in measuring without a process for applying what is learned to future activities and investments. The KPIs tracked and the assessment process provide valuable guidance to direct choices for future strategies and tactics.

Simple Ways to Start Measuring

Clearly, we can choose from a variety of criteria, approaches, and tools to measure the effectiveness of a social media campaign. Some marketers, however, will want a simple start before they dive in and develop a full measurement program for their social media marketing campaigns. This list highlights a few metrics that provide a good start:[27]

- *Content consumption*: who is interacting with and consuming the brand-generated and consumer-generated content? Is it who you want to consume your content?

- *Content augmentation*: who is adding to or changing your content by continuing the conversation with response posts? In what ways is the content augmented? Is it consistent with what you want from the campaign?

- *Content sharing*: at what rate are those exposed to the brand messages sharing the content with others using share tools? Does the rate of sharing suggest campaign momentum?

- *Content loyalty*: how many consumers have subscribed to branded content with RSS feeds or by registering for site access?

- *Content conversations*: who is discussing the brand? Who is linking to brand websites? What is the comment-to-post ratio?

- *Content engagement*: is the number of friends to brand profiles growing? Are people contributing content like comments and photos?

CHAPTER SUMMARY

What is the role of metrics in social media marketing programs? How do the metrics used in decision-making vary at different levels of the organization?

Metrics are measures to which marketers can compare results that relate to specific marketing objectives. Metrics allow us to determine the extent to which our strategies have been successful, if at all. Without metrics, we would be unable to assess the effectiveness of our campaigns. The Social Media ROI Pyramid links the choice of social media metric to the decision focus at each level of the organization—business, marketing, and social media execution. It recognizes that different metrics are used for decisions about revenues and costs, marketing strategies, and tactical campaign elements.

How can the marketing funnel, customer journey, and levels of engagement guide marketing objectives and the appropriate choice of KPIs?

Each stage of the market funnel aligns with the stages in the customer journey, from awareness to purchase. There are performance metrics that are relevant at each of these stages. For instance, reach and impressions are more useful metrics for assessing awareness but clickthroughs and referral to owned media sites will be more informative for gauging consideration and conversion. Engagement also varies from more superficial indicators to metrics that better assess emotional involvement. The key takeaway is that the right KPIs should be selected for the objective being assessed.

What are the steps in the DATA approach to measurement? What types of metrics are used?

We organize a measurement plan according to a four-step process known as the DATA approach: define, assess, track, and adjust. This process allows us to clearly specify what the program should accomplish for the organization and then confirm the plan works. If it doesn't, the DATA approach encourages the organization to modify the plan to make it more likely it will yield the desired results.

One way to describe social media metrics is in terms of what they measure: activity metrics measure the actions the organization takes relative to social media. Interaction metrics focus on how the target market engages with the social media platform and activities. Interaction measures include the number of followers and fans, comments, "likes," recommendations and reviews, and the amount of shared content. Return metrics focus on the outcomes (financial or otherwise) that directly or indirectly support the success of the brand. They include return on investment measures, cost reduction measures, and other performance metrics.

How do we calculate social media ROI?

ROI is a measure of profitability. It captures how effective a company is at using capital to generate profits. To determine ROI we assign a financial value to the resources we use to execute a strategy, measure financial outcomes, and calculate the ratio between inputs and outcomes. Return on investment answers the question, "How much income was generated from investments in the activities?" When we apply this concept to a brand's investment in social media marketing, we call the measure social media return on investment. SMROI answers the question, "How much income did our investments in social media marketing generate?"

How is A/B testing used to assess the costs and value of social media tactics?

A/B testing uses experimentation to vary the individual design elements in social media tactics and compare the subsequent performance and cost. Using this technique enables social media marketers to optimize decisions such as CTA, headline hook, content type, channel, image, and so on.

How do we track social media results?

Forward tracking requires the analyst to develop tracking mechanisms prior to launching the activity or campaign. Forward tracking is the most accurate approach because it enables the account team to develop a mechanism to track exactly the data desired. Coincident tracking begins during the activity or campaign. This method relies on data we gather at the point of interaction or point of sale. Reverse tracking is conducted after an activity or a campaign has concluded. This approach also uses residual data and may include primary data collection such as surveys to assess the effects of the campaign. Companies may use an enterprise platform, the analytics tools offered by each SNS, Google analytics, and other third-party sources and APIs as data sources. Information and assessments are organized in a social media performance dashboard.

REVIEW QUESTIONS

1   What is a metric? What is a KPI?
2   Why is the Social Media ROI Pyramid useful in selecting appropriate KPIs?
3   Explain the meaning of SMART objectives.
4   How can marketing managers apply the DATA process to evaluate social media marketing efforts?
5   Describe the differences among activity metrics, interaction metrics, and return metrics.
6   What is A/B testing and how is it used?
7   What kinds of adjustments might marketers make after the metrics are assessed?

EXERCISES

1   Identify a student organization that uses social media to promote its activities and membership opportunities. Briefly review the social media zones in use by the organization and define three SMART objectives for the organization's use of social media.

2   Using the SMART objectives developed in Exercise 1, identify two metrics appropriate to measure the success of each objective.

3   Explore the insights offered for each of the social network sites you use. What can you conclude about your use of social media on each channel?

4   Explore a few free social media analytics tools. Based on your experience, what value do you think enterprise platforms provide to social media marketers?

CHAPTER NOTES (access all weblinks listed here at: https://study.sagepub.com/smm3e)

1   John Heggestuen, "The Death of Social ROI," *Business Insider*, October 22, 2013, www.business insider.com/the-myth-of-social-roi-2013-10 (accessed November 12, 2013).

2   J. Sterne, *Social Media Metrics* (Hoboken, NJ: Wiley, 2010), p. 4.

3   Michael Stelzner, *2016 Social Media Marketing Industry Report*, Social Media Examiner, www.social mediaexaminer.com/wp-content/uploads/2016/05/SocialMediaMarketingIndustryReport2016. pdf (accessed June 16, 2017).

4   *CMO Survey Report: Highlights and Insights*, CMO Survey, August 2015, https://cmosurvey.org/wp-content/uploads/sites/11/2015/09/The_CMO_Survey-Highlights_and_Insights-Aug-2015.pdf (accessed June 22, 2017).

5   Sterne, *Social Media Metrics*, p. 4.

6   Forrester Research, "Measuring the Total Economic Impact of Customer Engagement: A Multi-Company ROI Analysis," September 2008, Commissioned Study, www.healthyworkplaceproject.com.cn/media/134747/case%20study%20economic%20impact%20-%20customer%20engagement. pdf (accessed July 5, 2017).

7   J.R. Roy, "Marketing Metrics and ROI: How to Set Up a Measurement System That Can Double Your Profitability," 2009, www.mktgsensei.com/AMAE/Marketing%20Research/Marketing%20Metrics%20Made%20Easy.pdf (accessed July 5, 2017).

8   Adapted from Jeremiah Owyang, "Framework: The Social Media ROI Pyramid," Web Strategist, December 13, 2010, www.web-strategist.com/blog/2010/12/13/framework-the-social-media-roi-pyramid (accessed June 22, 2017).

9   Ibid.

10 Fraser Likely, David Rockland, and Mark Weiner, "Perspectives on the ROI of Media Relations Publicity Efforts," Institute for Public Relations, 2006, www.instituteforpr.org/research_single/perspectives_on_the_roi (accessed December 26, 2010).

11 Arvind Narayanan and Vitaly Shmatikov, "De-Anonymizing Social Networks," presented at IEEE Security & Privacy '09, http://randomwalker.info/social-networks (accessed October 19, 2010).

12 Karola Karlson, "Learn More vs. Sign Up vs. Download? What's the Best Call-to-Action?" AdEspresso, February 24, 2017, https://adespresso.com/academy/blog/learn-vs-sign-vs-download-whats-best-call-action (accessed June 22, 2017).

13 Charlene Li and Josh Bernoff, *Groundswell* (Boston, MA: Harvard Business Press, 2008), p. 113 (note that Groundswell includes similar tables for calculating the ROI of ratings and reviews and of a forum).

14 Jason Stampler, "The ROI of Blogging, and Whether Jonathan Schwartz's Blog Pays for Itself," *Computer Business Review*, April 4, 2006, www.cbronline.com/blogs/technology/the_roi_of_blog (accessed December 27, 2010).

15 Recommended readings include Jeffrey, "Social Media Measurement: A Step-by-Step Approach;" Murdough, "Social Media Measurement."

16 Roy, "Marketing Metrics and ROI: How to Set Up a Measurement System That Can Double Your Profitability."

17 Kevin Lee, "Know What's Working on Social Media," Buffer, March 7, 2017, https://blog.buffer app.com/social-media-analytics-tools (accessed June 22, 2017).

18 Ibid.

19 "The World's 50 Most Popular Brands, Annual Rankings 2016," Infegy, https://top50.infegy.com (accessed June 22, 2017).

20 Alexis Madrigal, "Dark Social: We Have the Whole History of the Web Wrong," *The Atlantic*, October 12, 2012, www.theatlantic.com/technology/archive/2012/10/dark-social-we-have-the-whole-history-of-the-web-wrong/263523 (accessed June 22, 2017).

21 "The Power of Sharing Data," RadiumOne, October 28, 2016, https://radiumone.com/wp-content/uploads/2016/11/RadiumOne-Sharing-Data-Report.pdf (accessed June 22, 2017).

22 Madrigal, "Dark Social: We Have the Whole History of the Web Wrong."

23 "The Power of Sharing Data," RadiumOne.

24 "Tourism Ireland: Social Media Case Study," Brightspark Consulting, www.brightspark-consulting.com/tourism-social-media (accessed June 22, 2017).

25 Mark Henry, and Brian Harte, "A New & Simple Way to Measure Social Media ROI: Social Equivalent Advertising Value," Tourism Ireland, www.scribd.com/tourismireland (accessed June 22, 2017).

26 "Social Media Insights by Industry," Social Bakers, www.socialbakers.com/social-media-content/industry-social-content (accessed June 22, 2017).

27 Michael Brito, "Measuring Social Media Marketing: It's Easier Than You Think," *Search Engine Journal*, June 30, 2007, www.searchenginejournal.com/measuring-social-media-marketing-its-easier-than-you-think/5397 (accessed August 7, 2011).

Visit **https://study.sagepub.com/smm3e** for free additional online resources related to this chapter.

PART 5

Social Media Marketing in Practice

Case Zone—
10 Case Studies

Case Study for Part I *Foundations of Social Media Marketing*

Case Study 1—Social Advocacy Around the World

Karen Mishra, East Carolina University

Many nonprofit organizations use social media due to its low cost and wide reach. These "social communities" are places where organizations can provide influential information about their cause, as well as create a community of followers who believe in their cause and co-create content through their followership. Nonprofits use social communities to increase awareness and cement brand loyalty.

Recent studies about nonprofit social media use found that Facebook and Twitter are the top social media channels used by nonprofits.[1] Despite the widespread use of Facebook and Twitter, researchers find that nonprofits are not utilizing the positive aspects of social media as much as they might.[2] For instance, nonprofits use social media more to push out communication rather than create a dialogue with the communities they are trying to serve.[3] Many nonprofits are now pursuing a form of "social advocacy" by using social media to both inform and help their followers take action.

Lovejoy and Saxton found that there are three primary uses of social media for nonprofits: 1) information, 2) community, and 3) action.[4] Many nonprofits harness the information they are sharing with their communities to advocate for them to take action in some way: donate money, share information with others, or give their time.[5] Obar defined advocacy as "the act of championing, supporting or advocating a specific viewpoint or cause."[6]

Pack for a Purpose (PfaP) is a nonprofit with a mission to change the way people think about packing for their global travel. Pack for a Purpose (www.packforapurpose.org) began with Rebecca and Scott Rothney's first trip to Africa and the realization that they were allowed two suitcases each and a carry-on to the flight. On the next flight in Africa, they only had a luggage allowance equal to the weight of their carry-on. Not wanting to waste "free shipping" on their next trip, they used their four suitcases to take soccer balls and school supplies for a local school. Their tour operator, Wilderness Safaris, supported the school.

From this experience, Rebecca founded Pack for a Purpose in 2009. PfaP encourages travelers to pack five pounds of requested supplies in their suitcases and deliver them when they arrive at their destination. This form of "social advocacy" is not only educating travelers about how they can make better use of their luggage, but is encouraging travelers to take action and commit to make a positive impact with their extra luggage on their next trip.

PfaP has partnerships with accommodations and tour companies all over the world. These participants submit needs lists requested by the community projects they support. When travelers know where they are traveling to, they simply click on that specific country, find the needs list, and choose which supplies they would like to take with them. For instance, if you are traveling to Turkey, the Ritz-Carlton in Istanbul takes all the supplies Pack for a Purpose travelers drop off (such as school supplies and clothing) and delivers them to the elementary schools they support.

Pack for a Purpose is an all-volunteer organization. From the webmaster to the graphic designer, individuals volunteer their time because they believe in the mission. The website went live in December 2009. Since then, PfaP has used a variety of social media to get the word out to other travelers. The organization uses Facebook, Twitter, Instagram, Pinterest, YouTube, and LinkedIn. Its motto is "Small Space. Little Effort. Big Impact."

PfaP has built its social media presence with the use of college interns. PfaP first started out with only Facebook, but over time, new interns have added new social media channels. By using all of these social media platforms, PfaP has expanded its outreach enormously, informing world travelers how they can make a difference. In exchange for their time, Rebecca makes them homemade chocolate chip mint cookies (hot out of the oven and delicious!) in her home. A dedicated office in her home is the world headquarters of Pack for a Purpose and is where the interns work. Rebecca is such an inspiring leader that these interns love learning from her and enjoy giving her new ideas to promote her cause.

Andrew, an intern from NC State, commented on his experience with PfaP: "I'm so grateful that I was able to intern at Pack for a Purpose during my junior year at North Carolina State University. I learned so much from Rebecca Rothney, including what it means to be passionate and goal-oriented about one's profession. I introduced Pack for a Purpose to Instagram as a way to visually engage more travelers and help spread the word about the organization. Because photography is so immediate it's a great way to influence and inspire others."

Most recently, Rebecca initiated a fundraising effort ("action") to buy 500 pairs of Be Girl (begirl.org) underwear. This underwear allows young women in South Africa to stay in school every "day of the month." She used both Facebook and Twitter for her campaign, which both educated her followers about this issue and advocated for young women. This "social advocacy" campaign had excellent results. In less than three months, Rebecca raised the money necessary to purchase all 500 pairs of Be Girl underwear.

Discussion Questions

1. What is more important for a non-profit: the zone of social community or the zone of social commerce?

2. How has this social advocacy channel in the zone of social community built momentum for the PfaP cause using altruistic impulse?

3. Examine all of the ways that PfaP uses social media. What area would you improve? Why and how? Which social media site would you follow? Why?

4. How has PfaP been effective for building community? What could they do to improve their sense of community around PfaP?

5. What type of social advocacy group would you start? Why and how?

Case Studies for Part II *Social Media Marketing Strategy and Planning*

Case Study 2— Strategic Social Media Plan: First & Main, an Outdoor Shopping Mall

Donna C. Wertalik, Virginia Tech University

Not long ago, First & Main shopping center was entering a metamorphosis—starting a crucial time in its existence, which would come to have a lasting impact not only on the shopping center as an entity of its own, but also on each of its tenants. In a dynamic process, the center unveiled a new brand persona and offerings relative to entertainment, dining, and varied shopping experiences. Research suggested that the shopping center required the development of an online and offline marketing campaign to target consumers in a more strategic manner.

With these efforts came the goal of enabling the shopping center to host a recognizable digital tone among the Virginia Tech population. This included building an attitude that would be known to many young professionals, both in the area and visiting. Conversations needed to boast identifiable characteristics and quality dialogue to propel new discussions. New discussions needed to have life, lasting impact, and an intriguing yet informal and upbeat tone. The strong social push would ideally be shared across multiple platforms and would become an enjoyable staple within the local social community.

First & Main needed a brand voice that would inspire people to enjoy life, would bring to light the trends associated with the industries encompassed in the shopping center, and would be a resource for the latest activities and information in Blacksburg. It needed a brand that would act upon the following core goals:

- Draw students into the current shopping center through social media campaigns.
- Build momentum for new stores and coming entertainment.
- Excite students on campus.
- Utilize social media channels to engage the community.

With all of that in mind, a cyclical and tactical process was formed with the theme of "conversation" in mind:

Strategic Goals

1. Build awareness.
2. Create community.
3. Excite/engage students.
4. Drive traffic into First & Main.
5. Track progress and continue to modify to build digital domination.

Execution Steps

- Step 1—Curate: create content that our community will view and interact with in the social space.
- Step 2—Facilitate: manage and continue conversation with proper resources built to operate dialogue.
- Step 3—Monitor: risk management will secure proper usage of our social voice, making sure actions comply with an appropriate message.
- Step 4—Manage: top-level management will oversee activity throughout each stage of the process to align the First & Main vision.

The next actionable tasks were overarching ideas that would then become formulated tactics, covering all angles of the goals and needs outlined above. Through building momentum, building awareness, creating community, engaging students, and increasing store visits, First & Main would become a center of communal entertainment and excitement.

Tactics

Social Media

- *Task*: develop a strategic content calendar for First & Main with strategic messages on Facebook (Case 2 Figure 2a).
- *Goal*: drive consumers to First and Main during university-centric events as well as locally sponsored nights such as "Kids Night," "Senior Citizen Day," and "Hokie Night."
- The role the social platforms would play would be as interchangeable parts in a machine of engagement, managed via a pre-populated campaign calendar:
  - Twitter—news sharing source
  - Facebook—centrally promote events
  - Instagram—share photos and encourage tagging of contextually relevant ideas.

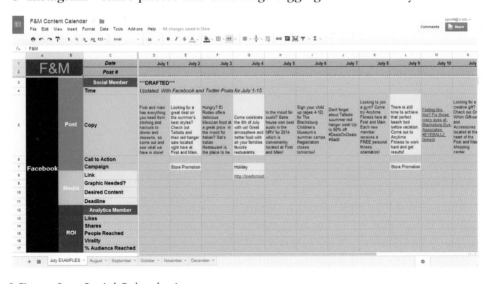

Case 2 Figure 2a Social Calendar Image

Online Coupons and Contests

- *Task*: use trackable coupons paired with social campaigns to attract crowds during peak weekends or events. Build upon existing relationships and sponsorships with tenants to include in gift bags, on swag, and in raffle items.
- *Goal*: utilize incentives and involvement as the primary recruiting source for new visitors in the center.
- Utilize playful pop-ups such as the First & Main Prize Wheel to draw the attention of non-existing consumers, while keeping the existing users involved.

Event Presence

- *Task*: exhibit at a walkthrough trade show such as the university's extracurricular, introductory fair—GobblerFest—and display table props, posters, a virtual video, and a game.
- *Goal*: reach out to multiple clubs, organizations and individuals with different needs. Advertise these events on social media to cross promote!
- There is large potential at this event to reach into the Greek life on-campus with a campaign aimed at fraternity and sorority participation.

Case 2 Figure 2b   Facebook Events Image

Miscellaneous Projects

- Long Term
  - Cumulus: utilize this mixed program to reach Wytheville, Bluefield, and Pulaski with the goal of involving high school sports, and offer satellite programs to drive traffic to First & Main and Nascar events.
  - Gaming App: create a simple gaming application to showcase the shops within the center, as seen in the image in Case 2 Figure 2c. Build a rewards program into the game to encourage multi-use action.

Case 2 Figure 2c   GamePlay

- Short Term
  - ○ Design and purchase a First & Main tent and flags for both internal and external use at events.
  - ○ Create a plan of action for each event to outline the audience, goals, measurable metrics, and more before even setting up.
  - ○ Include: game rules, prize ideas, social entry requirements, designs, etc.

Tactical Logistics

- Considered Return on Investment.
- Tracked all engagements, impressions, hashtags, and influencers through Radian 6 technology, Hootsuite, Commun.it, and other data mining platforms focused on ROI.
- Assessed and modified marketing strategies on a weekly basis to determine impact by channels and engagement.

Timeline

- 8/25—Welcome Back Week
- 9/5—GobblerFest
- 9/17—Business Horizons Career Fair
- 9/22—Homecoming Week
- 12/01 —Grand opening of new major entertainment tenant, Franks Cinebowl

Budget

- $250,000

The proper implementation of this plan required timed planning, failed predictions, unexpected successes, and imperfect details. The end goal was to make a difference in the purpose of the shopping center for all customer types. With consistent movement in the right direction on this front, success was met with increased tenants, more specialized and sponsored events, and major boosts in social engagement, which continues to bring in new customers at a remarkable pace.

Case Study 3—Strategic Social Media Plan: A University Business School

Donna C. Wertalik, Virginia Tech University

In efforts to build a central voice in the Pamplin College of Business at Virginia Tech, a 12-week plan evolved. This plan found a meeting place at a crossroads between education, social media placement and experimentation, and content marketing. A set of social media channels was developed as the source for those seeking academic news, trends in social media marketing, and engagement within the college and across campus. In this initiative, the goal was to reach an audience that consisted of current and prospective students, alumni, and leaders in academia.

With the intent to develop a robust community of influencers on all platforms within a specific timeframe, many steps had to be taken and dynamic metrics had to be followed and maintained. At the end of the project, the college would ideally have an all-knowing tone among the student and professional body as well as an exciting attitude with a passion for the business world. The college sought fewer casual conversations and more thought-provoking, share-worthy discussions. The students' words would eventually inspire action within the college and social networks, while allowing those with a passion for business to have fun among fellow enthusiasts.

With all of that in mind, how would success be measured and reached? Basics had to be set—in a case like this, with so many intricacies and so many potential critics, it's the little things that would matter the most. It began with a three-tiered system in regards to the social tone, voice, and personality, which would aim to encompass the following criteria:

- *Knowledgeable*—always current with what is happening in the college and business worlds.
- *Progressive*—inspiring and broadening ideas with a fresh business perspective.
- *Engaged*—starting, sharing, and continuing the conversation.

The next step in the evolution of this strategic plan was building a process to work by. By combining curation, facilitation, monitoring, and management, the team would continuously reach goals.

After coming full circle on the process, measurement was again questioned. What metrics would be appropriate to analyze action items in this plan? In what ways would measurable goals be attained? The scale of success was broken down into four major goals, each harboring a quantifiable KPI, as well as a tool that would harness those numbers.

Finally, creativity had to be addressed. Social media is of course an art, a marketing tool, and so much more than just a means to communicate. Using periodical themes, the 12-week plan would become a four-part plan. Timely elements of each period, such as national holidays, university events, and trending topics would be helpful in focusing on and creating conversation. Between each period, goals and metrics and engagement could be analyzed, and within each period, new ideas would be brainstormed and implemented.

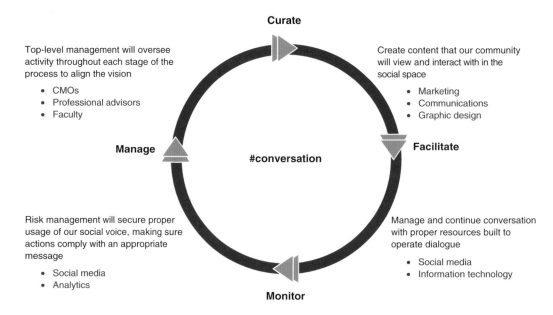

Case 3 Figure 3a   The Process

Goal	KPI	Metric (selection)
Awareness	Website traffic	Google Analytic Hootsuite-Page Views, SEO ranking
Acquisition	Average time spent per page/article downloads	Google Analytic Hootsuite Clicky Bounce Rate
Influence	Shares, re-tweets	Google Analytic Hootsuite Klout
Outcomes	Total # of website followers, Klout score	Google Analytic Hootsuite Klout

In a single semester, the social plan would be launched with themes as the central strategic element to work by.

- Period 1 (Jan. 28—Feb. 24): Determination
  - Focus on all elements of a student's life—fun, love, education, job-seeking, history, success
  - Super Bowl, Valentine's Day, Business Horizons Fair, Black History Month
- Period 2 (Feb. 25—March 24): Tradition
  - Ring Dance, American Red Cross Month, St. Patrick's Day

- Period 3 (March 25—April 21): Ut Prosim, So that I May Serve

  ○ The Big Event, 3.2 for 32 Run, Relay for Life

- Period 4 (April 22—Graduation): We Are the Future

  ○ Emphasize accomplishments of graduates (jobs, internships, etc.)

Through periodic breakdown, the systematic process, and the graphical goals, the approach consisted of a team and some simple action items. Starting with a content calendar and moving through multiple social channels individually required a very genuine human aspect throughout. If that was ignored, strategic analysis would mean nothing. By nurturing that role during the 12 weeks, the following items could roll out with more influence than even planned:

- Create a comprehensive editorial content calendar across platforms to expand engagement and reach

  ○ *Team role*: develop a comprehensive content calendar—with a goal of leading up to three blog posts per week, five to seven tweets per day, and one to three Facebook posts per day—publish and monitor.

- Maintain an active Twitter channel

  ○ *Team role*: identify influential professors, students, and alumni—contacts. Secure a minimum of 15% influential Twitter followers by target date.

- Build an engaged Facebook channel

  ○ *Team role*: post one to three status updates per day that encourage readership of blogs, conversation, and Twitter following. Secure a minimum of 10% influential "likes" by target date.

- Keep an updated blog

  ○ *Team role*: utilize targeted keywords and promotion on Twitter and Facebook; measure success based on traffic analysis through Google Analytics (SEO and AdWords) to establish and grow blog readership.

Through the execution of each one of these shifting parts, it became evident that this was not just an experiment; it was something that could benefit the college in the coming years in all areas. Prospective students, enrolled undergraduate and graduate students, and alumni could all focus in and share thoughts, creating irreplaceable and influential connections. Between generations, industries, cities, and even simple social likeness, groups could engage on a level they had not experienced previously. By working through a plan that was specific, measurable, attainable, relevant, and timely, success was reached at a fast pace with few obstacles.

Case Study 4—Travel and Social Media: The Grand Ole Opry

Caley Cantrell, Virginia Commonwealth University Brand Center and Brad Perry, Authentic

The travel and tourism industry most likely has a love/hate relationship with the Internet. On the one hand, the Internet can make for smarter and savvier travelers, eager to see the world. On the other hand, online travel aggregators, like Expedia and Kayak, make it harder and harder to find someone who isn't traveling with some kind of deal in their pocket.

The Internet can "get you there" and "put you up for the night." But when it comes time to determine what you'll do once you get where you're going—whether for vacation or business—travel and tourism is shifting from business-to-consumer to consumer-to-consumer. We make informed choices on where to go and what to do when we arrive at our destination based on crowd-sourced information from friends and family, and platforms like Pinterest and Instagram.

"Traveler-generated" content is seen as more credible, more authentic, and a form of insurance in spending our vacation dollars. We want to make informed choices before we leave and during our time away. We look for real experiences to make memories and to share with the folks at home. We pay it forward when we then share our travel smarts and success with our communities. Can travel brands, destinations, and venues be credible in these conversations and use them to increase visits?

Destination—The Grand Ole Opry?

The Grand Ole Opry is a weekly country-music stage concert in Nashville, Tennessee, which through the years has presented the biggest stars and legends of the genre. The Opry was founded November 28, 1925 as a one-hour radio "barn dance," and represents the longest-running radio broadcast in US history.

The Grand Ole Opry is an American icon, showcasing a mix of legends and contemporary chart-toppers, performing country, bluegrass, folk, gospel, and comedic skits. As an American icon, the Opry attracts hundreds of thousands of visitors from around the world and millions of radio and Internet listeners.

The city of Nashville itself is booming, having become something of a travel mecca. As a getaway destination, people head to Nashville for food, nightlife, shopping, and southern hospitality. The success of the recent television show *Nashville* has only fueled the popularity.

The Issue for the Grand Ole Opry

Over the years the Grand Ole Opry has remained extremely relevant and revered by its core country fans. But it needs to win over fans (and tourist traffic) outside that segment, especially visitors under 40. Can the Opry get more than its fair share of Nashville's rising popularity?

Social Media and the Grand Ole Opry

Like many tourist and entertainment destinations, Opry marketing has increasingly centered on an approach that puts social first. Social allows the Opry to do more with less money and to create more immersive experiences. Targeting opportunities with social are far better than broadcast channels. The Grand Ole Opry is active on Facebook, Twitter, Instagram, and YouTube as well as establishing a growing presence on Pinterest and Snapchat. But are they taking full advantage of these, and other platforms?

The Challenge

Develop a cross-platform social media campaign to help increase awareness and drive consideration of taking a trip to the Grand Ole Opry among a new and relevant target audience—that is not core country music fans and that is 20 to 40 years of age. Include relevant consumer, brand, and content insights. Attention should be paid to the current social media content Opry features across platforms. What new paid and earned content and platforms would you recommend adding to the mix? In lieu of specific budget figures, please provide recommended KPIs.

Discussion Questions

1. This is a two-prong assignment. It is a tourism challenge and it is a "choice of entertainment" challenge. Which comes first?
2. How would you set about segmenting the broad target audience of adults aged 20 to 40? Are there situational, occasion-based, or affinity groups that might emerge as priorities or low-hanging fruit?
3. How can your recommendations be as turnkey as possible for Opry and also feel "on-brand"?

Case Studies for Part III *The Four Zones of Social Media*

Case Study 5—Native Advertising: Novel or Deceptive?

Jennifer Zarzosa, Henderson State University and Sarah Fischbach, California Lutheran University

Lisa attentively pays attention to the posts her network of friends and family have posted today on Facebook. After all, this is the best way of getting her news and connecting with what's going on in the world. In fact, Lisa usually only gets her news from Facebook and Twitter anyways. She always makes sure to stay connected with her favorite brands and publishers. Lisa loves when she gets live updates—it makes her feel like an insider.

Today's feed features the usual content: cute dog videos, funny memes, happy birthday wishes, inspirational quotes, vacation pictures, and how-to-cook videos. As Lisa scrolls down her Facebook feed, she watches a cute dog video (of course), shares the funny meme, comments "Happy b-day!" and loves the inspirational quote.

Then, Lisa comes across a suggested post by The Gap. Lisa notices her friends Amanda and Marc both like The Gap. The post features the top five fashion trends for the summer. The post has many likes, loves, wows, and even angry faces as well as comments and shares. Eager for more information, she clicks the "learn more" button. Lisa loves the styles she sees on the landing page and adds a pair of denim jeans and a bright yellow crop top to her cart and checks out shortly.

Online advertising has come a long way since the early days when banners, pop-ups, and pop-unders were the prominent form of online advertising. Critics argue banner ads cause wear-out and banner blindness while pop-ups and pop-under ads are usually blocked. Critics claim this type of online advertising is intrusive and therefore ineffective. Consumers have become mobile first, decreasing the use of desktops, which makes desktop online advertising formats obsolete. In response, advertisers have developed new ways to engage with consumers and facilitate interaction.

Native advertising blends organic and commercial content seamlessly in order to break through the clutter. According to the Federal Trade Commission, native advertising—sometimes called sponsored content—is the practice of blending advertisements with news, entertainment, and other content in digital media. It refers to advertisements that more closely resemble the content in which they are embedded. Native advertising represents more than a third of its advertising revenue for many publishers.

Advocates of native advertising maintain consumers have been conditioned to ignore traditional online advertising. Therefore, advertisers can use native ads to better engage the reader by mixing commercial content with organic content creatively. Social media in-feed ads have distinct benefits over traditional online advertising. Many times in-feed ads have engagement markers (e.g. comments, likes, loves), blend well with organic content, and are endorsed by those in one's network through online word-of-mouth; all of which increase the likelihood of engagement. As a result, publishers also benefit by receiving more advertising revenue. Social media in-feed ads such as Facebook-sponsored posts and Twitter-promoted tweets comprise about 39% of native advertising. Additionally, publishers such as *Forbes, The New Yorker, Fast Company,* and *The Atlantic* use advertorials or branded content, another form of native advertising.

Critics of native advertising contend consumers cannot identify native advertising as advertising clearly. While social media in-feed ads are effective, in that they blend well with organic content, it is unclear whether consumers can recognize the in-feed ad as an advertisement with commercial intent. Therefore, native advertising could be a form of deceptive advertising. Is the in-feed ad novel or deceptive?

The FTC recommends clear and prominent advertising disclosures using visual cues such as shading and borders, and text labels that are explicit, large, and visible to avoid deceptive advertising. Despite this, there is no consensus on disclosure language and visual cues to signal native advertising for publishers. Consequently, publishers use different disclosure language varying in ambiguity—sponsored, suggested, promoted, branded content, and presented. When consumers are unable to recognize native ads, opponents of native advertising claim it violates trust between the reader and the publisher. Historically, there has been a divide between editorial and advertising content. The line is now blurred.

Discussion Questions

1. How would you classify social media in-feed ads?

2. How are social media in-feed ads different from display ads and organic social ads?

3. Why is Lisa more likely to click on the call to action for a social media in-feed ad than a display ad?

4. Do you think Lisa noticed the Facebook suggested post by The Gap was a native ad? Why? If she did, do you think she thought it was deceptive?

5. Based on your own experiences with native advertising, how do you believe native advertising should be regulated?

6. Imagine you are creating disclosure language standards. Describe how you would create the disclosure language standards in terms of visual cues and text labels.

Case Study 6—A Social Media Conference Community
Alan J. Seymour, Consultant

Sport marketing has contributed to a new revitalization of marketing activities and trends. Whenever the author ventures and delivers lectures, seminars and workshops, the conversation always returns to the belief that sport is the oxygen of the masses and that audiences respond with vibrancy and commitment.[7] These are now the vital tools of fan response and voice for sports marketers.

Overview

This case is an exercise in social media communities and their ability to come together for effective business dialogue among students, academia, and practitioners. As a university academic in sports marketing, the plan had been to launch new programs of studies in sport marketing management, and to promote this social media was the *preferred* vehicle of choice.[8]

Background

The conference was set up as a launch of the new BA undergraduate course in Sports Marketing at the University of Northampton. The intention was to use the conference to raise awareness of the new degree to enhance the credibility of the university in the sports business market, and to bring together the communities of sport in students, academia, and practitioners. The initial and subsequent conferences used various *marketing mix* processes and for the first time social media was integral to this. The agendas and assembled speakers plus the invited delegates reflected the above approach.[9]

The conference theme was sponsorship and crowdfunding with special emphasis on new media and powers of connection through social media platforms in communications.[10] The new opportunities to debate and discuss topics that may not necessarily be on the main agenda was an important feature in the choice of *theme*. The emergent importance and involvement of audiences in crowdfunding as a new addition to sponsorship options provided the *hook* for delegates and speakers to be attracted to the conference and join the sports community around the conference subject.

Discussion Questions

1. As the conference director, with your social media team, assess and appraise the various social media platforms you would incorporate into a social media campaign.
2. Devise and set up campaign initiatives to deliver a new conference sports community using the special processes that social media management could bring to this campaign. The community should be specifically drawn up as a sector/cohort that meets a pre-planned agenda of relevancy and selectivity in the type of conference design you have envisaged in your plans.

Case Study 7—#NikeAirMaxDay: The Creation of a Social Brand Event

Emma Reid, University of West of Scotland and
Katherine Duffy, University of Glasgow

Sneakers have evolved from being functional footwear to being a fashion staple underpinned by brand loyal consumers and a subculture of #sneakerheads with their own language, rituals, and sneaker culture. These sneaker enthusiasts use social media, blogs, and forums (such as NikeTalk, Sole Collector, and Hypebeast forums) and attract consumer novices to experienced collectors, discussing new releases or 'drops', debating 'colorways', admiring and validating finds, and sharing care and maintenance tips.

The business model has changed so much in the last decade. Companies rely on the web to push product, and moving inventory to brick-and-mortar locations has dwindled … quick strikes and hyperstrikes have meant that sneakerheads have to stay on their toes and near their phones at all times. The demand for product coupled with the ease of distribution has seen releases change from every month to, often, bi-weekly. Why send to a shop when you can simply put the shoe online every weekend?

The fascination and obsession with sneakers has moved from underground street culture to a mass consumer trend. Instead of billboards or television adverts, Nike has cultivated the #sneakerhead community and sneaker drops spread through social media in Instagram posts, tweets, blog posts, and dedicated Facebook groups. Nike's biggest selling product range is the Air Max brand. Now in its thirtieth year, there have been many versions of Nike Air Max released, offering both athletic comfort and fashion. Nike knows it has a devoted, unwavering customer base and uses that to its advantage.

Beyond the Product—the Commercial Holiday

Nike went one step further and created its own day of celebration—Nike Air Max Day. Held on March 26, this day coincides with the launch of the first generation of Air Max Trainers in 1987 and in fact the preceding month is fast becoming a key date in #Sneakerhead calendars. Nike uses this day as an opportunity to build awareness of new product launches, drive consumer anticipation, encourage consumer content creation and sharing, and as a way of building relationships between consumers and the brand. This branded holiday marks a shift in how brands are approaching brand engagement in terms of social promotion from both the brand and consumer fans. Offline events included a Nike Air Max bus that toured Toronto (with art installations and branded vending machines), pop-up 'Sneakeasy' locations across four cities, and in-store promotions.

Online, Nike used social media to take engagement out of the retail store and include user-focused gamification, fan art, social influencers, and e-WOM to build anticipation and mobilize the existing fan community:

- Consumers had the opportunity to vote for new 'hybrid design' shoes, created by 12 Nike RevolutionAirs, which would be released in the future.
- Nike encouraged people to wear their beloved sneakers on March 26 and snap a picture of them using #airmaxday, mobilizing Instagram and Twitter users as word-of-mouth for its products and ethos.

- Fans were encouraged to vote for a re-release of an iconic Air Max sneaker. This led to the re-release of the user-demanded Nike x Atmos Air Max 1 Elephant.
- Social media influencers and ambassadors including Kevin Hart and Neymar also shared images of their own Air Max on social media.

How Did the #AirMaxDay Hashtag Perform on Social Media?

Data collected using the Brandwatch social listening platform (www.brandwatch.com) found that the hashtag #AirMaxDay was used 41,000 times on social media between February 1 and March 26, a 64% increase year over year; 26,000 unique users discussed #AirMaxDay on social media, up from 18,000 the previous year. The most significant change was the 600% increase in the use of the hashtag on Instagram, with 12,213 user-generated posts on the image-sharing social network.

From this it is clear that #AirMaxDay continues to grow in popularity on social media, and that image sharing and visual storytelling are the most important ways for fans to communicate with and about the brand. Analyzing the Air Max brand fans offers some interesting insights that are demonstrated in the social media content created by fans:[11]

- *Emotional engagement*: whereby the ownership, the covetedness, and appreciation of the different versions of Air Max has meaning in the day-to-day life of the consumer, evidenced through tweets discussing desired purchases and favorite editions, seen in comments such as "Nike takes all of my money in March."
- *Self-identification*: where fans (sneakerheads) find ways to identify with and communicate and build networks with like-minded fans, through the utilization of the #AirMaxDay hashtag, use of sneakerhead language, participation in forums, and posting images of wearing favorite Air Max sneakers on the day itself.
- *Cultural competence*: the understanding of the brand, knowledge of previous editions of Air Max, understanding of the value and scarcity of the rarer versions, knowledge of where to purchase, and use of language unique to the sneakerhead community.
- *Auxiliary consumption*: the collection of related products—for this consumer group, unboxed Air Max sneakers have a high value. Furthermore, the scarcity and rarity of different versions and 'deadstock' are shown in the high resale value.
- *Production of content*: clearly indicated in the huge volume of fan-generated content shared and engaged with on social media.

Rather than linear, broadcast-based advertising and marketing, Nike has adapted to the changing media landscape and adopted a flexible tactic that works in its favor. As shown from the data, Nike has an amazing opportunity to work directly with these hugely loyal and engaged fans in the social sphere. Encouraging fans to create and share user-generated content, to interact directly with the brand, and be involved in decisions around designs will help keep Nike at the top of its game.[12]

Discussion Questions

1. Nike is one of the first brands to develop its own 'holiday'. J.Crew has also launched its own #NationalStripesDay. Suggest how another global brand with a highly engaged social media community could create its own day of celebration.

2. Nike uses Air Max Day to tap into an already thriving online community of sneaker-heads. How can Nike use social media to learn more about this community?

3. For future Air Max Days, how can Nike use the #AirMaxDay hashtag to reach new audiences without alienating the existing highly engaged community?

4. Suggest other ways that social media and other forms of digital marketing and technology could be used to help celebrate #NikeAirMaxDay.

Case Study 8—Pokémon GO: A Revolution in Social Gaming

Clay Gransden, Liverpool Hope University

In the summer of 2016, the twentieth anniversary of Pokémon, the Pokémon GO app was released. The game was developed by Niantic who collaborated with Nintendo, by way of the Nintendo Company.[13] Pokémon of course is no small brand; it is currently in the top 30 licensed brands worldwide.[14] Pokémon as a brand has diversified over the years and has many strong interests in the entertainment and gaming industry. There have been over 280 million video games sold worldwide, $670 million (approximately) accrued in box office revenue, and 21.5 billion trading cards shipped worldwide.[15] Combining this strong brand with a new form of gaming to create a totally immersive advergame has created quite a buzz. To really grasp the impact of the game it is important to first understand how the app works.

The game itself revolves around catching, evolving, or hatching each Pokémon and registering them on the in-game catalogue called the 'Pokédex.'[16] Each player is helped along the way by visiting Pokéstops (that are places in the real world), which when visited reward the players with in-game items to help continue their journey through the experience.[17] The game utilizes a mix of both VR and GPS tracking which is perhaps one of the reasons for its success.[18]

The game not only makes you explore where you live, but also encourages players to get outside and walk through gamification. In February 2017, Phil Keslin, the chief technology officer at Niantic, stated that 8.7 billion kilometers have been walked in-game, which is the equivalent of walking to Pluto.[19] The impact of this social game is incredible, and there have been claims that the game could add an estimated 2.825 million years of additional lifetime to its US users.[20] The game transcends those social games that have come before; it does not have the traditional features of leaderboards and in-game messaging. This is a game played through an electronic device that encourages you to work together with others in the real world and converse with others in the real world.

It is, of course, not the first game to do so; Niantic also released a game called Ingress which had similar features.[21] Ingress uses the same system of integrating GPS into a gaming app. It has been said that without the original gamers from Ingress there would in fact have been no Pokémon GO, with much of the data being used from the former to help with the formation of said Pokéstops.[22] Without the power of a licensed brand, Ingress did not have the same impact, with 20 million downloads compared to Pokémon GO's recent claim of 650 million downloads.[23]

Pokémon GO as of February 2017 has now amassed a massive $1 billion dollars.[24] This is the quickest of any app and places it as one of the highest grossing apps of all time.[25] One of the main reasons behind this are the microtransactions and in-game purchases that can take place within the app. Similar to the other games that have grossed $1 billion, Pokémon GO allows the player to purchase extra items to assist in the game.[26] The game is also free to play, and this duality seems to be one of the driving principles of many of the other top grossing apps in the marketplace.

If you are a hardcore gamer there is plenty to do; including the levelling up system, which has yet to be maxed by any player (without the use of bots).[27] For casual gamers you can still pick up and play the game without being disadvantaged by not putting the hours in.

The game also has appeal for those who played or watched the original iterations. There is an integrated camera system within the game which enables players' content to be shared through personal networks.

One thing that is clear about Pokémon GO is its success; it has amassed an enormous player base in a relatively short time and accumulated an incredible amount of money. The game has also reinforced Pokémon as a brand creating demand for other merchandise to rocket, in some cases increasing the value of some of the trading cards to as much as $10,000.[28] Unfortunately, there has been a slowdown in people playing the game since its launch.[29] But, with Pokémon now in its seventh generation and boasting a staggering 801 creatures, there is potential to continue to add content.[30] This humble app has revolutionized mobile gaming; with the advent of VR and more powerful devices being released, this is an exciting time to be using social entertainment for marketing.[31]

Discussion Questions and Exercises

1. Pokémon Go was available to download on the 20th anniversary of the first Pokémon game release. Why might celebrating this anniversary be particularly beneficial to this type of brand?

2. What factors contributed to the game's success?

3. Find examples of businesses using Pokémon Go to their advantage.

4. After the initial buzz of Pokémon Go died down, player numbers also dropped. Investigate the most recent Pokémon Go events/updates and create a timeline. Create a new event/update which may create interest and bring players back.

5. Download Pokémon Go and investigate the in-app purchases. Why might someone part with their money to purchase certain items/services? Compare and contrast these in-app purchases with other top games such as Candy Crush Saga and Clash of Clans.

6. Identify a brand, and describe and critique the present social entertainment efforts employed (if any). Suggest improvements to the social entertainment effort. Use theory as well as examples from industry to analyze your strategy.

Case Study 9—Social Media Is Gateway to eBook Sales Success: Amazon Kindle eBooks

Thomas S. Mueller, Appalachian State University

The Amazon Kindle eBook brand is one of the most popular forms of digital publishing in today's social community. As of early 2016, the direct-to-consumer online retailer was selling 1.06 million eBooks (paid downloads) per day. Consumers spent $5.75 million per day during a recent month, with $1.76 million of those sales directed to author royalties. Though it is somewhat undocumented regarding distribution, authors received an additional $140 million in funds from Kindle Unlimited, Amazon's subscription reading service.[32] The industry as a whole is generating over $2.1 billion in sales annually.

It is interesting to note that as established publisher sales decreased, eBooks written by independent authors increased.[33] During an assessment in 2016, 56 of Amazon's 100 top-selling eBooks were self-published titles. Topically, the bestselling independent authors write about paranormal activities, romance, thrillers, urban fiction, suspense, and science fiction. With the ascent of digital titles on Amazon and other sources, industry experts posit that printed versions of books will become a niche market, similar to the effect noted in magazine and newsprint.[34] Digital publishing strategist Ben Thompson applies *aggregation theory* to the process, suggesting that sales portals like Amazon eliminate intermediaries, which allows independent publishers to avoid publishers and go direct to consumers.[35]

With a substantial faction of the *social publishing* market operating independently, advertising and promotion become the responsibility of the author. One portion of an author's time is allocated to writing the novel, while the other half of the time is invested in *social commerce*, which includes marketing to expand the author's fan base. The challenge is to differentiate an eBook from millions of competitive titles, then convince readers to download the digital offering onto a Kindle reader or other digital device. Pre-selling is essential to assure return on investment for the self-published author. One viable and affordable option is to build a social media marketing plan. Social media platforms provide opportunities to develop leads, generate a follower list, leverage other prominent users, access large topical groups, and promote content "teasers" that showcase your upcoming eBook.[36]

Most eBook authors develop a social media plan through content generation. These are most often short, concise articles of 250 to 500 words. Most successful social media plans offer shorter posts, with frequent placement. Social media content is usually housed in a blog, such as Google's Blogger platform, or the highly customizable WordPress.[37] It's important to claim a URL that is unique and specific to the author and her or his work. A strong URL, along with key search words included in blog post titles, can help the author's social media content climb in ranking on search engines.

Social media portals such as LinkedIn and Google+ offer each user a personal landing page, but much more is available through groups and communities, where individuals share common interests. For example, a fashion community in Google+ hosts 557,000 followers.[38] A marketing communication group in LinkedIn has collected 621,000 members.[39] And, the LinkedIn Book Marketing group has 28,000 members.[40] It is essential to identify a topical group to understand the relevance of posts, how interaction and replies work, and who posts the top viewed submissions. Authors can integrate into these platforms by reading posts, replying to posts, and finally crafting content that resonates with potential readers. Some authors incorporate introductory promotional comments on their upcoming eBook. It is important for authors to remember that blatant selling is not admissible; posted content must provide value and prove interesting to other group members.[41]

Facebook has been the most influential platform for many eBook authors. It has grown to over 1.4 billion users worldwide, with 70% checking their feed multiple times each day. eBook authors create a "landing page" for their profile as an author, or sometimes for a specific title. The challenge is to direct friends from the page to a personal website, and to target specific Facebook users who are profiled as sharing an interest in the eBook topic. Some authors host events or make promotional offers to engage users and increase traffic, which can be measured through *social media data management*. Mark Dawson initially started writing for a traditional publishing firm. His sales were weak and he transitioned to self-publishing. After learning how to leverage Facebook, Mark invested time and energy and now earns over $450,000 per year.[42]

Video platforms such as Vimeo and YouTube have been integrated into the social media promotion of eBooks. YouTube, the predominant player, was purchased in 2006 for $1.65 billion by Google. YouTube currently reports that it generates over 1 billion views per month.[43] Successful eBook authors have integrated YouTube segments into their social media plans, including interviews or "teasers" that offer special introductory offers at eBook launch time.

It's beneficial to cross-promote YouTube posts across Facebook pages and embedded content in visual sharing sites such as Pinterest and Instagram. Studies indicate that the human brain assimilates images 60,000 times more quickly than text. eBook authors are intentional about visual sharing; Instagram is predominantly 18 to 24 female (56%) and allows space to share images. Pinterest represents a female and male audience, with two thirds between the ages of 18 and 24. One half are located outside the United States. It allows users to aggregate content that appeals to their interests and sensibilities. The author's challenge is to entice user engagement, create awareness for the latest published eBook, and generate reader feedback, which can channel into digital book reviews. Many authors use the visual advantage to promote their eBook through storytelling in multiple posts.[44]

A social media platform that serves as the "messenger" for all social media activity is Twitter. Each message is limited to 140 characters, which can in turn be reposted and shared. Twitter now has 320 million monthly users, with over 1 billion monthly visits.[45] Savvy eBook authors use Twitter to include "@" user handles to attract other key authors, or hashtags to create topical searches. Twitter can also steer followers to other platforms, where blog or web content has been placed. Some have also leveraged Twitter's new live video broadcast program Periscope to promote special programs and activities.

Some of the most highly successful eBook authors are also prominent podcast hosts. Technology entrepreneur James Altucher has published 11 books, including the *Wall Street Journal* bestseller *Choose Yourself!* Altucher's unique position in the marketplace is that he lost his fortune, earned it back, and then lost it again. He now publishes eBooks such as *Reinvent Yourself* and promotes his projects on the popular "James Altucher Show" podcast, which is accessible on podbay.fm and iTunes.[46]

One social media opportunity that is sometimes overlooked is within the Amazon portal itself. An Amazon author page can showcase the author, include a biography, feature a compilation of the author's Amazon Kindle publications, and link to other social media content such as Twitter or personal blogs.

Most anyone can become a digital author, but not everyone can sell books. The holistic author understands how to write, publish, network, create, associate, and entertain. Social media presents the gateway where authors and customers connect in the open and unregulated marketplace.

Discussion Questions

1. Every eBook author is challenged to build reader sales through targeted social media marketing. If an author has just finished a historical book on the Civil War, what social media groups might provide interested members? Run a search in LinkedIn and Google+ to explore options.

2. Historical documentarian Ken Burns created a 1990 television series on the Civil War for the Public Broadcasting Network (PBS). Find Mr Burns' Twitter user handle, then write a tweet that would include both user handle and hashtag to link his work with a new eBook on the Civil War.

3. An eBook author has just self-published an expert's guide to gardening, with a large array of color photos embedded in the publication. How would you leverage Pinterest and Instagram to announce the launch of the book?

4. Choose a topic, then create a book title for that topic. What order of social media would you utilize to make the announcement to potential readers?

Case Study for Part IV *Social Media Data Management and Measurement*

Case Study 10—Mila: Leveraging Social Media for Market Research

Ilenia Confente and Paola Signori, University of Verona

Mila is a milk cooperative of 2,600 small dairy farmers in northern Italy (South Tyrol). The dairy industry represents a unique agribusiness sector: dairy production is an agricultural commodity and milk is produced daily, year round.[47] Milk and dairy products belong to a global supply chain which encompasses multiple countries, each with unique production practices and consumer markets. The typical firm in this industry is small or micro, but this has changed recently thanks to new technologies and skills that are allowing farmers to manage larger organization. In Italy the milk industry is characterized by an increased concentration of retailers in the last few decades. This phenomenon is a cause of unbalanced power along the supply chain, and some innovative small producers are reacting with marketing innovation and market research in order to adopt a pull strategy, avoiding the buying power of intermediaries. In addition, consumers' preferences are increasingly driving the entire industry, so it is critical to understand their motivations and perceptions. In these scenarios companies need to evolve their marketing strategies toward "u-marketing, ubiquity marketing," which means to be always present with always connected users, everywhere. This is possible thanks to the presence of technology that enables consumers to have access to the application when needed and desired. Social media allow them to share their real-time events and feelings through written posts or pictures.

Mila, serving several European markets, adopts social media for several purposes. One of them is to improve data collection and research on such markets. Mila began its marketing innovation in March 2016 when it faced the need to better understand consumers' online content that is constituted not only of written posts but also a growing number of images. So, due to the lack of advanced technical skills, Mila decided to outsource this activity to Maxfone, a digital agency that since 2008 has been specializing in 3.0 digital communication services and technologies for companies. Maxfone, through SocialMeter Analysis and Photostream platforms, monitors text messages, tweets, blogs, Facebook and similar posts, Instagram images, and other social media applications where posts and conversations are occurring. These data are mined and screened to generate a live stream of data focused on a client brand and its parent firm. This stream then enables Mila to engage consumers in relevant and empathetic ways as they post about events and interactions with the brand. Over time, the digital agency was able to generate insights to the behaviors associated with the images in real time (with a service called Photostream by SocialMeter Analysis). The real-time analytics aspect is revolutionary and critical if brands are to tap into the conversations, events, and behaviors appropriately; timing is critical for relevant participation. The first action Mila decided to take involved both the activation of the Photostream service and management of Mila's social network official accounts (Facebook, Twitter, and Instagram). Thanks to this, Mila is now able to collect and analyze in one place (and screen on its website) the visual content spontaneously shared by its customers.

Visual content (that can be labeled as "Pics of Mouth") is, in a certain way, replacing or integrating the written content (word of mouth) in social media. The success of Instagram, Pinterest, and similar platforms confirms this increase and many are the opportunities for customers to share their daily lives online.

Such visual data collection and analysis allow the company to learn more about consumer behavior and preferences, to innovate products and to understand the consumption process, and consequently to stimulate brand awareness. For instance, Mila can observe and investigate the way in which customers use products and find out, for example, the most common food pairings with cheese, what people dunk in their milk, where they eat their yogurt, and the most appreciated flavors. This information is then used and integrated into the most commons ones usually withdrawn from the Web—the written reviews and posts— by Mila to meet the needs of its customers when it comes to launching new products, or partnerships, or to innovate them.

Such ways to conduct market research through crawling both textual and visual posts from social network pages have revealed a previously ignored demand for Mila products that comes from far outside South Tyrol, and that extends to Italy's central regions. On a daily basis, customers asked for information on where to buy the Mila products in their city. This is what pushed Mila to start working on a product search engine that was soon embedded in the Mila website, allowing visitors to find the nearest seller and the products available, even far away from South Tyrol.

Discussion Questions

1. How was Mila able to do market research through social media? Is there any difference in doing so between small enterprises and large companies?

2. What kind of information can Mila collect about consumers' habits from Photostream analysis regarding its target? Why is this information helpful to conduct market research?

3. Why is there a need to collect visual contents rather than mere written posts? What can they add to the company in terms of data and information?

4. What metrics could Mila apply to measure the effectiveness of the campaign?

Notes to Case Studies

1   Chao Guo and Gregory D. Saxton, "Tweeting Social Change: How Social Media Are Changing Nonprofit Advocacy," *Nonprofit and Voluntary Sector Quarterly*, 43:1 (2014), 57–79; Jonathan A. Obar, "Canadian Advocacy 2.0: An Analysis of Social Media Adoption and Perceived Affordances by Advocacy Groups Looking to Advance Activism in Canada," *Canadian Journal of Communication*, 39:2 (2014).

2   Kristen Lovejoy, Richard D. Waters, and Gregory D. Saxton, "Engaging Stakeholders Through Twitter: How Nonprofit Organizations Are Getting More Out of 140 Characters or Less," *Public Relations Review*, 38:2 (2012), 313–18.

3   Kristen Lovejoy and Gregory D. Saxton, "Information, Community, and Action: How Nonprofit Organizations Use Social Media," *Journal of Computer-Mediated Communication*, 17:3 (2012), 337–53.

4   Ibid.

5   Guo and Saxton, "Tweeting Social Change.'

6   Obar, "Canadian Advocacy 2.0.'

7   See A.J. Seymour (EASM Conference, *Fandom & Followers*, Coventry UK, 2014) cited in B.J. Mullin, S. Hardy, and W.A. Sutton, *Sport Marketing*, 4th edn (Champaign, IL: Human Kinetics, 2014), p. 461.

8   Other source and related materials include: https://sites.google.com/site/actionreplays/home/ sports-marketing-conference; https://sites.google.com/site/actionreplays/home/sports-marketing-conference/sportsmarketingconferenceatnorthamptonbusinessschool2010; www.youtube.com/ watch?v=7h3U7gRv3H4 (all accessed July 17, 2017).

9   Additional source materials available at: https://sethkirby.wordpress.com/2013/06/06/the-future-of-sport-marketing-insights-perspectives-conference; www.eventbrite.co.uk/e/the-future-of-sport-conference-tickets-5340216732#; https://twitter.com/search?q=%23UNFutureofSport&src=hash; http://fcbusiness.co.uk/blog/?p=629 (all accessed July 17, 2017).

10 Additional materials available at: www.facebook.com/events/1023858767710583; www.eventbrite. co.uk/e/future-of-sport-conference-sponsorship-crowdfunding-tickets-26520848572#; https://uwstaffnews.files.wordpress.com/2016/10/agenda.pdf; https://twitter.com/fosconf; https:// twitter.com/sportmarketing1/status/792299888973414400; https://twitter.com/i/moments/8166637 69438941188 (all accessed July 17, 2017).

11 R. Kozinets, "Brand Fans: When Entertainment and Marketing Intersect on the Net," in Tracy Tuten (ed.), *Enterprise 2.0: How Technology, E-Commerce and Web 2.0 Are Transforming Business Virtually* (Santa Barbara, CA: Praegar Publishers, 2010).

12 Further suggested reading: Remington Guest, "Your Definitive Guide to Sneaker Slang," Coveteur, October 28, 2016, http://coveteur.com/2017/04/18/sneaker-guide (accessed June 22, 2017); R. Kameir, "Just Instagram It: How Nike Is Using You to Sell More Shoes," Complex, January 14, 2014, http://uk.complex.com/pop-culture/2014/01/nike-instagram-social-media-strategy (accessed April 10, 2017); R/GA, "Air Max Day," www.rga.com/work/case-studies/air-max-day (accessed April 10, 2017); J. Sawyer, "Nike Is Opening SneakEasy Pop Up Shops in Four Cities for AirMax Day," High Snobiety, March 16, 2017, www.highsnobiety.com/2017/03/16/nike-sneak-easy-pop-up-shops (accessed June 22, 2017); T. Battle, "How Sneaker Culture Has Changed in the Past 10 Years," Complex, February 22, 2016, http://uk.complex.com/sneakers/2016/02/how-sneaker-culture-has-changed-in-the-past-10-years (accessed April 10, 2017).

13   Marguerite Ward, "How the Mastermind Behind 'Pokémon Go' Got His Start," CNBC, July 27, 2016, www.cnbc.com/2016/07/27/how-john-hanke-the-mastermind-behind-pokemon-go-got-his-start.html (accessed February 20, 2017).

14   "The Top 150 Global Licensors," License Global, May 1, 2016, www.licensemag.com/license-global/top-150-global-licensors-2 (accessed February 27, 2017).

15   "Pokémon In Figures," The Pokémon Company, www.pokemon.co.jp/corporate/en/data (accessed February 10, 2017).

16   "Pokédex," Pokemon.Com, www.pokemon.com/us/pokedex (accessed February 10, 2017).

17   "Catch Pokémon in the Real World with Pokémon GO!", Pokemongo.Com, www.pokemongo.com/en-us/explore (accessed February 10, 2017).

18   "MWC 2017: Pokemon Go Creator Says Mixed Reality Will Beat VR," BBC News, March 1, 2017, www.bbc.co.uk/news/technology-39126033 (accessed March 1, 2017).

19   Google Developers, "Google Developers Day at GDC 2017." Filmed [February 2017]. YouTube video, 6:24:03. Posted February 2017.

20   Tim Althoff, Ryen W. White, and Eric Horvitz, "Influence of Pokémon Go on Physical Activity: Study and Implications," *Journal of Medical Internet Research*, 18:12 (2016), 11.

21   "Ingress," Ingress.Com, www.ingress.com (accessed February 17, 2017).

22   Ariel Bogle, "How the Gurus Behind Google Earth Created 'Pokémon Go'," Mashable, July 11, 2016, http://mashable.com/2016/07/10/john-hanke-pokemon-go/#dUWt9_ePtkqP (accessed February 15, 2017).

23   "Employment Opportunities," Niantic, www.nianticlabs.com/jobs (accessed February 15, 2017); Christopher Dring, "Pokémon Go Downloads Hit 650M," Gamesindustry.Biz, February 28, 2017, www.gamesindustry.biz/articles/2017-02-28-pok-mon-go-downloads-hit-650m (accessed February 28, 2017).

24   Jon Russell, "Report: Pokémon Go Has Now Crossed $1 Billion in Revenue", Techcrunch, February 1, 2017, https://techcrunch.com/2017/02/01/report-pokemon-go-has-now-crossed-1-billion-in-revenue (accessed February 10, 2017).

25   Dean Takahashi, "Pokémon Go Generated Revenues of $950 Million in 2016", Venturebeat, January 10, 2017, http://venturebeat.com/2017/01/17/pokemon-go-generated-revenues-of-950-million-in-2016 (accessed February 10, 2017).

26   Sarah Needleman, "How Mobile Games Rake in Billions," WSJ, July 28, 2016, www.wsj.com/articles/how-mobile-games-rake-in-billions-1469720088 (accessed February 10, 2017).

27   "Trainer Max Level—Pokemon GO Wiki Guide," IGN, February 15, 2017, http://uk.ign.com/wikis/pokemon-go/Trainer_Max_Level (accessed February 15, 2017).

28   Andrew Griffin, "Your Old Pokemon Cards Could Now Be Worth Thousands," *The Independent*, July 21, 2016, www.independent.co.uk/life-style/gadgets-and-tech/gaming/pokemon-go-helps-make-old-pokemon-cards-worth-thousands-a7148846.html (accessed February 10, 2017).

29   Dean Takahashi, "Pokémon Go Generated Revenues of $950 Million in 2016", Venturebeat, January 10, 2017, http://venturebeat.com/2017/01/17/pokemon-go-generated-revenues-of-950-million-in-2016 (accessed February 10, 2017).

30   "Pokédex," Pokemon.Com, www.pokemon.com/us/pokedex (accessed February 10, 2017).

31   Alexander M. Clark and Mathew T.G. Clark, "Pokemon Go and Research: Qualitative, Mixed Methods Research, and the Supercomplexity of Interventions", *International Journal of Qualitative*

Methods, 15:1 (2016), http://journals.sagepub.com/doi/full/10.1177/1609406916667765 (accessed February 20, 2017).

32   "February 2016 Author Earnings Report: Amazon's Ebook, Print, and Audio Sales," Author Earnings, http://authorearnings.com/report/february-2016-author-earnings-report (accessed February 9, 2017).

33   "No, E-Book Sales Are Not Falling, Despite What Book Publishers Say," *Fortune*, http://fortune.com/2015/09/24/ebook-sales (accessed February 8, 2017).

34   Ibid.

35   Ben Thompson, "Are Ebooks Declining, or Just the Publishers? Oyster Goes Out of Business, Media Notes," Stratechery, September 24, 2015, https://stratechery.com/2015/are-ebooks-declining-or-just-the-publishers-oyster-goes-out-of-business-media-notes (accessed June 22, 2017).

36   Sarah Quinn, "How to Promote Your eBook with Social Media," Social Media Examiner, November 10, 2015, www.socialmediaexaminer.com/how-to-promote-your-ebook-with-social-media (accessed February 8, 2017).

37   Katy Takaoka, "10 Types of Social Media Platform," SBT Virtual, April 14, 2016, http://sbtvirtual.ca/10-types-social-media-platform (accessed June 22, 2017).

38   Jim McLaw, "Fashion," Google+, https://plus.google.com/u/0/collection/EKEXX (accessed February 9, 2017).

39   "Marketing Communication," www.linkedin.com/groups/59008 (accessed February 9, 2017).

40   "Book Marketing," www.linkedin.com/groups/1848415/profile (accessed February 9, 2017).

41   Quinn, "How to Promote Your eBook with Social Media."

42   Dave Chesson, "How to Advertise a Book on Facebook," KindlePreneur, June 8, 2016, https://kindlepreneur.com/how-to-advertise-book-facebook-facebook-ads-for-books (accessed June 22, 2017).

43   Vanessa Page, "The Top 6 Companies Owned by Google," Investopedia, May 20, 2015, www.investopedia.com/articles/personal-finance/052015/top-6-companies-owned-google.asp (accessed June 22, 2017).

44   Sue Zimmerman, "Should You Go on Pinterest or Instagram for Your Business? 7 Facts to Consider," Agora pulse, April 1, 2015, www.agorapulse.com/blog/pinterest-or-instagram-for-business (accessed June 22, 2017).

45   Matej Njiri, "How Big Is Twitter," Techinfographics, March 21, 2016, https://techinfographics.com/how-big-is-twitter (accessed June 22, 2017).

46   "The James Altucher Show," Podbay, http://podbay.fm/show/794030859 (accessed February 15, 2017).

47   Sources include I. Confente and P. Signori, "Creating Value within the Dairy Supply Chain," in M. Sargiacomo (ed.), *Accounting and Management of the Agribusiness Industry* (London: McGraw-Hill Education, 2016), pp. 159–88; D.J. Flint, P. Signori, and S.L. Golicic, *Contemporary Wine Marketing and Supply Chain Management* (New York: Palgrave Macmillan, 2016); Mila: www.mila.it/en/home.html; P. Signori and D.J. Flint, "Digital Marketing Innovations and Their Role in Service Ecosystems, the Exchange of Value and Social Impact," in T. Russo-Spena and C. Mele (eds), *What's Ahead in Service Research? New Perspectives for Business and Society*, Proceeding of the 26th Annual RESER Conference (2016), pp. 259–72.

Sample Social Media Marketing Plan

GONOW Vacations

Introduction

GONOW is a tourism planning agency that provides custom tours to fulfill tourists' personal interests, and in particular, their passions. People are passionate about all kinds of things like food, history, culture, architecture, activities such as yoga, and more. GONOW links people's passions with vacation packages. This plan provides GONOW with a detailed map to follow as it develops social media marketing messages to support its marketing plan. The core strength of GONOW's product offers is custom vacation packages tied to passion points for the target audiences such as family fun, history, food, and so on.

The brand will follow its existing brand architecture as it develops its social media presence. There is an existing brand identity guide that will be followed to ensure consistency across all marketing channels in terms of logo design, brand name, imagery, tone, and voice. The brand's position is "GONOW brings legendary life experiences to people who value doing over having, and recognize that there is no better time than now." The brand's promise is to provide these life experiences when and where the target audience wants. The brand's tag line is Live With Passion, Go Now.

Situation Analysis

Travel businesses have many opportunities and many threats. Direct spending on leisure travel by domestic and international travelers totaled $683.1 billion in 2016. Nearly 80% of trips are for leisure, rather than for business purposes. Top leisure activities include visiting relatives and friends, shopping, eating, and sightseeing. These activities do not relay the cultural trend of vacations tied to specific hobbies and passions. For instance, even a passion as niche as "cheese" appeals to relevant travelers as they plan for meaningful, unique vacation experiences. Unfortunately for GONOW, travel is an extremely competitive industry with competition from other travel agencies, hotels, destination marketing organizations, online travel booking sites, credit card services, DIY (do it yourselfers), and more.

SWOT Analysis

The following SWOT analysis captures the key strengths and weaknesses within the company, and describes the opportunities and threats facing GONOW.

Competitive Audit

A competitive audit of the top two competitors for customized vacation packages revealed a strong presence for both on all major social network channels. The competitors participate regularly on these channels with a focus on imagery, especially using Instagram as a communication channel. An analysis of the last month's posts showed that the competitors are posting regularly but are not responding to follower questions and comments. The titles used for posts also do not differentiate the brands in terms of the brand positioning statements. There is room for GONOW to excel in response, service, and differentiated messaging. More details are provided in the full report of competitive activity by social media zones and channels.

Table A1   SWOT Analysis

Strengths	Weaknesses
• Truly unique experiences tied to audience interests • Excellent staff, with exceptional training on locations and ability to provide high-quality, personalized service	• Struggle to continuously create new and unique experiences while maintaining quality • Lack of brand awareness • High acquisition costs per customer
Opportunities	**Threats**
• Strong market value for travel spending, which continues to grow • Focus on experiences over materialism as a cultural trend worldwide • Fatigue among some consumers for investing time to search for deals and destinations	• Terrorism around the world dampens enthusiasm of consumers for long-range destination trips • Internet and sites like Expedia encourage DIY options for travelers • High number of agency competitors, as well as competition from destination marketing organizations (DMOs), hotels, and tourism sites • Economic concerns limit consumer confidence for discretionary spending • Travel spending tends to be seasonal, focused on holidays and summers

Self-Audit

GONOW uses a corporate persona in each of its social profiles. The persona is consistent with the brand's personality as an authoritative expert on life experiences including culinary, historical, and cultural opportunities related to a variety of geographic destinations. GONOW's participation on social media has been sporadic. At times there have been regular posts, but not always. In addition, too much of the information is filler content that does not add value to the target audience. Refer to the full analyses of GONOW activity across each social channel for specific details.

Reviewing the brand identity manual is important as GONOW seeks to systematically utilize social media for marketing. GONOW is the expert planner for unique destinations that bring your passions to life. Their mantra is "life experiences." Their tag line is "Live With Passion. GONOW." Their sub-messages speak to specific passions among the target audience, such as history, food, sports, wine, music, outdoors, and so on.

In developing and executing on the social media marketing plan, GONOW will ensure that all communications are aligned with its brand identity manual. The tone and voice will align with its brand personality of experience sensei.

Objectives

Because travel is such a competitive industry, the primary objective is to gain awareness of the brand. The social media marketing plan will seek to accomplish the following objectives:

1. Increase brand awareness of GONOW and its relationship to passion destinations and experiences for tourists. Specifically, the plan seeks to increase awareness by 10% among target audiences within six months of the plan launch.
2. Elevate GONOW's share of voice as a premier travel agency for passion destinations, resulting in a 5% lift over competing travel agencies.
3. Drive traffic to GONOW's e-commerce website, resulting in traffic increases of 10% or more within one month of plan launch.
4. Increase bookings for passion vacation packages by 15% over last year.
5. Reinforce relationship with past customers to drive repeat business.

Target Audience

Research of travelers of high-dollar vacation packages identified three primary target audiences: 1) families, 2) unattached travelers, and 3) bucket listers. Families account for 49% of travel spending overall. However, families tend to be budget conscious and choose kid-friendly options over passion-driven interests. Unattached travelers travel without kids and may or may not travel with other adults. They represent 24% of travel spending. They are interested in exciting, buzz-worthy trips and experiences but they also need accommodations that provide a social element to their vacations. Bucket listers are those who are actively seeking once-in-a-lifetime experiences. They view these vacations as goals that they achieve and check off the list, one by one. Historically, bucket listers were older travelers, but in recent years, the concept of a bucket list has resonated with consumers of all ages. Social media sharing provides consumers a way to share, promote, and document these bucket list accomplishments. Bucket listers fit well with the value proposition for GONOW in that they tend to seek unique, rare, and somewhat scarce experiences. Such experiences align well with the message of passion that GONOW leverages in its brand positioning.

In terms of geographic segmentation, GONOW has few limitations. Its vacation packages can include destinations around the world. Most of its past customers have originated in the United States, the United Kingdom, and Australia. Increasingly, though, GONOW is seeing interest in passion vacations in several Asian markets, especially China, Singapore, and Japan.

Overall, GONOW's target audiences are affluent, cosmopolitan, educated, and Internet savvy. They are capable of making their own vacation plans using online resources, but they value expertise in creating a unique vacation package that allows the travelers to focus on the experience rather than the hassles of basic details in planning. They don't mind paying top dollar if they believe that the experience is sufficiently unique and the services provided are thorough.

In terms of social media, the target audiences are active on Facebook and Instagram but vary in their use of Twitter, YouTube, and review sites like Trip Advisor. They are primarily motivated by affinity, and secondarily by validation. Content on social media sites should inform the audience about potential bucket list opportunities and how to maximize these experiences and help them to share these unique experiences with their social networks.

Social Media Zones and Channels

GONOW will utilize owned, earned, and paid media in its social media marketing plan. Owned media includes distributing content on the GONOW website. In earned media, GONOW will distribute content via YouTube, Facebook, Instagram, Twitter, Snapchat, and any other channels that ultimately relate to target audience interests. GONOW will also submit content to journalists and develop content posts that are interactive to create opportunities for target audience engagement and message amplification. GONOW will use paid advertising on social media channels to accomplish reach goals for the target audience and to promote distributed content for additional engagement. GONOW will work with influencers in each passion area to highlight its ability to design custom experiences. For instance, influencers in the areas of food, history, and music will highlight bucket list experiences with an authoritative view.

The zones will include social community, social publishing, and social commerce. The channels will include content on GONOW.it, Facebook, Instagram, YouTube, and TripAdvisor. In addition, content will be submitted for potential use on websites related to the key passion areas of food, wine, and history. The zone of social community will be used throughout the year at an ongoing rate of engagement. The zone of social publishing will be ongoing but specific content published and promoted will be targeted throughout the year to align with seasonal interests and the brand's content calendar. The zone of social commerce will be an ongoing effort, specifically with a goal of generating reviews on Trip Advisor and other sites, to promote the credibility of the quality of experiences offered by GONOW. People will be able to post reviews and other UGC directly from the Passion List app.

Objectives can be mapped to strategies and tactics as shown in Table A2.

Table A2   Mapping Objectives to Strategies and Tactics

Strategic Objective	Strategy	Tactical Objective	Tactics
Create brand awareness	Expose target audience to brand in the zone of social community Encourage use of Passion List app to dream of travel-related experiences	Build brand presence in social communities Post interesting and interactive messages Engage in conversations with fans and influencers Promote links to high-value content Encourage app adoption and ongoing use to plan bucket list experiences	Develop brand profiles in selected SNS (e.g., Facebook, Instagram) Post daily in each network Respond to comments and questions daily Use influencer list to enhance reach by passion category Use paid ads in SNS to promote Passion List app
Acquire share of voice to exceed that of direct competitors	Organic messages, socially published content marketing, buzz from target audience and posts generated from app	Create and publish content that demonstrates value Invite reviews and ratings from happy customers as credible evidence of value	Create content that includes hero content as well as filler content to ensure fresh and interesting messages are always available across social channels

(Continued)

Table A2   (Continued)

Strategic Objective	Strategy	Tactical Objective	Tactics
	participation, and reviews exceed that of competitors	Respond to target audience comments	Tie content to targeted passion experiences of food, wine, history, etc.
			Use app to request UGC for Facebook and Instagram during passion experience participation
			Use email marketing to request reviews 10 days after conclusion of vacation experiences
Drive traffic to GONOW website and reservation specialists	Social community and social publishing posts will include links to GONOW.it and clickthroughs will be encouraged with use of call to action and incentives (mix of paid and organic posts)	Offer advanced content for visitors to website such as printable and shareable itineraries, digital photo album templates, recipes, and other high value content tied to passion experiences	Develop and deploy Facebook and Instagram advertising campaigns tied to family vacations and bucket listers, with targeting by special interests
			Split test calls to action, imagery, and incentive offered to optimize traffic
Generate demand/ acquire customers	Create desire and demand using zone of social commerce	Follow up with leads that clickthrough to acquire high value content offers from paid social ads	Keyword monitoring generates alert for follow-up from sales team
		Use emotional imagery in content posted across social channels	Influencer initiatives focused on specific sales goals
		Use group deals and crowdsourced lists to drive sales	Periodic group deals for passion topics announced on SNS
Retain customers/ build loyalty	Engage, delight, inspire, thank, and reward customers using zones of social community and social commerce	Invite customers to share experiences with UGC created during vacations	Invite UGC tied to each campaign and SNS (e.g., Featuring taste of the south – Who has a favorite recipe for Ocra? Share yours, rate others, and win!)
		Build fan relationships with gamification that rewards ongoing participation and highlights expertise to leverage validation motives	Thank contributors and offer coupon or other reward
		Reward reviews and ratings and other WOM communications	Monitor brand mentions and respond, or alert internal teams to potential crises
		Listen and monitor	
		Respond to questions and comments	

Experience Strategy

The experience should provide value to the target audience and encourage engagement through participation and sharing of the experience with others. This will be accomplished by creating valuable content aligned to each key passion by season and providing the Passion List app, which participants can use to plan their bucket lists. Content will be tied to seasonal elements and holidays as well as to top hobbies around which vacations can be planned. Each passion interest will have a dedicated content theme, which can serve as the foundation for content and engagement. Themes will include "the taste of" to appeal to foodies, "a look back in time" to appeal to history buffs, and "if I were a" to appeal to sports enthusiasts. The brand name, GONOW, will be tied to each message as a dual call to action and brand identifier.

In addition, posts will include interactivity such as polls and invitations for people to share UGC content that documents their bucket list accomplishments. For instance, posts about culinary tours might end with the words, "Go when? GO NOW!" A tactical implementation of the strategy is the development of a Passion List app which will enable users to create their own custom bucket list, check off list accomplishments, and share images and comments about their various bucket list experiences. The app will work on mobile devices and post to Facebook and Instagram as users create bucket lists, check them off, and share elements of their experiences.

The tactical plan will link passions to the annual, monthly, and daily content calendars and include high level messaging, special offers, and promotional tie-ins across each major passion point (e.g., food, wine, history, sports). Content will include videos, articles, infographics, and photography, shared across GONOW-owned media properties as well as social channels. UGC content tied to content themes will also be invited and distributed. Some of this content will be automatically generated as the audience uses the Passion List app. The app will enable users to develop bucket lists tied to travel related to their passions, travel itineraries, photo albums, and more and share these with their social networks via Facebook and Instagram. For instance, a focus on culinary passions will include video vignettes with chefs from popular destinations, tips for shopping local produce at area farmers' markets, playlists of songs tied to the area culture, and suggested recipes using local ingredients. Hashtags will be tied to each element such that the GONOW brand will resonate with each passion experience: Experience the Taste of Peru: Go Now; Experience the History of Scotland: Go Now; Experience the Music of Austria: Go Now.

Tactical elements include branching (social presence of brand personality), contributing (providing high value content), friending (participating in social communities), informing/broadcasting (promoting brand and specific vacation offers), clustering (using content tied to passion interests), collaborating and seeding (using influencers to develop suggested itineraries for target audience and to amplify reach), crowdsourcing (inviting UGC content related to travel experiences), incentivizing (offering special content and deals in exchange for social engagement and use of Passion List app), selling (supporting purchase decisions with social content, offers, and reviews), and serving (using social media as a channel for customer service).

Activation

Activation of the strategy will require the development of content that can be distributed and promoted across all social channels while remaining relevant and providing value to the target audience. This will be accomplished with the development of an annual content calendar, a list of themes (tied to the bucket list experience categories), and creation of content including videos, articles, photos, and sales promotions.

Table A3   Strategy Activation

Passion	Theme	Topics	Content Type	Target Channel
Food	Local ingredients The taste of Recipes	Spring brings When in [Rome] Recipe of the month	Article How-to videos Local chef vignette videos Images Recipe cards Live tastings	YouTube Facebook Instagram Pinterest
History	Images of the past Events worth remembering Cultural heritage	On this day The story of Wonder why	Articles Virtual reality/360-degree video recreations Images of historically significant locations Polls Suggested itineraries	Facebook YouTube
Sports	Golf Soccer Adventure Niche	Performance secrets of champions Amateur or pro? A day in the life Fantasy leagues	Infographics How-to videos Polls Suggested events	Facebook Instagram YouTube Gamer's Hive Twitter Gaming

Specific details will be developed in the tactical plan but will include daily posts to Facebook and Instagram, weekly posts to YouTube, paid advertising on all three social networks, and responses to all messages tagging GONOW on social channels. Posts will follow the 80–20 rule with only one promotional message for GONOW travel packages for every four posts of content of value to the target audience. Of those four posts, two will be based on filler content, one on original content, and one on original, hero content.

A major component of the social media strategy is the Passion List app. This requires custom development and testing. The app will need to provide planning tools that result in individual and personalized lists, itineraries, and artifacts (e.g., photos), which can be retained by the users as well as shared organically via social media channels including but not limited to Facebook and Instagram.

The app will be launched by influencers in each major passion category including chefs, sommeliers, history experts, and so on. These influencers will create suggested bucket lists with links to packages offered by GONOW.

The social media staff includes a social media marketing manager and a writer. Assistance with app development, video creation, and other custom content elements will be provided on an ad hoc basis using creative agencies.

The budget will be detailed specifically in the tactical plan, but will be limited to $200,000 for app development, and annual expenditures of $10,000 for photography and video assets, $15,000 for ad hoc agency work, $50,000 for influencer seeding and accompanying content, and the cost of salaries and benefits for two social media marketing staff members.

Measurement

The effectiveness of the plan will include measures of goal attainment including brand awareness, share of voice, website traffic, and bookings for travel experiences in each passion category. In addition, engagement with individual post types will be assessed to identify the type of content that resonates most with the target audience as well as the most effective channels and timing of posts. Listening will provide alerts for customer service opportunities, leads, and insights into developing trends in hobbies and interests.

Specific metrics measured, maintained, and assessed will include reach, engagement in the form of likes and shares, response rates to CTAs and interactive invitations for engagement, usage of Passion List app including recency, frequency, and time spent, sentiment expressed toward GONOW and passion interests, share of voice across social channels, return on earned media, and return on investment. Activity and interaction metrics will be assessed daily, weekly, and monthly. Performance metrics will be assessed annually.

INDEX